# THE ABINGDON PREACHING ANNUAL 2003

# THE ABINGDON PREACHING ANNUAL 2003

COMPILED AND EDITED BY
## David N. Mosser

ASSISTANT EDITOR
## Karen Dies

ABINGDON PRESS
*Nashville*

THE ABINGDON PREACHING ANNUAL 2003
*Copyright © 2002 by Abingdon Press*

*This book is printed on recycled, acid-free, elemental-chlorine–free paper.*
**ISBN 0-687-08199-8**
**ISSN 1075-2250**

All scripture quotations unless otherwise indicated are from the *New Revised Standard Version of the Bible*, copyright © 1989, Division of Christian Education of the National Council of the Churches of Christ in the United States of America. Used by permission. All rights reserved.

The scripture quotation marked CEV is from the *Contemporary English Version*, copyright © 1991, 1992, 1995 by American Bible Society. Used by permission.

The scripture quotation marked JB is from *The Jerusalem Bible*, copyright © 1966 by Darton, Longman & Todd, Ltd. and Doubleday, a division of Random House, Inc. Reprinted by permission.

Scripture quotations noted KJV are from the *King James* or *Authorized Version of the Bible*.

The scripture quotation marked NASB is from the *New American Standard Bible®*, Copyright © The Lockman Foundation 1960, 1962, 1963, 1968, 1971, 1972, 1973, 1975, 1977. Used by permission.

Scripture quotations noted NCV are from *The Holy Bible, New Century Version*, copyright © 1987, 1988, 1991 by Word Publishing, Nashville, Tennessee 37214. Used by permission.

The scripture quotation noted NEB is from *The New English Bible*. Copyright © The Delegates of the Oxford University Press and The Syndics of the Cambridge University Press 1961, 1970. Reprinted by permission.

Scripture quotations noted NIV are taken from the *Holy Bible: New International Version®*. Copyright © 1973, 1978, 1984 by the International Bible Society. Used by permission of Zondervan Publishing House. All rights reserved.

Scripture quotations marked NKJV are from the *New King James Version*. Copyright © 1982 by Thomas Nelson, Inc. Used by permission. All rights reserved.

Scripture quotations marked NLT are from the *Holy Bible, New Living Translation*, copyright © 1996. Used by permission of Tyndale House Publishers, Inc., Wheaton, Illinois 60189. All rights reserved.

Scripture quotations marked RSV are from the *Revised Standard Version of the Bible*, copyright © 1946, 1952, 1971 by the Division of Christian Education of the National Council of the Churches of Christ in the United States of America. Used by permission. All rights reserved.

"September 1, 1939", copyright 1940 & renewed 1968 by W. H. Auden, from *W. H. Auden: The Collected Poems* by W. H. Auden. Used by permission of Random House, Inc.

02 03 04 05 06 07 08 09 10 11—10 9 8 7 6 5 4 3 2 1

# CONTENTS

CONTENTS

## APRIL

## MAY

CONTENTS

CONTENTS

# INTRODUCTION

The book you hold is relevant to lectionary preaching. A lectionary is a standard table of Scripture readings that may be used for worship or teaching in churches. Although there are many designs for lectionaries, both formal and informal, this book directs itself to the ecumenical 1992 *Revised Common Lectionary*. Can others, say nonlectionary preachers, find the *Abingdon Preaching Annual* useful? Certainly! The *Annual* includes prayers and calls to worship. It incorporates benedictions and meditations for preachers. The *Abingdon Preaching Annual* also consists of 156 sermons arranged by a lectionary template, but the lectionary binds no one to it. The lectionary is merely a tool for preaching.

Why would preachers use the lectionary? Naturally, there are many reasons to use the lectionary and here follow only a few. First, in a world of increasingly biblical illiteracy, the lectionary gives a three-year tour through the most noted passages. Second, it allows the laity to participate more fully in the preaching event, in that they can study the Scripture prior to worship. Third, the lectionary can aid in Christian education when all Sunday school classes are able to learn about the same biblical text. Fourth, it encourages preachers to employ the whole breadth of Scripture. Both Old and New Testaments receive consideration—it also promotes preaching text that may not be from the preacher's favorite "hobby horse" texts. The lectionary is a tool to help people learn, hear, and absorb what the Bible offers to modern people—life abundant.

I would like to offer a word of caution, however. Like many entities in life, a book like *The Abingdon Preaching Annual* offers either a blessing or a curse. The curse comes in the form of a temptation to use someone else's work as our own. In a hurried day when preachers can download the sermon *du jour* in five or fewer minutes, it is tempting to delete our work in preaching. I once was startled to open a neighboring church newsletter and find an article that I had written plagiarized word for word. The only difference between the two articles was the name signed at the conclusion. Many of the *Abingdon Preaching Annual* writers are at the tops of their fields. Because this is so, I urge you not to let their fine work tempt you to do less for your own unique congregation than God calls you to do. Rather, my hope is that this book will provide a mental conversation on biblical texts with the authors.

Most of us do not hear many other people preach, but we can see how others might handle or preach the same topics on which we preach. This is the blessing of a book like the *Abingdon Preaching Annual*. We can look at others' approaches, exegesis, and application and check to see if it resonates with our understanding of God's word and our human experience. In this sense, I hope and pray that this book will engage us as partners in the preaching dialogue that we all need. After all, preaching is not simply a virtuoso performance by solitary individuals. Rather, it is a community event shared by all those who gather to worship the God in whom we all "live and move and have our being" (Acts 17:28).

The slogan of the Peace Corps speaks well to the enterprise of preaching: "The toughest job you'll ever love." Preaching is hard work. It takes time and energy. Preaching includes not only biblical study and an understanding of theology but also a real grasp of the human condition. No preacher will succeed if he or she does not understand both Scripture and the people for whom it is authoritative. This is the work of preaching—bring God's holy word and God's holy people into a conversation about faith and life and God in Christ. My hope is that this *Abingdon Preaching Annual* will become a partner in your conversations about Scripture, preaching, and your congregation. I hope this book is a work of love—both in its gathering and in its broadcasting the good news of Jesus Christ.

David Mosser

# SERMONS FOR SPECIAL DAYS

# TRANSFORMATION: THE NAME OF THE GAME

PHILIPPIANS 3:12–4:1; ROMANS 12:2

*One of the nonliturgical days that many preachers face is what we may call "Senior Sunday." Many churches celebrate "Senior Sunday" to embrace, recognize, and encourage students who move from one phase of life to another. No longer children, these high school graduates will either move toward the working world or continue education at an institution of higher or vocational learning. Either way, our students leave the nest of home to venture into a wider world. This sermon tries to acknowledge student achievements. We also want them to remember that their church prays for them, loves them, and has high hopes for their future.*

This is Senior Sunday, and as a church, we want to wish you well, congratulate you, and thank you for representing our church family so well. You are a class that gives older folks hope about what we refer to as "the younger generation." But we want to do more than simply slap you on the back and congratulate you. We want to bless you in the name of God. We want you to remember that as you begin to move from your childhood homes and make your way into the world—as students or workers or both—that you take part of us with you wherever you go. In a sense, our own hopes go with you as you grow into and toward your own hopes and aspirations.

A resourceful preacher on such a day as this might quickly turn to some biblical passage or another to share various pieces of biblical wisdom. The Bible is full of wisdom, and we stand and sit here as a people shaped and formed by this collection of books we call the Bible. Therefore, looking to the Bible on a day like today seems as natural to us as "checking a pay phone for forgotten coins." However, if you know your Bible, then you immediately sense that I have a problem.

The problem is that the Bible in general, and Jesus in particular, have little by way of wisdom to offer seventeen- and eighteen-year-old people. This problem of lack of direction for today's youth seems like a giant oversight on the part of those who wrote the Bible. However, if we think about the problem for a moment, the answer may have been under our noses all the time. In Jesus' day, children were children until the time of their *Bar* or *Bat Mitzvah*. These two *Mitzvahs* (one for boys and one for girls) are synagogue ceremonies that mark both the end of childhood and that young person's entry into adult life. It happens in the life of a Jewish youngster at the age of thirteen. A Protestant equivalent of this ceremony is confirmation. At confirmation, we as a church recognize that those who were children in the eyes of the church have now assumed an adult confession or profession of faith. Do you see the answer to our problem? In Bible times, there was really no such thing as a teenager. One was either a child or an adult. A person was either pre-Mitzvah or post-Mitzvah, but there was no truly accurate category in between.

We, however, have a category of age that stands between being an adult in the fullest sense of our understanding and our understanding of what constitutes being a child. As graduates you stand in that "twilight zone" between being a child and being an adult. You are a child because there are many things that you cannot legally do—yet! At the same time, each of you is reasonably mature, and there are not many questions about it. So now what do we do? I think we want to look at what reasonably mature people do as they wait to fully mature. "Who might that include?" you may ask. The answer concerns each person in this sanctuary. We are each on our way to becoming what God has created us to be. None of us have arrived yet, and few of us want to get to the point that we stop growing in wisdom or in grace. We all want to become better people, more mature in our faith and in our relationships with other people, especially with regard to people whom we care about deeply.

When speaking of maturing, Christians speak of transformation. In the church we call this "Spiritual Formation"—being formed in and by the spirit of God. No matter what your age, transformation of God's people is the chief task of the church. We are interested in the formation of individuals. The church is also interested in the formation of congregations. Paul writes for us words that we all live by if we are Christian. He writes, "Do not be conformed to this world, but be transformed by the renewing of your minds, so that you may discern what is the will of God—what is good and acceptable and perfect" (Romans 12:2). What does this mean? It means simply that as living and breathing human beings we are on a quest to find out who we are. It is a lifetime search, and no one worth his or her salt ever finishes the quest.

Americans are "always on the way to someplace else," writes *Harper's* editor Lewis H. Lapham.

> If America is about nothing else, it is about the invention of the self. Because we have little use for history, and because we refuse the comforts of a society established on the blueprint of class privilege, we find ourselves set adrift at birth in an existential void, inheriting nothing except the obligation to construct a plausible self, to build a raft of identity....
>
> Who else is the American hero if not a wandering pilgrim who goes forth on a perpetual quest? (Lewis H. Lapham, "Who and What Is American?" *Harper's Magazine* [January, 1992]: p. 46)

A sign of a healthy church or the sign of a healthy spiritual person is one who takes Paul's admonition or advice to heart—to "not be conformed to this world, but be transformed by the renewing of your minds, so that you may discern what is the will of God." Transformation or the quest for life's meaning—this is the name of the game. Transformation lets God change you into what God created you to be. God takes the stuff of brain and heart and shapes a unique creature—*you*. Walker Percy's character out of his novel *The Moviegoer* [New York: Alfred A Knopf, 1962, p. 13] had it right. This character said, "The search is what anyone would undertake if he were not sunk in the everydayness of his own life.... To become aware of the possibility of the search is to be onto something. Not to be onto something is to be in despair." Thus, all of us have a choice: the quest or the despair of a common and unreflective person. As your pastor, I wanted to remind you of this choice. I also want to remind you that this choice is not undertaken only on your high school graduation. Rather, it is a choice that you will make over and over in your life. You sit in a sanctuary full of people who also must make these decisions daily.

Naturally, we all have our ways of going on the quest. Some do it watching television. Others quest for the meaning of life in video games or searching for pleasure in even more questionable pursuits, such as overindulgence in alcohol or drugs. But one way or another, we either quest or quit. At about eighteen, I found my way into a quest for life's meaning and the wisdom that I could find therein by reading some pretty heavy stuff for a high school student. Given the fact that television in my growing years consisted of only three networks—ABC, NBC, and CBS—I had few alternatives to discover what was "out there." So, I read, and I read a lot. I read Albert Camus, Jean-Paul Sartre, Fyodor Dostoyevsky, and a host of other "pointy-headed" authors, as my friends called them.

I am a Christian today because I searched and searched among the wisest and most thought provoking people I could find to read. Finally, however, I came to the awareness that what my little church had tried to teach me had a lot of merit. My church had long before introduced me to a person named Jesus. By thoroughly investigating what other profound thinkers had said about human life and life's meaning, I finally concluded that Jesus was wiser than all. Jesus had plenty to teach me. Jesus taught me about what life means and how I might fit into a community that said following Jesus was the most important and meaning-filled thing I would ever do. They told me this when I was six, ten, and eighteen, and I still believe the people who taught me and loved me.

To you seniors I want to say one thing: You will all be transformed. Each of you will take your own path and make your own quest. But don't forget that the primary reason for the church and its message is simply to transform people from mere biological creatures to something much more magnificent. As Psalm 8 puts it:

What are human beings that you are mindful of them, mortals that you care for them? Yet you have made them a little lower than God, and crowned them with glory and honor. You have given them dominion over the works of your hands; you have put all things under their feet, all sheep and oxen, and also the beasts of the field, the birds of the air, and the fish of the sea, whatever passes along the paths of the seas. (Psalm 8:4-8)

We, as your church, want you to be transformed. We want you transformed from young people eager to discover yourselves and the world into individuals who find yourselves in the everlasting and loving arms of the God we know most fully in Jesus Christ. I want you to notice something interesting. Some of the most important symbols of the Christian life are symbols of transformation—the caterpillar into a butterfly and death into life. Jesus took a cross, the symbol of shame and dishonor, and by his death and resurrection he transformed the cross into a symbol of hope. May God take your life and make you a symbol that love is superior to hate and that hope is greater than despair. These are the ends of the quest that we hope and pray that you make. And remember we are all pulling for you on every step of your quest. Amen. (David Mosser)

# THE RITUAL OF THANKSGIVING

## LEVITICUS 7:11-15

*This sermon was preached on All Saints Sunday near the conclusion of a sermon series titled "A November Full of Thanksgiving." The sermon series examined thanksgiving comprehensively as a fundamental character trait of Christians. These sermons also acknowledged that thanksgiving is regularly an experience difficult to articulate for Christians. One aim of these sermons was to facilitate a believer's understanding that they are Christian stewards over the thanksgiving God gives them.*

The day following an emotional memorial service for one of our congregation's most beloved members, I sat in a hotel lobby waiting for a taxi. While in that lobby I listened to a young woman give the same polite, but decidedly routine, speech to each and every customer checking out of the hotel.

"Yes, sir. Thank you for choosing our hotel. We thank you for your business and hope the next time you return to our city you will choose to lodge with us. Thank you for your decision to stay with us."

The only problem with this particular "ritual of politeness" was that she delivered this speech precisely and in a monotone voice. The young woman's voice never wavered from one customer to the next. I could only imagine some poor soul being locked out of his room, appearing in the lobby in a bath robe or towel, standing in front of the young woman and her giving the same speech.

This illustration is a bad example of ritual. No one ever intended the idea of ritual to be words spoken by rote, without feeling or meaning. When you recite the Pledge of Allegiance, do you repeat it without feeling and then say it has lost meaning for you? I hope not. Anyone can turn our meaningful rituals into dry and pointless sets of words and actions, but ritual has a deeper—and what I would like to call a teaching—purpose. Ritual helps us pass along those meanings and interpretations of our common life together that are bigger than the words we use to explain them. This is why ritual is so important in the life of faith.

Ritual helps people act out their faith. Ritual tells others about the things we hold dear, although most of us could not articulate why these things are so important to us. Ritual is also important in the church realm, although many modern people forsake it. They forsake ritual because they do not understand that for the past two thousand years the church has tried to help people value life and faith in ways that we can scarcely articulate. Prior to the existence of the church, Israel too, celebrated the rituals of faith. Read our lesson from Leviticus:

> This is the ritual of the sacrifice of the offering of well-being that one may offer to the LORD. If you offer it for thanksgiving, you shall offer with the thank offering unleavened cakes mixed with oil, unleavened wafers spread with oil, and cakes of choice flour well soaked in oil. With your thanksgiving sacrifice of well-being you shall bring your offering with cakes of leavened bread. From this you shall offer one cake from each offering, as a gift to the LORD; it shall belong to the priest who dashes the blood of the offering of well-being. And the flesh of your thanksgiving sacrifice of well-being shall be eaten on the day it is offered; you shall not leave any of it until morning. (Leviticus 7:11-15)

For Israel, the ritual in worship was a way not only to celebrate the people's faith in God but also to teach Israel's young to value the things that the community of faith valued. Our Leviticus lesson concerns what we might call "the ritual of peace offering." Israel carries out this ritual in thanksgiving because although they know that they ought to be thankful, thanksgiving is something we live less than we know we should. Thanksgiving, for Christians especially, is a way of life. Perhaps it is this attitude that makes Paul's later statement so compelling: "See that none of you repays evil for evil, but always seek to do good to one another and to all. Rejoice always, pray without ceasing, give thanks in all circumstances; for this is the will of God in Christ Jesus for you" (1 Thessalonians 5:15-18).

Of course, people are not born thankful. Someone must teach us to be thankful, just as someone must teach us how to pray. It was not some quirk of the Gospels that one of Jesus' disciples asked him, "Lord, teach us to pray, as John taught his disciples"

(Luke 11:1*b*). It is for this reason of good behavior and deport-ment that concerned parents worry so much about their chil-dren's manners, politeness, and gratitude toward other people. These kinds of concerns bring youngsters to school-like events such as a cotillion or another rite of passage event. As you may know, a cotillion is designed to teach young people the meaning of manners and etiquette.

Ritual helps people get into the groove of good habits. Leviti-cus—as deadly as it may read to modern people—reminds the faithful that God values more than mere words of praise and thanksgiving. Thanksgiving, rather, becomes a way of life—a liv-ing response to God's gift of bountiful life to God's people.

All Saints Sunday provides the church—us—a ritual mode to remember those persons who have lived among us. Those who showed us what it means to be Christian. When we read the names and hear the chimes of our departed brothers and sisters in faith, these rituals remind each of us of our own mortality. We will all, sooner or later, have our own names read and chimed. Our worship ritual reminds us what is important—although many of us could not put this moment into words. What we remember is so much larger than our understanding of it. Ritual is a practice to remind each of us that too often we stand in the presence of greatness, yet we often forget it. Worst of all, we often fail to rec-ognize the simple greatness of other people.

When I was nine years old I walked across the street with my father to be with a family who had just learned that their sixteen-year-old daughter died as a result of heart surgery complications. I was too young to realize just how difficult that walk across the street was for my father. He and the girl's father were good friends. In the midst of stunned and profound silence, one of the men in the living room suggested, "Let's pray." As we bowed our heads, I remember thinking that I had never seen a group of grown-ups so intensely sad and completely powerless. Yet, in their own ritualized way, they turned toward God because God was the source and the end of all that they were. Ritual helps us remember that life's most profound moments—both in joy and in grief—must finally and completely be handed over to God.

Today we hand the lives of our saints over to God, but we keep their memory alive in our worship and in our hearts. We celebrate the ritual of thanksgiving to God because God has put these important people into our lives and given us a memory of them that never fades. We are thankful to God because that is our proper response. I only pray that through our ritual of thanksgiving we can remember that God really does give us gifts of people who make living life worth the while. Amen. (David Mosser)

# REFLECTIONS

*Introduction to the Monthly Meditations*

Imagine going to a financial planner and discovering that he or she has recently declared bankruptcy. Or, for a slightly more bizarre example, imagine going to an obese doctor, who smokes and drinks, for motivation to "get in shape." Every profession has negative stereotypes of its practitioners. We all know of "crooked lawyers" or "corrupt judges," but do any of us preachers want to be "unspiritual" spiritual leaders? Yet, for many of us, being spiritual and attending to the prayer life we so highly recommend from the pulpit becomes elusive. Many things seduce us. First, most preachers are so harried that we leave little time to cultivate our own spiritual gardens. Second, we so focus on other's needs that too often we neglect our own. Third, we too regularly handle sacred means with utilitarian ends in mind. We read the Scripture for sermon ideas rather than letting the voice of God speak to us through the Scripture. Fourth, in the constant handling of holy things, we too often become immune to the Holy's life-giving power for us. The reasons the Spirit eludes human creatures are as legion as the number of people who fail to allow God into their lives.

For these reasons, and many others, the *Abingdon Preaching Annual*'s tradition is to offer twelve monthly meditations written by preachers for preachers. Among those who contributed these meditations are four homiletics professors and two pastors who among them account for more than sixty years of pulpit preaching. Each of these writers knows all too well the seductions that the pulpit and its responsibilities impart to those who preach in and out of season. These meditations have been written with your spirit in mind.

In recent years, given the general despair over the moral state of our nation, our culture is revisiting the idea of virtue and character. There is a certain irony as the "free love, Woodstock, and anything goes" generation becomes leaders that there is now a new bellow for ethics and morals in the public arena. After the many instances of school violence, even down to the six-year-olds among us, people are taking a harder look at our hard-won freedoms. One of these freedoms is to live a life that befits the gospel.

All this talk of morals and character means that most thinking people are on the same page. We need a new focus and new direction or we will do ourselves in. As Pogo said so eloquently: "We have met the enemy and he is us!" For pastors and preachers, we become part of those who want to lead people toward the life of the Spirit. The difficulty, however, is that most of us are so drawn into the "professional ministry" that we often have little time or energy left to cultivate our spiritual core that God gives us to be leaders for Christ.

This brings us, as it most often does, to the topic of Spiritual Formation. Honestly, like most of you, I'm not sure what this means. Being from a Wesleyan tradition, I suppose Spiritual Formation has to do with the idea of practicing spiritual disciplines. These naturally include activities such as meditating, praying, fasting, studying, spiritual reading, alms giving, and worshiping. One thing I do know is that we all need time and a means to deepen our lives in God so that we can deepen our relationships with other people and ourselves. Leo Tolstoy once wrote with great insight: "Everybody thinks of changing humanity and nobody thinks of changing himself." Most of us know the absolute truth of Tolstoy's statement. We see it, we live it, and we think we understand Tolstoy's sentiment every day.

We have provided these monthly meditations as a gift of quiet reflection for you—the preacher. We have not intended these meditations to be "sermon fodder" nor do we intend them as something from which to get some good ideas. Rather, we furnish these spiritual reflections purely to allow preachers to have a spiritual moment or two. These are clearly for you to read and meditate over. I pray that they may speak to your soul. May these monthly meditations give you a grasp on the spiritual life that God wants each of us to possess as a divine gift to God's people. (David Mosser)

# REFLECTIONS

### ❦

# JANUARY

**Reflection Verse:** *"I know all your ways; and look, I have set before you an open door which no one can shut." (Revelation 3:8 NEB)*

There is no time in which people become more acutely aware of their past and hopeful of their future than at the beginning of a new year. We tend to reflect on our past, regret our mistakes, contemplate the future, and make resolutions. People want to do and be better. This offers the preacher an unusual annual opportunity to encourage and help people turn loose of the negative parts of their past and appropriate to the power of God to help them do what they cannot do on their own.

Many years ago Louisa Fletcher Tarkington wrote a perceptive poem entitled, "The Land of Beginning Again." It begins and ends with a verse which is almost a universal wish.

> I wish there were some wonderful place
> Called the land of beginning again
> Where all our mistakes,
> And all our heartaches,
> And all of our poor selfish grief,
> Could be dropped like a shabby
> Old coat at the door,
> And never be put on again.

Do we not all, periodically, wish that could happen to us? We would do it at once if we just knew how. But, one does not live long without learning that this is not easy, even when it feels necessary.

There is something about the past that troubles all of us, even if it is nothing more than the nagging belief that we could do better if we had another go at it. Burdens and baggage of the past constitute such a terrible load for so many people! Until we can get rid of some of what we are carrying, we cannot take on more.

Admittedly, some of the burdens of the past are real. They cannot be dismissed with a wave of the hand. They represent the residue of old errors that have left scars and, sometimes, open wounds. Some of them are unfulfilled obligations that, whether they were wise or unwise, must still be met. Not all of the baggage of the past is imaginary or unreal, but much of it is.

All of us carry some baggage from the past that could be laid aside and never picked up again because it does not exist in reality. Our unwillingness to let go of the past hurts; our ignorance about how we may be forgiven and our blindness and insensitivity to the joys we could experience when we put unnecessary baggage aside keeps us a prisoner of the past. Only God knows how we hurt as the result of unresolved aspects of the past! Only God knows what we may become if we could be free of our unresolved and unredeemed past!

The Bible tells us we can be free. We can lay aside the anchors we have been dragging and gain dominion over the obstacles and burdens in life. I do not mean to be casual about your past, for who would be insensitive enough to be casual with people about the places where they hurt, the emotional "hot spots" of life? Our emotional and spiritual pain is serious business and should not be treated in a cavalier fashion. I cannot forgive sins or redeem the past for you. I cannot even do that for myself. I can only tell you where it can be done. The Bible teaches us that we do not have to be a victim of our past—unless we want to.

The Bible is filled with the idea of beginning life over again. Early on, that concept of new beginnings became necessary in the life of God's creation. It runs like a thread throughout the whole Bible. Jesus came into the world to personify and actualize the whole transaction. His mere coming should have been enough; but he came, lived among us, taught us, suffered and died for us, and exemplified to us in every way how we may be free. When Nicodemus, the gentle and learned Pharisee, came to inquire of Jesus, the Master told him that he would have to be born again. Nicodemus tried so hard to intellectualize the process. He pointed out to Jesus that it is impossible to be born again. He raised astronomical problems with the process. He literalized what was spiritual and, therefore, missed the point. The marvelous thing about what Jesus taught was not so much that you *must* be born again, but that you *can* be born again.

God has set before us an open door. No one can close it. However, it is up to us, individually, to make the decision and effort to walk through it. Whatever loose ends may be lying out there in the past, God can help us gather them into new beginnings. Forgiveness is for the asking. "If we confess our sins, he who is faithful and just will forgive us our sins and cleanse us from all unrighteousness" (1 John 1:9). "As far as the east is from the west, so far he removes our transgressions from us" (Psalm 103:12).

While some people are haunted by the past, there are others who are lured to it, like a moth to the flame. The past is used as a place of comfort and security in a world of chaos and change. Some psychologists say that people who are threatened in ways they cannot handle tend to return to earlier levels of development (the past) for security. Those who constantly return to the past for security are in as much danger as those who flee from it and are haunted by it. Sometimes people keep going back to their past hoping it will improve. There is nothing more futile than trying to create a better past. There is a country song that has a very sad line in it about the past: "It looks like looking back is all I have to look forward to." If all our happiness is in the past, we are not likely to be happy again. You cannot live with the past when it is gone. Don't try! Your story will be too sad to tell. It is better to trust the uncertain future.

January is a wonderful time to teach and preach about forgiveness and deliverance from the past, and hope for the future. (Thomas Lane Butts)

# JANUARY 5, 2003

## *Second Sunday After Christmas*

**Worship Theme:** Jesus is the Word made flesh. Jesus dwells with his people just as the Word of God has dwelt with the faithful through the ages. We celebrate not only God's creation but also that God works within creation and Christ to continually renew God's covenant with God's people.

**Readings:** Jeremiah 31:7-14; Ephesians 1:3-14; John 1:(1-9), 10-18

### Call to Worship (Psalm 147:12-20 RSV)

*Leader:*    Praise the LORD, O Jerusalem! Praise your God, O Zion!

***People:***    **For he strengthens the bars of your gates; he blesses your sons within you.**

*Leader:*    He makes peace in your borders; he fills you with the finest of the wheat.

***People :***    **He sends forth his command to the earth; his word runs swiftly.**

*Leader:*    He gives snow like wool; he scatters hoarfrost like ashes.

***People:***    **He casts forth his ice like morsels; who can stand before his cold?**

*Leader:*    He sends forth his word, and melts them; he makes his wind blow, and the waters flow.

***People:***    **He declares his word to Jacob, his statutes and ordinances to Israel.**

*Leader:*    He has not dealt thus with any other nation; they do not know his ordinances.

**All:**    **Praise the LORD!**

**Pastoral Prayer:**

Gracious Lord, we gather at this festive time to praise and sing to your holy name. We have spent time with loved ones who constantly prompt us to recall that you give life as a precious gift. You only ask that we not squander this gift. Help us value the fellowship that we enjoy. Remind us that the early church "devoted themselves to the apostles' teaching and fellowship, to the breaking of bread and the prayers" (Acts 2:42). For us life cannot be lived at any higher level. Raise again our awareness that you give us life to share with others and not only those of our own kind. Rather, you have called us to be both salt and light—a city set on a hill (Matthew 5:13-14). Thus, as we count our Christmas blessings let us not forget all those for whom Christ died. Give us the spiritual energy to love those who are different from us. Help us reach out with food, clothing, and a word of encouragement to others. Let us be for others the love that you have been for us. In the name of Christ, we pray. Amen. (David Mosser)

# SERMON BRIEFS

## CHRISTMAS: A VISION OF CHRIST'S HOPE

### JEREMIAH 31:7-14

No one can live without hope. Hope is the energy that makes the future possible. Hope is the antidote to despair. Hope is to life what wind is to fire; it is the one essential ingredient if people are to construct new lives for themselves.

In these beautiful verses we catch something of the prophet's energy of hope for his people. Terrible things have happened in Israel. Institutions have been destroyed; families have been uprooted and displaced. Old securities have melted in the fire of historical chaos, and despair is the order of the day. The exile to

Babylon has dictated that nothing in Israel's life will ever be the same. The glorious worship of the temple is gone forever. The bright and secure days of Israel's life under strong kings seems like a distant memory. The people are languishing in a foreign land; the songs of the heart forever silenced by the lament of despair and longing.

Into this bleak condition comes a strong word from the prophet Jeremiah to the exiles: God is going to do a mighty work of restoration! The place where you are is not the final place of your lives! Look and see; listen and hear: "See, I am going to bring them from the land of the north, and gather them from the farthest parts of the earth, among them the blind and the lame, those with child and those in labor, together; a great company, they shall return here" (Jeremiah 31:8).

This prophecy is an energizing word for a desperate people in what appears to be a hopeless situation. It is always crucial to have someone speak the word of hope! Paul wrote about faith, hope, and love and said that the greatest of these three is love. No one would argue with that. But for some moments in life and for some people, the greatest word is the word of hope. It is the mission of Jeremiah to speak this word to his people as creatively and as forcefully as he can. His ministry in this text offers guidance to the church as it proclaims the faith of Christ to the world. There is no higher calling or more holy work than to be the speakers of hope to a hurt and confused and lost people.

The spirit of Christmas is found in Jeremiah's promise of restoration: "I will turn their mourning into joy, I will comfort them, and give them gladness for sorrow" (31:13b). Into a world laden with the heaviness of ceaseless activity and endless consumption has come a word of hope for a new way of living. No longer do we have to toil for that which does not satisfy and live for that which is transitory. A new word has been spoken, indeed, has been born, and we are invited to embrace it and let it embrace us. Life will be different because of what God has done in Bethlehem.

Perhaps the best way for the church to use this text from Jeremiah on the second Sunday after Christmas is to remind itself of the ministry of hopeful proclamation. We have experienced something that the world may not perceive. God has come in

Christ, making all things new. Our proclamation should be as creative and as bold as we can dare to make it as we direct lives to the restoring fountain of grace. It is so vitally important for someone to be able to perceive the "not yet," the hope that is still unseen, and paint a picture of that dawning day for those weighed down by present circumstances. Those who speak such a word offer a ministry that has the power to revitalize people and bring new shape to present reality.

It has been suggested that when beginning a significant work one should always "have the end in mind." It is against the vision of what is ultimately desired that all work is done in order to arrive at the desired outcome. Jeremiah is speaking a word about the end of exile. It is not yet realized, but now the people have a vision of what that end looks like. They are energized to live creatively in the sure and confident hope that God will restore their lives. Such is the vision of the church in this season of Christmastide. From such vision we dare, in the words of the hymn, to "live tomorrow's life today!" (*The United Methodist Hymnal*, "There's a Spirit in the Air," no. 192). (Chris Andrews)

## PRAYING FOR THE SEAL OF PROMISE

### EPHESIANS 1:3-14

While cleaning up a long-neglected stack of files in my office, I found a note that contained these words of wisdom: "People who worry are stuck in the past. People who are anxious are consumed by the future." I had no recollection from which lecture or event I captured this phrase. However, the truth of it came back to me.

When we worry, we are looking back at the past with a sense of dread. We sense that our faults and mistakes will pursue us. We build scenarios in which our past unfolds to cause us grief in the future. Anxiety over that future fuels our imagination to picture ways we will fail, be unhappy, or suffer because of the power of our circumstances.

The opening chapter of Ephesians contains a two-part prayer. The first part is a prayer of blessing offered to God. The second part is a prayer of intercession for the reader. The opening prayer is hymnlike in its energy and ecstasy, serving to reinforce the reader's sense of being in the care of a loving and active God. It is easy to recognize that prayers of blessing of this sort grow from a life of prayer.

Prayer helps us interpret our past in a new way. Paul's life of prayer and worship provides deep reflections about God and significant experiences of God. New understandings and interpretations emerge. As we first encounter Paul in Acts, we discover what Paul believes about the past. The past serves as the arena in which the law condemns an imperfect humanity. Paul, in that part of his life, chooses to be the instrument of a judgmental God seeking to maintain the purity of the law.

As Paul grows in the experience of Christ, the past becomes a lifeline to God. He looks at his life through a new set of lenses. Paul comes to believe that God has sought the redemption of the daughters and sons of God since the foundation of the world. God seeks to bless, to re-create, and to redeem. The gifts of forgiveness and reconciliation move through the currents of time and reach their completion in the sacrifice of Christ. God's generous initiative of grace moves Paul to experience a rich thanksgiving and gratitude as if the heavens had opened up a virtual shower of spiritual blessings.

Prayer awakens the imagination. A new world of options and opportunities flood the soul when we experience God's grace moving to include us. God's plan is to gather us into a new purpose to be lived out in God's future. We are delivered from the hopelessness of believing that we must search for God. We live in the joy of knowing God is searching for us. A spirit of thanksgiving replaces our despair. Our actions and witness glorify God, as the true purpose for our lives unfolds.

The joy that is reflected in Paul's opening doxology is the joy of living fully in the present. The past is overcome in God's grace and the future is opened by God's mercy. The present becomes the scene in which our lives become hymns of praise to God's glory.

A man came into my office at the time we encountered Ephesians in a Disciple Bible Study. New to the church and a self-proclaimed doubter, he described experiences in life that had become patterns of pain in his present day. As his eyes misted over, he related that he had become aware that God had been searching for him all along and that he had resisted. He had come to believe that wherever he was found by God that point would become the point at which forgiveness could overcome the past, and he could start all over again. Why should I have been surprised? After all, Paul said that when you hear the word and believe the gospel of salvation you are marked with the seal of the promised Holy Spirit. (Bob Holloway)

## THE ETERNAL IN THE MUNDANE

### JOHN 1:(1-9), 10-18

In her book *At Home in Mitford,* Jan Karon writes of a time when Father Tim, an Episcopal priest, heard a horrible scream from the sanctuary of his church. As he came closer, he began to understand the anguished words which made up the scream: "Are . . . you . . . up . . . there?"

> Father Tim slid into the pew across the aisle and knelt on the worn cushion. "You may be asking the wrong question," he said quietly.
> Startled, the man raised his head.
> I believe the question you may want to ask is not, 'Are you up there?' but, 'Are you down here?' " (Jan Karon, *At Home in Mitford* [New York: Penguin Putnam, Inc., 1996], p. 182)

What an appropriate question for this time when our celebration of the birth of our Savior has been put behind us! For a few weeks, we focused on the nearness of God, on Emmanuel, God with us. But now, as we move back into our daily routines, thoughts of Christ are often discarded with the used wrapping paper or boxed up with the nativity scene to be brought out next year. God once again retreats to the heavens, no more the Word that dwelt among us, full of grace and truth.

John's Gospel calls us to remember, however, that the Word was made flesh and dwelt among us. This Word, the Word that was at the beginning, the Word that was with God, the Word

37

that was God, became something we can grasp. Christ, the Word, certainly is "up there," but we must never forget that he is also "down here." We can see that Christ is dwelling with us still, if only we ask the right questions and look in the right places. It is these continued occurrences of incarnation that we must seek if we are not to take for granted our lives as children of God. How can we see the eternal in the mundane?

To see the Word made flesh, we must realize that all of life can be a sacrament. We must find ways to transform our daily routines into conveyors of God's truth and grace. Perhaps we do this by being aware of the gifts of the things which fill our days. If we say a prayer of thanksgiving for our car each time we place the key in the ignition, perhaps the rush hour traffic will seem less burdensome. If we say grace not only over meals but also over our work, perhaps we will begin to see our chores as gifts from a loving God. If we celebrate the transitions in our lives, such as retirements, birthdays, and relocations, perhaps we will see more clearly how God works in those times.

Even more important, we must learn to see our relationships as sacraments. Humans are created in the image of God; therefore, we should most clearly be able to see God in each other. How would life change if we made a special effort to make everyone we meet feel better than they did before we met? What would happen if we secretly did nice things for friends and strangers, seeing how much good we could do without getting caught? Maybe we could see the Word become flesh not only for them but also for ourselves.

The sacred moments when the eternal touches the temporal leave a permanent mark on all who experience them. If we look for God "down here," we will be able to say truly that, like John, we have seen the glory of God. The Word, the glory of God, is continually being made flesh, revealing God to us. The darkness has not overcome the light, and the Son, who is close to God's heart, continues to make himself known to us in the flesh. (Melissa Scott)

# JANUARY 12, 2003

*Baptism of the Lord*

---

**Worship Theme:** God's spirit hovers not only over the face of the waters but also over the lives of God's people.

---

**Readings:** Genesis 1:1-5; Acts 19:1-7; Mark 1:4-11

**Call to Worship (Psalm 29:1-4, 9-11)**

> *Leader:* Ascribe to the LORD, O heavenly beings, ascribe to the LORD glory and strength.
>
> ***People:*** **Ascribe to the LORD the glory of his name; worship the LORD in holy splendor.**
>
> *Leader:* The voice of the LORD is over the waters; the God of glory thunders, the LORD, over mighty waters.
>
> ***People:*** **The voice of the LORD is powerful; the voice of the LORD is full of majesty.**
>
> *Leader:* The voice of the LORD causes the oaks to whirl, and strips the forest bare; and in his temple all say, "Glory!"
>
> ***People:*** **The LORD sits enthroned over the flood; the LORD sits enthroned as king forever.**
>
> ***All:*** **May the LORD give strength to his people! May the LORD bless his people with peace!**

**Pastoral Prayer:**

As we come before you in worship this day, O God of All, help us each to remember our baptism. Remind us that your sacred waters

39

give us drink, cleanse us, and allow us to grow. Baptism does for us what water does for us. In our time many of us fail to realize just how short our lives would be without water. So dry, too, are our lives without you. As Jesus had the Holy Spirit fall upon him at his baptism, may we, this day, sense a new spirit within us as we remember the sacredness of the baptismal moment. May the sacred memory of you continue to nurture and sustain our lives before you, O God. Grant us our prayers and once again make us your people. In the name of Jesus, we pray. Amen. (David Mosser)

## SERMON BRIEFS

## WHEN GOD INVADES THE EMPTINESS

### GENESIS 1:1-5

Isaac Newton had a model of the solar system in his office with the sun in the center and the planets surrounding it. A fellow scientist came into his office and exclaimed,

> "My! What an exquisite thing this is! Who made it?"
> Sir Isaac Newton replied, "Nobody." The scientist looked amazed as he said skeptically, "You must think I am a fool. Of course somebody made it, and he is a genius."
> Sir Isaac Newton got up, walked around his desk, and put his hand on the shoulder of his friend as he said earnestly, "This thing is but a puny imitation of a much grander system whose laws you and I know. I am not able to convince you that this mere toy is without a designer and maker; yet you profess to believe that the great original from which the design is taken has come into being without either designer or maker. Now tell me, by what sort of reasoning do you reach such incongruous conclusions?" (Anne Graham Lotz, *The Glorious Dawn of God's Story: Finding Meaning for Your Life in Genesis* [Dallas: Word Publishing, 1997], p. 3)

Genesis, the book of beginnings, opens with the story of creation. It includes two accounts (1:1–2:4a and 2:4b-25). The author of Genesis does not attempt to prove God's existence but rather assumes God's preexistence before time and space. The Gospel of John begins with a similar affirmation of faith: "In the beginning was the Word, and the Word was with God, and the Word was God.... All things came into being through him, and without him not one thing came into being" (John 1:1, 3a). Genesis assumes that God is the creator/designer of heaven and earth.

After the writer states his initial assumption, he describes three specific actions and affirmations of faith in which God is actively involved. In all three actions, the emphasis is on God's involvement, not on how God did it. The first action describes God creating form and substance out of nothing, or emptiness (v. 2). The second action describes God creating order out of chaos (v. 2). The third action describes God creating light that penetrates darkness and the endless cycle of day and night (vv. 3-5).

The description of earth as it existed in the beginning is frightfully similar to the lives of so many people living today. Their lives are formless, with no shape or center. Their lives are void of meaning, joy, and satisfaction. They are attractive on the outside, but they are empty on the inside. Their lives are dark with depression, ignorance, and separation from God.

As we begin a new year and look at the mostly empty calendar in front of us, the text invites us to let the Spirit of God invade our own lives. If we will allow God into our lives, God will fill our emptiness with purpose and meaning, God will bring order out of the chaos, and God will illuminate the darkness of our world with light! (Bob Buchanan)

## NO BLISS IN IGNORANCE

### ACTS 19:1-7

Initiation into Christianity was, is, and perhaps should continue to be an involved task not to be taken lightly. In the baptismal rites practiced in the fourth and fifth centuries, catechumenates underwent the *apertio,* or opening, during which their eyes, ears, and nostrils were anointed to receive spiritual impressions and divine truths. What did Jesus say regarding his parables? "Let anyone with ears to hear listen" (Mark 4:9). Without being opened, one is unprepared to receive the mysteries of the gospel. This would otherwise cheapen them and oneself. As

Philip Zaleski has observed, one would not be able to discern ambrosia from earthly foods, such as a hamburger from a fast-food restaurant (Philip Zaleski, "The Night Journey of Nicodemus," *Parabola,* vol. 23, no. 4 [1998]).

Paul is opening this dozen disciples to the freedom of the Spirit. Repentance is confining, as it is associated with the Law. The Holy Spirit is freeing. While this freedom is not license, neither is its center given. Paul is merely the access to something that is beyond him, something of which Apollos seems to have been unaware. The Holy Spirit, as we and this dozen discover, spontaneously ignites the fire of spirituality within the tortuous route in the world of our souls. Paul is opening these people, as Welsh poet Gerard Casey would say, "to the Divine in the proper way precisely, in the darkness of our desolation."

One has only to think of the famous triptych known as the Isenheim Altarpiece, by the sixteenth-century painter Mathis Grünewald. Depicted among the mourners of the crucified Christ is John the Baptizer. He is pointing to the Savior. Into the world's darkness he came, bringing light, truth, and real knowledge of God. And not unlike Prometheus, who was chained to the rocky ledge of the Caucasus for bringing fire and knowledge to human beings from Mt. Olympus (and would thereby be terribly popular with the good folks in Corinth), Jesus is punished for his salvific grace. And into the dark void left in the lives and hearts of his followers by his death, resurrection, and ascension, his Holy Spirit came as Jesus promised it would.

It is a bit perplexing that for one so well versed in the details of Jesus' earthly life, Apollos should know little, if anything at all, about the Holy Spirit. But then, we are told a little earlier (Acts 18:24-28) that Apollos was appreciated by Priscilla and Aquila (whom Paul had taught), and they took him aside to teach him that part of the gospel, the knowledge of the Holy Spirit, so he would no longer be ignorant.

The gospel was—and is still—meant to be heard. The Dominican mystic, Meister Eckhart, once told of another master who said that hearing was more noble than seeing because one learned more wisdom through active listening, and in listening we live more wisely. I recall a poster in a sixth-grade classroom which read, "The Lord gave me two ears and one mouth so I could hear twice as much as I speak."

These would-be followers had not yet heard about the Holy Spirit. So when they listened to the words Paul spoke concerning the Spirit, the doors of possibility were opened. They received the Holy Spirit, and like those who had gathered in the Upper Room to pray and subsequently received the Spirit themselves, these people—about a dozen in all (!)—prophesied and spoke with tongues that the gospel might be heard by others through them. They found their bliss: not in ignorance but in the divine spark of the Holy Spirit. (Eric Killinger)

# THE IDENTITY BAPTISM GIVES

## MARK 1:4-11

As we look at how the Gospel writer introduces the gospel of Jesus Christ, we see John the Baptist fulfilling the prophecy of old, calling for everyone to "prepare the way of the Lord" (Isaiah 40:3a). Verses 4-8 tell of John preparing the whole Judean countryside and all the people of Jerusalem, the center of Jewish religious life, to repent of their sins and get ready for the One whom God is about to send. This is much like the Old Testament prophets prophesying about the next king to come. This time, however, we see that God is going to act in an earth-shattering way. God is going to act in a way that is unique for all of creation.

John distinguishes himself from the One who is to come. Coming from a tradition that sounds much like that of the Qumran community or a Jeremiah-like figure, John humbly prophesies about his role and the greater role of the One after him. Ritually, John will wash everyone with water through baptism in the river, but the One to come will penetrate everyone's soul to purify his or her life with the Holy Spirit.

The focus here leads to the introduction and the baptism of Jesus. Verses 10-11 help us to understand that what is happening here is no small thing. Rather, the introduction of Jesus has cosmic significance. The heavens are ripped open and God reveals Jesus as having the unique status as the Son of God! Jesus will be the agent of God's salvation and redemption. The tearing open of heaven reminds us of the beginning of times as God brought all

43

of creation into being. Even more significant, *torn* is the same word that is later used to describe the curtain of the temple being ripped apart at Jesus' death (15:38). All of these events have cosmic significance! The curtains that have been hung to try to give order and structure to a godly life have actually become walls that divide people from each other and from God. The curtains will be torn down with the coming of Jesus. The Gospel writer jumps right into the middle of God's action on earth as Jesus' identity is made known.

As we approach Jesus' baptism, we notice that both John and Jesus are coming from the wilderness as a place for preparation. This reminds us of our Old Testament faith stories of others who had to go through the wilderness before entering into the promised land. Can we enter the promises that God has for us until we have traveled through the wildernesses of our lives? How does the wilderness prepare us for the future? What does it mean to prepare? How do we prepare the way of the Lord? Just as water was used in purification rituals, how does our baptism open us to the Holy Spirit so that we might be purified? Can we testify as to what it meant to us to allow the Son of God to come into our lives?

Just as Jesus' identity was made clear to Jesus at baptism, so our identity is made clearer to us at our baptism. We are publicly making it known that we are trying to follow Jesus. Each of us is unique to God, and through our baptism, God will mold us into our unique identities. Maybe what we need in our lives is to allow God to rip open our hearts and minds so that we can repent and change directions toward God's ways. (Ryan Wilson)

# JANUARY 19, 2003

## *Second Sunday After the Epiphany*

**Worship Theme:** God calls us to glorify God in our bodies and work because it is God who created us for a mission to all creation.

**Readings:** 1 Samuel 3:1-10 (11-20); 1 Corinthians 6:12-20; John 1:43-51

### Call to Worship (Psalm 139:1-2, 13-18 RSV)

*Leader:*    O LORD, thou hast searched me and known me!

**People:**    **Thou knowest when I sit down and when I rise up;**

*Leader:*    Thou discernest my thoughts from afar.

**People:**    **For thou didst form my inward parts, thou didst knit me together in my mother's womb.**

*Leader:*    I praise thee, for thou art fearful and wonderful. Wonderful are thy works! Thou knowest me right well;

**People:**    **My frame was not hidden from thee, when I was being made in secret, intricately wrought in the depths of the earth.**

*Leader:*    Thy eyes beheld my unformed substance; in thy book were written, every one of them, the days that were formed for me, when as yet there was none of them.

**People:**    **How precious to me are thy thoughts, O God! How vast is the sum of them!**

THE ABINGDON PREACHING ANNUAL 2003

*All:*    **If I would count them, they are more than the sand. When I awake, I am still with thee.**

**Pastoral Prayer:**

O God, you remind us not only who we are but also that your claim on us is our call to ministry. Too often we think that you only call the ordained to ministry. But from the beginning, you fashioned yourself a holy people and gave them the task to be "a light to the nations" (Isaiah 42:6*b*; 49:6*b*). Therefore, as you created us, you also gave us as a gift to all people. Renew in us that burning desire to be your people. Give us the courage and energy to be beacons to others for the sake of your name. We confess that we cannot accomplish this mission without a contact to the divine, given in your beloved, Jesus Christ. May we look to Jesus, our Messiah, for sustenance and nurture. This is our holy prayer, in Jesus' name. Amen. (David Mosser)

# SERMON BRIEFS

## HERE I AM

### 1 SAMUEL 3:1-10 (11-20)

Kenneth Chafin relates that as a professor of religion he has his students prepare a sermon from either First or Second Samuel. Each semester one-third of the sermons came from 1 Samuel 3:1-10, which describes Samuel's call to ministry. He reasoned that these young people responded to this passage so overwhelmingly because they could identify with Samuel's search. These students had not stood before a burning bush, as did Moses, nor did they have a vision in the temple of God, as did the prophet Isaiah, but most were young children or teens when they heard the voice of God calling their name. They also had their own Eli, a wise friend who helped them understand the voice of God.

The clergy ranks need people—young and old—to step forward when they hear God call them to "professional" ministry. God does not call all people to be pastors or missionaries, but God does call us by name to fill ministry roles such as Sunday school teaching, ushering, visitation volunteers, choir members, and hundreds of other roles of service. The church needs both men and women who, like Samuel, will say those three important words, "Here I am."

## I. Here I Am Through Listening (vv. 4, 5, 6, 8)

Gerard Reed wrote, "I'm often haunted by the title of Professor Neal Postman's book *Amusing Ourselves to Death*. He argues that the best symbol for modern America is Las Vegas, Nevada, a city humming with frantic people, continuously aglow with the glare of neon signs, devoted to letting the good times roll!" (Gerard Reed, C.S. *Lewis and the Bright Shadow of Holiness* [Kansas City: Beacon Hill Press of Kansas City, 1999], p. 127). Reed's belief is that people are literally committing suicide with addictions, amusements, and diversions, which numb the soul and distract us from eternal concerns. We cannot hear God's voice for the noises surrounding our lives.

If we are to hear God's voice we need to quiet ourselves from the outside distractions and simply listen. Samuel listened to God's voice. Samuel heard God speak in the silence of the night. A popular tune when I was a teenager said, "Silence is golden." How true, but how rare in our age. My plea for this generation is to take time to be silent before God and listen to what God says. Step back from the noise and concentrate on the still small voice that still whispers in any ear that listens.

## II. Here I Am Through Persistent Availability (vv. 5, 6, 8)

It is one thing to listen and another to be actively available. Each time God called Samuel's name he thought it was Eli and without hesitancy went to Eli and said, "Here I am!" Samuel was saying through his action, "Eli, I don't care how often you persist; I am available. I'm here for you!" How available are you for God's use? How available are you for others?

Availability includes: affirming, forgiving, helping, listening, giving, caring, impacting lives—get the picture?

## III. Here I Am Through Service (v. 10)

Ted Engstrom tells about rummaging through a desk at home and discovering a flashlight that he hadn't used in a year. He wasn't surprised when he flipped the switch and discovered it didn't work. He unscrewed it and attempted to remove the batteries but to no avail.

In a last-ditch effort and tug, they came loose! But the mess was horrible. He wrote, "Battery acid had corroded the entire inside of the flashlight. The batteries were new when I'd put them in, and I'd stored them in a safe, warm place. But there was one problem. Those batteries weren't made to be warm and comfortable. They were designed to be turned on—to be used" (Craig Brian Larson, *Illustrations for Preaching and Teaching: from Leadership Journal* [Grand Rapids: Baker Book House, 1993], p. 223).

So God called Samuel to be used. Samuel, at his young age, understood the call. Do you at your age?

God is calling your name. Your positive response should be, "Here I am. Your servant is listening." (Derl Keefer)

# THE BELIEVER AND SEXUAL IMMORALITY

## 1 CORINTHIANS 6:12-20

Paul's attempt to address the various concerns at the church at Corinth turns to specific prohibitions regarding sexual immorality. The church at present exists in a world inundated with sexuality. Thus, the message of this text will sound prudish and legalistic in the ears of present-day hearers. Yet, with the proliferation of pornography and sexual immorality in this technological age, this message is vital.

## I. False Principles Lead to False Christian Living (vv. 12-13)

It appears that Paul quotes some Corinthian believers who flaunted their "liberty" without restraint. Paul reviews two false principles that lead these mistaken believers to live promiscuously. The first principle is that they believed everything was permissible for them. But Paul quickly retorts that everything is not beneficial to the Christian and that a believer is not to be mastered by anything. His point is powerful to a modern society's addictive pattern: Our freedom in Christ is not intended to make us a slave again to the things that bound us before coming to faith in Christ. There are limits in the proper exercise of the Christian's freedom. Behaviors that are enslaving and not beneficial should be avoided. If we are slaves, we are slaves to Jesus Christ alone.

The second false principle is a dualism of sorts. Food for the stomach and stomach for food encapsulates the thought that what is done to the believer's physical body does not affect the spirit or soul. The faulty argument was just as the body digested food and had no effect on the believer's spiritual life (cf. 1 Corinthians 8:1-13), so then behaviors such as sexual promiscuity did not affect the believer spiritually. Paul's response is quite blunt; God will destroy both stomach and food, for the body is not intended for sexual immorality. Instead of a dualism, Paul posits God's sovereignty and principles of human stewardship. The body is for the Lord and the Lord is sovereign over the human spirit and body.

## II. Proper Principles of Christian Discipline (vv. 14-17)

Paul points to the more important principle that the divine and pure power that raised Jesus Christ from the dead is the same power that will also raise our bodies. This first indicates that our bodies have significance in that they will experience resurrection. Thus, they should be properly treated as vessels of honor. Second, the believer's body is a member of Christ (v. 15). That is, we are part of the Body of Christ in soul and in body. From this principle, Paul asks the Corinthians to query: Should we unite members of Christ with a prostitute as one with her in body? The very idea of Christ united with a prostitute is a clear violation of any believer's moral conscience.

Third, Paul moves to the implication of a believer engaging in sexual immorality. When one sexually unites with a prostitute, that person is "one" with her in body. The scriptural principle remains true, the two become one flesh. However, Paul notes that a believer has an even higher union with the Lord in Spirit. This relationship encompasses body and soul. The proper first principles will dictate the proper restraint in the believer's behavior when living in liberty.

### III. Proper Christian Response to Sexual Immorality (vv. 18-20)

The practical matter has yet to be resolved by Paul. How then should a Christian, who has freedom, behave as it relates to sexual immorality? Paul does not direct the believer to prepare and battle the problem of sexual immorality. This sin is particularly potent as a sin against the believer's own body. The sin against the believer's body is highlighted when viewing the fact that the believer's body is the temple of the Holy Spirit. God is to be honored by our bodies; believers are not to be enslaved by the desires of their flesh.

Therefore, the practical response to the temptation of sexual immorality is not to "stand and fight" but to flee. This is a total avoidance of the possibility of engagement in the struggle. Practically, in today's society, believers must avoid or purposely turn from sexual immorality. The only way to properly respond to sexual immorality whether it is pornography, fornication, adultery, and so forth is to flee from it at the first realization of its potential. Anything less will likely ensnare and enslave a believer. (Joseph Byrd)

# NATHANAEL: NO NAME NO LONGER

## JOHN 1:43-51

Good news! My mother hung up the phone but quickly picked it up again. As she dialed, she explained her excitement. My aunt and uncle, who had been waiting for years to adopt a child, had just received the call telling them a baby girl was waiting for them. Our phone did not stay on the hook for very long that evening; Mom just had to share the news with everyone.

Philip must have felt much like my mother did that night. At last, the long-awaited event had occurred. For generations, people had been saying the Messiah would come soon, and now, he finally had. Not only that, he had sought out Philip and made himself known. Who would have guessed this simple man from Nazareth, of all places, would be the one. Philip just had to tell someone. He quickly found Nathanael and burst out with the news, "We have found him—the one Moses and the prophets wrote about. It's

Jesus, the son of Joseph from Nazareth!" Nathanael's reaction was, to say the least, less than desirable. "Nazareth?! You're kidding, right? Nothing good could possibly come from there!" Even that lack of response could not dampen Philip's excitement. "If you don't believe me, come and see for yourself."

Nathanael must have been curious about this man who had his friend so worked up. He trudged up the road behind Philip, following him toward the stranger. Nathanael may not have known Jesus, but Jesus certainly knew him. "Here is truly an Israelite in whom there is no deceit!" Nathanael stopped in his tracks, mouth hanging open for a moment before he stammered, "Where did you get to know me?" Jesus answered, "I saw you under the fig tree before Philip called you." That was all it took. Nathanael's doubt and cynicism fell away as he recognized the one who stood before him. "Rabbi, you are the Son of God! You are the King of Israel!" (vv. 47-49). Jesus promised that Nathanael would see great things in the days to come.

The Bible doesn't tell us much more of Nathanael's story. He is not mentioned again until the last chapter of John's Gospel. There we see that he did indeed, as Jesus promised, see great things. After Jesus' resurrection, Nathanael went fishing with several friends. They caught nothing but continued to fish all night; they probably were not sure what else to do with their lives. Then, just as the sun came up, they heard a call from the beach, telling them to put their nets on the other side. They did, and the fish came pouring in. As they struggled to pull in the net, Nathanael watched in amazement as Peter jumped off the boat and began swimming toward shore—toward Jesus! There could be no greater sight. Here was the one who had been crucified and buried, appearing before the disciples he loved for one last meal together. Nathanael and the others quickly rowed ashore. Nathanael must have remembered, as he ate breakfast with the risen Lord, that day so long ago when he had scoffed at the idea that anything good could come from Nazareth.

The great things of Christ did not end with his resurrection or with the events witnessed by the apostles. They continue if we put our faith in the one from Nazareth who sees and knows us all and who says to each of us: "Come and see." May God grant us the willing heart of Philip and the wondering eyes of Nathanael as we seek to follow Christ's call. (Melissa Scott)

# JANUARY 26, 2003

## *Third Sunday After the Epiphany*

**Worship Theme:** When God manifests God's power in the world all things are possible for those whom God calls.

**Readings:** Jonah 3:1-5, 10; 1 Corinthians 7:29-31; Mark 1:14-20

**Call to Worship (Psalm 62:5-8, 11-12)**

> *Leader:* For God alone my soul waits in silence, for my hope is from him.

> **People:** **He alone is my rock and my salvation, my fortress; I shall not be shaken.**

> *Leader:* On God rests my deliverance and my honor; my mighty rock, my refuge is in God.

> **People:** **Trust in him at all times, O people; pour out your heart before him; God is a refuge for us.**

> *Leader:* Once God has spoken; twice have I heard this: that power belongs to God, and steadfast love belongs to you, O Lord.

> **People:** **For you repay to all according to their work.**

**Pastoral Prayer:**
God of the Universe, we understand that you give even disobedient prophets like Jonah a second chance to fulfill your mission to your world. When your divine Spirit captures our hearts, truly trusting people can accomplish great ministry for your creation. Give us the same sense of urgency to proclaim your truth to our world that captured Paul's heart as he worked with steadfastness

for your realm. Remind us that even in times of despair, your word is sufficient for us. Even as "John was arrested, Jesus came to Galilee, proclaiming the good news of God" (Mark 1:14*a*). Give us the same courage that Jesus had when, amidst his own grief, he nonetheless proclaimed a vital word of life for the people of his generation. Make us an earnest people who have the Word of Life for people in the clutches of death. We pray this in the name of Jesus, the Christ. Amen. (David Mosser)

# SERMON BRIEFS

## TWO PUZZLES

### JONAH 3:1-5, 10

There are two puzzles in the text today that one might consider. The first is how quickly the people of Nineveh responded to such a short sermon by Jonah. The other is the idea of God changing God's mind.

It is obvious that Jonah does not have much regard for the people of Nineveh. The scripture says the city is a three days' journey in breadth. Jonah takes only one day to get into the city as far as he cares to go. He does not even go to the center of the city. He did not even go to the king's court. The king has to hear about this event second hand (3:6).

Maybe Jonah is much like people in our society. We seem to have a fascination with violence. It sells newspapers. It brings people to the theaters. Living close to a NASCAR track, I was wondering to a friend why people would want to watch cars going around in circles for 500 miles. My friend said that people watch the first 400 miles to see the wrecks and the last 100 miles to see who wins. Maybe Jonah really wants to see Nineveh wreck. He does not want to see Nineveh win. We do know that when God does not destroy Nineveh, it disappoints Jonah (4:1).

So, going only one day's journey into the city, Jonah speaks one brief sentence then turns around and leaves. Maybe that was all God gave him to say or maybe Jonah was just doing and saying as little as possible to fulfill the "letter" of what God had told him to do. After all, Jonah had done everything he could to avoid this task. So, he says one sentence, "Forty days more, and Nineveh shall be overthrown!" (v. 4*b*). Then, miracle of miracles, everyone believes. They put on sackcloth and go on a fast. All of them do this, from the greatest of them to the least. Do you not wish that people would respond to your preaching in that manner? What is happening here?

In verse 10 we hear words that those who believe that God is immutable and unchanging do not wish to hear. God changes God's mind. Scripture is full of prophecy where God tells the people what God is going to do and then does it. For many, that is indeed a sign that God is God. How is it that God changes?

Jonah himself gives us the answer to these puzzles when he bemoans the fact that God relents and does not destroy Nineveh. Jonah says, "I knew that you are a gracious God and merciful, slow to anger, and abounding in steadfast love, and ready to relent from punishing" (4:2). The people did not believe Jonah. They believed God. It was not Jonah's eloquence or lack of it that brought the people to believe. It was the gracious work of God's mercy. Likewise, it is not God's nature to be the harsh, immutable, "god of doom." Rather, it is God's nature to be the God of hope, promise, mercy, and grace. Time and time again God acts to redeem God's people often after they have suffered the consequences of their actions in opposing God's will. God brings them out of Egypt, through the desert, into the promised land, and out of Babylon. Given the choice by our free will, it is God's nature to choose mercy. Is it not so with us also in our Lord Jesus Christ? God has acted once again and for all time to redeem God's people. Believe! (Tim Russell)

## LIVING LIKE A VISITOR

### 1 CORINTHIANS 7:29-31

Most people can relate to staying at someone's home for an extended trip. We are never truly comfortable regardless of the stellar hospitality of our host. The bed can be comfortable, but it is not ours. The recreational area can be entertaining, but we are still reserved; it is not ours. That is the kind of attitude or posture that Paul is articulating for believers by analogy here.

## I. Time Is Short and the Present World Is Passing Away (vv. 29, 31)

Regardless of one's eschatology, we cannot avoid Paul's sense of immediacy for doing the work of God. Time slips by, and believers have light only for a period of time to complete their calling and purpose. It is far too easy for believers in today's society to feel that there is no immediacy. Even when confronted by the death of other people or living through incidents that remind them of their own mortality, American believers live like their nonbelieving counterparts—without restraint in accumulating personal happiness.

When people recognize time is short a clear change in priorities and effort emerges. It has been said that no one on their deathbed wishes they had spent more time in the office. Usually, people focus on those things most dear to them: their family, their friends, and their faith. Somehow, present-day believers need a sense of their own mortality and the limitation of time to reshape their priorities and determine the best stewardship of their energy.

## II. The Posture of Visitation

Paul lists five areas of human life that should be affected by a consciousness of our brevity of time. In each of these five areas, believers should carefully reflect on how attached they are to this world's values and not the values of the kingdom of God.

**Marriage** (v. 29). Although marriage and family is an important aspect of human life and Christian homes, it is not the ultimate goal of a believer's life. Some people live for their families and find utter ruin if a tragedy occurs or if relationships disintegrate. This is not to devalue marriages and family nor slight the consequences of death and divorce. It is simply to place marriage and family in the proper perspective: second only to relationship with God and kingdom values. To sacrifice for one's family is laudable if it does not mean sacrificing spiritual commitment to God. No family member should demand that level of sacrifice. To succumb to that type of "extortion" is to have family values out of proper order.

**Grief** (v. 30). Certainly, grief is part of human experience, and we should not deceive ourselves with the unhealthy notion that believers should not grieve. However, there is a particular way that believers are supposed to grieve. A Christian's grief is tempered by hope (1 Thessalonians 4:13). That is, our faith in God causes us to view the death of someone with an eternal perspective and with trust in God.

**Happiness** (v. 30). The analogy here would not be Christian joy, but more along the lines of the temporal happiness that comes with favorable circumstances. People tend to live and make decisions all in an effort to increase their happiness. This is not proper steward-ship of a believer's energy and effort. The call for every believer is to bring glory to God in all that he or she does. Hence, our happiness is viewed as shifting and temporal and not the ultimate issue in deci-sion making.

**Wealth** (v. 30). Related to the concept in the following paragraph, Paul specifically addresses the "buying power" of people. This power is what we can afford to purchase. Paul's phrase calls for a simple lifestyle not caught up in accumulating wealth to purchase *things*. Interestingly, when people buy *things* the *things* tend to own the owner and demand his or her time for maintenance and attention. Better for the believer to be a steward. Material things purchased are not the personal possession of believers; they hold in trust mate-rial property placed in their care by God. Jesus made clear that there would come a day of accountability regarding the stewardship of material possessions.

**Material Possessions** (v. 31). This phrase also involves steward-ship but focuses more on the condition of one's heart. We are not to be engrossed by the *things* that are used in this life. A believer's life cannot consist of the material possessions. These *things* are tempo-ral. As Jesus taught, Christians are to value or treasure the things of heaven (Matthew 6:19-24). (Joseph Byrd)

# AN INVITATION YOU CANNOT REFUSE

## MARK 1:14-20

Our Markan text for this third Sunday after the Epiphany finds Jesus beginning his public ministry. Earlier in chapter 1, we see where the Savior of the world has been baptized by John the Baptist. He's been anointed by the Holy Spirit. He's been affirmed by God and tried and tempted by the devil in the wilderness. And now that he's been delivered from the desert, he is proclaiming that "the time is fulfilled, and the kingdom of God has come near; repent, and believe in the good news" (v. 15).

Interestingly, according to Mark, the first thing Jesus does in his public ministry is to summon people to follow him. Specifically, he calls Simon, Andrew, James, and John—fishers by trade—saying, "Follow me and I will make you fish for people" (v. 17). Mark, with a belief that Jesus' second coming could occur at any time, emphasizes in the calling of each disciple that "immediately" they left everything and followed him.

The Greek word for *call* or *called* here means *to invite* or *to summon*. It reminds me of when I was first invited to follow Jesus. Surely, it could do the same for any reader of the text. I was an athletic 14-year-old having a good time at a church camp in the mountains of Pennsylvania when I first heard that call. I was 20 when it really gripped me and "old things" started passing away; behold all things were becoming new. It was an invitation I could not refuse.

Have you received from Jesus an invitation you cannot refuse? Jesus calls us, hoping that we will follow him to places and possibilities yet unknown. Still, whenever I read this text, I'm always confronted with the question: *What was it that caused Simon, Andrew, James, and John to drop everything and follow him?*

Well, I believe an initial hint is found in verse 15 when Jesus says the time is fulfilled. I believe that the four fishermen recognized that it was time for them to do something different with their lives. Perhaps they were at a transition. They enjoyed fishing; history shows us that after the Lord's resurrection they went back to it. But perhaps they were looking for something deeper in their lives, and here was Jesus offering them an opportunity of a lifetime, a new challenge—an invitation they could not refuse.

Such was the case for me in 1991. I'd been working in "corporate America" and just finished my Master of Divinity degree. I was making good money, living a comfortable life. Like the four fishermen, I was minding my own business, fulfilling the responsibilities of my vocation for that day. But there before me was an invitation to a greater, more powerful life—an invitation I could not refuse. I left my career behind, not knowing where the next paycheck would come from but knowing that "the one who calls you is faithful" (1 Thessalonians 5:24*a*). I've discovered that when the Lord wants you, the Lord comes at a time when you need to change directions. Christ's call is so compelling that even when you can't see what's ahead, you know that all will be well because Jesus is leading you. It's an invitation you cannot refuse.

In reading the text, I believe that these four common folk realized that Jesus could fill a void in their lives. The kingdom of God was near. The God of peace and harmony in the person of Jesus had come to be present with them.

I don't know of a soul in this world that does not desire peace and harmony to be present in our lives. With many of the socioeconomic challenges, the "isms" of life, and the family hardships that many persons face, numerous people just want to experience peace and harmony in their lives as they are going through their daily routines and struggles. Jesus provided that for these four fishing disciples. The kingdom of God had come near.

As a part of our men's ministry at Emory Church in Washington, D.C., several men and myself have covenanted to gather and pray at a local West Indian restaurant. The owners have allowed us to come in before they open in the morning and assemble ourselves for prayer. I remember one morning when three of the cooks came out and requested prayer from us. They were not churchgoers; the demands of survival often minimized their getting to church. But, as we asked them for their prayer requests, each of them without blinking an eye said, "We just want peace in our lives and the lives of our families." As they rose up from prayer that day, realizing a void was being filled, Jesus came by with an invitation they could not refuse. The kingdom of God had come near!

The four left everything as well to follow Jesus because he had good news! Repent and believe in Jesus, and our sins will be forgiven. In a bad news world, where children are killing children, where we have a high incidence of sexually transmitted diseases throughout the country, and where taxes are high and economic times can be rough, people need some good news. People will follow good news. When the Lord came with good news—news of a better way and a better life—it was an invitation they could not refuse.

Finally, I believe the four disciples immediately followed Jesus because they saw that he had a vision. They saw, in following him, the possibility of reaching something they never thought they could attain. In casting a vision, Jesus gave them hope. I would imagine that was powerful for people who did the same thing day in and day out. They were given a vision of hope, a vision of a tomorrow that could be better than the present. It was an invitation they could not refuse.

Jesus is always dropping by the doorstep of our lives with a call to greater possibilities at the time we least expect it, but at the time when we need to have him. Have you accepted the invitation you cannot refuse? Perhaps for someone, the time has come. (Joseph Daniels)

# REFLECTIONS

# FEBRUARY

**Reflection Verse:** *"Those who endure to the end shall be saved."* *(Mark 13:13 NLT)*

By February each year most of us are beginning to feel guilty because we are losing the battle to keep some of our more lofty resolutions. People need to be encouraged not to lose heart and give up. Just because you did not keep all of your resolutions does not mean you should abandon all of them. Encouragement is an important concept for the preacher to feed the flock—and more than likely, it would be good medicine for the preacher also.

When I was growing up in rural South Alabama during the Great Depression, there was an outbreak of hog cholera in our community. This was a matter of serious concern to a group of farmers who were sitting around the country store one Saturday afternoon discussing the matter. One old farmer seemed to have had more experience than the others, so they turned to him for advice about what to expect. He thought for a moment and then made this interesting pronouncement: "Well, it appears that them what gits it and lingers for a few days do better than them that gits it and dies right off."

Life is like that. Hang in there. Some days, and in some ways, survival is an achievement in and of itself.

A story emerged a few years ago about a very unusual person. Her name is Marie Balter. At the age of 17, she was suffering severe depression and panic disorder. She was misdiagnosed as schizophrenic and spent the next twenty years in and out of the Danvers State Mental Hospital. With the help of friends and the strength of her faith, she gained release from the hospital and from her misdiagnosis.

Her recovery was painful and gradual, but she was determined to take charge of her life. She got an apartment, got married, earned a degree in psychology from Salem State College and a Master's Degree from Harvard in administrative planning and public policy. Marie Balter later returned in triumph as administrator of the Danvers State Mental Hospital.

What a victory for Marie Balter! She made up her mind that she would not continue to be a victim. She said that she would not have grown one bit if she had not learned to forgive. "If you don't learn to forgive your parents, or your children, or yourself, you never get beyond anger," said Ms. Balter. "Forgiving is a way of reaching out from a bad past and heading out to a more positive future."

Not many of us will face problems of such magnitude. We may face a problem of that type but not that magnitude. Not many will experience such a dramatic victory over such a traumatic situation. But, we all have our problems, which are important to us. We are embattled by forces of evil and unfortunate circumstances that threaten our balance, our sanity, and sometimes even our lives.

We live in a dangerous world where accidents happen even to the most careful persons. If absolute safety is our goal, then being born was a fundamental mistake. We are beset by circumstances that are seldom under our control. Our lives are affected by the sins, mistakes, and poor judgments of other people. There is evil in the world, which brushes against our lives at unexpected times. There are natural disasters that capriciously destroy.

We are seldom able to control the forces that cause us grief and, no matter how hard we try or how careful we may be, we cannot avoid suffering, pain, and sorrow. Our greatest battle is not with any of these forces that lie beyond our control, as frightening as the specter of them may be. The real war is within. Our greatest battle is with ourselves. Most of our defeats have come because we have not learned to fight effectively against the enemy within. We can seldom control what happens to us, but we have a tremendous margin of control over how we respond to that event. That margin of control is more often than not the difference between victory and defeat.

When Marie Balter came out of the mental hospital, after having been kept there for 17 years under a misdiagnosis, she had some choices to make. If she had chosen to direct her energies against the people and the circumstances that caused her problem, she may well have gone back to Danvers Hospital, but not as Administrator. She would more likely have gone back as a patient. She could not change what had happened, but she could control how she responded. This was the key to her recovery and to her return to Danvers State Mental Hospital as administrator rather than as a patient.

One of the most insidiously dangerous developments in our lives is the compulsion to be perfect. This usually begins with the idea that the more perfect we are the more people will love and admire us. It does not seem to matter that the very premise of this perception is untrue. People will first admire but finally fear a person who appears to be perfect.

How many people do you know who are perfect or who think they are perfect? Are they people in whose presence you feel safe? I don't know about your experience with "perfect people," but mine is not very good. I really do not enjoy the company of "perfect people." They are a pain! I have never been helped much by "perfect people." If you were able to achieve perfection, your friends would distance themselves from you in direct proportion to the perceived perfection. The "perfect people" in Jesus' day were the Pharisees. Jesus did not like them. They did not like Jesus. Beware of the illusion of perfection. It is a real trap.

People who have a compulsion to be perfect begin to "fudge" when their performance does not measure up to their expectations. The inward battle is the struggle to accept one's humanity. We all suffer, somewhat, from wanting to appear better than we are. We put up some kind of front that leads others to think we have it "all together" when in reality we have some fundamental fragmentation. Sometimes we become so good at misrepresenting ourselves to others that we can literally fall apart before any of our friends realize what is going on. It is important for us to be able to forgive ourselves for not being perfect and to expect others to forgive us too.

People need to hear an encouraging word from the pulpit. In order to win the biggest battles in your life, it is important to do all that you can, but you do not have to do it all by yourself. There is help—human and divine. Hang in there! (Thomas Lane Butts)

# FEBRUARY 2, 2003

*Fourth Sunday After the Epiphany*

**Worship Theme:** The power of God is manifest in the healing and loving work of Jesus. God calls the faithful to emulate the ministry of Jesus' healing love.

**Readings:** Deuteronomy 18:15-22; 1 Corinthians 8:1-13; Mark 1:21-28

## Call to Worship (Psalm 111:1-8)

*Leader:* Praise the LORD! I will give thanks to the LORD with my whole heart, in the company of the upright, in the congregation.

*People:* **Great are the works of the LORD, studied by all who delight in them.**

*Leader:* Full of honor and majesty is his work, and his righteousness endures forever.

*People:* **He has gained renown by his wonderful deeds; the LORD is gracious and merciful.**

*Leader:* He provides food for those who fear him; he is ever mindful of his covenant.

*People:* **He has shown his people the power of his works, in giving them the heritage of the nations.**

*Leader:* The works of his hands are faithful and just; all his precepts are trustworthy.

*All:* **They are established forever and ever, to be performed with faithfulness and uprightness.**

**Pastoral Prayer:**

Gracious God, you know our frame and the intent of our heart. You, O God, know that we are people who create idols out of nothing. Yet, you love us all the same. Help us to recognize those things in our lives that attempt to replace you as our center and focus as believers. When we see the so-called demons of our age, help us to confront and name them. Give us the strength to overcome evil in the manifold ways that evil reveals itself in our lives. Grant us a vision of Jesus, who rebuked demons and freed people to live lives that befit the gospel. Impart to us the spirit of Jesus, who knew who he was and lived according to your claim on his life. Let today be a day in which we solemnly recovenant to be your sacred people—the chosen people of our day. We pray this in Jesus Christ's holy name. Amen. (David Mosser)

# SERMON BRIEFS

## MOSES AND LIFE'S TRANSITIONS

### DEUTERONOMY 18:15-22

Edwin Friedman was a rabbi and systems thinker who wrote a great deal to help churches understand whether or not they function in healthy or unhealthy ways. He wrote that a successful transition depends more on how the present leader departs than on the efforts of the successor. Problems occur when the longtime leader does not openly deal with his or her own grief with the people. Transitions can also be made more difficult if the leader lives out the belief that no one else can really do as well. Most often this becomes evident when a former leader participates in triangles with the new leadership and longtime church friends.

Moses has faith in God's care and provision for God's people. He is actively dealing with the concerns that people will have in major transitions in their life together. It is important to note that the faith Moses articulates to the people is that their nation can also be important in the life of an individual, and it is individuals who must navigate the often turbulent waters of personal transitions. This article of faith is important to the meaning of the season of Epiphany.

The first thing Moses declares is that God will raise up leaders. In times of transition people need a presence that connects them to God. Moses is clear in his affirmation that God will raise up leaders who will be capable of discerning God's presence. In all likelihood, this story is remembered to describe roles that persons will be called of God to fulfill. The early reader would be able to recall the people God called and who fulfilled the role of prophet in the history of the people of Israel. Christians can see this promise fulfilled in Jesus. In Jesus we find the love and presence of God most clearly revealed. In Jesus we find the presence of God incarnate in human life.

In times of transition people need the presence of God in ways that communicate the character of God. Jesus said that he came to give sight, to heal, to set free, and to proclaim the kingdom of God. Parables are how Jesus most often revealed the character of God. The shepherd seeking the lost sheep, a father looking down the road for a son, or a woman scouring her household for a lost coin imply to us what is in the heart of God. In the life of Jesus, we experience a God who welcomes little children, invites scoundrels to lunch, and includes people caught in the act of sin. For people asking what will become of us, God is revealed as one who acts to help and to lead.

This passage from Deuteronomy invites us to consider where we are in the transitions of our life. We are invited to find whose words of comfort and hope have been helpful in our life's forward progress. In the season of Epiphany we look first to the person of Jesus as that one whose presence and word for us has been the truth by which we can live. In Christ's sacrificial love for us we know we are moving to the promised land.

A curious kind of affirmation ends this portion of Moses' teaching. Sometimes we will hear a word that does not prove true. We are advised not to be frightened. Apparently, the Word of God will always find its way to us in our searching. In Epiphany we celebrate that the Word of God has come with a light that the world cannot extinguish. (Bob Holloway)

# SPIRITUAL MATURITY

## 1 CORINTHIANS 8:1-13

The Corinthian believers had asked Paul certain questions, which he took time to answer in his letter to them. In this text he is answering a question regarding food that had been used in pagan rituals, offered on the pagan altars, which was common in that day among Gentiles. It is easy to brush this text off as irrelevant to the modern church because such pagan rituals are not part of our societal customs. However, there are important principles about how we should relate to one another here, particularly as maturing believers.

## I. The Value of Human Knowledge (vv. 1-3)

Setting this topic in context, Paul "levels the playing field" in pointing out the limited spiritual value of human knowledge. It is not that faith is irrational; however, kingdom principles are very often "transrational." Knowledge that is common to all humanity has a result of "puffing up." That is, human knowledge tends to give one a false pride and arrogance. In dealing with questions of spiritual maturity, there is no room for arrogance among those who are more mature. Such arrogance will negate the effort in edifying all of the believers involved. The primary focus should be God knowing us, not our knowledge. God's knowledge of us is rooted in our love for God. If we fully commit ourselves to loving God and following God's direction, we can address controversial situations in the Body of Christ with an eye toward pastoral edification of God's flock.

## II. Truth of Spiritual Reality (vv. 4-6)

Having set the proper tone for the discourse about food offered to idols, Paul begins to address the topic specifically. Those who have been converted know that an idol is nothing because the believer knows that there is only one God. Paul acknowledges that even if there are some creatures of a spiritual nature, they all are subordinate and inferior to the one true God from whom all things come. Believers live for this one God, and our priorities reflect our loyalty to God alone. Moreover, believers recognize the singular Lordship of Jesus Christ through whom all things came into being and through whom we live. Thus, our views of demonic or "other world" realities need to be kept in the perspective of the sovereignty of God and the Lordship of Jesus Christ.

### III. Newer Believers and the Posture of Mature Christians (vv. 7-13)

Paul recognizes that not all believers have come to fully embrace the truth of God's sovereignty and the Lordship of Jesus Christ. Some believers, newer to the faith (or immature), become accustomed to their worldly context of false or erroneous beliefs that they have weak consciences in their "superstitions." For them, to partake in food used in a pagan ritual is to partake in defiled food. But Paul notes the truth that food does not affect us in our spiritual walk with God, reminiscent of the words of Jesus in Matthew 15:11. There, Jesus said, "It is not what goes into the mouth that defiles a person, but it is what comes out of the mouth that defiles."

The response of the mature believer is not to be one of ridicule toward the less mature believer, however. In fact, Paul indicates that the more mature believer is to be more aware of the less mature. He warns the mature in verse 9, not to allow their freedom to become a stumbling block to the weaker believers. The potential danger is that a flagrant demonstration of liberty can negatively influence the immature to act against their weak conscience. They are "destroyed" by the "knowledge" of the mature—a clear violation of the purpose that God gave such "knowledge" to mature believers. Christ is unhappy when we act and live in an uncaring way toward the immature believer. So, the posture of the mature is reflected by avoiding the behaviors that would bring condemnation to weaker believers, in consideration and concern for their growth. (Joseph Byrd)

## LEADERSHIP WITH AUTHORITY

### MARK 1:21-28

More and more in my travels as a pastor, I observe people looking for leadership that can transform lives and situations in deep and powerful ways. The fact that the 2000 presidential election was so close reflected that neither candidate convinced the majority that he had the authority people needed to change their circumstances for the better.

Dionne Warwick was right when she sang several decades ago that, "What the world needs now is love sweet love." But I've been telling my congregation that what the world needs more of now is strong, spiritual leadership, people from all walks of life who will take authority in leading people to have life and have it more abundantly because of a deep and abiding relationship with God.

This was confirmed for me even further at a seminary graduation not long ago. Mike McCurry, the former press secretary for President Bill Clinton, gave the keynote address and spoke of his experiences around leadership in the White House. He told the graduating class of Doctor of Ministry candidates that what our country needs more than anything is strong, spiritual leadership. He said in essence that in the United States, we have "a plethora of information but a paucity of leadership."

When Jesus came to Capernaum and on the sabbath attended synagogue to teach, he came with authority. He came with a life that was connected to his power source—God. He spoke with authority and lived with authority. When we are in relationship with God, allowing God to feed and nurture this relationship daily, we will find that, like Jesus, we can do the same. We'll even find that, like Jesus, we can teach with authority. Like Jesus, our teaching will astound and amaze people—even transform people—causing them to follow the Christ. This will arise not because of our own doing but because of the fruit God will produce in us—the results coming from having an abiding relationship with God.

The scribes were ineffective in transforming people's lives through their teaching because they lacked a firm connection with the God of transformation. They relied on their position of authority rather than God's divine authority. Positional authority without power leaves churches suffering. It also leaves hurting people unchanged in a world where people need to be healed.

At present, we have too many people in our denominations and churches who are functioning like scribes. We are leading by position and not with power. Many churches are dying, and mainline denominations struggle for this very reason. As a result, we see people leave one church for another, because they're searching for that power that they've seen and heard can strengthen their lives.

Troubled people who come to church want to know where they can find help and, more important, who can help them. Troubled people coming to church want to be taught by people operating in divine authority. Troubled people want to learn so that, as healed people, they can live and teach with authority themselves. When we lead with God's authority, teaching with God's authority, healing comes to those around us. Transformative events begin to happen around us.

The factual evidence is right in our text, for as Jesus continued teaching with authority in the synagogue, a man with an unclean spirit emerges and is changed. Leading with authority will cause demons to tremble. For even demons recognize divine power and have to flee. When we lead in the power of Jesus, demons—unclean spirits, behaviors, attitudes, and habits not of God that seek to control us—must go. As the text reveals, when Jesus is present, evil cannot remain. When we lead in the authority of Jesus, works of the flesh seeking to control us such as fornication, impurity, idolatry, sorcery (our modern day drug abuse), strife, jealousy, anger, dissensions, envy, drunkenness, carousing, and so forth have got to go. When we lead with authority, by the power of Jesus these spirits must come out of people. The Lord was not afraid to speak with authority and live with authority, and as he did, lives were changed for the better. When we follow his example, lives will be changed.

When I was ordained, I recall the bishop laying hands on me and saying, "Take thou authority as an elder of this church. . . ." When we take it, lead with it, and live by it, the world will be a happier, healthier place. The church will be much stronger. (Joseph Daniels)

# FEBRUARY 9, 2003

*Fifth Sunday After the Epiphany*

**Worship Theme:** The Lord God is almighty. The Lord has no equal in earth or in heaven. Jesus uses the divine power to preach good news and heal the infirm.

**Readings:** Isaiah 40:21-31; 1 Corinthians 9:16-23; Mark 1:29-39

**Call to Worship (Psalm 147:1-7a, 20)**

> *Leader:* Praise the LORD! How good it is to sing praises to our God; for he is gracious, and a song of praise is fitting.
>
> *People:* **The LORD builds up Jerusalem; he gathers the outcasts of Israel.**
>
> *Leader:* He heals the brokenhearted, and binds up their wounds.
>
> *People:* **He determines the number of the stars; he gives to all of them their names.**
>
> *Leader:* Great is our Lord, and abundant in power; his understanding is beyond measure.
>
> *People:* **The LORD lifts up the downtrodden; he casts the wicked to the ground.**
>
> *Leader:* Sing to the LORD with thanksgiving;
>
> *All:* **He has not dealt thus with any other nation; they do not know his ordinances. Praise the LORD!**

**Pastoral Prayer:**

God of Grace and God of Glory, in you we move and live and have our being. As we worship your holy splendor this day, keep before us the wonder and majesty of creation. Help us be good stewards over nature's resources, for you have entrusted them to us as a sacred responsibility. May we hand on to future generations our natural world in a condition that is better than the condition in which it was passed on to us. The prophet tells us that you, O Lord, give "power to the faint, and strengthens the powerless" (Isaiah 40:29). Help us draw from your divine strength to be the people you created us to be. Let us reach out to others as you first reached out to us in love. We pray this in the holy name of Jesus. Amen. (David Mosser)

# SERMON BRIEFS

## DOES GOD ANSWER PRAYER?

### ISAIAH 40:21-31

You might ask, Why even ask such a question? Does God answer prayer when we ask? Well, sometimes it seems that our prayers are unanswered. Good people pray for good things such as the health of a loved one but eventually stare at an empty chair at the dinner table. The heavens are deafening by their silence. Or, possibly our prayers seem unanswered because we misunderstand the nature of prayer. If our petitions include only "gimmie, gimmie" from a perceived heavenly Santa Claus, then we may not always receive the answers we anticipate. Or if we see prayer as a sort of spiritual hocus-pocus in which we utter the right incantations and are guaranteed results, we may be disappointed. One man actually said to me, "If I abide in him and he abides in me, God has to do what I say, right?" Or, possibly even more tragic, some may have given up on prayer altogether. This attitude may range from, "Well, God already knows, so why ask?" to a quiet resignation that prayer goes nowhere. As a result we simply don't pray. So, the question *Does God answer prayer?* may not be so far-fetched after all.

71

I believe that God answers every prayer. God hears and answers every prayer, believer or unbeliever! Be advised though that God may not answer every prayer in the way we think God should. I believe that it was John Claypool who stated that God answers every prayer: some with a *yes,* some with a *no,* and some with a *wait.* Often God says Yes! Emphatically, enthusiastically God responds, "Finally! I have been waiting for you to ask. This is in my will for you. I am delighted that we agree." On other occasions, God wisely says, "No! This is not best for you." If a three-year-old asked for a sharp knife, would you hand it to him or her? Doesn't Garth Brooks sing "Thank God for Unanswered Prayers"? God may respond, "Wait a while. You are not ready to receive this." God may be waiting for us to act on the answer we received yesterday before answering our petition of today.

Our text responds to our curiosity of how God does answer prayer. Again, Claypool is helpful. He writes that God responds by miracle, collaboration, and strength to cope. Sometimes, maybe more than we realize, God responds with an outright miracle or rescue giving us "wings as eagles" and lifting us up out of the situation. Something occurs for which there is no other explanation except God. God acts, not necessarily contrary to nature but perhaps contrary to nature as we know it. Then, on other occasions, God says, "Let us collaborate or cooperate together to bring about our desired result." It is often nothing short of amazing how God's strength combines with our weakness when we are willing to work with God. We can "run and not grow weary." Then, there are those times (more than we wish) when God gives us strength to cope. Some days the best we can do is to merely "walk and not faint." Often we can only hang in there and endure. But is not the ability to simply persevere also an answer to prayer? Paul seemed to think that his ability to cope with his "thorn in the flesh" was an indication of the sufficiency of God's grace.

I believe that prayer, allowing for the awkwardness of our words, is an expressed trust in the gracious nature of God and God's ultimate will for our lives. God loves us unconditionally and, in every situation, seeks to conform us to the image of God's Son! (Romans 8:28-29). Who wouldn't want to pray to a God like that? (Gary Carver)

# THE CALL TO MINISTRY

## 1 CORINTHIANS 9:16-23

The heart of Paul's call and purpose in ministry is demonstrated in a graphic way in this passage. The Body of Christ needs to rediscover the purpose and motivation for our existence and find fresh passion and compassion in the working out of our ministry. Having a clear perspective on our role in the larger scheme of God's plan and keeping God's purposes before us will keep us on the path of effective ministry.

## I. The Role of the Minister (vv. 16-18)

The primary role that Paul viewed for himself was to proclaim the gospel of Jesus Christ through preaching (see 1 Corinthians 2:1-5). However, Paul also knew that in discharging his duties to preach, he had no place to boast because his preaching came from an inward compulsion. So strong was this passion for the gospel that he exclaims, "Woe to me if I do not proclaim the gospel (v. 16)!" He was no hired hand with rhetorical skills that he should be compensated for his services. Paul simply was being a good steward of what God had entrusted to him as one who proclaims the gospel. He was able to offer the gospel free of charge, as a herald sent by the King.

## II. Passion-Compassion of Ministry (vv. 19-23)

The minister is a person of liberty and yet has connected himself or herself to people in a servant role, with the purpose of winning as many people for Christ as possible. This causes Paul to step out of his comfort zone and personal preference and to change his approach to effectively minister to a wide range of audiences. He identified with several categories of people: Jewish, Gentile, and weak. Paul was willing to identify with the wide array of people for the purpose of winning some to faith in Jesus Christ. It was for the sake of the gospel and his desire to share in the blessings of the gospel that Paul was willing to press beyond his own comfort level.

In general, the church lacks this kind of passion for the kingdom of God and compassion for people. This lack of passion is reflected in the pride and unwillingness to associate and identify with people of varying ethnic, social, and gender backgrounds. Yet, when God's compassion fails to consume us with passion, we also fail to be gospel stewards. We may take care of our church buildings and administrative structures, stay within budgets and maintain the policies that six subcommittees developed through months of drafting. Yet, have we lost something in all of the busy religious work? Such a description of ministry seems dissonant from the ministry that Paul has described.

What should we be doing? Returning to the foundation of our own faith and realizing our place to be participants in God's wonderful work of grace will refresh and ignite both our passion for the Kingdom and our compassion for the people of God. When we dedicate ourselves to what the heart of God desires and God's purposes and take serious time to reflect and listen to the guiding divine voice, we will find effective and rewarding ministry. This ministry makes an eternal difference in the lives of people.

Here is the challenge for ministry in the twenty-first century. We are not hired hands to diffuse our expertise (although Kingdom ministry must be competent). We are to be inwardly compelled to bring to God's household all of God's lost children. Our message in this technological era is no different than that of the apostle Paul and neither should our purpose and motivation. (Joseph Byrd)

# CAN YOU STAND THE PRESSURE?

## MARK 1:29-39

People often underestimate the pressure that comes to an individual doing ministry. The multitude of problems, needs, and concerns pastors face can be overwhelming. What begins as a single need soon evolves into a heavy burden. Before we know it, we can find ourselves having to function under a great deal of pressure.

Our lectionary text for this week gives a vivid picture of this pressure. As Jesus pressed forward in his public ministry bringing hope and transformation to troubled people's lives, the burden Jesus carried became heavier and heavier. It started with just a single event, the healing of Simon's mother-in-law from a fever. At verse 32, however, we see Simon, Andrew, James, John, and others bring to Jesus all who were sick or possessed with demons. Soon the whole city of Capernaum was gathered around the door where Jesus was staying, in hopes of being healed.

Jesus was under great pressure. No doubt, every faithful servant of God—clergy and laity—comes to points in our service where we are overwhelmed by the demands of ministry. We find ourselves under enormous pressure, for people come to us needing relief from many problems, needs, and concerns. There is the mother who needs a mentor for her wayward son. There is the household that has witnessed the breadwinner lose his or her job, needing rent money to keep the family from being evicted. Couples have marital problems. The list goes on and on. Sometimes in ministry, people arrive in droves needing help here and now. Suddenly, you find yourself under great pressure. Can you stand the pressure?

Surely it was a question Jesus had to face, and it is a question we, too, must answer. As we track the concluding verses of our text, we discover that Jesus leaves us a model. This model offers a discipline to handle ministry pressures. When verse 35 rolls around, we find that Jesus was able to stand under the pressure because he first cultivated a prayer life. Jesus carved out time in his busy schedule to talk with God in prayer and have his battery recharged, so to speak. As we read this Scripture and others in the Gospels, we find that Jesus made it a habit to rise before dawn and go pray in a deserted place. He found a time and place to be alone with God.

It is in "alone times" with God that we can reflect on all that is happening to us, with us, and around us. It is in "alone times" with God that we can allow God to speak to us about the sorting of life's priorities. It is in "alone times" with God that the ordering of our steps must surface if we are going to stand under the pressure. It is in quiet prayer, before the alarm clocks go off, the radios blast, and the phone starts ringing with demands from the outside, that we can get our daily marching orders from God. In prayer, we can daily receive a divine road map from God enabling us to stay focused on those things Jesus wishes us to accomplish. Jesus also tells us those things we need to leave for others to do.

When we start each day with prayer, we can stand the pressure because our spiritual batteries have been recharged. As the text reveals, the agendas of others will not deter us from accomplishing what the Lord places before us. In verse 37, Simon and his companions bring an agenda for Jesus. "Everyone is searching for you," he says. That "everyone" was, no doubt, those people whom Jesus was unable to heal just yet. Notice the Lord's response. He says, "Let us go on to the neighboring towns, so that I may proclaim the message there also; for that is what I came out to do" (v. 38). From the early morning prayer, Jesus had his day's purpose set. Jesus focused on getting it done.

As ministers of the gospel—clergy and laity—we desire to meet everyone's needs. Jesus reminds us, however, that we will not be able to reach everyone; that is God's business. God will provide. As we arise in prayer, allowing God to recharge our batteries and provide us with divine marching orders, we can press forward daily with the purpose of reaching those God intends for us to reach. In prayer and with a clear purpose, like Jesus, we will be able to proceed with power—proclaiming the message of good news and healing people from behaviors, habits, and attitudes not of God, which seek to control us. Daily, we will be able to stand under the pressure because God orders our steps.

Can you stand the pressure? (Joseph Daniels)

# FEBRUARY 16, 2003

*Sixth Sunday After the Epiphany*

---

**Worship Theme:** God asks certain things of disciples, but true faith reveals that service to the Lord is its own reward.

---

**Readings:** 2 Kings 5:1-14; 1 Corinthians 9:24-27; Mark 1:40-45

**Call to Worship (Psalm 30:1, 4-5, 10-12)**

*Leader:* I will extol you, O LORD, for you have drawn me up, and did not let my foes rejoice over me.

**People: Sing praises to the LORD, O you his faithful ones, and give thanks to his holy name.**

*Leader:* For his anger is but for a moment; his favor is for a lifetime. Weeping may linger for the night, but joy comes with the morning.

**People: Hear, O LORD, and be gracious to me! O LORD, be my helper!**

*Leader:* You have turned my mourning into dancing; you have taken off my sackcloth and clothed me with joy, so that my soul may praise you and not be silent.

**All: O LORD my God, I will give thanks to you forever.**

**Pastoral Prayer:**

On this Sabbath day, O God of all days, make us mindful of the yoke of discipleship. As Jesus told us, "My yoke is easy, and my burden is light" (Matthew 11:30). Therefore, as we strive to be better and more faithful disciples, O God, keep in our hearts that certain knowledge that Jesus is our Lord. Allow and inspire us to

77

pay homage to Jesus by serving others with glad and generous hearts. Remind us that it is often the most difficult people to love who so desperately need the love of Jesus. Keep us in your fold. Help us meditate day and night on the things that please you. Most of all, O God, let us embrace our salvation as the precious gift it is. As stewards over your mysteries, may you find us faithful. We pray this in Jesus' name. Amen. (David Mosser)

# SERMON BRIEFS

## CLEANLINESS IS NEXT TO GODLINESS

### 2 KINGS 5:1-14

One morning while taking my daily constitutional, I saw a new pickup truck with these words emblazoned on the rear window of its cab: "I'm not spoiled—just well taken care of."

The more I ponder this message, the more I like that little piece of insight. Poor old Naaman. He was spoiled. He lived to serve at the discretion of his king, a powerful man and apparently well pleased with his mighty warrior. Undoubtedly, Naaman would have had the best: the best chariot and horses for battle, the best servants and soldiers, the best clothes and weapons, and perhaps, the best wives. All the best a man of his stature could want he had achieved. And yet, he was plagued with leprosy. Oh, it may well have been any number of skin diseases from scrofula to rosacea, for had it been true leprosy, he would not have had the strength to fight.

But to his good fortune, a female captive from Israel knew of Elisha, the prophet in Samaria. This is an interesting point since the Samaritans and Israelites seem never to have been on particularly good terms with one another. At any rate, Naaman, a man of achievement, asks his Aramaic master for permission to follow up on the information he has garnered. Travel documents are drafted and sealed, an expense account is granted, and Naaman is off to the Holy Land.

The king of Israel is perplexed. Leprosy in any form was forbidden within the city gates. It said so in the rule books, zoning laws, and statutes in the law library. What was the king of Israel supposed to do? This went against everything in the law. It went beyond the pale. Today he might have cried out, "This isn't Lourdes! People don't come here for cures." So he had little recourse but to rend his robes in fear and loathing. No tact. Too much exclusivism. No diplomacy here.

Like the good Samaritan in a future parable of one Jesus of Nazareth, Elisha pipes up and says, "I'll take care of him." He is the true prophet in the best sense; that is, he knows the difference between his ethnic ideas and the elementary ideas they enclose. But his prescription is so dispassionately and disappointingly simple that Naaman can't believe it. He thought making the pilgrimage to Israel was tantamount to being religious. Being religious was equivalent to obtaining a cure: calling on the name of God, passing a hand over the diseased spot, and incanting some mumbo jumbo. Perhaps a shamanic dance to boot. Oh, well. It was not to be. Naaman fumed. He could have bathed at home, saving himself the stress and nuisance of the trip! Had he been retired, we could imagine him sitting at home with his chin on his hand, "chewing the fat," remembering when. However, his body said, "You know, you're not giving me anything to do here, so I'm just gonna sign off"—or however it goes in Aramaic. His servant, thank God, knew that he had to do this simple thing. Had he been ordered to slay a dragon or jump through fire to rescue some poor distressed damsel to obtain the cure, Naaman wouldn't have batted an eye. But take a bath—albeit a ritual one?

But this was a spiritual journey at its best. Seven immersions in the Jordan symbolized cleansing the self on the way to wholeness. Naaman, like the rest of us, needed to be right and still within himself before being still and knowing God is God. Perhaps it helped Naaman realize he could no longer be spoiled but rather could be well taken care of. (Eric Killinger)


# CHRISTIANITY AIN'T FOR SISSIES!

## 1 CORINTHIANS 9:24-27

The apostle Paul has been called many things: boastful, fervent, daring, stubborn, antiwoman, zealous, just to name a few.

But he rarely has been called wishy-washy for being too pliable or flexible. However, he might be so accused if one looks closely at 1 Corinthians 9:19-23. "I make myself a slave to everyone. . . . I have become all things to all men so that by all possible means I might save some" (vv. 19, 22*b* NIV). Too flexible? Paul? Say it ain't so!

There are some who say that the church has become too flexible in seeking to reach the unchurched. We have to adapt to the times to reach a consumer-oriented market. Agreed? But how far do we go? What about this current worship with choruses and rock bands? We know that we need to tile and repaint the church nursery, but how do we know if this music business is a fad or a fixture? "It was good enough for my generation, why isn't it good enough for theirs?" we hear people ask. We, like Paul, want to reach everyone, but where do we draw the line? How flexible can we be and still be true to the integrity of the gospel?

Like it or not, the church is in transition. Some say we will be in transition for the next 30 to 40 years. We have not set foot in these waters before. Paradigms shift so rapidly! We used to talk about shifting trends in the 1960s, but now major changes occur every two to four years, not every decade. What can we do in days of such rapid transition?

We don't have all the answers; neither did Paul. Paul does, however, give us a clue in his letter to the troubled church at Corinth. We must remember that his time was similar to ours in that faith in Christ had brought radical change to many believers with no road maps to guide them. Paul's own faith, too, was a theology in process. His evangelistic style varied with the audience. So, what was the constant factor, the consistency that gave his ministry integrity and effectiveness?

In our text Paul would say "Keep spiritually fit!" Using a well-known sports analogy, he would urge them and us to exercise spiritual discipline. We cannot control everything in a rapidly changing world, but we can control ourselves. For Paul, spiritual formation involved the "strict training" of practices such as prayer, fasting, solitude, and perseverance. We can be "God's athletes," who condition and train ourselves in order to be used by God to benefit others.

Chattanooga native Reggie White, future NFL Hall-of-Famer,

is quoted as saying, "Football is one thing—but life with God is everything. What really matters is what is on the inside." Here is the true battleground! When we can win the battle on the inside, we can win the battle on the outside. The cry today, from young and old alike, is for practical guidance on how to live the life of Christ. People want to know how to live a life with God! How well has the church done in providing such help in spiritual formation?

Paul's exhortation is set in the background of the Isthmian Games, the athletic festival held in Corinth every two years. The athlete's "perishable wreath" is illuminated because the victory wreath at the Isthmian Games was made of withered celery.

Another example is that of Gary Player responding to someone who said to him, "I'd give anything if I could hit a golf ball like you!" He would reply, "No you wouldn't. . . . Do you know what you have to do to hit a golf ball like I do? You've got to get up at 5:00 every morning, go out to the golf course, and hit a thousand golf balls! Your hands start bleeding, and you walk to the club house and wash the blood off your hands, slap a bandage on it, and go out and hit another thousand golf balls! That is what it takes to hit a golf ball like I do!"

If athletes would push themselves to the limit to win a pathetic crown of withered vegetables or to the point of bleeding, how much more should we maintain self-discipline to obtain a crown that lasts forever? As Paul says, "Follow my example, as I follow the example of Christ" (1 Corinthians 11:1 NIV).

Christianity ain't for sissies! (Gary Carver)


## CAN'T KEEP IT TO MYSELF

### MARK 1:40-45

Our text for this sixth Sunday after the Epiphany serves as the concluding healing story found in the first chapter of Mark. Jesus is now active in his public ministry, spending much time healing the sick and casting out demons from suffering people.

As we approach this final pericope of the chapter, we encounter a man suffering from leprosy. Leprosy is a contagious skin disease, a disease so abhorred by society in that day that individuals who contracted it were banished from their communities, often forced to live in colonies outside city gates. Lepers were considered outcasts, much like those suffering from AIDS. Reentrance to the community for a healed leper could only occur through the temple priest who was given the responsibility of proclaiming the individual clean or unclean.

This leper, however, refused to endure this outcast status. In fact, he demanded deliverance from it. And as we encounter him in verse 40, he has submitted himself fully to Jesus in worship, yearning persistently for the Lord to heal him and believing with great faith that Jesus could heal him. "If you choose," he said to Jesus, "you can make me clean." When outcasts pursue Jesus with a bold faith that demonstrates a belief and trust that God can transform our suffering situations, God through Jesus Christ will do so. No doubt this man in Capernaum heard about the healings in the region. His demonstration of faith was the leper's first step to find healing for this cursed disease.

When Jesus sees his faith, he is moved to pity. With compassion, Jesus responds. Jesus' compassion raised Lazarus. Jesus did it in the raising of the son of the widow at Nain in Luke. Jesus often revealed compassion. Here in Mark, he does it again. We serve a compassionate God who, seeing our suffering, our faith, and our circumstances, often moves to make us well.

Jesus simply reached out his hand and touched him and immediately, verse 42 says, the leper was made well. Jesus, and Jesus alone, can cause the seemingly impossible to suddenly become possible, even in the twinkling of an eye.

Jesus sternly warns the now healed man not to say anything. Jesus did so because Jesus' time of suffering had not yet come, and he did not want any confusion to come over his mission. But the man, overjoyed because of the mercy rendered to him, just couldn't keep it to himself. He just had to proclaim freely and to spread the word that yes, Jesus can heal even lepers as well as the greatest of society's outcasts.

Some people might suggest that this man was disobedient. He did not obey the command of the Lord. On its face, this argument would be correct. But if you've ever been labeled an outcast, and the Lord has delivered you, then you can't keep it to yourself. For the joy you feel is so overwhelming that you've just got to tell somebody of the Lord's goodness.

Have you ever been an outcast? Have physical ailments, the "isms" of life, family dissension, or division ever isolated you from others? Have you experienced Jesus rescuing you from the pain and agony associated with it? I've been there before. When deliverance comes, you can't stop singing. You can't stop shouting. You can't stop telling others. Life becomes an eternal celebration. We don't receive word in the text that Jesus complained about the man's proclamation. It may have caused him to reroute a few plans, but who can complain about a soul giving thanks to God like this man. His testimony drew multitudes to Jesus.

If only more souls who've experienced the delivering hand of Jesus from outcast situations would tell their stories, how many more souls would be saved? In the name of Jesus, don't keep your testimony to yourself! (Joseph Daniels)

# FEBRUARY 23, 2003

*Seventh Sunday After the Epiphany*

---

**Worship Theme:** God in Jesus Christ shows his people how to live by the spirit of the law and not simply by the law's letter.

---

**Readings:** Isaiah 43:18-25; 2 Corinthians 1:18-22; Mark 2:1-12

**Call to Worship (Psalm 41:1-3, 12-13)**

Leader:    Happy are those who consider the poor; the LORD delivers them in the day of trouble.

**People:**    **The LORD protects them and keeps them alive; they are called happy in the land.**

Leader:    You do not give them up to the will of their enemies.

**People:**    **The LORD sustains them on their sickbed; in their illness you heal all their infirmities.**

Leader:    But you have upheld me because of my integrity, and set me in your presence forever.

**People:**    **Blessed be the LORD, the God of Israel, from everlasting to everlasting.**

**All:**    **Amen and Amen.**

**Pastoral Prayer:**
Eternal God, our lives are empty and lack meaning until we acknowledge that we are your people. You, O God, have revealed yourself to your people in a number of ways. We not only know you through the law given to Moses but also in the words of the

84

prophets who tell us that you "will make a way in the wilderness and rivers in the desert" (Isaiah 43:19b). Finally, in Jesus we see that you have defeated the final enemy—death. Create in our time and place a confidence in your word that the carnal world of sin cannot shake. Give us the fortitude to do what is right, even when taking the path of least resistance seems so much easier. Help us teach our children the power of your grace and mercy, O God. Make us again your faithful community held together by the covenant you made with us in Jesus. We pray this in Jesus' holy name. Amen. (David Mosser)

# SERMON BRIEFS

## THE GIFT OF FORGETTING

### ISAIAH 43:18-25

A well-known politician whose notorious private life had gotten him into trouble with the voters was visiting a senior center in an attempt to refurbish his reputation. He approached one of the seniors who was playing bingo and clearly did not want to be interrupted. She barely looked at him, so he asked rather grandly, "Madam, do you know who I am?"

"No," she replied, "but if you'll go to the nurse's station, the woman behind the desk will be able to tell you who you are."

There are circumstances in which forgetting the past is not only advantageous but also necessary in order to make a new beginning. In the reading from Isaiah, God is so distressed over the people's unresponsiveness that God decides on a reversal of policy: God wants them to forget "the former things," "the things of old."

Should we forget Abraham, Sarah, Miriam, and Moses? Should we stop telling the stories about God's deliverance of our ancestors in the faith? Surely not—the gift of remembering them is a treasure that guides and sustains us—but this great poem wakes us up to the fact that God doesn't want us to focus solely on yesterday and fail to see God's working in fresh, creative ways now. "We've always done it this way" is no justification for refusing to follow a new path God may be opening.

The Hebrew prophets knew the truth of what the epistle writers proclaimed many years later: God's redeeming love comes purely as grace. God remains faithful even when we are unfaithful. Paul says God affirms us through Jesus, the "Yes" of all God's promises (2 Corinthians 1:20). Isaiah declares to the weary exiles in Babylon that God is "about to do a new thing."

The "yes" and the "new thing" are not deserved. The exiles have just about worn God out with their superficiality and indifference. They're living in the big city now, and their attitudes toward a life of worship in service to God are not unlike attitudes in our own society. They (and sometimes we) are either too busy, too bored, or too bothered by personal cares to give full attention to God. They, as well as we, don't understand that a life without prayer and praise is shapeless and tedious.

Isaiah is convinced that these exiles wouldn't be a conquered people far from home in the first place if they had not turned away from their purpose in life, which is to praise God. God's exasperation mounts throughout the poem. The people have failed to recognize that they were formed by God for the single purpose of living, from birth to glory, lives that are, in Charles Wesley's words, "lost in wonder, love, and praise."

We worship a living, responsive God whose promises abide but who knows how to do "a new thing" when the situation calls for it. The exiles in Babylon could only think of the way things had been, but God is always ready with an unexpected way out of the morass created by human failure. It is time to wake up to the future, to praise the God who cuts a way through the thickest wilderness and brings rivers to the driest desert. The God who gives drink to the wild animals will surely have water for God's people who thirst for a new way of life.

One other positive point about the gift of forgetting: God knows how to forget too and promises to forget all our failings: "I will not remember your sins" (v. 25). This is not a "senior moment." God has an *intentional* lapse of memory, not because we deserve God's selective amnesia but because that's who God is: the One who chooses to make us new people, sins blotted out, *for God's own sake*. The most remarkable statement Isaiah makes here is that God's own joy comes from making us new. The waters in the desert are our waters of baptism. God does remember us and knows our name. God calls us through the waters to newness of life. (Blair Meeks)

# GUARANTEED!

### 2 CORINTHIANS 1:18-22

Recently, when high winds took down three large trees on our property, I called my homeowner's insurance agent and was told, "Yes, you do have tree removal!" I was elated! However, when another agent called, he began to specify the conditions under which I was covered. He said something about if it occurred on Thursday afternoon between 2:15 and 2:30 and if the tree fell across third base at Turner Field. In short, I was not covered. The yes became a no!

On another occasion, however, I returned an automobile to the dealer with a defective power window switch. The car went out of warranty just five days earlier. The dealer said, "No problem! We will stretch the warranty out to the end of the month." The cost of the switch was more than three hundred dollars. Their guarantee was good! Their yes was a yes.

Believe it or not, Paul was accused in our text by the Corinthian church of saying both yes and no. Because he had changed his plans to visit there, some were saying that Paul was wishy-washy, vacillating, talking out of both sides of his mouth, two-faced, like a "worldly person."

In our text, Paul does an amazing thing by grounding his defense in the character of God. He implies that he is faithful "As surely as God is faithful." He also suggests that we must remember that our salvation is not dependent on our faithfulness, but God's. We, too, are sometimes vacillating, fickle, and wishy-washy. We are sinners, sometimes unfaithful to God. But God always is faithful to us. We do sing "Great Is Thy Faithfulness, O God."

Paul continues his defense by stating that Jesus is God's proof that he is always faithful to his promises. God's promises to Abraham, David, Isaiah, and the entire nation of Israel found their fulfillment in Jesus. It was not a reluctant, qualified, degrading Yes, but one that was emphatic, resounding, ever enthusiastic to which one can say "Amen." In fact, the entire Old Testament is read and interpreted through the lens of its fulfillment in Jesus. Some would say that all of history is understood through such a view! History is His-story! Jesus is God's yes to all his promises.

Jesus once told a parable of two sons who were asked by their father to work in the field. One said yes but meant no, as he did not go to the field to work. One said no, but later said yes and went to the field to work. Which did the will of the father? Well, neither! The latter did better, but the will of the father was to say yes and then be true to one's word by working in the field. God's yes is always yes, and we see that promise in Jesus.

Paul concludes his defense by saying that God gives us the Holy Spirit as a guarantee that he will not only keep his promises but also fulfill his promises in us. God has "anointed" us, given us a place in God's plan. God has set his "seal of ownership" on us, giving us authenticity. God has given us the Holy Spirit as a deposit (earnest payment), guaranteeing what is to come.

Does this mean that God will never say no to us? Of course not! God will always say no to our selfish perversions, our schemes to control or manipulate, our efforts to dominate or abuse, and our plans to organize for selfish ends. But, on the other hand, God will always say yes to our highest prayers, our noblest ambitions, our best dreams, the potential God has placed within us, and our desire to make the world a better place. And God always says yes to us when we seek to depend on God and to center our lives around God.

Some have read the book, *She Said Yes!*, the story of Cassie Bernall. In the horror that was Columbine, Cassie was asked by a terribly sick individual if she was a Christian. Cassie said, "Yes!" It cost Cassie her life! There is a price to pay when we say yes to God, though one hopes not as extreme as Cassie's. But whatever the cost, it is worth it to hear God say yes to us. Guaranteed! (Gary Carver)

# THERE'S ALWAYS A CROWD AROUND JESUS

## MARK 2:1-12

For Christians today, this story adds life to the meaning of discipleship. The friends of the man with paralysis are literally carrying their mission on their backs. Their faith is visibly displayed as they physically help the man with paralysis get to Jesus.

I think it is important for those of us who live in predominantly Christian areas to take this story to heart. You see, there will always be a crowd around Jesus. There are people proclaiming Christ everywhere you turn. All of them are claiming to be faithfully following God. Some are seeking to follow; some are just curious; some are skeptical; and some are even looking to destroy Jesus. Sometimes it is the people that need Jesus the most who have the hardest time getting to him. And often, it is the "church crowd" who become the blockade for others wanting to reach Jesus. Some will watch and say, "If that's what being a Christian is all about, then I don't want anything to do with it." Others will genuinely want to get to Jesus, but the crowd becomes moblike and won't allow that person to get to Jesus.

What we must remember is that it doesn't matter what the crowd is doing. Rather, we must seek to be faithful no matter what the crowd is doing. Many claim to follow Christ, but many people are only crowded around him. For churches, we must respect and learn from other Christian churches, but we must faithfully respond to where God is leading our own congregation. How will we find our way through the crowded streets of this religion we call Christianity? We must not just crowd around Jesus, but rather we must be faithful to Jesus by bringing the ill and hurt to Jesus. We must weave our way through the crowd so that Jesus' love can be spread.

Verses 6-7 discuss a group of people in the crowd and their reaction to the scene. They don't really like it when others get to Jesus. Why do we get upset if someone else is forgiven? Can we not be happy for that person? Do we feel that if another person is forgiven that we are less loved? Is being in the "in crowd" mentality still forcing us to want others out of "our" crowd, the "right" crowd? Are we still acting immature in our relationships? If others aren't just exactly like us, does it mean that either their faith or our faith is invalid?

In the case of the four in our story, their faith called them to act as partners and take their friend to Jesus no matter the obstacles. Maybe the people who are on the right track of discipleship are the faithful who partner with one another in order to help others get to Jesus. We see that partnering in faith heals and saves the man with paralysis. Whenever we can get people to Jesus without indoctrinating our preconceived notions, lives are changed for the better.

Individually, we can ask many questions. Does our faith matter to God? Does our faith affect this world? Does our faith make a difference for the kingdom of God? As a church, does our combined faith have the capacity to save or heal someone?

Can you find yourself in the middle of the crowd? The crowd will always be flocking around Jesus, but only a few will have the faith to help others find their way through the crowd to Jesus. One thing is for sure: Through the power and authority of Jesus, we can make a difference. Maybe it will be through our faith that Jesus can tell someone in need, "Take your mat and go home" (v. 11 NIV). When we get people to Jesus and allow Jesus to work in their lives, everyone will be amazed and will praise God. (Ryan Wilson)

# REFLECTIONS

# MARCH

**Reflection Verse:** *"Then you, together with the Levites and the aliens who reside among you, shall celebrate with all the bounty that the* LORD *your God has given to you and to your house."* *(Deuteronomy 26:11)*

I suppose that *celebration* and *Lent* are two words that are seldom, if ever, found together. *Lent* equals penitence and sacrifice; *celebration* equals, well, fun and frolic. Yet, I want to suggest that celebration must be a part of Lent if Lent is to have its full power in our lives. I think the old book of Deuteronomy is helpful to make this connection.

When the Hebrews urged one another to bring their firstfruits to the sanctuary—the results of their hard labors for themselves, their families, and their communities—they demanded two things: memory and celebration. Memory was first, but not just any memory. Not the memory of the hard work they had done. Not the memory of their past successes or failures as workers, parents, citizens. The first declared memory was spoken to the priest in the sanctuary: "Today I declare to the LORD your God that I have come into the land that the LORD swore to our ancestors to give us" (Deuteronomy 26:3b). It is *God's* actions that are first remembered and announced. One might say that the service begins with doxology; doxology does not follow the offering but precedes it.

That primary memory of God's great gift of land is followed by the memory of God's great work of salvation. The closest thing we find to an Israelite creed begins, "A wandering Aramean was my ancestor," and continues with an account of God's victory in Egypt and God's gift of the land of promise. Interestingly, the word usually translated *wandering*, suggesting the nomadic origins of the Israelite forebears, can also be translated *perishing* or *dying.* This dual meaning is important. Israel remembers its past not simply as nomadic but also as perishing. Without God's action, they would have died in their wandering; they would have found no final place of rest; they would have perished, forgotten and alone.

The ancient announcement places the emphasis squarely on God, who makes possible any actions on our part, actions that must always be seen as reactions to the prior actions of a God who loves us unreservedly. Earlier in Deuteronomy, we read that the choice of Israel in Egypt was made for one simple and incredible reason: "It was not because you were more numerous than any other people that the LORD set his heart on you and chose you—for you were the fewest of all peoples. It was because the LORD loved you and kept the oath that he swore to your ancestors" (Deuteronomy 7:7-8*a*). It is only God's love for us that makes possible our love for one another. The first letter of John in the New Testament (see especially chapter 4) was hardly the first ancient writing to make that central claim of the gospel!

Yet, it is never enough merely to announce a memory. If a memory is to have present power, it must be shared. In short, it must be celebrated. After the gift has been presented in the sanctuary, after the memory of the great actions of God have been proclaimed, then it is time to party! Memory is made for celebration; memory means little unless it is re-presented in joyous celebration. But watch out! Not just any sort of party will do. Note carefully the guest list. "Then you, together with the Levites and the aliens who reside among you, shall celebrate." Two groups are singled out for this celebratory party. Although there has been considerable discussion concerning the origins and work of the Levites, two things can safely be said. First, the Levites had no property of their own and were to remain landless. This requirement no doubt was a great hardship in a community that measured much of its wealth and power in terms of ancestral land. Second, most indications are that the Levites did the menial tasks in the worship of Israel. Perhaps we could say that they were the communion stewards, the candle wax cleaners, the lightbulb changers of their day. In short, they were persons with little power. Even their earlier teaching function was eventually usurped by the scribes. To invite a Levite to the party is to invite a marginalized person.

So, too, is the second group who is to attend the party—the aliens. These were foreigners who were living in Israel for a certain period of time for any number of reasons, including employment, escape from persecutions in their homelands, and slavery that had turned to freedom. One could imagine many undocumented workers among this crowd, persons who did not quite sound, or look, or act like the Israelites we know.

So the party to celebrate the memory of God is a decidedly odd one. "Custodians" and "wetbacks" head the list of guests! If that sounds peculiar, and certainly unlike the most recent parties I have attended, it is not strange at all in the world of Deuteronomy. After all, in Moses' listing of the Ten Commandments in chapter 5, he says that we all should celebrate the Sabbath because of an important memory we all should have: "Remember that you were a slave in the land of Egypt, . . . therefore the LORD your God commanded you to keep the sabbath day" (Deuteronomy 5:15). Without the power of God's gifts to us, we *all* are slaves and are doomed to remain enslaved forever.

Of course, Jesus knew the importance of the right guest list for giving a party. In Luke's Gospel, when he noticed how guests at a party that he attended were elbowing one another to get to the best seats in the house, he suggested they think differently about their proper places. "When you give a luncheon or a dinner, do not invite your friends or your brothers or your relatives or rich neighbors, in case they may invite you in return, and you would be repaid. But when you give a banquet, invite the poor, the crippled, the lame, and the blind. And you will be blessed" (Luke 14:12-14a). The constant and clear memory of what God has done for you must lead to a new form of community wherein those on the margin are brought into the center of the circle with those who traditionally have the power. Why? Because without the loving gifts of God, we are all on the margin.

Memory and celebration are the hallmarks of a proper Lenten observance. But only the right sort of memory and the right sort of celebration, with the right sort of guest list, will finally do in this new world of grace and gift, freely offered by the God who stands at the center of all of our lives. (John Holbert)

# MARCH 2, 2003

## *Transfiguration Sunday*

**Worship Theme:** Those who yearn to see a vision of God see it in the life, teaching, death, and resurrection of Jesus, the Messiah of God.

**Readings:** 2 Kings 2:1-12; 2 Corinthians 4:3-6; Mark 9:2-9

**Call to Worship (Psalm 50:1-6)**

Leader: The mighty one, God the LORD, speaks and summons the earth from the rising of the sun to its setting.

**People: Out of Zion, the perfection of beauty, God shines forth.**

Leader: Our God comes and does not keep silence, before him is a devouring fire, and a mighty tempest all around him.

**People: He calls to the heavens above and to the earth, that he may judge his people:**

Leader: "Gather to me my faithful ones, who made a covenant with me by sacrifice!"

**All: The heavens declare his righteousness, for God himself is judge.**

**Pastoral Prayer:**

O God of the mountain, inspire us today with a vision of your splendor on the mountaintop of Transfiguration. Just as you transformed Jesus before Moses and Elijah, let us see the dazzling truth of Jesus as did Peter and James and John. Because

Christ is your beloved son, may he be for us a guiding light that illumines our path of discipleship. Create moments in each of our days where we behold his glory for ourselves. Create also in us, O God, a passion for ministry to our world, which is so needy. May we be vessels of both divine encouragement and godly truth. Too many of our brothers and sisters live in the shadows that the world casts upon them. Let us be part of your light that shines to give hope and a good word to those in need. Finally, stir us to hear anew the words of life you offer, O God, to all people. In the name of Jesus, we pray. Amen. (David Mosser)

# SERMON BRIEFS

## ESCAPE VELOCITY

### 2 KINGS 2:1-12

It is difficult when a mentor departs the course of our lives. We have only to think of how the disciples of Jesus felt when he left them. Although they were neither desolate nor destitute because of the arrival of the Holy Spirit, their sadness was extremely keen.

In the last century, *mentoring*—for which some were born while others had it thrust upon them—became something of a byword for children and teens badly in need of postmodern heroes, heroines, and role models. Robert Oppenheimer had his followers who helped develop the Manhattan Project. Freud had his circle. Artists gathered around whoever of their own was the most prominent, be it Picasso or Thomas Hart Benton. Ann Landers and Abigail van Buren have their disciples, as do Oprah and Martha Stewart. Who can tell what will happen when Oprah passes on? Holes will be left in the interwoven fabric of the lives Oprah has touched. Even Elisha rent his robes when the fiery chariot and whirlwind came forth to carry his mentor, Elijah, home.

Do you recall the movie *Pollock*? In the city where I lived, it showed in only one theater, which may say something about the state of our reception of biographical films. When I think of

Jackson Pollock, I envision a man who embodied creativity, intelligence, and a deep sense of soul despite his alcoholism and manic depression. He was a sage and had the restlessness of a dire prophet, not unlike Elijah. Behold a noble artist who traced a path to the Absolute.

Intrigued by the visualizations evoked in the film, I went back to its source, the Pulitzer prize-winning, controversial biography of Pollock, itself a screenplay waiting to happen (Steven W. Naifeh and Gregory White Smith, *Jackson Pollock: An American Saga* [New York: Clarkson N. Potter, 1989], pp. 789-93). The last chapter, "Escape Velocity," holds one spellbound and is uncannily reminiscent of this story of Elijah's ascension. It fits: Pollock is the Elijah of the American art scene in the 1930s, 1940s, and early 1950s; Elisha is represented by Pollock's disciple, Ruth Kligman (accompanied by her friend, Edith Metzger, a refugee from the turmoil of persecution in Nazi Germany because she was a Jew—another similarity to both Elijah and Elisha as well as Pollock, who also wanted to escape. Remember "I alone am left" (1 Kings 19:10*b*)? The Oldsmobile is the flaming chariot, its engine the fiery horses. The eyewitness account and the police and coroner's reports tell us everything for Pollock was silent, except for the air rushing by, like the divine whirlwind.

We often know that something is about to happen whenever the number three is mentioned in the Bible. Three times Elijah told Elisha that the Lord was compelling him to stop along the way to the finish line: at Bethel (the city of God), at Jericho, and finally at Jordan, where a fiery chariot picks up Elijah and delivers him to God. Jonah was in the belly of the great fish three days and nights prior to being spat out onto a beach near Nineveh. Jesus of Nazareth was in the tomb three days and nights before the Resurrection. Three times Edith Metzger screamed to be let out, and three times Ruth told her to be quiet, that it would be all right, and warned Pollock to slow down. Pollock expected, as Elijah did, that he would lift off at any time. The biographers note he had achieved escape velocity. The car/chariot gone. All he knew was gone and he was free, not falling but flying, fully conscious and arrested in space. (Eric Killinger)

# LIGHT ON MISTAKEN NOTIONS

## 2 CORINTHIANS 4:3-6

I grew up with the mistaken notion that everyone in the Bible, with notable exceptions such as Judas and Jezebel, were paragons of virtue. I thought that I needed to be just like Abraham, Isaac, Jacob, and David until I began to read that they, too, had problems just like everyone else. I also had a mistaken notion about the New Testament church. I felt as if we needed to take the church back two thousand years to exactly fit the New Testament pattern. Then I read about Corinth. This was not a perfect church and definitely was a shaky example for any congregation to follow. I guess I had to admit that people then were like people now. Churches then were like churches now, warts and all. We all have problems. The church is a home for sinners. Where such people dwell there is eventually disagreement and criticism.

Even Paul heard such criticism! I am referring to Saint Paul, missionary to the Gentiles, writer of words considered to be Holy Writ! Yes, that Paul evidently was criticized for sermons that were less than effective. "Well, Preacher, our church isn't growing. Souls aren't being saved. Could it be your preaching?" Paul defends the lack of converts by saying that the "god of this age has blinded the minds of unbelievers" (v. 4a NIV). He replies that there is another formidable team on the playing field that serves to thwart his best efforts. This fact must never discourage us or even be used as an excuse for doing nothing. It is the task of every church, that century or ours, to find creative ways to present the gospel so that it will be heard. It is the vocation of every Christian, their age or ours, to understand those to whom we present the gospel and to present it through images and language to which they can relate.

Paul also had to answer the criticism that he was too much concerned about himself. Now, I can identify with Paul here. I, too, have used personal illustrations (in fact, I am doing that right now!) and stories about my boring childhood to the extent that the messenger has often stood in the way of the message. But give Paul some slack! They criticized him personally. They forced him to talk about himself. Paul probably added fuel to the fire when earlier he challenged them to imitate him (1 Corinthians 4:16, 11:1)!

Is there a way out of this quandary? We should remember the words of the prince of preachers, Phillips Brooks, when he said, "Preaching is ... truth [expressed] through personality" (*The Joy of Preaching* [Grand Rapids: Kregel Publications, 1989], p. 1). It is often difficult or unnecessary to separate the truth from the personality that presents it. The gospel is not so much a set of abstract truths to be announced as it is a way of life to be lived. Would anyone want to hear a preacher who does not live the life about which he or she speaks?

Paul responds, "We do not preach ourselves, but Jesus Christ as Lord, and ourselves as your servants for Jesus' sake" (v. 5 NIV). His defense is the essence of the gospel itself—Jesus is Lord. When we profess that Jesus is Lord and we are not, light comes from God through Christ. Just as Saul of Tarsus recovered from his blindness to see the light of God through Christ, we see the light of God, just as in the original creation (Genesis 1:3). We understand that Jesus is the light that illumines history, the Bible, God, and even ourselves. Through Jesus the light dawns on us that we can indeed love God because God first loved us. Through Jesus the light dawns on us that we can love our neighbors as ourselves, warts and all. (Gary Carver)

# A DAZZLING MOMENT

## MARK 9:2-9

This passage speaks of the now and the not yet. There are moments in life when the curtain between the present and the future is drawn back, and we glimpse just for a moment what tomorrow holds. It is a glimpse of truth, a glimpse of God that can see us through life.

A teenager is playing one-on-one basketball with his dad. His dad shoots and misses. The boy steps back and shoots. It is a perfect shot; and for just a split second, which seems eternal, father and son contemplate the reality that the son, once taught by the father, is now better, even greater, than the father.

The father good-naturedly acknowledges that the son has made a better shot. The son smiles but doesn't answer. For one small moment both of them have been given a glimpse of the future: the day when the son takes his father's place, when the father moves to the other world, and the son carries on. Seeing the future changes them a bit.

Frederick Buechner had taught for five years and then went to New York City to write. He was in turmoil about his future, even considering the CIA or advertising as a career. It was the first time in his life that he attended church regularly, and it occurred because there happened to be a church on his street whose preacher was the famous minister, George Buttrick.

The moment came during one particular sermon preached by Buttrick. It came really around four words that never appeared in the sermon when it was printed, words that were ad-libbed or dreamed up as if they were meant just for him. Buechner says on such holy threads hang the destiny of us all.

The mountaintop experience of the text suggests that Jesus is crowned again and again in the hearts of people who believe in him. That inward coronation takes place among (and here are the four words that moved Buechner) confession, tears, and great laughter.

To say that Buechner was born again (as he says of himself) is to say too much because in many ways he remained the same. But to say that he was not born again is to say too little. This was a moment when something too precious to tell was glimpsed in the dusk like fireflies—something that determined his whole life.

Time stops; silence reigns; God steps forward with a vision, a power, a memory, which guides all the rest of our lives.

That day on Mt. Tabor, Peter, James, and John knew who was standing in front of them. It was a dazzling moment, a glimpse of the future, a Messiah who had come to make all things new. In the daily events of our lives, the God of grace and power, of beauty and majesty, of love and forgiveness comes to you. These moments reveal the now and the not yet. On such holy thread hangs the destiny of us all. (Wayne Day)

# MARCH 9, 2003

*First Sunday in Lent*

---

**Worship Theme:** As disciples of the risen Lord, too often we are tempted to let the *good* substitute for the *best*.

---

**Readings:** Genesis 9:8-17; 1 Peter 3:18-22; Mark 1:9-15

**Call to Worship (Psalm 25:1, 4-7, 9-10)**

*Leader:*    To you, O LORD, I lift up my soul.

*People:*    **Make me to know your ways, O LORD; teach me your paths.**

*Leader:*    Lead me in your truth, and teach me, for you are the God of my salvation; for you I wait all day long.

*People:*    **Be mindful of your mercy, O LORD, and of your steadfast love, for they have been from of old.**

*Leader:*    Do not remember the sins of my youth or my transgressions; according to your steadfast love remember me, for your goodness' sake, O LORD!

*People:*    **He leads the humble in what is right, and teaches the humble his way.**

*All:*    **All the paths of the LORD are steadfast love and faithfulness, for those who keep his covenant and his decrees.**

**Pastoral Prayer:**

O God, we acknowledge the beginning of our wilderness journey with Jesus toward the cross. As we gather to worship, we know that sometimes the path of discipleship is a difficult one. We often stray because the cost of making decisions that are just and true and right seems too high. Yet, we ask you, O God, to hold up for us the example of Jesus who "knew no sin, so that in him we might become the righteousness of God" (2 Corinthians 5:21). Remind us that Jesus has already explored and charted a path through each of our wildernesses. He clears the path for us so that we too might know the newness of life found in him. Give us the courage of our convictions and remind us daily that Jesus always travels before us. Jesus is "the pioneer and perfecter of our faith" (Hebrews 12:2). For this we give you thanks, O God. Amen. (David Mosser)

# SERMON BRIEFS

## A COVENANT OF GRACE

### GENESIS 9:8-17

The season of Lent is a time of spiritual evaluation and renewal. It is a time that leads us to revisit the covenant between God and humankind. The text focuses on Noah and the covenant of grace that God established following the Great Flood.

A friend recently sent me the following email. "All I really need to know about life, I learned from Noah's Ark." (1) Don't miss the boat. (2) Don't forget we're all in the same boat. (3) Plan ahead—it wasn't raining when Noah built the ark. (4) Stay fit—when you're 600 years old someone might ask you to do something really big. (5) Don't listen to critics, just get on with what has to be done. (6) For safety's sake, travel in pairs. (7) Two heads are better than one. (8) Build your future on high ground. (9) Speed isn't always an advantage; after all, the snails were on the same ark as the cheetahs. (10) When you're stressed, float awhile. (11) Remember, amateurs (given directions by the master builder and teacher) built the ark; professionals built the *Titanic*. (12) The woodpeckers inside were a larger threat than the storm outside. (13) No matter what the storm, when God is with you, there's a rainbow waiting.

Following the Great Flood, once again God instructs humankind to "be fruitful and multiply, and fill the earth" (Genesis 1:28). Humankind is to preside over creation in order to enhance, celebrate, and dignify it. The sanctity of human life is established, and God unqualifiedly states that every human being is of ultimate value. However, God makes an irreversible decision and commitment regarding his relationship with humankind and creation. In verses 11*b*-13, God resolves, "Never again shall there be a flood to destroy the earth. . . . This is the sign of the covenant that I make between me and you—for all future generations: I have set my bow in the clouds, and it shall be a sign of the covenant between me and the earth."

Nothing has changed about humankind or creation or waters or floods. God has changed. God has made a decision about the grief and trouble of God's heart. The flood has not eradicated evil from the face of the earth, but we are assured that a revolution or reformation has taken place in the heart of God. The relationship between Creator and creature is no longer in a scheme of retribution. A reformation has occurred in the heart of God and our covenant with God is now based on unqualified grace. No matter how provocative creation becomes, God will "never again" destroy creation by a great flood.

Step into Noah's sandals for a moment. After the Great Flood, God knew that every time Noah or one of his sons sinned and every time Noah heard of someone else's sin, he would be terrified that the clouds would start rolling in and God's judgment would fall. God knew that Noah would live in constant fear, analyzing the sin in his own life and the sin in the world, trying to determine how much was too much. The rainbow reassured Noah that the preservation of the human race did not depend on human goodness or sinlessness, but on God's word and God's promise of grace. (Bob Buchanan)

## SAFETY IN NUMBERS

### 1 PETER 3:18–22

In the number of the disciples gathered in the community of faith, there is encouragement in the face of persecution and confident hope for the future: "Lord, I want to be in that number."

"Nice service, Pastor . . ." We are grateful for the encouragement. But, we often fail to grasp the seriousness of what we are about in worship. We forget the "death-to-life" joy to be found as Christians gather. "I once was lost but now am found," indeed! Most of the time the only thing we are conscious of losing is a set of car keys or the quarter for the Sunday school offering.

**I. In gathering in the number of the faithful, we find encouragement in the face of adversity (3:20).**

The readers of 1 Peter were reminded that following Christ is serious business. To be a follower of Jesus, at the end of the first century, could mean the loss of position and family and sometimes death. The writer knows that readers are tested by persecution and are in danger of walking away from their faith. So the writer sends them a letter to strengthen their faith saying, "Don't worry: Christ has saved a place for you. You, though few in number, will be saved by the water of baptism, just as Noah was saved from the waters of the flood."

We, as postmodern believers, know about persecution. We no longer expect culture or social convention to "back up" our faith. But we are not alone: There is safety in numbers, even if those numbers are small. Other believers stand beside us, a part of the "royal priesthood—God's own people" (1 Peter 2:9).

**II. Set apart by a hostile world, we are learning what it means to be a "new generation of saints" (3:18).**

Believers know what it means to be "marginalized." We are also "set apart" to proclaim the riches of God's commonwealth. The root word for *saint* and *set apart* is the same. What we need is a "new generation of saints," set apart in baptism to live life in a world given over to death.

Do you share in the victory and realize your specialness? God does. In the beautiful film *Tender Mercies,* singer Mac Sledge finds worldly salvation through the care of a woman and her young son, who take him in and give him one more chance. Mac is once again made to believe that there is redemption in relationship and hope to be found around a family hearth. And finally, Mac finds himself, along with the boy, waist deep in a baptismal pool at a rural Texas church.

After the baptism, Mac and the boy are riding back home in a pickup, across the rural Texas landscape. Neither says a thing until finally, the little boy says, "Well, we've done it, Mac. We was baptized. But I don't feel any different. Do you?"

And Mac replies, "Not yet."

### III. In the act of baptism, we are reminded that we are set apart to a future filled with life (3:21-22).

Yes, there is danger in the water of baptism. The early Christians knew that it could mean exclusion and alienation in this world. There is danger in the flood waters. There is a danger of us going down and not coming back up. Like the cartoon character who goes under once, then twice. Will we be finally overcome by the danger in the water? We will, unless there is an ark, a ship of salvation to bear us up. And that ship of salvation is ours in the church, and there is still a little water around in baptismal fonts to remind us of all from which we have been saved. That water also reminds us of how good God is. (Don Holladay)

## PREPARE AND RESPOND

### MARK 1:9-15

Have there been points in your life when you asked if God would ever do something to help you? This passage assures us that God will act decisively in our lives, and then it calls for us to act decisively toward God.

In verses 9-11, Mark shows us from the very beginning the identity of Jesus. He is God's Son. The heavens being ripped apart tell us up front that the divine is doing something magnificent in this world. The Spirit descending is like the anointing of a new king. The voice affirms that Jesus is the unique Son of God. God is doing something awesome for all of creation!

We see in verses 12-13 how Jesus is sent from baptism into the wilderness to be tested. Jesus sees the temptations of the world and how Satan can use his forces against the Good News. Jesus identifies with the sins of the people, and then accepts his role for ministry as God's beloved Son. Where Adam, Eve, you, and I have failed, Jesus will not. Therefore, the church looks to this passage for Lent. The forty days of Lent commemorate Christ's forty days in the wilderness.

During Lent, God invites us to reflect on our own lives and our own shortcomings. Lent is often a season of fasting and penitence. It is a time of introspection to evaluate our priorities, values, goals, and faith. We remember our baptismal vows and the new life that we promised to live. We ask that God will work in our lives so that we can make the changes we need to make.

In verses 14-15 we see Jesus coming through the wilderness unblemished. Then, we see that the introduction of the kingdom of God is shown by Christ's victory over Satan. The reign of God is seen clearly in God's Son, Jesus, overcoming evil. Because of Christ's victory, we are then called to repent and believe. These are continuous action verbs that emphasize the ongoing nature of following Jesus in discipleship. We realize that God requires a radical change of heart and mind if we are to be true disciples. The continuous actions of repenting and believing help us realize the discipline that is involved in following Jesus. The season of Lent helps us to refocus on that disciplined life.

The kingdom of God is at hand, and we continually get glimpses of the kingdom wherever Jesus is. As we focus on Lent, we depart with the image of Jesus preaching to us. Although this may seem minor, the spoken Word of God is a powerful word. God has given us a Living Word seen through the decisive act of God in Jesus. Are we ready to open our hearts to God's unique revelation? What is holding us back from receiving the Good News? Does Jesus' victory over Satan matter to our lives? When the Word is offered to us, we are left to decide. Will we repent and believe? (Ryan Wilson)

# MARCH 16, 2003

*Second Sunday in Lent*

**Worship Theme:** God's relationship with God's creation—and this is especially true for humankind—God reflects in covenant commitment.

**Readings:** Genesis 17:1-7, 15-16; Romans 4:13-25; Mark 8:31-38

**Call to Worship (Psalm 22:23-31 RSV)**

> *Leader:* You who fear the LORD, praise him! all you sons of Jacob, glorify him, and stand in awe of him, all you sons of Israel!
>
> *People:* **For he has not despised or abhorred the affliction of the afflicted; and he has not hid his face from him, but has heard, when he cried to him.**
>
> *Leader:* From thee comes my praise in the great congregation; my vows I will pay before those who fear him.
>
> *People:* **The afflicted shall eat and be satisfied; those who seek him shall praise the LORD! May your hearts live for ever!**
>
> *Leader:* All the ends of the earth shall remember and turn to the LORD; and all the families of the nations shall worship before him.
>
> *People:* **For dominion belongs to the LORD, and he rules over the nations.**
>
> *Leader:* Yea, to him shall all the proud of the earth bow down; before him shall bow all who go down to

the dust, and he who cannot keep himself
alive.

*All:*     **Posterity shall serve him; men shall tell of
the Lord to the coming generation, and
proclaim his deliverance to a people yet
unborn, that he has wrought it.**

**Pastoral Prayer:**
Gracious Lord, help us remember today the great biblical
covenants by which you define yourself and your people. Help us to
recall not only the great covenants of old, like those you made with
Abraham, Moses, David, and the House of Israel but also the
supreme covenant you made with your people in Jesus Christ. In
addition, we too make sacred covenants and vows. Remind us of the
many covenants that we make by virtue of friendship, marriage,
church membership, and especially the covenants we make with
you. Daily we renew our covenant. Help us so live as to uphold the
vows we profess. Grant us the courage to be your people. Guide us
as we fulfill the covenants for which you make life worth living and
dying. We pray this in Jesus' holy name. Amen. (David Mosser)

# SERMON BRIEFS

## A COVENANT OF HOPE

### GENESIS 17:1-7, 15-16

"When Abram was ninety-nine years old, the Lord appeared to
Abram, and said to him, 'I am God Almighty; walk before me,
and be blameless. And I will make my covenant between me and
you, and will make you exceedingly numerous.'" It wasn't the
first time the Lord made such a promise. Twenty-four years earlier, God promised, "I will make of you a great nation, and I will
bless you" (Genesis 12:2).

God changed Abram's name to Abraham, which means "father
of nations," yet Abraham was a long way from being the father of
a nation. All Abraham had to show was one child that was the

107

result of an arrangement that his wife had made with a servant girl. When Abraham heard the voice of God again after an extended period of silence, he must have been tempted to say: "Give me a break! We haven't talked for years. Why are you bringing up this subject again?"

When God told Abraham that Sarah would give birth to his son, he doubted the Lord even further. Verse 17 says that Abraham fell on his face, not to worship God but to laugh. God's plan sounded absolutely ridiculous and humanly impossible. "Whoever has heard of a one-hundred-year-old man and a ninety-year-old woman giving birth to a child?"

The nature of the covenant between God and Abraham was similar to the suzerainty treaties. A suzerain, a dominant power who overcame another power, would form an agreement or covenant by which their relationship would be established. The greater power would guarantee the well-being of the lesser power, while the lesser power or individual would guarantee loyalty and service to the greater power. The covenants that God made with his people originated in God's loving, caring heart and were designed to introduce individuals to God's gracious presence and protection.

The author of this covenant of promise and hope to Abraham is El Shaddai or "God Almighty." God possesses all-sufficient power and is able to do what is humanly impossible. Almighty God committed himself to give Abraham three things: the land, a child, and an infinite number of descendants. Faith is believing the impossible even when we have to wait for a while.

El Shaddai expected some practical responses from Abraham. God expected Abraham to "walk before me, and be blameless" (v. 1). The Hebrew word translated *blameless* means *whole*. It was sometimes used to describe an animal without blemish. When applied to a person, it does not mean sinless perfection but rather that his or her approach to God should be *whole*hearted.

Oswald Chambers once wrote,

> Faith never knows where it is being led, but it loves and knows the One Who is leading. . . .
> . . . The life of faith is not a life of mounting up with wings, but a life of walking and not fainting.

(Oswald Chambers, *My Utmost for His Highest*, "March 19" [Uhrichsville, Ohio: Barbour Publishing, 1963])

Living under the promises of God empowers us today. We do so because we know that God always keeps his promises. (Bob Buchanan)

# THE REVOLUTIONARY CHURCH

## ROMANS 4:13-25

Across history, the letter to the Romans has revolutionized the church. Augustine, Luther, and Karl Barth all sat with the book of Romans open on their knees when God showed them what the church could be. Romans continues to bring new life to the church. We will be surprised, however, to learn that the carrier of this message is an old man named Abraham, "as good as dead" (v. 19).

Why Abraham? Why should Paul not pull some popular Roman hero out of his hat? There were Jewish Christians in the Roman church, to be sure. But Paul's main audience was Gentile. So what does Abraham teach us that we need to know?

## I. Abraham teaches us that "it [all] depends on faith" (4:16).

In the story of Abraham and Sarah, God is the real hero. God tells Abraham over and over that he and Sarah will be the parents of a blessed nation. But it is up to Abraham to believe.

Here, the gift and the reminder is that the Jewish faith, as with all human religion, is not contrary to the truth of faith. Abraham, properly understood, is one who shares the truth that "it [all] depends on faith." Religious practice is not contrary to faith: It is good when it grows out of faith. It is evil when it becomes a substitute for faith.

## II. Abraham shows us that "faith depends on God."

As we read the first four chapters of Romans, we realize that we are "a part of something big." It is a story written, if you will, from the perspective of heaven. Can it be possible that Paul sees from the perspective of heaven? In fact, he writes of himself, "I know a person in Christ who ... was caught up to the third heaven ... and heard things that are not to be told" (2 Corinthians 12:2, 4).

Yet, Paul could not resist telling the vision. In the first four chapters of Romans, we have a "biography of God." Here, God turns human sin in the direction of life, through the gift of faith.

When we look from the perspective of heaven, human achievement, even an exalted religious system, becomes trivial. That is a revolutionary word that saves the church whenever it takes its structures, its pieties, its doctrines too seriously. It all depends on faith, and faith depends on God.

## III. The faith of Abraham will bring revolution wherever it is found because God will respond to faith with fulfillment of the promise.

Abraham is a central character in several New Testament texts. Yet he is really nothing more than another example of the power of God to work miracles (v. 17). In Paul's Roman letter, faith is fulfilled in God granting the gift of Isaac. We call it "the righteousness of God ... through faith for faith" (Romans 1:17).

Once again, we learn that Abraham is one among a host of examples of those who respond faithfully to God's sovereignty. God is the real hero: in the promise to Abraham, in the gift of faith, and in the fulfillment of the promise. Past, present, and future: "The Lord God, who is and who was and who is to come, the Almighty" (Revelation 1:8).

Abraham surely had a plan for his life. Was he looking forward to his retirement in Haran? All his plans, however, were brought up short. He left, taking his family with him, hanging a sign on his doorknob: "Gone to the promised land." In his "hope against hope," he became dependent on the one who is the Author of Hope and the Keeper of Promises. (Don Holladay)

110

# THE PROFITS OF OUR FAITH

## MARK 8:31-38

Jesus said to his disciples, *Take up your cross. If you want to be my disciples, you have to lose your life for my sake.* What do the disciples say? *This is a hard saying. Give us something easier. Talk about the good shepherd, or the waiting father, or the birds of the air and the flowers of the field. This is a hard saying.*

Philip Yancy, a writer, once began to think about the literally hundreds, thousands of people that he had interviewed. Of course, these people were from across the spectrum of humanity, but he divided them into two categories of people who fascinated him: people he called *stars* and people he called *servants.*

The *stars* were the people who were icons of our civilization. They were the great television, sports, theatrical, and political personalities: the Elizabeth Taylors, the Michael Jordans, the Madonnas.

The *servants* were people who were relief workers in Bangladesh, the Ph.D.s who translated the Bible into obscure languages in South America, and those people who worked in inner cities. He said he was surprised, as he got to know these great TV, movie, and sports personalities, at how generally unhappy they were. They had troubled marriages, tormented psyches, and self-doubts—not all of them but, by and large, a majority of them.

He said he was prepared to be inspired by the *servants* and to admire them. However, what shocked and surprised him was how much he wound up envying them. Low pay, long hours, no-applause people who gave themselves to the poor and unedu-cated—he wound up envying them. He said he felt that these people, as opposed to the stars, were the truly blessed. They were the ones who were lucky. They were the ones who were favored. They were the ones who were graced.

A mother sees her baby for the first time, and she looks the baby over from head to toe. In looking over the baby, she finds that something is wrong; there is some abnormality or defect, some handicap or trouble. It crosses her mind to push the child away or distance herself, or maybe to give the child to someone

111

else. Instead of that, she draws the baby even closer to her heart. She gives herself to that child and loses herself for that child. In doing so, in some unexplainable way, what should be drudgery and self-denial, trouble and difficulty becomes an unimaginable source of love and strength, power and insight, meaning and purpose. That which she had thought of rejecting becomes the most important part of her life.

Will Willimon, Walter Wink, and other scholars have suggested that in the last three hundred years of enlightenment, we have so given ourselves to reason, so given ourselves to the tangible world that it has plunged us into a kind of *me, me, me* and an *I, I, I* and a *dog-eat-dog* world where the material things count more than anything else.

The text suggests another way: Take care of your soul by getting in touch with real life. What does it profit an individual or a nation, a city or a church; what does it profit a person if he or she gains the world but loses his or her soul? (Wayne Day)

# MARCH 23, 2003

*Third Sunday in Lent*

---

**Worship Theme:** The cross is not only God's answer to the world's strength and wisdom but the very sign of God's power over creation.

---

**Readings:** Exodus 20:1-17; 1 Corinthians 1:18-25; John 2:13-22

**Call to Worship (Psalm 19:1-4a, 7-10, 14 RSV)**

*Leader:* The heavens are telling the glory of God; and the firmament proclaims his handiwork.

**People:** **Day to day pours forth speech, and night to night declares knowledge.**

*Leader:* There is no speech, nor are there words; their voice is not heard; yet their voice goes out through all the earth, and their words to the end of the world.

**People:** **The law of the LORD is perfect, reviving the soul; the testimony of the LORD is sure, making wise the simple;**

*Leader:* The precepts of the LORD are right, rejoicing the heart; the commandment of the LORD is pure, enlightening the eyes;

**People:** **The fear of the LORD is clean, enduring for ever; the ordinances of the LORD are true, and righteous altogether.**

*Leader:* More to be desired are they than gold, even much fine gold; sweeter also than honey and drippings of the honeycomb.

*All:*    **Let the words of my mouth and the meditation of my heart be acceptable in thy sight,
O LORD, my rock and my redeemer.**

**Pastoral Prayer:**
Day by day, O Lord, we pray that truth and justice might win
the day. Yet, all too often, we see the evil in this world continue to
crush the spirits of people who seek a sincere relation to the
divine. Often we seem at the edge of despair. Yet, in your manifold grace and mercy, show us that in Jesus good can conquer
evil, and hope can thwart despair. In Jesus' cross we see "God's
foolishness is wiser than human wisdom, and God's weakness is
stronger than human strength" (1 Corinthians 1:25). May this
announcement of faith continue to guide our steps as we strive to
be a covenant people. May the faith you, O God, have shown in
your people be reflected in our daily walk with you. We pray for
the victory of right over might in the name of Jesus Christ. Amen.
(David Mosser)

# SERMON BRIEFS

## A COVENANT OF LIFE

### EXODUS 20:1-17

A professor of clinical psychology in a small liberal arts school in
Ohio has suggested, "Maybe the Ten Commandments are mis-
named. They ought to be called the ten hardest things we try to do in
life—honoring our parents, dealing with adultery, attempting to get
off the treadmill for one day each week, and not feeling jealous about
what other people have. These topics aren't ancient history—they are
core issues that most of us struggle with in our personal lives."

In Judaism, the stone tablets of the Ten Commandments are
visible in the sanctuaries of most temples and synagogues. In
Islam, the Ten Commandments are respected and included as
part of the highly developed guidelines given to Muslims on how
to live a spiritual life. In Buddhism, the Five Precepts that form
the basis of Right Behavior are almost identical to several of the

Ten Commandments. In the Sermon on the Mount, Jesus reinforced the value of the Commandments when he said, "I have not come to abolish them but to fulfill them" (Matthew 5:17 NIV).

Religious leaders and scholars have been interpreting the Ten Commandments since Moses received them. Regardless of your religious tradition (Judaism, Christianity, Islam, or Buddhism), the Ten Commandments contain spiritual lessons that create meaning, growth, and richness in your everyday life.

However, we need to remember that the Ten Commandments are rooted in God's grace. The preamble not only identifies God as the author of the Ten Commandments but also declares that they are rooted in God's grace. The Jewish people didn't have to do a thing to be saved but stand still. Verse two reminds the Israelites that God's grace preceded the law.

The Ten Commandments are designed to protect and provide. The Ten Commandments are more than a list of moral absolutes, which shackle people with arbitrary burdens. They are blueprints for living. Unfortunately, most of us don't like rules. We are inherently rebellious. While many of the commandments are negative, there are at least two positive reasons for every command: God wants to protect us from any unnecessary harm and God wants to provide us a rich and meaningful life.

The Ten Commandments focus on our vertical relationship with God as well as our horizontal relationships with one another. The first four commandments concern our vertical relationship with God. The last six commandments concern our horizontal relationship with fellow human beings. Even Jesus acknowledged that life is lived on the vertical plane as well as the horizontal plane. One day a Pharisee, an expert in Jewish law, approached Jesus and asked,

"Teacher, which commandment in the law is the greatest?" He said to him, " 'You shall love the Lord your God. . . .' This is the greatest and first commandment. And a second is like it: 'You shall love your neighbor as yourself.' On these two commandments hang all the law and the prophets." (Matthew 22:36-40)

Our relationship with God affects the way we relate to other human beings. Conversely, the way we relate to each other affects our relationship with God. (Bob Buchanan)

# THE GOD WITH SKIN ON

## 1 CORINTHIANS 1:18-25

As a mother tucked her little daughter into bed, she told her to have sweet dreams and proceeded to exit the room, turning the light off as she left. Her daughter asked to stay with her on this particular evening, as she was feeling a bit uneasy about sleeping alone. Her mother reassured her that everything was all right and told her she would leave the door cracked. But the little girl insisted she stay with her. "Honey, everything is fine," said the mother, "and don't forget that God is with you." Then her daughter replied, "But Mommy, tonight I need a God with skin on."

Isn't this what we all need—a God with skin on?

Jesus was the God of Abraham, Isaac, and Jacob with skin on. Emmanuel, God with us, living in a little dusty town called Nazareth. He grew into adulthood and shared every facet of human life. One facet was troublesome to the disciples and his contemporaries, namely, Jesus was crucified. The God with skin on died a human death. This truth has been a thorn in the theological side of people ever since.

This kind of language is illogical. God cannot die! This language is an idle tale for some; furthermore, it is madness to claim God died. This language is a roadblock on the road of faith, one we cannot detour if, on faith, we accept the resurrection.

But for those who are on a salvation journey with God, the language of the cross is the language of human struggle and pain, and we all can associate with this truth. People suffer and die every day for all sorts of reasons. The Gospels portray the good news that God put skin on so that we might be saved. God took it upon God's self to journey with us, traversing the great divide between God and humanity in the person of Jesus the Christ. And what does it get Jesus? A cross.

Perhaps the reason some Christian traditions use a plain cross and not a crucifix is that the picture of a human being hanging on it is too much to bear. We are not ashamed of an empty cross. It doesn't appear to be all that foolish. Just two boards intersecting. We adorn it by coloring it in gold and adding jewels to it. Thus, we have attempted to reduce its stumbling block character. It doesn't look so foolish if it looks cultured.

But no matter how hard we may try to explain it away; no matter how much we adorn it; no matter if we make it the centerpiece of our faith, we Christians cannot avoid addressing the most mysterious aspect of the Gospels—the crucifixion of Jesus. It's ugly. It's insane. It's unjust. It's embarrassing.

The God with skin on was murdered.

The God with skin on was hung on a cross, crucified.

It makes no sense. It's offensive. It's unbelievable.

Yet, paradoxically, the crucifixion is God's gift of good news. The crucifixion is the centerpiece, the very core of the good news. Without it, there is no good news. Without the cross, the Christian faith is but an empty message. Without the cross, there is no resurrection. The cross of Jesus Christ is the power and wisdom of God incarnated for the sake of all people. Out of injustice comes justice for the whole world; out of turmoil comes peace for the whole world.

Only a God with skin on could have done this, and his name was Jesus, the Crucified. This God puts skin on every day when you and I live and suffer, and even die, with those who need a God with skin on. (Mike Childress)

## OLD COVENANTS DESTROYED: LIFE UNDER THE LAW

### JOHN 2:13-22

It was a day when sacrificial theology ruled, the time when Jesus preached and taught. Much like a Middle Eastern street market or a busy American holiday craft show, the path to the temple was crowded, tempting, and frustrating. Jesus saw worshipers being driven by guilt rather than gratitude, frustration rather than joy, and fatigue rather than renewal as they walked the dusty streets of Jerusalem to the temple. Near the temple people found vendors trying to convince them to buy beautiful, specially blessed animals for the sacrifices in the temple or to exchange their own goods and wares for the acceptable sacrificial coins to donate. It was life under the law in those days of Judaism. Worshipers didn't have much choice if their own animals bore blemishes or their means of making a living didn't include raising animals acceptable for sacrifice in God's holy temple. Jesus could see that life under the law was destroying lives rather than purifying hearts. Jesus could see that people had become so invested in life under the law that the purchase of temple donations and sacrificial items was more important than simply worshiping God. Too many were so obsessed with luxurious trinkets to show their "righteousness" that they forgot to honor God's temple as a holy place, a place of worship and fellowship.

We are not all that different from those early worshipers of God. A group of people who are scared to be together in economic diversity, we may be afraid that little gifts and offerings aren't big enough. Or, we think that others with more money or fewer responsibilities should pull the weight for us. We hold back a donation until we get our way on an upcoming church project or doctrinal stance. Such temptations toward selfishness or feelings of inadequacy are all the results of letting life under the law guide us.

Jesus came to proclaim a new law—not a destruction of the old law but rather a fulfillment of it. "Destroy this temple, and in three days I will raise it up" (v. 19). Not just the temple of Jerusalem, not the temple of God's Ten Commandments, not the temple of modern day ethics or church rules and regulations. But rather, the temple of Jesus himself would be destroyed—a prediction Jesus' disciples struggled to understand. Jesus' body was destroyed so that believers might put to rest guilty hearts, resist temptations to power and judgment, and overcome frustrations with not being "good enough." Jesus' body was raised up so that believers might know the joy of life in Christ, the excitement of following God, the abundance of hearts full of love. Those are the pure hearts that God wants for our lives. Those are the pure hearts that people tried to achieve through animal sacrifice or large financial gifts. But, pure hearts are given freely and graciously by God through Christ Jesus—that's the new covenant God has made. For those who don't know Christ, this is the message most needed: God is waiting to shower that love and freedom that gives us a heart to love one another and God abundantly. For those who know Christ, the much-needed message is that a pure heart is assured, and God's love is with us, no matter what. (Mary Scifres)

# MARCH 30, 2003

*Fourth Sunday in Lent*

---

**Worship Theme:** God lifts up the Son of Man so that the world might believe in the power, mercy, and grace of God.

---

**Readings:** Numbers 21:4-9; Ephesians 2:1-10; John 3:14-21

**Call to Worship (Psalm 107:1-3, 17-22 RSV)**

*Leader:*    O give thanks to the LORD, for he is good; for his steadfast love endures forever!

*People:*    **Let the redeemed of the LORD say so, whom he has redeemed from trouble and gathered in from the lands, from the east and from the west, from the north and from the south.**

*Leader:*    Some were sick through their sinful ways, and because of their iniquities suffered affliction; they loathed any kind of food, and they drew near to the gates of death.

*People:*    **Then they cried to the LORD in their trouble, and he delivered them from their distress;**

*Leader:*    He sent forth his word, and healed them, and delivered them from destruction.

*People:*    **Let them thank the LORD for his steadfast love, for his wonderful works to the sons of men!**

*All:*    **And let them offer sacrifices of thanksgiving, and tell of his deeds in songs of joy!**

119

**Pastoral Prayer:**

Almighty God, hear our prayer this day. As we move toward Jerusalem and the divine work that you will do there, let us understand the plight of the disciples as they watch their mentor move with purpose toward the world's destiny. Too often we forget, O God, that we cannot see from your divine perspective. Too often our daily problems seem so large and unmanageable. However, when we turn to you, we find hope and comfort. May the words of our conversation and the acts of our will reflect the love you have for your world, O God. Make us those people for whom the gospel "wears well." May others see in us the spirit of Jesus, who taught us how to love one another. Help us confess our sins and know that with true confession there is truly mercy with you. Make us those people who know the gift of redemption. We pray this and all things in the holy and righteous name of Jesus Christ. Amen. (David Mosser)

# SERMON BRIEFS

## WHEN IN THE PITS, LOOK UP—TO GOD

### NUMBERS 21:4-9

I recall on one occasion my wife and I slaving in the kitchen to provide our children with a meal the likes of which they had not had nor would they ever forget. We spared no excesses. The finest tableware and the best ambiance we could afford were not too much for our children. As we prepared the meal, the children would take turns running into the kitchen and asking, "When is supper going to be ready? We're starved!" This coaching would happen periodically until called to eat. Finally, we all gathered around the table, said the customary blessing, and heard the first words from one of the children: "I don't like this stuff!" We were speechless, utterly dumbfounded. After all the hard work, after going to the limits of human ability (at least our ability), all they could do was say they didn't like it?

Perhaps our children's reactions were strangely similar to those of the Israelites toward God and Moses when they found themselves on the Exodus journey. "The people spoke against God and against Moses, 'Why have you brought us up out of Egypt to die in the wilderness? For there is no food and no water, and we detest this miserable food'" (v. 5).

My wife and I didn't bring out any poisonous snakes, although we ourselves felt snakebitten by their response. No, we simply encouraged them by saying, "This is it. Eat it, or go hungry!" I don't recall either child leaving the table.

The people of God in the Numbers episode are in the pits, so to speak. Grumbling and complaining are items on their menu. Instead of looking up to God they are looking down at what's going on around them. Their view is upsetting, and they take it out on Moses.

This is a marvelous parable about the journey of faith that God's people are called to make in every generation. Who among us has not complained to and against God when things didn't go our way? What church family has not gotten caught up in the game of impatience and complained because the church is not progressing as expected? The journey of faith is at times an arduous and demanding pilgrimage. More akin to the pace of a snail is God's timeline. Racehorse faith is seldom the mode of God's will. Consequently, we get bogged down, and rather than respond with gratitude to God for guidance, we moan that nothing is happening. We are a people who get bored easily in our day. If things are not always happening that are exciting and continually whetting our appetite for fun and excitement, then we pull up to the table of God's grace and say things like, "We don't like this stuff. Why can't we be a church like the one down the street where they have everything, and we have hardly anything? We detest the miserable state this church has become!" Quite frankly, the church finds itself in the pits more often than not. We are more apt to look down at what is occurring around us rather than look up to God for help.

When the Israelites looked down they not only found themselves in the pits, they found that they were not alone: "The LORD sent poisonous serpents among the people, and they bit the people, so that many Israelites died" (v. 6). Did God really send the serpents to bite the people as a result of their ingratitude? Would God be so vindictive as to punish the people for

121

their lack of faith? The people come to Moses and are convinced that the infestation of serpents is a direct consequence of their arrogance toward God. What is going on here?

This story is not about a vindictive God. This story is about an arrogant people and a merciful God.

The gist of this story is this: Whenever people of faith are tempted to look down, to look around and see what is wrong with the church, life, or the world, we are called to look up. We are called to focus on God and God's rescuing and empowering love. This will make all the difference in the world in whether we choose life or death. God asks us to choose life. So the next time you and I find ourselves in the pits of life, we must make a choice. What will we choose? (Mike Childress)

# NOTHING BUT A QUICK FIX

## EPHESIANS 2:1-10

### I. Background

Some scholars think Ephesians is not actually the work of Paul. It is at least, however, the work of someone who thinks with the mind of Paul and lives by the spirit of Paul. It is a good introduction to Paul's theology and his other letters.

In 2:8a we have the introduction, middle, and conclusion of Paul's experience and thought: "For by grace you have been saved through faith."

And what is salvation? It is resurrection from death in sin to life in the Spirit, as a gift of God.

### II. Situation

Most people don't think in theological terms. In our time, the problem is not that we are dead in sin, separated from God. The problem is that, for whatever reason, we aren't having a good time. We're sure we can have a good time if we can just get more of what we want and less of what we don't want. If we could just get more money, more sex, more power, more notoriety, more drugs, or more booze, life would be good. If we could just have fewer worries, illnesses, in-laws, rainy days, hangovers, or dandelions, life would be good. We don't need less sin; we need more good times.

Modern culture is onto something here. The purpose of life *is* to have a good time. Jesus himself says it: "I came that they may have life, and have it abundantly" (John 10:10).

### III. Problem

The biggest obstacle to a good time, however, is not a bad time, a hard time. God gives us a special grace to handle hard times. The biggest obstacle to a good time is a *partial* good time, a *false* good time, fool's gold that glitters compared to real gold that is solid through and through with grace and life.

A false or partial good time almost always feels good at the moment but makes feel bad in the long run. A true good time makes us feel bad at the moment but is good for us in the long run.

Partial good times that make us feel good at the moment but make us feel bad later? Drugs and booze. Promiscuous sex. Adultery. Overeating (Beware the church buffet!). Mindless TV. These can feel good in the moment but can put us on the run from our conscience and the Spirit of God.

True good times that may feel bad (at least make us feel bored) at the moment but make us feel great later? Exercising. Fasting (and dieting). Praying for our enemies. Singing hymns the preacher chooses just because he or she knows we can't stand them! Being nice to someone we don't like. Sacrificing for the sake of those we love, and should love. Tithing. Meditating.

### IV. Solution

To a modern congregation I would ask this question, *Why are you not having a good time?* Because your soul is dead, and the reason your soul is dead is because you're *trying* to have a good time!

Trying to have a good time always leads us to the partial good times, the quick fixes of what feels good at the moment.

We are "created in Christ Jesus for good works" (v. 10). If we forget about trying to have a good time and follow the way of Christ—accepting God's gift, living as saved people, doing good to those who harm us, not just trying to get more for ourselves but sharing with those in need, respecting God's creation and God's creatures—well, then, let the good times roll! (John Robert McFarland)

# THE LAW OF LOVE

## JOHN 3:14-21

This scripture, like the Hebrew Scriptures for this Lenten season, is a scripture about God's covenant with humanity. The covenant history is a rich one to explore in the Lenten season, particularly as it culminates in the Law of Love. And yet, even after Christ's resurrection, humanity never fulfills its part of the covenant. Caught up in the rules themselves, overly invested in making the covenant work through human effort, and forgetting the spirit of love in which God offers this covenant, even the best of Christians seldom can claim to live by the Law of Love constantly and consistently. And so, John's Gospel, which warns so direly of the evil and darkness of false belief or arrogant unbelief, would seem to condemn. Are all sinful people condemned because of a love for the darkness instead of the light? Our scripture says No! John's Gospel offers its most beloved hope in these passages: "God did not send the Son into the world to condemn the world, but in order that the world might be saved through him." "For God so loved the world that he gave his only Son, so that everyone who believes in him may not perish but may have eternal life" (vv. 17, 16).

The great news of the Christian covenant is God's refusal to give up on humanity. That's the story of grace. The scripture readings teach us that God has ultimately decided there is only one rule in this covenant with humanity: God must obey the law of love. This scripture reminds Christians in the Lenten season that God's light is mightier than any darkness. God's grace is sufficient to cover any imperfection. God's powerful love is stronger than any death.

But John does not let us forget that such grace and light and love are facing real forces in this world. The forces of sin and darkness and death are genuine and powerful, and humans have the ability to align themselves with such forces. When we do so, we become the "evil" who "hate the light" because of our fear that our "deeds may ... be exposed." The call to Lenten disciplines, alongside the Christian tradition of Lenten studies and sacrificial living, helps us remember to be among "those who do what is true" that we might "come to the light, so that it may be clearly seen that [our] deeds have been done in God" (v. 20). Such deeds are not done because we are the mighty ones but because we have put our faith and trust in Christ Jesus. Such truth is not the result of perfect living but rather trust and hope in God's promise of eternal life in Christ Jesus, a life of love and grace that begins now and goes into eternity. Such a life is worthy of God's calling; such a life is an honor to Christ's sacrifice; such a life is a joy to the Holy Spirit's presence.

In living the life of faith, in trusting Christ's gift by giving our belief and hope to God, we become lovers of the light, lovers of God, lovers of the one who will always love us. In this new covenant through Christ Jesus, God has placed a trust in humanity, a hope and a belief that we will come to the light and shun the darkness. No matter how many times we turn to the darkness, God hopes again for our repentance—our return to the light. This hope is God's covenant with us, God's promise to always abide by the Law of Love. (Mary Scifres)

# REFLECTIONS

# APRIL

**Reflection Verse:** *"We must obey God rather than any human authority."* (Acts 5:29)

Those of us who love the Hebrew Bible and who welcome the lectionary as a valuable tool for our preaching are often sad after Easter because Acts displaces the older testament all the way through the day of Pentecost. The good thing about this fact is that it forces some of us to look at texts that we would not normally tackle. That is, finally, the great value of the lectionary, however any particular lectionary may have many shortcomings.

So, in the Sundays after Easter we find texts concerning Acts; for example, Acts 5:27-32. And in that text we find prominently displayed the command to witness. Let me be honest about this word—it makes my skin crawl! There used to be on my campus every Friday a man who would "witness" to the students, any and all students, who came within the sound of his trumpet-like voice. He shouted, harangued, cajoled, abused, incensed many of them, and certainly me, in the course of his furious monologues. For one solid hour he sent all of us to hell and ensured us that hell was far from full and would readily accommodate any others who refused to heed his dire warnings of the wrath to come. Although he was laughed at, made fun of, and verbally assaulted in many decidedly subchristian ways, such things only confirmed in him the conviction that he was serving the cause of the Lord. I found him pathetic, little short of a lunatic.

But several years after he ceased coming around for his weekly sermons, I am not quite so sanguine about him as I once was. After all, many prophets of the past have said any number of things that brought ridicule and danger to them, too. I especially question my easy dismissal of this man when I read this passage from Acts. The book speaks of the astonishing growth of the early Christian communities, and much of that growth came through witnessing to large crowds and among religious authorities who were less than pleased at their words and their success. In the story recorded in Acts 5, the apostles are all tossed into prison, but they miraculously escape only to return to the witnessing that got them thrown into prison in the first place. So, the high priest demands that they all appear before him in order to warn them against any more of this witnessing. " 'We gave you strict orders not to teach in this name [the name of Jesus], yet here you have filled Jerusalem with your teaching and you are determined to bring this man's blood on us' " (v. 28). Note that the religious authorities do not debate the content of the preaching; they are far more concerned about the violence that such witnessing can cause. Their use of the word *blood* provides a chilling summary of their fears: Speaking of Jesus' shed blood may soon lead to their own shed blood.

But now Peter and the apostles say, " 'We must obey God rather than any human authority' " (v. 29). And that sentence provided the loudmouth preacher I mentioned with the ammunition he needed to vent his righteous anger on all of us heathen. He was convinced he was obeying God rather than human authority, and the very rejection we offered him proved his point.

How am I ever to know whether he was truly speaking for God in his rantings or simply a deranged, slightly unhinged, weirdo? Who has the right, or the courage, or the temerity, to stand up and speak on behalf of God? Every preacher who does precisely that week after week needs to ask this question regularly. What gives us the right to speak the Word of God?

The Bible provides thoroughly mixed messages on the question. Deuteronomy 18 ensures us that a true prophet speaks for God. But what is the definition of a true prophet? "If a prophet speaks in the name of the Lord but the thing does not take place or prove true, it is a word that the Lord has not spoken. The prophet has spoken it presumptuously; do not be frightened by it" (Deuteronomy 18:22). How long do I wait to see whether it "proves true," and how am I really to determine just what "proving true" means? In the amazing story of Saul and Samuel in 1 Samuel 15, the old prophet Samuel thunders to Saul that " 'the Glory of Israel [God] will not recant or change his mind [*nāḥam* in Hebrew]; for he is not a mortal, that he should change his mind [*nāḥam*]' " (1 Samuel 15:29). Yet in this very same chapter,

God precisely does "change his mind" and says so quite directly: "I [change my mind *(nāham)*] that I made Saul king" (1 Samuel 15:11). Quite obviously, Samuel, the supposed great prophet of God, is not always to be trusted to know all that God does. Is it possible that prophets need to have a large dose of humility to go along with their extra portions of zeal?

Perhaps that is finally what made me uncomfortable about that shouting prophet; he was just so *sure* that he was right. There was no trace of humility in him in the face of an awesome God who is sometimes more hidden than easily and readily revealed. None of us, neither he nor I nor you, have a phone line to God, a cellular device that always registers the divine will with digital clarity. Let me admit that I would welcome the stark certainty of Peter and the apostles as they stood in the teeth of an enraged High Priest and his religious councils, but I do not ever expect such certainty this side of paradise.

I think the wise old teacher, Gamaliel, in Acts 5 speaks a word to me about these matters. You might find his words helpful, too. He reminds the religious leaders that persons claiming to be prophets have risen again and again in history, and one after the other they have gathered some followers, raised much enthusiasm, and inevitably perished. Indeed the two he mentions, Theudas and Judas the Galilean, are at best footnotes to specialized histories only. He urges that this Peter and his followers may be little more than one of them. Because, he says, "If this plan or this undertaking is of human origin, it will fail; but if it is of God, you will not be able to overthrow them—in that case you may even be found fighting against God" (Acts 5:38*b*-39)!

Maybe Deuteronomy's way of testing the truth of a prophetic utterance is not so far-fetched after all: It must "prove true." So what do I say about my shouting preacher? If there is truth in him, it will stand the test of time. What do I say about my own preaching? If there is truth in it, it will stand the test of time. How much time? That is not for me to say. In humility, I must wait and trust the remarkable words of Habakkuk. "Though the fig tree does not blossom, and no fruit is on the vines; though the produce of the olive fails, and the fields yield no food; though the flock is cut off from the fold, and there is no herd in the stalls, yet I will rejoice in the LORD; I will exult in the God of my salvation" (Habakkuk 3:17-18). And, we should add, *I will wait and see if it really is of God.* (John Holbert)

# APRIL 6, 2003

## *Fifth Sunday in Lent*

---

**Worship Theme:** One of the profound benefits of God's covenant with God's people is the forgiveness of sin. When we accept God's forgiveness we enter into God's covenant.

---

**Readings:** Jeremiah 31:31-34; Hebrews 5:5-10; John 12:20-33

**Call to Worship (Psalm 51:1-4, 9-12)**

> *Leader:* Have mercy on me, O God, according to your steadfast love; according to your abundant mercy blot out my transgressions.

> *People:* **Wash me thoroughly from my iniquity, and cleanse me from my sin.**

> *Leader:* For I know my transgressions, and my sin is ever before me.

> *People:* **Against you, you alone, have I sinned, and done what is evil in your sight, so that you are justified in your sentence and blameless when you pass judgment.**

> *Leader:* Hide your face from my sins, and blot out all my iniquities.

> *People:* **Create in me a clean heart, O God, and put a new and right spirit within me.**

> *Leader:* Do not cast me away from your presence, and do not take your holy spirit from me.

*People:* **Restore to me the joy of your salvation, and sustain in me a willing spirit.**

**Pastoral Prayer:**

God of Justice and Mercy, hear the prayer of our hearts from the depth of our being. We ask for forgiveness for we "have been weighed on the scales and found wanting" (Daniel 5:27). We know in our hearts that we have done things that displease you. We have also failed to do the things that fulfill the holy covenant you made with us in Jesus Christ. O Lord, help us in our time of need. We want to do right, yet often it seems so complicated. Give us the courage to be your people and to treat others as our brothers and sisters in Christ. Give us a fresh start and forgive us our ignorance of your divine ways in the world. Let us embrace the forgiveness you freely offer us and may we extend that forgiveness to those who have wronged us. In all things make us charitable people in the name of Jesus. Amen. (David Mosser)

# SERMON BRIEFS

## A COVENANT WRITTEN ON THE HEART

### JEREMIAH 31:31-34

Jeremiah's relationship with his fellow Israelites was volatile. From Jeremiah's lips come some of the most severe language ever directed at Israel. He holds nothing back. Israel has broken faith with the covenant given at Sinai. Such actions have consequences, and God's response would be severe. Exile would be Israel's price for its sinfulness.

But Jeremiah also loved Israel as a parent loves a rebellious child. Yes, he spoke words of anger, hard words that made the people drive him away. But there were other words that Jeremiah spoke, words that must have made Israel's heart sing and its hope soar. The prophet spoke words about restoration and renewal. Nowhere among his words do we find any more beautiful and hopeful than the teaching about a "new covenant." The old covenant made at Sinai had been broken. Now there would be a new covenant, written not on stone but on the living tablets of the human heart. Only in this way could God establish a new order on earth.

The life of Jeremiah bears a striking resemblance to the life of Jesus. Their lives parallel each other in interesting ways. Both spent long periods in solitude, and both drew strength from the well of prayer. Each of them struggled with the hostility of their contemporaries in their hometowns, Jeremiah at Anathoth and Jesus at Nazareth. Both spoke against the religious representatives of the day. Jeremiah denounced the priests and prophets, while Jesus contended with the Pharisees and scribes. Both of them wept over what they saw coming to Israel as the result of apostasy, and each counseled against inordinate confidence in the Temple.

Most beautifully, Jeremiah anticipated the gospel—the Good News—in his teaching about the new covenant. On the night of his betrayal, Jesus was clearly referring to Jeremiah's prophecy when he inaugurated the "new testament" (covenant) in his own blood (Luke 22:20 KJV). All of Jeremiah 31:31-34 is quoted by the author of the Letter to the Hebrews (Hebrews 8:8-12) as the central element in the argument that in Christ all things have become new. To Jeremiah was granted a vision, unparalleled outside the New Testament, of that inwardness, universality, and perfect freedom, which exist within the relationship between God and human beings. In the teaching about a new covenant we see the pattern of the new life in Christ; here already we see the foreshadowing of the "glorious liberty of the children of God" (Romans 8:21 KJV).

Jeremiah teaches Israel that there is a faith that will carry them, as contrasted to a religion that they have to carry. His words about the new covenant are a wonderful illustration of the difference between law and grace, between works and faith. More important, Jeremiah is pointing to a faith that is personal. "No longer shall they teach one another, or say to each other, 'Know the Lord,' for they shall all know me, from the least of them to the greatest, says the Lord" (v. 34a). The day is coming when the God of Abraham, Isaac, and Jacob will be the God of every person, personally known and experienced. What a joy it is to experience such relationship! Personal faith is the secret to religious vitality.

There is an old story about romantic love. A bachelor professor, a young boy, and a teenager who has just kissed his girlfriend good night are all asked if they believe in romantic love.

The professor says, "Yes, I believe in romantic love. It is a phenomenon between two persons that leads to the propagation of the species." His is the evidence of scientific observance.

The young boy says, "Yes, I believe in romantic love because my sister is in love, and she acts in strange ways." His is the evidence of relational observance.

The teenager, who has just kissed his girlfriend, says, "Do I believe in romantic love? Oh boy, you bet I do!" His is the evidence of experience.

Jeremiah is foretelling a relationship with God that is experiential. He is pointing to a time when hearts will burn (Luke 24:32), like the disciples' experience on the Emmaus Road after meeting the risen Christ. Such is the power and joy of living faith! (Chris Andrews)

# WHAT JESUS' SUFFERING TEACHES US

### HEBREWS 5:5-10

Gregory J. Riley wrote a book entitled *One Jesus, Many Christs*. One of the many insights that he explores in some depth is that in the early days of the church, there were many differing views about Jesus. It would seem that the author of Hebrews is responding to claims that others have made. Hebrews, in a very systematic way, defines Jesus as the Christ. The author is particularly interested in our being in touch with the humanity of Jesus.

As we encounter this passage in Lent we are invited to reflect upon the sufferings of Christ, the human being. The image most closely identified with Jesus in that of high priest. As priest Jesus becomes willing to suffer. These sufferings are chosen and have a twofold meaning. Suffering reflects Jesus' willingness to submit in obedience as the Son of God and his identification with humankind. In this role there is the sense in which Jesus allows his character to be shaped and molded by his trials. In this role he becomes a willing pioneer from whom we can learn in our own challenges. In his obedience, Jesus completed the work that God had for him, and in this mystery, we are to see God's design for our salvation.

Following the author's lead, perhaps we are invited to consider our humanity and our relation to God in times of suffering, trial, and challenge.

We can see within the text the invitation to share the depth of our pain with God. Our doubts and fears and even our sense of isolation from God can be openly expressed. Jesus in the Garden of Gethsemane holds nothing back as he shares the longings of his heart and the pleas to be spared.

We are told that Jesus was heard. In our day and time it is not unusual for us to say *I am not being heard.* Usually it means that we are not getting our way or what we ask for. But in this passage, *being heard* is a much more profound experience. *Being heard* here means to know that Jesus experienced the vital presence of God. In that experience with God, Jesus was given a freedom over events even as it seemed his destiny was being limited by those events. I believe that there is a direct relationship between our emotional openness with God about what we are experiencing and our openness to experience God's presence and help.

There is also the invitation for us to trust God enough to dare to ask ourselves what our difficulties are teaching us. We are invited to dare to believe that in our suffering there exists meaning and purpose. Søren Kierkegaard, the Danish theologian, suggests that the way forward through suffering is to ask how we can offer it to God in obedience. Hebrews offers that same kind of spirit of hope and encouragement. It is clear that in his role as high priest, Jesus goes ahead of us. In his humanity we catch a glimpse of who we are becoming and who it is that does not forsake us.

The issue of suffering raises many questions that do not yield easy answers. This picture of Jesus helps us to live fully in the midst of the mystery. (Bob Holloway)


## THE ILLUSION OF SUCCESS

### JOHN 12:20-33

Success is usually measured in terms of power and prestige or money and possessions. Such a measurement is nothing new.

Jesus' followers probably hoped that his triumphal entry into Jerusalem meant that he would soon begin a "successful" campaign. The dream remained that Jews would revolt against the Romans and proclaim power. The dream remained that Jesus would reform Judaism so that God's law of love could guide. But no sooner had Jesus entered Jerusalem than he spoke strange words. Words about dying wheat that bears fruit; something about loving life causing us to lose life. Strange words, troubling words, words that give even the most enlightened modern-day Christian pause.

Even Jesus admits that his soul is troubled and confesses that he has thought of asking for release from his calling. It must have been an odd and awkward moment for his followers.

Then, words of triumph: "Now is the judgment of this world; now the ruler of this world will be driven out. And I, when I am lifted up from the earth, will draw all people to myself" (vv. 31-32). Followers who still dreamt of power and prestige might have grasped onto those words, ignoring the rest. But John is a careful writer and refuses to allow us off the hook as he reminds us that these words are "said . . . to indicate the kind of death [Jesus] was to die" (v. 33).

As readers of this Gospel, we can't ignore the haunting truth of this passage: Jesus is not interested in the illusion of worldly success. He knows that falling in love with the things of this world will not bring eternal life; passion for earthly prestige will not even bring the joy now that most people hope for. And, that's the bottom line for Jesus: Eternal life begins now, not later. Joy in God's spirit of love is something that brings eternal life immediately because we are living that eternal life here and now. But Jesus knows that joy is hard to come by when the seduction of temporal things is all around.

Most people can probably recount stories of some very wealthy or powerful persons who are unhappy, even miserable, with their lives. We know that money can't buy love or happiness, but we still pursue economic gain. We state that power corrupts, but we still seek it. The "ruler of this world"—the temptations to power and corruption, to success and gain, to self-centeredness and cruelty—that ruler was driven out for one brief moment on Easter morning, in the moment of resurrection, in that triumph of life over death, light over darkness. But even for those who know the story, who believe in Christ's power of life over death, we face the temptation to rule this world with our desire for power and success. The Scripture refuses to let us forget: "Those who love their life lose it, and those who hate their life in this world will keep it for eternal life" (v. 25). Jesus is not asking followers to be dour, unhappy people who hate this world; rather Christ is reminding us to love God first, love others and ourselves more than we love the things of this world, "this life" if you will. For it is that latter love, the love of things, the love of power, the love of success that will lead us most certainly into darkness and destruction. But the love of God, self, and others is the love that will lead us into eternal light and eternal life. (Mary Scifres)

# APRIL 13, 2003

## *Palm Sunday*

**Worship Theme:** Jesus parades into Jerusalem as a hero, only to be scorned, mocked, and crucified by week's end. In the irony of Passion/Palm Sunday God reveals God's love through Jesus' ministry.

**Readings:** Isaiah 50:4-9*a*; Philippians 2:5-11; Mark 14:1–15:47

### Call to Worship (Psalm 31:9-10, 14-16)

*Leader:* Be gracious to me, O Lord, for I am in distress; my eye wastes away from grief, my soul and body also.

**People:** **For my life is spent with sorrow, and my years with sighing; my strength fails because of my misery, and my bones waste away.**

*Leader:* But I trust in you, O Lord; I say, "You are my God."

**People:** **My times are in your hand; deliver me from the hand of my enemies and persecutors.**

*All:* **Let your face shine upon your servant; save me in your steadfast love.**

### Pastoral Prayer:

Almighty God, do not hinder us from hearing your holy word that comes to us by way of Scripture, the prophets, and the teachings of Jesus. Make us people who live by the word that comes from your divine mind. May we walk through life by the statutes, ordinances, and laws of Christ. These rules for the life of faith guide us into living the trustworthy covenant given for our edification by your mercy and grace. As the people of God, we need the direction that your gracious and divine hand provides. Help us heed the word that dwells among us, and give us newness of life. Continue to lift the example of Jesus, who "humbled himself and became obedient to the point of death—even death on a cross" (Philippians 2:8). May Jesus' servant example ever be before those who claim Christ as Savior. May we bear the likeness of Jesus on our holy way. We pray this in Jesus' name. Amen. (David Mosser)

## SERMON BRIEFS

## THE SERVANT GOD CROWNED KING

### ISAIAH 50:4-9a

Our older son, a father himself now, has always disliked parades and will go out of his way to avoid them. The reason, we think, is that once when he was a small boy, we unwittingly took him to the strange and fascinating Fasching parade in Basel. Fasching is a centuries-old, Swiss-Protestant answer to Mardi Gras. It occurs during Lent, and rather than encouraging a party atmosphere, the custom was intended to bring about Lenten penitence and the contemplation of mortality. Ancient masks are brought out of storage from the city museum, and whole brigades of grotesquely masked men process down the street to funereal marches while clowns work the crowds, setting off fire crackers and poking fun at unguarded foibles. The whole thing was supposed to strike fear in the hearts of the unrepentant. Most parade-goers are merely amused, but our two-year-old buried his head in his father's neck and didn't want to look at anyone in a mask or clown makeup for years.

Our Palm Sunday processions are joyous occasions with waving branches, glad shouts, and songs, but this parade in its origin also had an edge, one that makes us want to hide our faces in fear. Jesus is knowingly riding toward the forces of death, and the people are shouting "Hosanna! God save us!" Hosanna is not Hallelujah. Palm Sunday is not yet Easter. What lies ahead for Jesus is abuse, humiliation, and painful death at the hands of the Roman executioners. Even so, we are reminded that Jesus is truly king and that God exalts him even as he is crucified.

Isaiah's words highlight the paradox that Jesus' exaltation is utterly linked with his humiliation. Like the servant of Isaiah 50, Jesus, even in the events of his trial and crucifixion, is the victor not the victim. Jesus rode a lowly work animal into Jerusalem and was hailed as king. Jesus with silent dignity endured the mockery and the disdain of Rome's representatives and raised up the kingdom God had given him. Jesus' "lifting up" on a cross became his glorious "lifting up" by God, giving him a name above every name.

According to the ancient hymn, Jesus *willingly* "emptied himself, taking the form of a slave [household servant], . . . humbled himself and became obedient to the point of death" (Philippians 2:7-8). God's promise in Isaiah and in Philippians is that God will stand with the servant who is obedient and faithful and that God will exalt the one who is humiliated and abused for God's sake. Neither Isaiah nor Paul glorifies suffering for its own sake, but these writers do reveal that suffering for the sake of God's justice can bring about good for others.

Jesus became a household servant for us, died for us, and thus we know him as our king. But when the crowd honors him as king, the parade is politicized. He is seen as a threat to Caesar, to all powers who oppose God's rule. Jesus bears the "Hosannas" and later the derisive taunts because he is sure that God will vindicate him. He knows the Hebrew Scriptures and remembers the assurances made in Isaiah. God teaches and sustains the suffering servant. In *God's* court no one will dare pronounce him guilty. "I have set my face like flint, and I know that I shall not be put to shame; he who vindicates me is near" (v. 7*b*). The gospel songs tell us, "Satan is busy, but God is near," and we know that Jesus' steps will be ordered in God's word.

Isaiah 50:4-9*a* declares God's promise of long ago to stand with the oppressed and those who serve God through troubling times. The speaker in these verses is vulnerable and relies totally on God. Christians have long seen in Isaiah's suffering servant an image that reveals the meaning of Jesus' suffering. In its original setting this song affirms God's relationship to Israel and offers comfort to the suffering exiles of Isaiah's time: God is there for the faithful. The encouragement is timeless, however, and the promise of God's enduring presence extends to all who follow Jesus in risking humiliation and physical harm to affirm God's will for life. (Blair Meeks)

# JESUS WAS NEVER FULL OF HIMSELF

### PHILIPPIANS 2:5-11

Have you ever heard it said of a person, "Oh, she's just full of herself." Usually this means, in a joking sort of way, that the person is lighthearted and fun. It can mean the contrary. In a serious vein, this caricature can mean the person is arrogant and sees himself or herself as the author of his or her state of being. According to the Gospels, neither description could characterize Jesus the Christ. In fact, according to the writer of Philippians, Jesus was empty of himself, if such a characterization were grammatically correct. "Though he was in the form of God, [he] did not regard equality with God as something to be exploited, but emptied himself" (Philippians 2:6-7a).

What does it mean to empty oneself? The way the writer puts it, one could get the picture that to empty oneself is no more difficult than emptying a glass of water. What did Jesus do in order to empty himself? Three things jump from the text: servitude, humility, obedience.

## I. Servitude

To be truly human is to serve others. The highest calling from God is for a person to serve others. Whether it was prophets, apostles, or you and me, God calls us to serve. This is what Jesus did, and this is what Jesus expects of disciples. *Service* means "getting your hands dirty" in ministry. *Service* means putting yourself, literally, in other people's situations, and the best way to do that is to share their station in life, even if that be compromising one's social, political, and religious customs. Jesus never reached out to others by first checking out their social, political, and religious position in matters. These things meant nothing to Jesus, and they should mean nothing to the church. The call of service to others by God means, first, getting down off of our high horses.

## II. Humility

To be truly humble is not to discriminate among people or, sociologically speaking, to profile people. Jesus shared his community with tax collectors, harlots, murderers, atheists, government officials, fisherfolk, and the religious elite. Jesus didn't find it beneath him to eat, worship, and enjoy social events with the worst and the best of people. This is humility at its best. We shouldn't find it "humiliating" to do the same. The world divides people into races when in reality there is only one race—the human race. When all is said and done, there is only one thing that matters to God when it comes to loving and forgiving people—that they be human! Jesus lived this truth.

## III. Obedience

To serve others as Christ served just doesn't happen over night. And we certainly aren't born with a serving attitude. Such a life is learned behavior. To be selfless in the face of another person's dilemma, regardless of whether we know them or not, just doesn't happen due to one's innate helpful proclivity. To be a disciple of Jesus, we have to intentionally put ourselves in situations that will change us. The word *disciple* has for its root meaning the word *discipline*. As Christians, we are to unlearn some things we have acquired over the years, namely, we must pick our friends. It is not a choice for the Christian whether he or she will serve. Obedience to God means to do just what Jesus did: Furnish love and care, justice and peace indiscriminately. If this doesn't change a person, there is nothing that will work to make disciples of Jesus Christ.

These three things—servitude, humility, and obedience to God's way—won't make us full of ourselves; they will make us full of Jesus! Nothing more beautiful, nothing more gracious, nothing more loving can happen to a person than this. (Mike Childress)

# IN THE CROWD, WAVING

## MARK 14:1–15:47

We are now at the first moment when it is recognized that, indeed, the Son of Man is going to suffer and die. The woman with the alabaster jar is the first to recognize who Jesus is and what is going to happen—that indeed the Son of Man must suffer and die and be resurrected in order for the kingdom of God to come upon this world.

In the events of Holy Week and Palm Sunday, we learn about ourselves. Few of us would have stood with the woman. Some might have taken the sword and tried to use violence in the face of approaching suffering. Some might even have hid or run the other way. Few could take the extraordinary action of the woman with the alabaster jar. She has not only the sensitivity to truly understand what is happening but also the courage to act. The act itself is a minicrucifixion for her because she must give up everything and suffer in order to be who God calls her to be. She is very much alone in her understanding and her action. It brings her nothing but ridicule and scorn.

For some reason, following Christ requires going against the grain. It requires seeing the world not through the eyes of the powerful but through the eyes of the poor.

In my city a reporter went undercover as a homeless person. He lived for a week on the streets as a homeless person. He was beat up. He was robbed. He slept in abandoned cars and homeless shelters. Of all the places he went for help, there was only one place where people looked him in the eye, touched him, and called him by name. It happened to be a Methodist church.

When the reporter's week on the street was complete, he wrote an extensive story about his experience for the newspaper. His experience so moved the church that helped him that it mounted a city-wide crusade to raise the money for a Day Center for the homeless, which would help people get off the street.

The events of Holy Week are dominated by what happens to Jesus: conspired against, anointed for burial, denied, betrayed, captured, tried, sentenced, mocked, crucified, and buried. Jesus

141

identifies with the common people, and it is this identification that creates for us mercy and grace.

What we all want is a hero who will come in and set things straight—a powerful, dominant figure who will move the world in a new direction, get rid of the false prophets and crooked leaders, clean up the place, and establish a new rule. We want powerful and bold action from a great leader who will set right the mess of our lives and the injustices of our world.

Jesus prepares the way for that to happen, but at the end of the week, the ball is in our court—the necessary action now must be ours. Jesus' action is to be the suffering servant, to identify with the little and the least. He calls us to recognize that in imitating him, we find the new life even if it is in what we would consider the strangest of places.

Few people realized as the woman spent all she had on oil to anoint his body, as she violated the religious and secular customs of the day and scandalized those who watched her that she herself was becoming part of this new kingdom that Jesus in his death and new life was bringing to the world.

The problem we have as human beings is that most of us are in the crowd waving palm branches not knowing who this Jesus is. Most of us are there with the disciples who cut and run. Few of us are with the woman who gives all she has to the Christ. (Wayne Day)

# APRIL 18, 2003

## *Good Friday*

---

**Worship Theme:** The only goodness in Good Friday is the goodness God brings out of Jesus' suffering and death. Without the pain of Jesus' crucifixion there is no joy in the resurrection of Jesus as our Christ and Lord.

---

**Readings:** Isaiah 52:13–53:12; Hebrews 10:16-25; John 18:1–19:42

**Call to Worship (Psalm 22:1-5, 11, 22-23a, 25-27 RSV)**

| | |
|---|---|
| *Leader:* | My God, my God, why hast thou forsaken me? Why art thou so far from helping me, from the words of my groaning? |
| *People:* | **O my God, I cry by day, but thou dost not answer; and by night, but find no rest.** |
| *Leader:* | Yet thou art holy, enthroned on the praises of Israel. In thee our fathers trusted; they trusted, and thou didst deliver them. |
| *People:* | **To thee they cried, and were saved; in thee they trusted, and were not disappointed.** |
| *Leader:* | Be not far from me, for trouble is near and there is none to help. |
| *People:* | **I will tell of thy name to my brethren; in the midst of the congregation I will praise thee: You who fear the LORD, praise him!** |
| *Leader:* | From thee comes my praise in the great congregation; my vows I will pay before those who fear him. |

*People:*    **The afflicted shall eat and be satisfied; those who seek him shall praise the LORD! May your hearts live forever!**

*All:*    **All the ends of the earth shall remember and turn to the LORD; and all the families of the nations shall worship before him.**

**Pastoral Prayer:**

God of Mercy, we come to worship as confused as ever about life and our part in it. We remember the sacrifice of Jesus on the cross and wonder what part we might have played in the injustice that visited him had we been there. We sing "Were You There," and we wonder what it would have been like. Would we have deserted this innocent person who died for us? Would we have denied Jesus like Peter? Would we have run from Jesus' presence like the other disciples? In these questions our vulnerability stands as an eternal question before us. Forgive when we are weak and indecisive. Forgive us when we turn our backs on those crucified by the harshness of modern life. Inspire us by your Holy Spirit to reach out to others as Christ reaches out to us. This is our prayer in Jesus' name. Amen. (David Mosser)

# SERMON BRIEFS

## WERE YOU THERE?

### ISAIAH 52:13–53:12

Some disciples ran away; some watched from far off. The women stayed nearer the cross, and Jesus, still the leader and teacher in his dying hours, called his mother and the disciple whom he loved even closer. Who would dare to be there? Who could stand to look? "So marred was his appearance, beyond human semblance. . . . He was despised and rejected by others; a man of suffering" (vv. 52:14*b*, 53:3).

Since the time of the evangelists, we have borrowed the unmatched poetry of Isaiah's fourth Servant Song to tell the horror of the crucifixion. Down through the centuries the words echo. "Surely he hath borne our griefs" (v. 53:4*a* KJV). "All we like sheep have gone astray" (v. 53:6*a* KJV). The phrases thunder from Handel's *Messiah,* and they are uttered in the sheer silence of despair by those lost in grief over their own failings.

Jesus in all his humanity suffered deeply, and Isaiah's suffering servant helps us to know what Jesus suffered on Good Friday: "He had no form or majesty that we should look at him, nothing in his appearance that we should desire him" (v. 53:2*b*).

Isaiah's words are a corrective to our tendency to spiritualize Jesus, to dismiss his anger and impatience, his vulnerability, his pain and weakness. We want radiance and dazzling purity. The presence of our beautiful Savior is uplifting, puts a smile on our faces. But were you there with our Savior who was lifted up on the cross? The appearance of the crucified One is not beautiful but "marred"; he is "one from whom others hide their faces" (v. 53:3). In this he is like the sick and wounded, the forgotten and rejected, the ones he has come to save. "He was oppressed, and he was afflicted. . . . By a perversion of justice he was taken away" (vv. 53:7*a*, 8*a*). We would rather not be there, rather not see the face of this one who was wrongly condemned to death.

If you were there, if you heard Isaiah's words—all of them—you will find, even in the darkest hour, a promise: "See, my servant shall prosper; he shall be exalted and lifted up, and shall be very high" (v. 52:13). Even in the midst of pain and death God offers hope: The wounded one is our healer. "But he was wounded for our transgressions, . . . and by his bruises we are healed" (v. 53:5). Even in the midst of oppression and injustice, there is a future to imagine: The one who was himself oppressed and afflicted calls us to stand with him and with all who, like him, suffer the abuses of the powerful. His appearance astonishes us and will also "startle many nations" (v. 52:15*a*) and shut the mouths of kings. "Through him the will of the LORD shall prosper" (v. 53:10*b*).

Were you there? If you were there, if you were able to look at the one crushed by pain, "cut off from the land of the living" (v. 53:8*b*), you are also able to come early in the morning to the tomb with Mary Magdalene and the other women. They watched and waited and came to bathe the body and anoint it with spices. Those who can look into the face of the suffering Jesus, who can touch death

145

and not turn away, are called to the garden, called to the tomb. If we are there, if we are at the cross and at the tomb, we, like Mary, will look into the face of the risen Lord, we will hear him call our name. The wounds will still be visible but so will the light. As Isaiah promised ages ago: "Out of his anguish he shall see light. . . . The righteous one, my servant, shall make many righteous" (v. 53:11).

Were you there? Were you there with the suffering and the rejected? Were you there with the righteous one who poured himself out to death? (Blair Meeks)

# THE GREAT ERASER

## HEBREWS 10:16-25

Okay. I admit it. When I was in elementary school, I often got into trouble. Nothing really bad but I constantly tested and tried my teachers. You see, I liked to talk and have fun with my friends when I was supposed to be doing other things. Suddenly, the class would grow quiet and I would hear the sound of chalk on the board as my name was written, along with those of others. That you did not want to happen. That meant you were in trouble. You had to stay in at recess and do chores or suffer whatever punishment the teacher sentenced (lots of time it was to read and write things, especially the assignments we didn't do while talking). If you got your name on the board several times in one week, you ended up with the principal. But at the end of the week, our teacher had this giant eraser. I don't know where she got it, but it was huge. She took that eraser and erased our names from the board. We also had to get cloths and water to wash the board. I don't know exactly how to describe it, but when our names were erased and washed away, it felt good. It kind of felt like we had a new start—until the next week anyway!

It seems to me that the writer of Hebrews has an even larger eraser in these wonderful words. He quotes Jeremiah 31:31-34 about the new covenant God will make with the people, which will bring them closer than they have ever been to God. But this would require a very large eraser. It would require forgiveness and grace. It would require the cross! Through the cross, through the sacrifice of our great High Priest, which was his very life, we are forgiven. God remembers our sins no more! They are erased forever. What an eraser!

I remember when I first began to understand and experience what this really meant. It was after my own baptism. I remember feeling so clean, so new. All of that came back to me recently when my daughter managed to find every bit of dirt in our backyard. I could not see a clean spot on her. I took her inside and ran warm water for her bath. She loved it. She watched curiously as the water and all the soil began to drain away. "Look, Daddy," she said. "The dirt is all gone." It was. She looked shiny and clean.

There is a mountain stream not far from our house. I walk on a trail that runs beside it. You can hear it long before you see it. It sings through the forest. Many are the times I have sat there and felt such peace simply in its presence. But one day I managed to dislodge some stones that tumbled down into the crystal clear water, stirring up the water and turning it muddy. As I looked on the water continued to flow, and soon all the mud, the soil was taken away. It was clean again as if it had never happened. And that is how I feel when I remember my baptism and what Christ has done for me. We still can get dirty. But we are God's children. God has cleansed us. God has erased for all time our sins and remembers them no more—all because of Christ and what he did for us on Good Friday! Thanks be to God! (Bass Mitchell)


## BETRAYING THE BEST

### JOHN 18:1–19:42

Jesus had carefully chosen a small group of close followers, the disciples. Jesus must have known that when times get tough, many followers fall away. Some will deny ever having followed. Others will betray the leader whom they earlier loved and trusted. And so, of the hundreds of people who followed Jesus during his years of ministry, a dozen very special people gave their lives to follow Jesus, to hear and heed his lessons, to learn as he taught so that they could also become leaders. As we read this passage of Scripture, we are surely and oddly struck that Judas was one of these twelve. Judas, who sold Jesus for some silver and a brief moment of fame, was one of the twelve.

Jesus must have suspected that possibility as well. Students of human history know that leaders are often betrayed by close friends and confidants. Jesus knew this possibility. And so, he had a few select amongst the twelve who were perhaps his closest friends and allies: Peter and James and John, the three who occasionally go off alone with Jesus and learn and see unique things in those times apart from the others. Did Jesus know that one of them would sit in the courtyard during his trial and deny even knowing him? Whether Jesus knew or not, nothing could prevent the pain and sorrow he surely felt when facing those denials and betrayals. Perhaps one of the most powerful parts of the Good Friday lesson is that Jesus suffers such human agony on the journey toward death. Very few of us will ever face being murdered or executed; very few of us will be defendants in an unjust trial; very few of us will be tortured or imprisoned; very few of us will know the day or time of our deaths in order to say "Oh, this is what Jesus went through." But almost all of us will face the denial and possibly even the betrayal of people who once were close to us. Friends fall away; loved ones become vicious adversaries; leadership teams become bitter rivals; a church body turns into a divided house. Betrayal is part of the human condition. Often betrayal is not a product of bad leadership or bad people. For Jesus was betrayed, and Jesus was the best that would ever be. Even the best can be betrayed. That is the condition of this world that still struggles with sin and sorrow.

Jesus knows this part of the condition. Jesus lived that betrayal right here with us. And so, on this Good Friday, we are given the promise that our own sufferings are not endured alone. Jesus has endured the very worst of them alongside us. We will face betrayal in our lives. We will be denied by people who once seemed to love and care for us. Good Friday reminds us that even the best cannot avoid such sorrows. But perhaps when we remember that even the closest followers of Jesus became the producers of such sorrow, we are encouraged to avoid becoming Judas or Peter to those whom we love and especially to God. Perhaps we can find a little more courage to avoid those daily betrayals and denials that cause such great sorrow to God and to those who love us. If we found that courage, if each of us avoided being the betrayer more times than not, this world would surely be more of an Easter place each and every day. (Mary Scifres)

# APRIL 20, 2003

*Easter Day*

---

**Worship Theme:** Christ is risen, indeed. Today we proclaim what gives all life meaning and value. Hallelujah!

---

**Readings:** Acts 10:34-43; 1 Corinthians 15:1-11; John 20:1-18

**Call to Worship (Psalm 118:1-2, 14-19, 24 RSV)**

*Leader:*   O give thanks to the LORD, for he is good; his steadfast love endures forever!

*People:*   **Let Israel say, "His steadfast love endures forever."**

*Leader:*   The LORD is my strength and my song; he has become my salvation.

*People:*   **Hark, glad songs of victory in the tents of the righteous:**

*Leader:*   "The right hand of the LORD does valiantly, tthe right hand of the LORD is exalted; the right hand of the LORD does valiantly!"

*People:*   **I shall not die, but I shall live, and recount the deeds of the LORD.**

*Leader:*   The LORD has chastened me sorely, but he has not given me over to death.

*People:*   **Open to me the gates of righteousness, that I may enter through them and give thanks to the LORD.**

***All:***       **This is the day which the L**ORD **has made; let us rejoice and be glad in it.**

**Pastoral Prayer:**

Today is the day of Easter. With the great multitude around the world and through the centuries, we believers shout, "Hallelujah! Salvation and glory and power to our God," who has saved us from the sting of death (Revelation 19:1). We give you thanks today, O God, for by the resurrection of Jesus you prove your great love toward us. Inspire us this day that you rule over both sin and death. Give us the confidence that our faith in you will solve the riddle of life and our problem of pain. Although we often suffer, remind us that our suffering has a greater purpose than we can see on this side of the grave. Let us live in confidence that you watch over the faithful both by day and by night. Let us make a joyful noise on this most holy day. May we revel and rejoice in our Lord Jesus Christ, in whose name we pray. Amen. (David Mosser)

# SERMON BRIEFS

## PETER PRESENTS THE GOSPEL IN BRIEF

### ACTS 10:34-43

Peter cannot prevent himself from remarking on the extraordinary scenario that found him addressing a Roman centurion who had actually sent for him. This was certain proof that God is a *prosopoleptes,* an acceptor of persons. Surely we cannot hear this message too often! In our limitation and sinfulness, we are quite adept at finding the barriers that divide us. The "isms" of cultural exploitation (sexism, racism, ageism, classism) are collective projections of individual sin and the refusal to embrace God's acceptance of all people. No defined group has a monopoly on the God revealed in Jesus Christ. As church leaders, this should give us pause for thought. Before rounding up the "usual suspects" to provide leadership for the church in some fashion, we are reminded that God does not show partiality. Others are also called who depend on our effectiveness as "people brokers" to thrust them into situations in which they become the visible Word of God. Laypersons are called to significant ministries by virtue of their baptisms. While our roles within the church may differ, our identities are constant: We are first and foremost baptized Christians. After all, God shows no partiality.

God sends Jesus to *euaggelizo*, bring good news to the world. This is the sacred function of preaching. As preachers, we are obligated to skewer the injustices of society, hammer on the sins of self and the multitudes, and point out the disparity between what we do and what we are called to do. Yet, we must not forget that ultimately we are called to pronounce the good news. The stakes are simply too high to do any less. Our congregants face a troubled and troubling world bearing pains and suffering we cannot know. They require the glad tidings of the gospel.

Peter provides this very commodity for Cornelius. In simple form, he relates the basic components of the gospel. Jesus taught and performed acts of healing; he was crucified and arose from the dead. Sending the disciples forth, Jesus offers forgiveness for sins even as he promises to be the judge of the living and the dead at the *parousia*, the last judgment.

In the diverse theological climate of the day, preachers must know that many times the pews are filled with persons with varying interpretations of the Scriptures. Fundamentalists profess to treat all books of the Bible as literal history. I differentiate between the many types of narrative and literature found in the Bible but primarily read the Gospels as historical witness containing mysteries I cannot rationally explain. Others follow the lead of the Jesus seminar members in demythologizing and deconstructing the Scriptures to "boil down" to the most factual account that rational methodology can provide. Regardless of our hermeneutical diversity, we can find unity in essentials and keep learning through constant inquiry into the ministry and identity of Jesus of Nazareth.

While attending seminary, I had an opportunity to interview Albert Outler. Outler in his final years had an interest in paranormal phenomena and he allowed for future intersections of science and biblical narrative that cannot presently be explained. He allowed for the presence of mystery. The gospel message demands to be approached with respect for the vitality and revelation potential. Exegetical endeavors cannot become textual autopsies that render the message dead. We can know that Peter preached the gospel with passion and conviction. Anything less simply does not inspire people then or now. (John Fiedler)

# RESURRECTION PREACHING

## 1 CORINTHIANS 15:1-11

John S. McClure wrote:

> When your preaching empowers a congregation it must express power *with* others. It must invite church members to stand with others who live in very different situations, and help church members to find others who stand with them in their situation. In other words, preaching must reach across boundaries and connect people, creating new communities of commitment and hope. (John S. McClure, *The Roundtable Pulpit: Where Leadership & Preaching Meet* [Nashville: Abingdon Press, 1995], p. 13)

McClure calls this enterprise an exercise in *integrative power*. Paul's letter to Corinth provides a solid foundation to draw this church together. Paul reached across boundaries—geographical, political, and religious—to integrate the church. Paul based his theological presentation on the one central theme that is uniquely Christian: the resurrection of Jesus Christ.

However, a lot of preaching could be suffering from something the apostle Paul pointed out to the Corinthian church. It doesn't lead anywhere. John Killinger notes,

> Christian preachers . . . have a mighty theme—how God has acted in Christ to give us wholeness of life in the eternal family—and it is important that our sermons embody that theme. There is nothing more trivial than preaching that misses it. Ministers are called to preach the gospel, not offer commentary on what is happening to hairdos and hemlines. (John Killinger, *Fundamentals of Preaching* [Philadelphia: Fortress Press, 1985], p. 163)

In any cultural context, preaching that avoids giving people hope based on Jesus' resurrection, doesn't lead anywhere. This kind of preaching is empty and unempowering for the hearer.

Too often this results in relegating preaching to a talk rather than a message from God. Thus, the sermon's author in this case is the preacher and not God. People don't come to hear a word from the preacher; people come to church to hear a word from God.

Undoubtedly, Paul had a difficult time convincing some of the Corinthians that the message he preached was not of his authorship. Like the disciples who received the message from the women following their return from the empty tomb, it all seemed like an idle tale (Luke 24:11). There were those in the Corinthian church who thought Paul had concocted the story of the Resurrection. He writes them to reiterate the contrary. Preaching the good news of Jesus Christ is a gift from God. It is not a message that originates with the preacher. People needed to be reminded that the gospel is established in people's lives by God's Spirit, and the preacher is but a conduit through which God brings the good news. Putting it another way, the preacher's sermon is to point away from himself or herself and point directly to God.

Paul's letter can be a powerful reminder for preachers in that we need to refresh everyone's memory of what this good news exactly is: "Christ died for our sins, in accordance with the scriptures; that he was buried; and that he was raised to life on the third day, in accordance with the scriptures" (1 Corinthians 15:3-4 JB) These are what I would call the three prongs on the fork of salvation. Preaching that avoids these three things is not preaching at all, and it is preaching that doesn't lead anywhere. It is preaching that misses the mark. When preaching, however, is immersed in these three things, it is preaching that can change people, change situations, and even change the world. It is preaching that leads somewhere. It is preaching that leads people to Christ. (Mike Childress)

## THE POWER OF EASTER

### JOHN 20:1-18

When the women rose early on that first Easter morning, they were focused on their task at hand: finishing the preparation of Jesus' body for burial. Friday had been a living nightmare. There was Jesus' mockery of a trial and his crucifixion. The friends of

153

Jesus rushed to get the body down from the cross and take it to a borrowed tomb for its final disposition. Through tears of grief and the shock of disbelief, they carried out their grim task.

Sabbath had been the most somber, dismal experience ever. Instead of worship and wonder, there was only doubt, disillusionment, and despair. Sleep had been fitful, and the morning brought a reminder of the task that lay before them. The task made them revisit their grief, still fresh from Friday, as they returned to the garden tomb.

The Gospel of Mark mentions something that John's Gospel omits. In all their anguish, no one thought ahead to ask one of the men to accompany them. The women wonder aloud, "Who will roll away the stone for us from the entrance to the tomb" (Mark 16:3b)? The stone was a formidable barrier. As the stone fell into the notch carved out for it in the rocky earth, it sealed the tomb's entrance from animals and the grave robbers. It would take a lever and a concerted effort to remove it so that these faithful women could approach their task.

To their surprise, the stone had been rolled away. The body was gone. This was no robbery, no trickery, no hoax or deceit. The women were the first witnesses to the resurrection, and the fulfillment of a hope and a faith that says, "for God all things *are* possible!" (Matthew 19:26b, emphasis added by author).

The text proclaims again the best elements of the good news, which we need to hear often. God's love cannot be stopped, even by death. Despair is never so dark that the light of Christ cannot illuminate our lives. The least likely of persons, in this case the women instead of the apostles, can be used to tell God's message of hope, love, and peace. It is great to see and believe, but it is even better to have not seen and still have faith.

When you are down on the church, embittered by empty religion, and broken by bitterness, remember this: God has the power to roll away the stone from whatever tomb in which you find yourself. Easter is not a memory, a moment, a false doctrine, or an empty search for eggs. Easter is about encountering the reality of the God who was one of us and is with us still. This Easter, allow the power of the Holy Spirit to touch your hardened heart again, and be prepared to be moved. No stone—no one—is too great for the touch of the Master's hand! (Gary Kindley)

# APRIL 27, 2003

## *Second Sunday of Easter*

---

**Worship Theme:** Life in the resurrection of Jesus Christ brings the church of God together in fellowship and prayer. We are the Body of Christ.

---

**Readings:** Acts 4:32-35; 1 John 1:1–2:2; John 20:19-31

**Call to Worship (Psalm 133)**

> *Leader:* How very good and pleasant it is when kindred live together in unity!
>
> **People:** **It is like the precious oil on the head, running down upon the beard, on the beard of Aaron, running down over the collar of his robes.**
>
> *Leader:* It is like the dew of Hermon, which falls on the mountains of Zion.
>
> *People:* **For there the LORD ordained his blessing, life forevermore.**

**Pastoral Prayer:**

During this season of Easter, O God of New Life, we gather to sing and thank you for giving us a second chance to be the people you created us to be. Let us rejoice in our good portion of Jesus' life, death, and resurrection. Resurrect us too, dear God, for we so want to be faithful disciples. May your spirit of love and hope permeate our assembly. Make us like those first disciples who loved one another. Jesus taught us that the marks of discipleship could be seen in our love reflected in daily life. Make us people who not only speak words of love but also, in fact, love others. Remind us that those brothers and sisters we encounter daily are also people for whom Christ died. Give us the grace and perseverance to be your people. Open us to new life and abide with us. Send your Holy Spirit to be our encouraging advocate. In Jesus' name we pray. Amen. (David Mosser)

# SERMON BRIEFS

## RADICAL POWER

### ACTS 4:32-35

In the midst of the struggles and tragedies of life, communities bond together and friendships form. We find a similar situation in this selected passage. Jesus' crucifixion and resurrection propelled believers into a close-knit group; their bonds were strong. Both unity and vision characterize this early Christian community mentioned in Acts. The company of believers is described as having one heart and mind, in which their lives are lived in accord with one another.

Most communities, organizations, and groups rarely are known for such a harmony and peace. How did these people live sacrificially and with unity? This community offers a fascinatingly unique response as they deal with the struggle of life after Jesus. Their actions take hold of our attention; they tackled the issue of materialism. No one claimed personal ownership but people sold their possessions as needs became known. Wow. It appears that greed, selfishness, and individuality are absent from the fabric of this community. Although the individual response is not emphasized, what strikes the reader is the power of a unified, corporate response. Indeed, it is baffling to understand how a community appears to overcome personal interests for the sake of the group. How could these people be so generous and so selfless?

The company of believers responded to the gospel of Jesus Christ. Their response, although unusual in our times, is to say the least, radical. While Jesus was present on earth, he preached for people to be a light unto the world and the salt of the earth. I can only imagine this community understanding itself as the light of Christ and as an alternative to the ways of the world. Yet, they did not cease to be in the world or to separate themselves from the rest of society. They chose to live out their faith to the best of their abilities, and according to this passage, they cared for one another just as Jesus cared for the world.

Caring for one another was much more than sharing kind words. They took the radical approach of selling personal possessions to minister to those in need. I am amazed at this response because our culture promotes an attitude that we should care for ourselves by protecting our assets, a notion reflected in our society's emphasis on the accumulation of material wealth. Our society pretends that the person who takes the most toys to the grave wins the game of life. Indeed, the presence of greed was known in Jesus' day, and even now it seeps into our own communities and families. It has the power to debilitate our lives and deafen our ears to God.

The Christian community in Acts chose to fight greed. They sided with the idea of living a bold and powerful life by selling and sharing their possessions. Perhaps their actions were a response to the divine grace they experienced in their own, individual lives. Perhaps these people discovered grace—the grace that Jesus preached and lived out on earth—as a community through their generosity. The grace of Jesus Christ transforms lives and enables people to participate in miraculous work. It was no coincidence that this community had the power of unity and peace. In order for the group to have such power, individuals must have had their own personal experiences of both the resurrection and the grace of Christ. It is this kind of power that enables the community of believers to change and become a light unto the world. (Mark White)

## REAL COMMUNITY

### 1 JOHN 1:1–2:2

In an era of megachurches and subdivisions, it is all too possible to go through modern life without much of a connection to our community. It is no wonder that stories of people who have extraordinary community experiences are often newsworthy. There are pictures of neighbors building makeshift flood walls together, searching for a lost child, providing meals for a grieving family, and huddling together under Red Cross banners that remain fixed in our minds. The concept of community seems to be an ever-changing one in our twenty-first-century world, and yet the need for true community has perhaps never seemed so urgent and necessary.

The First Letter of John, like most of the New Testament epistles, speaks to a small community of Christians trying to grasp their new lives both in Christ and with each other. Throughout the letter, the author, whom I will join other scholars and call "the elder," encourages and admonishes this community as they struggle with their faith. Specifically in this passage, the elder tackles the meaning of true fellowship and its practical implications. Although we do not know what specific circumstances the community was facing, it was surely not too different from the recipients of Paul's letters. The fellowship was no doubt entering a different phase of their faith. The euphoria of their new lives in Christ had probably waned as they were forced to consider the real-life implications of their Christian commitment and the possibility that their earthly commitment might be extended, as the timing of Jesus' return became more ambiguous.

In the first part of this passage, the elder reminds the community of what has brought them together: the new life found in God and the Son, Jesus Christ. He reminds them of the experience that brought them together and gave them eternal life. It is the kind of recapitulation that every community of faith should have from time to time—a kind of reminder of why we're here and what it all means. For communities such as this one, and probably many of ours, it was important to be reminded of the common call and connection that binds us even beyond our differences.

The elder further elaborates on the meaning of true fellowship as chapter 1 progresses. First there is the restatement of the polarity of accepting God and rejecting God reminiscent to John's Gospel. God is light. The opposite of God (and righteousness) is darkness. If we walk in darkness, we do not have true fellowship with God or with each other. In other words, the community of believers is more than simply a group of people with similar experiences or beliefs. It is more than a group brought together by the quest for religiosity or security. It is in true community that Christ is made present. Because of Christ's presence in the fellowship of believers, the community has a moral responsibility to and with each other. Their individual actions as well as the seriousness with which they consider their commitment to God has an effect on the whole community.

Although we are two millennia removed from the Christian community to which the elder wrote, the difficulty of community is just as real to us. In our individualistic society, it is easy to become so busy "looking out for #1" that we lose sight of the real meaning of Christian fellowship. It means more than socializing or sharing the same zip code. Christian fellowship or community goes further than Wednesday evening supper and Sunday school socials. True fellowship happens when Christ is made present through the community. When the manifestation of community that seems so odd to us now, becomes the norm by which we live together, Christ is present. Our connection to God and each other then is made complete. (Tracey Allred)

# PRESCRIPTION FOR THE CHURCH

## JOHN 20:19-31

Anxiety is rampant in our culture, and the church is not immune from this plague that robs us of joy. Anxiety feeds fear and fuels anger, blame, and denial. The lack of trust that anxiety brings gives birth to suspicion, doubt, and despair. Our text reminds us that no one is immune and gives us a remedy to the malady of desperate anxiety that consumes us.

The text from John's Gospel reveals the mood and tension of the setting. The worry and confusion of the events of the last seventy-two hours have taken their toll on faith. The fearful disciples are huddled behind shuttered windows and barred doors, wondering what will happen next. Their fear is both understandable and justified. Persecuted for following Jesus, banned by Sanhedrin action from spreading the "heresy" of Jesus' teachings, no wonder the disciples are timid and trembling.

They are apprehensive, but Jesus calmly appears. "Peace be with you." He says it twice, just to be certain that they get the message. Jesus knows our needs, and Christ's prescription cuts through our fuzzy thinking and fragile faith. There is something amazingly calming about being in the presence of the Holy.

An eighty-five-year-old woman told me that she saw Jesus each afternoon behind the sheer curtains of her den window. "He comes most every day, about the same time," she reported. "I don't know if he is coming to take me or just to be with me, but either way it is nice that he comes." Jesus' presence cannot be stopped nor contained by the walls we build.

It is also good to remember that when we discover the Christ in our midst, there is a gift that accompanies him—the Holy Spirit. God's Spirit empowers and offers grace such that timid disciples begin preaching the Resurrection at the temple. No longer floundering in fear, they give birth to the church, or at least become midwives to the Holy Spirit.

It was Rabbi Edwin Friedman who taught for decades the importance for clergy to be a nonanxious presence in the midst of an anxious, hurting, and often troubled congregation. Whether church or synagogue, the process is the same and the dynamics of anxiety and fear rob faith communities of their power, purpose, and peace (Edwin Friedman, *Generation to Generation: Family Process in Church and Synagogue* [New York: Guilford Press, 1985]).

This text for the Sunday after Easter is appropriate, for as surely as the crowds show up on Easter Day, the Sunday after Easter can be a disappointment. Life goes on. The Resurrection is wondrous, but the routine of life with its doubts and difficulties remains. Reality sets in. John's text reminds us that we can handle the setbacks and sad failures of life because Christ brings peace. Surgeries fail, businesses go bankrupt, cancer consumes, relationships end, life is not fair, but Easter continues to burst forth. The calming and powerful presence of Christ can be discovered in our shuttered rooms and in our darkest valleys. God is with us. We are not alone. Peace be with you! (Gary Kindley)

# REFLECTIONS

❦

## MAY

**Reflection Verse:** *"Woman, why are you weeping?"* (*John 20:13*)

During Lent I participated in a spiritual formation group with five other people. We each agreed to fast from two things. My two were sugar of any kind and anxiety. This left me with nothing good to eat and lots of free mental time. I did better than I expected with the sugar but could not fast from anxiety for six weeks. I continued to experience anxiety regarding my own life, family, projects, and future. I continued to feel anxious about pornography on the Internet, worldwide abuse of children, racial segregation in my own community. My anxiety did not motivate me to action, however.

The result was that I did not feel spiritually ready for Easter. In church on Easter Sunday, as I sat with the choir, my mind began to wander. For some reason, I began thinking about those pieces of playground equipment we played on in grade school. The big, round, flat platforms with the metal handles—lots of kids could get on and whirl around if one would push with his foot. Other kids would try to jump on as the wheel came around, but if you couldn't grab the handle, you had to wait until it came around again to get on.

I looked around the choir and the congregation. They say misery loves company. I couldn't be the only one who didn't feel quite ready to experience the joy of Easter. There sits a tenor with his eyes closed whose third marriage just ended after only two months. There sits another member in his wheelchair in the aisle. He used to be a farmer and our church's Mr. Fix-it but is now elderly and has lost the use of his legs. His face is set in lines of pain that is not just physical. There sits a woman, who has served as chairperson of just about every committee at one time or another. Competent, comfortable, well liked, her face carefully serene, but everybody struggles with something, don't they?

I looked at the pastor standing before the congregation, confidently proclaiming the Resurrection. I wondered if he, as I have often done, had spent so much time creating spiritual experiences for other people during Lent that by Easter Sunday he feels like a dry well. I wondered if, deep down, he felt spiritually ready for Easter.

It has always fascinated me that, in the Bible, none of the disciples seems fully ready for Easter joy. All four Gospels concur that the Resurrection took them by surprise! The women bring spices to anoint his body. They wonder who will roll the stone away for them (Mark 16:3). They seek the living among the dead, and then are perplexed to find the stone rolled away and the body gone (Luke 24:2-4). They are filled with fear (Matthew 28:5). They don't know what to make of the empty tomb and neatly folded grave clothes (John 20:5-7). They weep with grief while the resurrected Lord stands close at hand. They were not spiritually prepared for Easter.

John's Gospel has the clearest depiction of this state of unreadiness. All that the empty tomb means for Mary is that Jesus' body has been stolen. She assumes the worst, not the best. Who would assume something that is too good to be true? She retraces her steps at a run and wakes Simon Peter and the Beloved Disciple. Who was this Beloved Disciple? Scholars debate. Maybe he was John Mark. Maybe Lazarus. Maybe Thomas. He could be any one of them. He could be any one of us. For whoever he was, John portrays him as one who "has become very sensitive to Jesus through love" (Raymond E. Brown, trans., *The Anchor Bible: The Gospel According to John [xiii-xxi]*, vol. 29 [New York: Doubleday & Company, Inc., 1970], p. 1005). Not a bad prescription for how we can get ready for Easter joy! In John's Gospel, the Beloved Disciple is the first to put two and two together. He is the first to stoop and look into the tomb and see the empty linen wrappings. He is first to believe that Jesus is risen!

But then he goes home, thinking, perhaps, "This changes everything, but I'm not sure how. Let me just mull this over a while before I tell anyone else about it."

Then there is Peter, the brash, big talker who, in a pinch, becomes a threefold betrayer. Bold as always, he goes into the tomb and sees the grave clothes. Luke fills in his response. He went home "wondering to himself what had happened" (Luke 24:12 NIV). Perhaps his guilt had numbed his faith. Perhaps he was thinking, "I'm not worthy of this Day."

The disciples go home. On Mary's second trip of the morning, she looks inside the empty tomb and sees something neither Peter nor the other disciple saw: two angels in white sitting at either end of where the body had been. They don't tell us where to find him or what to do. They just ask a really obvious question. "Woman, why are you weeping?" I have a theory that the angels, while Mary explains why she's weeping, are pointing behind her as if to say "turn around, turn around." See your resurrected Lord who, from now on, is always standing right behind you, whose presence does not depend on whether you are ready for him to be there or not.

According to all four Gospels, Easter is precisely for those who are not ready for it. Easter is for Peter, too distracted by guilt to take it in. Easter is for the Beloved Disciple, who believes in Jesus' resurrection but needs time to process what difference it makes. Easter is for Mary, weeping over her loss while her Lord stands behind her.

According to the story, Easter is for each of us, who is all of them.

Our retail culture doesn't give us much time to savor Easter. Like an impatient waiter whisking our plate away before we're finished eating, our culture tries to banish Easter from our awareness. On the day after Easter, grocery stores put the marshmallow chicks on the bargain table to make room on the shelves for Mother's Day knickknacks and gifts for graduates. But we have the fifty days of the Easter season until Pentecost stretching out ahead of us. We have a time of liturgical lingering. Days to weep. Days to pray. Days to ponder. Days to rejoice and bear witness to the Lord, who stands behind us healing our past, the Lord, who beckons from before us, promising us a future saturated with divine presence, which is fullness of joy. (Alyce McKenzie)

# MAY 4, 2003

## *Third Sunday of Easter*

**Worship Theme:** Repentance is a turning away from the sin of the world toward the grace and mercy of God. To repent means that one embraces the work of God in Jesus Christ, the Messiah of God.

**Readings:** Acts 3:12-19; 1 John 3:1-7; Luke 24:36*b*-48

### Call to Worship (Psalm 4)

*Leader:* Answer me when I call, O God of my right! You gave me room when I was in distress. Be gracious to me, and hear my prayer.

*People:* **How long, you people, shall my honor suffer shame? How long will you love vain words, and seek after lies?**

*Leader:* But know that the LORD has set apart the faithful for himself; the LORD hears when I call to him.

*People:* **When you are disturbed, do not sin; ponder it on your beds, and be silent.**

*Leader:* Offer right sacrifices, and put your trust in the LORD.

*People:* **There are many who say, "O that we might see some good! Let the light of your face shine on us, O LORD!"**

*Leader:* You have put gladness in my heart more than when their grain and wine abound.

*People:* **I will both lie down and sleep in peace; for you alone, O LORD, make me lie down in safety.**

**Pastoral Prayer:**
O God, we often confess we are your people. In us dwells a deep yearning to be what you made us to be. Often, however, we find that the road of discipleship is a high road—one that is difficult to walk upon and more difficult to stay upon. Help us, O God, stay the course of our confession. Remind us that true healing for our infirmity and for the sickness in our soul comes from Jesus, who you, O Lord, crowned as a "Wonderful Counselor" and "Prince of Peace" (Isaiah 9:6). Let us look to Jesus when our path is dim. Let us draw strength from Jesus when we are tempted to wander from the path. Let us pray to Christ in our time of need. Jesus is our shelter in every storm. May we cling to Jesus as the author of everlasting life. We pray this in Jesus' holy name. Amen. (David Mosser)

# SERMON BRIEFS

## A WITNESS TO HOPE

### ACTS 3:12-19

A man who is paralyzed is healed. Observers are amazed by the work of the healer, if not confused, and even suspicious of his actions. Peter responds to the need of the beggar who lived as the town's outcast. In defense of his work, Peter bears witness to the work of God. The idea of being a witness is not unusual in Acts; the first chapter alludes to this as Luke writes that the followers of Jesus Christ are to be witnesses to the work of God in all parts of the world (Acts 1:8).

At Solomon's Portico, Peter reacts to the confusion and surprise of those who witnessed the healing of the man by delivering a sermon. Perhaps some of the witnesses interpreted Peter's actions as the work of God. Others attributed the power of this healing completely to the power and piety of Peter and John. The Scripture, however, leaves the reader with the impression that some observers are skeptical of Peter and this act of healing. This is the same type of skepticism that Jesus encountered. Peter recognizes these responses and feels the urge to preach and bear witness to the power of God through Jesus Christ. Peter, in all likelihood, wants to clarify what just happened. He wants to set the record straight.

The events that have just unfolded are miraculous, if not unbelievable. Peter understands that this power to heal is the power of God acted through Jesus Christ. This is the same God who is the God of Abraham, Isaac, and Jacob. This is the God of Israel. Peter attempts to connect his faith with the faith of doubting Jews and opponents of Jesus. He urges his audience to consider that the faith in Jesus Christ, who healed the beggar is the same faith present in Judaism. The doubters and opponents, however, preferred to narrowly define and even limit God. A desire for certainty is generally accepted as an aspect of human nature, and therefore, it is not surprising that Peter's opponents have trouble believing in the power of Jesus Christ.

Peter contends that the limitations imposed by the Jews unfortunately shortened the life of Jesus and led to his crucifixion. Human error and the failure to recognize Jesus as the Messiah proved costly. Peter addresses this concern, but he does not end his sermon on a depressing note. He pleads with his doubters to repent. Peter wants the crowd to understand that God offers humanity a second chance, an opportunity to change and unite with God because of Jesus the Christ. Hope remains present despite all of the mistakes and sins of humanity. God provides each person the opportunity to change his or her mind, go in a new direction, and be healed. This good news is at the heart of Peter's sermon.

Peter sought the direction of God by bearing witness to the work of Jesus Christ in his life and in the lives of others. Both his actions toward the man who was paralyzed and his words to the crowd share an account and a witness to the power of God. This gospel message indeed encompasses all of life, and it works despite human failures and shortcomings. Peter had his limitations, but he also probably felt a deep calling to voice his experience of Jesus' resurrection in his own life and to the hope that is now present within him. He attempts to share the gospel message through word and deed, just as Jesus did while he was on earth. Is this not what Christian discipleship is all about, offering hope by sharing the good news of God with others through both conversation and action? (Mark White)

# ALLEGIANCE TO GOD

## 1 JOHN 3:1-7

As a youth minister, I find sin a challenging topic of discussion with teenagers. It is not because I do not think that sin is a real problem or that I have an "I'm okay, You're okay" kind of theology of sin. It is because of the incredible number of loopholes and gray areas that young people can always manage to identify. Sometimes it is a case of simply setting some wrong ideas right. But often their points are valid, and the ambiguity of being a human being prone to sin in a world where "having our cake and eating it too" is an acceptable philosophy of life is a bit problematic.

Although the community to whom 1 John was written was probably very different from the group of teenagers at my church, their struggle with sin is the same struggle felt through the ages. While we do not have specific details, the elder's comments regarding the community's attitude toward sin seem adamant. This passage is marked by the combination of loving encouragement and disappointed animosity found throughout the letter. At times, the elder speaks to the group using the familial language of parents and children, gently explaining the love of God. Then the elder's tone switches. He admonishes their devilish behavior and ignorance of what it means to be in relationship with God.

The first few verses of chapter 3 continue the elder's teaching regarding the Christian's status as a child of God. According to the elder, believers are not children of God because they have chosen or earned the title. On the contrary, it is because God has chosen them. God's love is unsolicited and freely given. Even though the gift is free, however, the believers have reciprocating responsibility in their lifestyles and treatment of others. In other words, while God's love is freely given to us with no strings attached, that love should be naturally reflected in the moral choices we make and in our treatment of each other. In verse 4, there is a change of tone but really a continuation of the earlier verses. It is because of the love of God that our attitude toward sin should be different. Here the elder sets the record straight on sin. Committing sin and being a child of God are not compatible. If someone thinks that they are a child of God and lives a life of sin, his or her allegiance is not to God but to the devil (the opposite of God).

Although the theological problems with this text go far beyond the realm of this sermon (for instance, it is perfectly possible for children of God to sin contrary to the implication of this text) this passage is still quite insightful. Many modern readers would probably view the elder's teaching as extreme. This is probably because we are much more attracted to the opposite end of the spectrum, which says that it's possible to be a child of God and sin as long as it's not a really bad sin or we try hard not to do it again. The word from this passage reminds us that sin should be taken seriously. As Christians, we should be ever aware of the possibility of sin and the importance of avoiding it. My youth are still correct in their difficulty grappling with this issue. The concept of sin and its many gray areas will most likely only get more complicated. The important thing to remember is that we were freely chosen even as sinners to receive a great gift from Jesus, whose life was taken for the very sins of those for whom he came. In remembering that great gift, those sins that so entice us should not seem so attractive. (Tracey Allred)

# REALITY CHECK—OVERCOMING DISTANCES

## LUKE 24:36b-48

Two themes springing from the same source evidence themselves in this passage. The first is the reality of the living Christ. The second is the overcoming of distance. Both of these themes spring from the resurrection of Jesus Christ.

The writer of Luke wants to show us quite clearly that this

Jesus, whom we crucified, is no longer dead. He is alive as the living Christ. He is physically present with the disciples. He is not a spirit. Whereas in John 20:17 Jesus tells Mary, "Do not hold on to me," here in Luke, Jesus invites the disciples to "handle" him. Then Jesus asks them for something to eat. A spirit does not do that. This is a real person. This is a real event. This is not a supernatural, special effects, occurrence. God raises Jesus from the dead as Jesus raised Lazarus. Jesus becomes the living Christ, and for a little while he is physically present with the disciples. In volume two of Luke's Acts account Jesus ascends into the heavens to return again as he has gone. The writer wants us to know that this is reality. This is the way it is.

The second theme is how this living Christ overcomes the distances that exist in this real world. Take for example the distance between knowing and believing. The risen Christ overcomes the distance in the plea, "I believe; help my unbelief" (Mark 9:24). Another distance in our lives is the distance between the pulpit and the pew. There are many distances in our lives: the distance between you and me, the distance between the rich and the poor, and the distance between what appears to be true and what is really true.

The risen Christ overcomes all of these distances because, in the resurrection event, God calls us to overcome the greatest distance of all: the distance between what we say and who we are. We are such pretentious creatures. One father encouraged his son to give up candy for Lent. The little boy asks his father what he and his mother gave up and the father said that they gave up liquor for Lent. The boy looked puzzled and reminded his dad that they drank liquor before dinner. The Father said that was sherry as opposed to hard liquor. So the boy said, "Well, Dad, I think I will give up hard candy for Lent."

Jesus says, "You are witnesses of these things" (v. 48). The word *witness* in Greek can also be translated as *martyr*. To be a martyr is not simply to talk about something you have seen but to live a certain way so that all around you know what you believe and what you see. You live this way even though it may cost you your life.

Reality is not a smug assurance that we have all the right answers. Reality is struggling to see the face of God in the everyday events of our lives. Reality is letting go of all those things that present a mask to God and to God's world. James Smart concludes an article by saying "Salvation is not a state of soul but a movement in history, an invasion of our blind and broken world by God's new world of grace and truth. There is no salvation for any of us unless we welcome that divine invasion each day afresh, and let ourselves be caught up and carried forward by it into a new future" (James D. Smart, "The Language Problem in Evangelism," in Rueben P. Job and Harold K. Bales, eds., *Issue One: Evangelism* [Nashville: Tidings, 1970], 51).

The reality of the Christ is that he lives still, and enters our lives, and changes us, and turns us around. That is repentance. That is the starting place to overcoming the distances in our world. That is overcoming the distance between what we say and who we are. That reality makes us true witnesses to these things. That reality overcomes all the other distances in our lives including the distance between life and death itself. (Tim Russell)

# MAY 11, 2003

*Fourth Sunday of Easter*

---

**Worship Theme:** Jesus is the Good Shepherd. A good shepherd will lay down his life for the flock. Jesus proves his goodness as a shepherd because he laid down his life for God's people.

---

**Readings:** Acts 4:5-12; 1 John 3:16-24; John 10:11-18

**Call to Worship (Psalm 23)**

| | |
|---|---|
| *Leader:* | The LORD is my shepherd, I shall not want. |
| ***People:*** | **He makes me lie down in green pastures; and leads me beside still waters;** |
| *Leader:* | He restores my soul. He leads me in right paths for his name's sake. |
| ***People:*** | **Even though I walk through the darkest valley, I fear no evil; for you are with me;** |
| *Leader:* | Your rod and your staff—they comfort me. |
| ***People:*** | **You prepare a table before me in the presence of my enemies;** |
| *Leader:* | You anoint my head with oil; my cup overflows. |
| ***All:*** | **Surely goodness and mercy shall follow me all the days of my life, and I shall dwell in the house of the LORD my whole life long.** |

**Pastoral Prayer:**

We pray to you this day, Merciful God, because you have provided for us the Good Shepherd. In the life of Jesus we see signs

171

and wonders. Jesus heals the sick, comforts the afflicted, speaks bold words of justice, and leads us through the valley of death. In Jesus' resurrection you, O God, show us a new sense of that hope. In Jesus' resurrection, O God, our fear of death is overcome by a new sense of joy in the name of Jesus. In Jesus' resurrection, O God, you reassure our hearts and give a new boldness with which we can live out our lives as disciples of the Good Shepherd. Inspire us to reach out to others in confidence. Remind us of the good news of Jesus as we confront the bad news of our world. Let us abide in Jesus forever, in whose name we pray. Amen. (David Mosser)

# SERMON BRIEFS

## IN THE FACE OF OPPOSITION

### ACTS 4:5-12

In order for opposition to exist, there must be another side to a story. Quite often this is depicted with good guys and bad guys, or more cleverly put, cops and robbers. The typical cop and robber story includes an interrogation, portrayed with the questioning of a suspected criminal under a spotlight. I imagine the authorities, with sweat dripping from the brows, are full of anger and contempt, while the suspect either trembles with fear or stares blankly at a spot on the wall, daring not to utter a word.

In Acts chapter 4, the reader discovers that Peter and John are the suspects, the ones being questioned by the authorities. If Peter and John lived in our time, I picture them placed under the spotlight and hounded for answers, although they are not filled with fear. Their interrogators are not the police but those representing the religious establishment; they hold the power. Ironically, it seems that power is at the heart of the issue that they have with Peter and John.

So what crime did Peter and John commit to deserve being detained and questioned? The answer lies in the healing of the man who was paralyzed. Peter reminds the religious representatives that his actions were merely a good deed performed in the name of Jesus Christ. Of course this was a good deed, but the religious authorities' concerns and apprehensions stem from the fact that five thousand people began to believe in the power of Jesus Christ following this healing. In all likelihood, these leaders feared losing their religious control to a growing, grassroots movement that favors and appreciates Jesus.

Jesus received a certain level of popularity even in his own day. Yet, the religious leaders, who were more interested in power and control than in Jesus' message, eventually offset this popularity. Could the same series of events happen to Peter as they did to Jesus? Notice their similarities. Both Jesus and Peter tried to meet people's needs. Both men collided with the religious leaders. The authorities, in response, attempted to silence them, but Peter could not keep quiet. He reminds the leadership that Jesus is "the stone that was rejected by ... the builders," and now he "has become the cornerstone" (v. 11). Peter is convinced that there is hope through Jesus Christ. The establishment, however, is alarmed that a "Jesus movement" will circumvent their power and doom their future. They fear the unknown. Jesus is mysterious, and therefore, the establishment does not know how to handle people who believe in him.

Peter seeks to clarify this mystery. Jesus, according to Peter, is the only person in whom salvation can be found. Salvation is both physical and spiritual, as in the case of the healing of the man who was paralyzed. Salvation, which comes through a faith in Jesus Christ, includes the forgiveness of sins and the offer of a new and bright future. Peter preaches that, through Jesus, people have hope and can move away from a stagnant faith, such as that of the establishment who worshiped their own power. He therefore urges the religious leaders to repent and worship God alone through Jesus Christ.

I doubt that Peter was excited about his interrogation, yet I imagine he reveled in the opportunity to share the gospel message with anyone who would listen. In the face of opposition and in the midst of an interrogation, God's Spirit worked through Peter, enabling him to heal the sick and lead people toward hope. Peter confidently exemplifies that this hope transcends worldly opposition and overcomes a stagnant faith. It is the hope found in Jesus Christ that is so powerful and contagious. (Mark White)

# THE ABIDING LOVE OF CHRIST

## 1 JOHN 3:16-24

I recently heard the story of a little girl whose mother was expecting a baby. It was her first sibling, and she was quite excited about the prospect of having a little sister. Her parents tried to explain to her that there was no guarantee that the baby would be a girl. She could just as easily end up with a little brother. With this, the little girl disagreed and matter of factly informed her parents that she knew she was getting a sister because she had asked God to bring her a sister. "What if the baby is born and it is a boy," her parents asked. The little girl responded, "I'll pray to God again, and he'll change the baby to a girl!" This humorous story makes us giggle about the theology of little children, but I have come in contact with quite a few adults whose thinking is not so far removed from that of the little girl.

This particular text, among other things, deals with the issue of asking with boldness before the Lord and receiving what we ask for. How easy our lives as Christians would be if we could merely isolate verse 22 and build our theologies on asking and receiving. We know, however, that this is not possible and so did the elder.

First, the community is reminded again of the implications of being children of God. Being loved by God and understanding that Christ laid down his life for us should profoundly affect how we treat others. Because of the sacrificial love that was given to us, we are called to love sacrificially. Here, the elder's teaching reminds us of James as he encourages the Christians that love is more than words; it is action. One cannot claim to be a child of God and ignore the needs of others or treat them poorly. Being in relationship with God means that the individuals have reciprocal responsibilities in the practice of their faith and in their daily lives.

It is this holistic practice of faith that makes the assertion in verse 22 possible. We cannot go to God with boldness if we are walking only half the walk, so to speak. Our whole life should reflect God and God's commandments. Theoretically, then, our desires and requests of the Lord will not be selfish but will uplift the whole community, and God will hear and answer. By emphasizing this important element of verse 22, the elder attempts to discourage the "wish list" kind of approach to God that often leads only to disappointment and a questioning faith.

Preaching this text is important, although it must be done with care. So many in our congregations have been disappointed and had their faith completely shaken when their earnest prayers seemed not to be answered or even heard. I'm not talking about the prayers of children for little sisters and puppies or even of adults for pay raises or new cars. Many committed children of God in our very congregations have stood boldly before God and begged for the healing of a loved one, the reconciliation of a relationship, or the lost soul of a family member, only to walk away empty-handed. Just as important as it is to vocalize this for your congregation is the emphasis of the rest of this text. God is greater than our hearts and knows everything about us. Believe in God and love each other, and God will abide in us. It is because of that abiding love that we never really walk away empty-handed, even if our desire isn't met. God is with us. God is in us and answers our prayers in a way that sometimes we cannot even imagine. Perhaps more important, we are never alone in our need or suffering. Sometimes, it is the very abiding love of God that is the answer we did not even realize we sought. (Tracey Allred)

# THE LEADING OF THE GOOD SHEPHERD

## JOHN 10:11-18

In this chapter, Jesus attempts to explain his identity and mission using the example of a shepherd. The use of this image tempts us to speak about shepherds: their job description, their place in society. And it also tempts us to rehearse the familiar image of Jesus carrying the lamb on his shoulders. I think these temptations arise because the text here is difficult, and a retreat to the surer ground of social analysis or sentimentality is often in order.

For Jesus, shepherding could be boiled down to two essential functions: laying down his life for the sheep and knowing the

175

sheep. Although both of these make a certain degree of sense, are they really the marks of someone who claims to be the Good Shepherd? Look at this from the point of view of the sheep. It is nice to know that your shepherd is willing to risk it all to protect you, but it is disconcerting to know your shepherd intends to be killed in the line of duty. Would you rather have the hired hand who runs away from the first wolf, or the shepherd who is killed by the first wolf? All having the Good Shepherd gains you is destruction by a later wolf who will march right over the mangled remains of your Good Shepherd. It is hard to see what could make this shepherd good.

Likewise, Jesus' claim to know the sheep and have the sheep know him is not easily understood. It is hard to speak of knowing someone like John's Jesus who is, frankly, very difficult to know, who seems to be speaking at a different level. The effect may be especially pronounced in this passage, as Jesus is speaking to those who "do not belong to this fold" (v. 16). The audience in chapter 10 never gets the point; they do not understand Jesus (John 10:6), and his words create division (John 10:19). Even those who wish to give Jesus the benefit of the doubt leap over all this shepherd talk, basing their respect for Jesus on his healing of the man born blind. But John's Jesus is hardly less confusing for those inclined to believe in him, as Nicodemus, the Samaritan woman, and Philip might attest. Yet, our knowledge of Jesus is to be like Jesus' knowledge of the Father. This is a deep knowledge, and it sounds impossible for us.

So we are left, at the end of verse 15, with these two central images: the Good Shepherd who gets killed and the Good Shepherd who claims to be known but remains a mystery. But with verse 16, Jesus begins to conjure up a future. The flock is larger than we had known. Jesus claims he will lead the whole flock in the future: "There will be one flock, one shepherd" (v. 16). This future leadership is based in Jesus' utter confidence in the resurrection.

The Good Shepherd lays down his life, not in a failed attempt to defend the sheep, but "in order to take it up again" (v. 17). God loves Jesus not because he dies an obedient death but because that obedient death is undertaken so that life may be taken up again. The role of the Good Shepherd is indeed exemplified in an obedient death for the sheep, but it is not exhausted by it. The Good Shepherd will die but will continue to lead. There will be one flock and one shepherd.

The Good Shepherd whom we supposedly know intimately yet who often confounds our understanding, will always be available to be known. And if we know Jesus as Jesus knows God, we can at least know that our relationship involves both love, which is expressed in death, and power, which is expressed in the end of death. (Don Polaski)

# MAY 18, 2003

*Fifth Sunday of Easter*

---

**Worship Theme:** When fully mature, vines tend to grow thick and interweave with other vines. When love grows and matures in believers, these believers interweave with God and other believers. We call this *church*.

---

**Readings:** Acts 8:26-40; 1 John 4:7-21; John 15:1-8

**Call to Worship (Psalm 22:25-31)**

*Leader:*    From you comes my praise in the great congregation; my vows I will pay before those who fear him.

*People:*    **The poor shall eat and be satisfied; those who seek him shall praise the LORD. May your hearts live forever!**

*Leader:*    All the ends of the earth shall remember and turn to the LORD; and all the families of the nations shall worship before him.

*People:*    **For dominion belongs to the LORD, and he rules over the nations.**

*Leader:*    To him, indeed, shall all who sleep in the earth bow down; before him shall bow all who go down to the dust, and I shall live for him.

*People:*    **Posterity will serve him; future generations will be told about the LORD, and proclaim his deliverance to a people yet unborn, saying that he has done it.**

**Pastoral Prayer:**

Gracious God, you have linked each of us who calls himself or herself a believer by the true vine, Jesus Christ. As you are the vine grower, we are the branches. We are connected by a love that overcomes every evil produced by the world. Continue to beckon us to abide in you, for you abide in us. Remind us that we are joined as a holy people by love and not merely any kind of garden-variety love. You, O God, have connected us with a divine love. As Jesus tells the disciples of old, he continues to tell us by the spirit, "Just as I have loved you, you also should love one another" (John 13:34). Out of this divine charity, O God of Love, you enable us to love not only our brothers and sisters but even our enemies. This kind of love is not our own doing. Rather it is a gift of your spirit. Nurture us in the love of Christ, in whose name we pray. Amen. (David Mosser)

# SERMON BRIEFS

## HOW FAR CAN THE GOSPEL GO?

### ACTS 8:26-40

Luke's emphasis in Acts focuses on the spread of the gospel to all people. Progressively, the gospel message moves from Jerusalem to the outermost parts of the world. It appears from Luke's perspective that there is no end for the gospel and no one that it cannot touch; but can the gospel really have such remarkable growth and reach so many people?

To answer this question, Philip and an Ethiopian eunuch enter Luke's story. Philip's role as the evangelist preacher is indeed important, but the role of the eunuch is utterly fascinating because it brings significance to the gospel story that has not before been witnessed. Up to this point, the message of Jesus Christ has remained confined to Israel and its religion. But as Luke emphasizes, the gospel's power speaks to others as witnessed previously by both the Samaritans, who were not seen as pure Jews, and now as the gospel encounters an Ethiopian.

The term *Ethiopian,* as used in the first century, presumably describes a black person from the lands south of Egypt. To the

179

Mediterranean mind, this area was the outermost part of the world, and a person such as the eunuch would have been a racial minority. He would have experienced people's curiosity and interest because he would have been seen as exotic, rather than being despised or ostracized for his skin color.

Obviously, the Ethiopian eunuch was a stranger in a distant land. So, we ask the question, *why was he in Jerusalem?* The story depicts the eunuch reading from the prophet Isaiah during his return home, and therefore, one could assume that he has some level of interest in Judaism. Was he a Jew, a Jewish proselyte, or simply, an interested Gentile? Regardless of his religious position, the eunuch tries to understand the words of Isaiah, which he is unable to do. He lacks the power to interpret and to comprehend the Scriptures, despite having significant civil power. Philip, however, has experienced the gospel and is empowered to interpret the Scriptures. Philip uses this opportunity to share the good news about Jesus. In response, the eunuch is so moved by this encounter that he requests Philip to baptize him.

There are several baptisms, including the eunuch's, recorded in Acts, and certainly, each baptism signifies a person's conversion and acceptance of the gospel message. It is intriguing, however, to note the order of these baptisms. Luke has already demonstrated that Jews and Samaritans alike have been moved by the gospel of Jesus Christ. The reader is also aware of the story of Cornelius found in chapter 10, which illustrates that the gospel is open to everyone, including the Gentiles. The Ethiopian eunuch's story, however, is sandwiched between these conversions, yet it demonstrates that the gospel is progressively spreading to all people, Jew and Gentile alike.

Human participants, like Philip, have an important role as the gospel grows and reaches new people. Philip, however, is not the primary mover in this story. Rather, it is divine intervention and movement that facilitates this advancing work. Philip is commanded by an angel of the Lord to get up. Then the Spirit of God prompts him to speak with the eunuch. Finally, the Spirit of the Lord snatches Philip away from the eunuch and places him in Azotus.

It is this mysterious work of God that advances the gospel message, not merely human effort. Through the work and power of God, the gospel advances by being inclusive, reaching Ethiopia and the outermost parts of the world. Christians today have the same opportunity as Philip. Individuals can allow God to use them in advancing the gospel by including all people, not setting any limits on either the gospel or for whom it is intended. Indeed, if we help spread the gospel, then there is no limit to how far the gospel will go. (Mark White)

## FINDING LOVE IN THE REAL CHURCH

### 1 JOHN 4:7-21

If you're looking for a church these days, they are easy to find. After all, there is practically a church on every corner. Within a three-mile radius from our suburban Virginia church, there are at least twenty other churches. It is a wonder then that so many folks are searching so hard to find a church. Some folks visit a different church each week hoping to find the right place. Many people church hop, staying a little while at one place and then moving on. Others have given up on the search, and choose to stay home and watch TV preachers as opposed to bothering with yet another church visit. Ministers, outreach committees, and anyone in the church who cares about reaching these searchers have probably asked these questions a number of times, *What is it that people are searching so hard for?* and *Why is it that we don't have it?* What do twenty-first-century searchers hope to find in a church? Is it charismatic leaders or innovative programming, or is it something else?

The author of 1 John seemed to have an idea of what his particular congregation needed most. It probably seems too simple to us, but the community of 1 John needed to realize that they were loved by God and, in turn, were to love one another. Though we do not have specific details of the circumstances faced by this faith community, as a group of first-century Christians, their lives were probably not easy. They were definitely persecuted for their beliefs. Families probably were split. Jobs were lost. Faith practices and meetings were forced into hiding with the ever-present threat of martyrdom. The community had, no doubt, already suffered great losses for their faith and may have been constantly poised for more. Yet, they were committed. They remained faithful although they struggled with outer and inner pressures. What was the adhesive of this community? What helped them to continue their journey? The love of God is the clear answer.

In 1 John 4:7-21, the elder reminds them again of the depth and meaning of that love. God's special love was revealed through the life and death of God's Son. God is the ultimate initiator of that love. It is not that we loved God first. God loved us first. When we accept that awesome gift of love, we should freely and completely love one another. It is the completion of God's love for us. God's love is forever present and abides in us. It is impossible to return God's love and hate our brother or sister. True love cannot hate. From earlier in 1 John, we can suppose that the love we are commanded to have for our brothers and sisters is not a lazy or inactive love. Loving each other means caring for the needs of one another—physically, emotionally, and spiritually. In this passage, the elder reminds the community of perhaps what is most important: Love is what binds them together. Without love, they could not survive.

Perhaps, that is what our churches are missing. There may be lots of church buildings with all kinds of programs and frills. There might be a family life center on every corner. Seminaries may even be turning out the most brilliant theological minds ever, but without the love that the elder talked about in 1 John 4, it is all wasted effort. Those who are searching will continue their search. Those who are firmly planted in a particular congregation will continue their church routine but without grasping what it's really all about. We need the elder's reminder perhaps even stronger than the first-century Christians. Our fellowship and commitment should be about nothing more than the love of God and the love of our brothers and sisters. (Tracey Allred)

# VINES AND FRUIT

## JOHN 15:1-8

Jesus proclaims himself to be the true vine, with God acting as the vinegrower. For the gospel's original hearers, this claim would resonate with passages in the Old Testament in which God tends a vineyard. In Isaiah 5, God plants a vineyard with choice vines on fertile soil, providing all the necessary care. But, left to its own devices, the vineyard produced wild grapes. Despite such promise, the vineyard betrayed the keeper of the vineyard. In response, God will arrange its destruction. Only at the end does the audience learn that they are the vineyard that produced bloodshed, not justice. In Isaiah 27, God again plants a vineyard. This time, God is always present, actively watering and guarding it. If any thorns or briers become evident, they will be burned. As a result, the vineyard is hyperproductive, filling the world with fruit. And, again, the vineyard is identified as the people.

What does it mean to add Jesus to this set of images? Jesus' reuse of this material fundamentally alters it. The conflict in Isaiah 5 is between God and the people. The people fail and are destined for destruction. Likewise, in Isaiah 27, it is the people who are called upon to act as a part of God's vineyard. Those who do not (thorns, briers) will be consumed, while the people as a whole will succeed. Jesus now claims to be the vine, so the nature of the conflict between God and the people must change. God can never threaten the entire vine. Total destruction is not an option, as that would mean God destroying God's own Word. But the conflict also cannot be understood as a conflict only within God—Jesus replaces the people as the focus of God's wrath and God's hopes. The people are still intimately involved in the story, only now they are in union with Jesus, God's Word. So while total destruction is ruled out, the expectations of the vinegrower need not be relaxed. Jesus' reuse of these texts keeps the sense of conflict between God and the people alive, while insisting that God and humanity have found their meeting place in Jesus.

There are still those, like the vines of Isaiah 5, who when left to their own devices, will betray God. They bear no fruit and are pruned away (John 15:2). There are still those, like the thorns in Isaiah 27, who resist God's reign. They will be burned (John 15:6). But if you abide with God, you will produce good fruit.

So, "abiding" is the solution. But this is hardly an explicit command: "I want all of you to go out there and abide!" A clue to the meaning here is found in a play on words. Jesus speaks of God pruning the vines that bear fruit in order to make them more productive. (God doesn't "prune" the dead wood, God lops it off!) The word for *prune* here more often is used in the sense of *cleansing* or *purification*. It is used to describe the "pure of heart" in the Beatitudes, for example. When Jesus speaks of cleansing the disciples by his words he uses a related word, clearly uniting God's pruning with his own purifying activity. In short, if you abide, you will bear fruit. If you bear fruit, you will be cleansed so you can bear more fruit. The abiding life means a life of constant pruning, or purification. This purification comes by attention to the words of the Word. (Don Polaski)

# MAY 25, 2003

*Sixth Sunday of Easter*

**Worship Theme:** Jesus tells his disciples, "You did not choose me but I chose you" (John 15:16). This fact of divine love reminds each believer that it is God who seeks us out, rather than the other way around.

**Readings:** Acts 10:44-48; 1 John 5:1-6; John 15:9-17

**Call to Worship (Psalm 98 RSV)**

| | |
|---|---|
| *Leader:* | O sing to the LORD a new song, for he has done marvelous things! |
| ***People:*** | **His right hand and his holy arm have gotten him victory.** |
| *Leader:* | The LORD has made known his victory, he has revealed his vindication in the sight of the nations. |
| ***People:*** | **He has remembered his steadfast love and faithfulness to the house of Israel.** |
| ***All:*** | **All the ends of the earth have seen the victory of our God.** |
| *Leader:* | Make a joyful noise to the LORD, all the earth; break forth into joyous song and sing praises! |
| ***People:*** | **Sing praises to the LORD with the lyre, with the lyre and the sound of melody!** |
| *Leader:* | With trumpets and the sound of the horn make a joyful noise before the King, the LORD! |

*People:* **Let the sea roar, and all that fills it; the world and those who dwell in it!**

*Leader:* Let the floods clap their hands; let the hills sing for joy together before the LORD, for he comes to judge the earth.

*All:* **He will judge the world with righteousness, and the peoples with equity.**

**Pastoral Prayer:**

O God, through the life of Jesus you have revealed to us how a life of faithful love emerges. In Jesus' life, death, and resurrection, you provide us an opportunity to claim newness of life. In Christ we each have a chance to repent and begin life anew. By your covenant in Jesus, we possess a reliable guide to the living of a meaningful life, a life full of value and concern for others. As we ponder the wonder of your world and the love you reveal in Jesus, O Gracious Lord, help us to consider the plight of the poor and needy among us. Help us reach out to others with the kind of holy love that you have first established for us in Christ. Make Jesus' example one that inspires in us a higher expression of faithful living. Give us this day our just portion and teach us to offer a just portion to others. In the name of Jesus we pray. Amen. (David Mosser)

# SERMON BRIEFS

## IS BAPTISM MECHANICAL?

### ACTS 10:44-48

This text is a reminder of the power of preaching. Although many in worship exchange polite pleasantries at the door with the preacher offering thanks for a good sermon, the truth is we never know how a given sermon influences others. I have had the experience of a person enthusiastically telling me what I said in a previous sermon while thinking to myself, "that's not what I said!"

We can know what we are saying, but we cannot know what the Holy Spirit pronounces into people's lives. We cannot know the chemical reaction to the preached word with a person's given emotional, mental, and spiritual state. For this reason, preaching is a powerful tool that must be respected and held sacred. Peter converts many and then offers the ritual of baptism.

It is important to note the chronology of what has happened. The people were converted and then were baptized. Baptism is an outward and visible sign of an inward reality. The conversion has already taken place and baptism is administered. Baptism is not a magical rite that mechanically changes the hearts of people. I once baptized a man who presented himself for the sacrament at the conclusion of worship. The next week he called me and said with indignation, "It didn't work. I still drink and beat my wife. Your baptism didn't take." Peter understood that conversion in response to the gospel is a prerequisite for baptism. Those who were circumcised were astounded to note again that God does not show partiality but rather made converts of certain Gentiles. Who, indeed, would withhold the water to baptize these?

There have been times when the institutional church has been unable to resist the temptation to blur the distinction between sacramental responsibilities and the pursuit of organizational goals. The most profound rewards of faith are free. We do not sell the sacraments. We do not raffle off salvation. We do not manipulate the grace of God. We cannot simulate Jonah by trying to second-guess the results of our messages. Rather we offer ourselves as conduits for the gospel message confident that it is powerful enough to accomplish the ends of the spirit. The text states that the Holy Spirit did *epipipto*, fall upon. This sounds as arbitrary as a piano falling on some unsuspecting soul. Competent preachers strive to master the message, but they cannot dictate the message's reception. Peter simply notes the reactions of many and provides them with a corresponding baptism.

The Holy Spirit is not only a prerequisite to baptism but also remains in the life of people after their baptisms. Baptism reflects God's gift of grace in Jesus Christ and the individual response to that gift. Present day churches display a broken witness when they refuse to recognize the baptisms of the other. Few things in the life of faith are as hurtful as having one's baptism denied on the basis of mechanical procedure (not enough water) or age (that child doesn't understand what is happening). Certainly infant baptism requires the supplemental preparation of rigorous instruction and a public profession of faith in order to have integrity. Scripture provides no direction regarding the age of those to be baptized and so disagreement remains. However, for those who present themselves or loved ones for this mark of the Lord, who can withhold the water to baptize them? (John Fiedler)

# LOVE EQUALS OBEDIENCE

## 1 JOHN 5:1-6

The tangled logic of 1 John 5:1-6 creates a challenge for anyone trying to discern the main idea. Certainly the author does not intend to be able to summarize his thoughts in one slide from a PowerPoint presentation or in a twenty minute Sunday morning sermon. Or does he? Despite the looping flow of the elder's argument, one thing remains consistent: an unshakeable focus on Jesus Christ. And is not this focus a mirror of life itself? Consider one hour or one week in your life. As Christians, our centering point is Jesus Christ, but the details of our lives flow in, around, and through that relationship. Such is the message of this passage. Sometimes the logic does not make perfect sense; nevertheless, our lives are to be lived through the lens of Jesus.

For the elder, life through Jesus is inseparable from obedience to God's commands. Because of our faith in Jesus Christ, who has died for our sins, we are able to conquer the world and obey God by loving "the children of God." Such a demand for obedience is not oppressive. It is as if the elder has said, "You, being born of God and having the love of Jesus, must obey God's commandments. Such obedience may seem hard, but it really isn't. Our faith in Jesus has already allowed us to conquer whatever in this world would prevent us from obedience." The elder wants his hearers to understand that God's commandments set expectations for our actions, expectations meant to protect and nourish our lives, not to squelch us. Such understanding comes from focusing on Jesus Christ.

The context here seems to be that a group has left the local community of Christians. Tensions are running high. People want to know how to respond, and loving "the children of God" is not foremost in their thoughts. Instead of focusing on polemics stemming from their differences, the elder simply addresses those with whom he still has an audience. The point of the matter is not what those who left the community are doing, but what those who remain in the community do. And their "doing," no matter how hard or ostensibly unfair, should look like love as commanded by God. This passage takes me back to junior high school. You will have your own version of this scene, but in my home it went something like this: "I am not her mother, I am your mother, and you may not wear that to school." Although not being allowed to wear the dreamed-of outfit seemed despotic, my mother regulated the way I acted in an effort to establish healthy parameters in which I could mature.

So what would a final summary slide look like for us? First of all, Jesus Christ would be at the center. *Everything* we do is grounded in our faith in the Son of God. Under that is love, the hallmark of our relationship with God. Beside love is an explanatory note that reads, "It equals obedience." Although only a side note, it is boldface. Love for God cannot be expressed without obedience to God. Growing from the letters of obedience is a flourishing tree of life. Our lives do grow in response to obedience to God. The branches flow in and out of Jesus Christ, again the center of our lives. Finally, over in the corner is a separate reminder: a thought bubble filled with other people. In his writing the elder reminds us that in the face of differing opinions we should focus on ourselves and not on what others do. (Karen Hudson)

## A DEEPER KIND OF FRIEND

### JOHN 15:9-17

The leader calls his followers together. The situation looks grim; their hour is upon them. But the leader proclaims that all who follow him will be counted as his brothers; their status will forever change.

This might seem to be a paraphrase of the passage from John, but it is actually a description of the famous "St Crispin's Day" speech from Shakespeare's *Henry V*. Henry and the remains of his army are seemingly trapped by the French. The inevitable defeat will come the next day. But Henry refuses to surrender to the French, choosing instead to inspire his army:

> We few, we happy few, we band of brothers;
> For he to-day that sheds his blood with me
> Shall be my brother; be he ne'er so vile,
> This day shall gentle his condition:
> And gentlemen in England now a-bed
> Shall think themselves accursed they were not here.

(The University Society, *Henry IV part II, King Henry V, Henry VI part I*, vol. 8 of *The Complete Works of William Shakespeare* [New York: The University Society, 1901], p. 101)

The final speech before what appears to be a certain death is a powerful rhetorical situation. Both Shakespeare's Henry and John's Jesus claim that the experience that will be faced by their followers will alter their relationships. Unlike Henry, Jesus has already demonstrated, through the washing of his followers' feet, that his followers should serve each other. Yet, while Jesus takes on the role of a servant in that passage, Jesus is still Lord and Teacher (John 13:13); and indeed, he is the example the disciples must follow. At that point, then, the disciples' relationships to one another have changed, but a reconfigured relationship between the disciples and Jesus is only implied. But we might expect developments in this area.

As Jesus' hour approaches, he returns to some of the themes in the foot washing sequence. Now the disciples are still to keep Jesus' commandments but are no longer described as Jesus' servants. Rather, they are now friends because they are fully aware of what their Master is doing.

*Friend* does not seem to fit this passage very well, probably because our culture, by and large, tends to evaluate friendship on its content, rendering it as sentimental attachment or temporary arrangement. Friendship makes no real demands. If it does, we are tempted to call it codependency. Shakespeare's image of brothers fighting to the last man against the enemy, while violent (and gender exclusive!), is at least arresting.

To understand this passage, then, involves reclaiming a different notion of friendship. Literally, Jesus calls the disciples here his "lovers," attaching the claim of friendship to the overarching theme of love in this section (both *phileo* and *agapao* are used). Of course, the term *lover* also has its own set of cultural understandings that might also obscure the meaning of the text, but we should not deny the real passion in the passage. Jesus deeply loves his followers; God deeply loves Jesus; the disciples are to follow the commands of their "Lover" so they may abide in God's love and love each other.

This passion, in addition, cannot be separated from the other passion: Jesus' suffering. Here is where friendship starts to make demands. Real love and real suffering are forever intertwined. When love hurts (not the loss of love but love itself), sentimentality goes out the window. When suffering is truly shared, love will be there. And, strange as it sounds, when love is there, God's joy will be made complete in us. (Don Polaski)

# REFLECTIONS

❦

# JUNE

**Reflection Verse:** *The "Spirit intercedes with sighs too deep for words." (Romans 8:26b)*

A few years ago my church sponsored the resettlement of a family of Bosnian refugees in our small Pennsylvania town. I volunteered to help them learn English. My assignment was to teach the unit on seasons and weather. I pulled up outside their apartment to be met by gusts of wind that signaled a late summer storm on its way. Once inside I taught them the words for the seasons helped by a picture book. I taught them the words for snow and rain and sunshine. But then we came to the word *wind*. How to explain *wind*? I looked it up in the dictionary. "Air in motion; a state of movement in the air; a current of air, of any degree of force perceptible to the senses, occurring naturally in the atmosphere, usually parallel to the surface of the ground" (*The Compact Oxford English Dictionary*, 2d ed. [New York: Oxford University Press, 1991]). I didn't know how to say that in Croatian. I tried hand motions and sound effects. They looked at me and then at each other.

Finally, in desperation, I took them outside, pointed to the trees, whose leaves were rippled by the vigorous breeze, and said, "wind!" They nodded and smiled in comprehension.

What is the Holy Spirit? The Holy Spirit is the Third Person of the Trinity. The Holy Spirit is the power of the living Christ at work in the hearts of the people and in the church. Theological definitions can be clarifying, but the best way to get to know the Holy Spirit is firsthand, by attentiveness to its work in our hearts and communities.

One thing we will hear if we listen closely to our inward lives during Pentecost is a deep groaning. Like labor pains, Paul says. Each of us is groaning with some mixture of guilt, remorse, sadness, or futility. When we fail to pray and feel scattered and irritable, we groan. When we sit down to pray but can only pray self-centered or mechanical prayers, we groan. When we are not sure what God wants from us, when we are convinced that we are unforgivable, we groan. As pastors we hear the groaning of God's people struggling with addictions, depression, the breakdown of relationships, and crises of faith. We ourselves groan with loneliness, with a sense of being overwhelmed by the tasks before us, or with the pain of criticism. As citizens of the community and world, we hear the groans of the abused and the hopeless. Even where there are no tears, there can be groaning. Paul hears all creation groaning in agony as a new world comes to birth.

When we groan, we sometimes write a false equation on the chalkboard of our minds: Groaning equals the absence of God. An experienced spiritual director once said, "Many of us believe it is up to us to pray in a way that reaches God. I believe we are in the presence of God at all times and that prayer is being attentive to that presence."

Paul offers us a corrective equation: Groaning means the presence of the Holy Spirit. When we groan, whatever the reason, even when we do not know the reason, it means that the Spirit groans with us. The Spirit searches our depths and prays in us. A young mother once said in embarrassment at a church Bible study, "I'm thirty years old, and I don't think I know how to pray!" She is not alone. We do not know God's will perfectly. We do not have strength in and of ourselves to do it. We do not even know our own deepest needs. So the Spirit assists us in our feeble efforts to pray "with sighs too deep for words." Our prayers are at times very selfish, and the Spirit cleanses and purifies them. The Spirit reminds us to pray for others. When we get weary of praying, the Spirit renews our spiritual strength as individuals and as a faith community. In fact, it is only because of the Spirit's presence in our hearts that we pray at all. And every time we do pray, it is because we have heard the Spirit's call and are answering it.

The Spirit searches our depths, surfacing our longings and aspirations, which are so deep that they cannot be expressed in mere words. The Spirit mediates them to God and then mediates God's longings and aspirations for us back to us. The Spirit prays for us, according to God's will.

Stephen Arrington was a navy frogman specializing in bomb disposal who had done several tours of duty rescuing downed pilots in Vietnam. Through a series of mistakes in judgment he became involved in piloting flights smuggling cocaine from Columbia to California. He became the fall guy in the John Delorean drug case, one of the most highly publicized cases of the 1980s. He was arrested and sent to prison to serve a four-year term. In his book *Journey into Darkness*, he recounts the sounds of a cell block at night: the weeping of the homesick, the cursing of the angry, and the screams of the assaulted. He recounts the events of one particular night.

> I had been lying on my bunk wide awake, thinking about the criminal bent my life had taken. I wondered whether I would ever be able to look honest people in the eye again. Some of the cocaine I had smuggled into California had no doubt filtered its way down into young hands. I wondered how I could ever atone for that?

Filled with emotion, Arrington recounts, "I asked the Lord if he was still there for me? . . . I didn't exactly hear anything; it was more like being filled with a word. The word was 'ALWAYS.' I felt it flow through my body and soul; it . . . brought me . . . sudden peace" (*Journey into Darkness: Nowhere to Land* [Lafayette, La.: Huntington House Publishers, 1992], 173). (Alyce McKenzie)

# JUNE 1, 2003

## *Seventh Sunday of Easter*

---

**Worship Theme:** God sent Jesus into the world to make people one in Christ's spirit. In Jesus Christ, God fulfills God's plan for all people.

---

**Readings:** Acts 1:15-17, 21-26; 1 John 5:9-13; John 17:6-19

**Call to Worship (Psalm 1)**

| | |
|---|---|
| *Leader:* | Happy are those who do not follow the advice of the wicked, or take the path that sinners tread, or sit in the seat of scoffers; |
| *People:* | **But their delight is in the law of the LORD, and on his law they meditate day and night.** |
| *Leader:* | They are like trees planted by streams of water, which yield their fruit in its season, and their leaves do not wither. |
| *People:* | **In all that they do, they prosper.** |
| *Leader:* | The wicked are not so, but are like chaff that the wind drives away. |
| *People:* | **Therefore the wicked will not stand in the judgment, nor sinners in the congregation of the righteous;** |
| *Leader:* | For the LORD watches over the way of the righteous, |
| *All:* | **But the way of the wicked will perish.** |

**Pastoral Prayer:**

God of Truth and Sanctification, you have come to not only give us the truth but also perfect us in it. As you give us Jesus to forgive us our sins, you also send a spirit that makes us perfect in your love. Help us receive the gift of Christ as we worship today. May the peace that you offer gain a foothold in our lives so that we too might know what it is to be a child of God. Turn the core of our being upward toward the life you offer in Christ. Give us a heart for our brothers and sisters and may we aid you in resurrecting them to new life in you. For giving us the mystery of the gospel, we thank you. Let us be about your business of sharing the good news to a world in need. For this and all things, we give you thanks. Amen. (David Mosser)

# SERMON BRIEFS

## KNOWER OF HEARTS

### ACTS 1:15-17, 21-26

The very act of Peter standing among the believers connotes representative leadership. Peter, known as the foundation rock of the disciples, takes this authority and acts in the interests of the collective (that is, the emerging Jerusalem church). The required number of disciples (twelve representing the twelve tribes of Israel) must be restored in anticipation of the age to come (Luke 22:29-30). In stating a need based on Scripture, Peter takes on the preaching task. He chooses a Scripture and interprets it for the occasion; he makes it revelatory. Revelation is always God's Word for a given people at a given place at a given time. Peter moves from the recollected words of Jesus to a present mandate: Find a new disciple. Preaching is always about articulating present mandates drawn from Scripture. Consequently, preaching requires a certain audacity. The very act of standing before the believers and announcing what needs to be done requires confidence and a strong sense of role. Albert Outler, United Methodist theologian, preached my ordination service in 1985. All during his sermon, Outler hammered on what ordination was not: not being spiritually superior to one's congregants, not being biblically superior to one's congregants, and so on. By the time he concluded, I think we ordinands were wondering for what purpose had we been set apart! We have been set apart to administer word, sacrament, and order in the life of the church, according to Outler.

In retrospect, we should give Peter credit for not saying, "We don't need to replace Judas. I can pick up his duties and do my own as well." Peter was willing to share the responsibilities and the joy of ministry. Representative leaders who embrace a heroic model of ministry ("I can do it all for all of you") condemn themselves to a ministry of limited scope and tenure. As Jethro scolded Moses in Exodus 18:17, "What you are doing is not good. You will surely wear yourself out, both you and these people with you. For the task is too heavy for you; you cannot do it alone." Consequently, in keeping with Scripture and effective practice, Peter pronounces the need to recruit a new disciple.

Now let's give credit where it is due. Peter pronounced a need and then did something rather remarkable: He actually did something about it. How many of us have participated in Saturday morning brainstorming sessions in which extensive ink was applied to multiple sheets of paper to identify needs and perhaps even goals, only to wonder a few months later, "What ever happened to those goals we identified at that leadership retreat?" Churches are infamous for being well intentioned but ineffective. As simple as it might seem, Peter identified a need based on Scripture, and then he put together the process and forum by which to meet that need. Peter was an action-oriented leader.

The process begins with nominations based on gift assessment. In other words, they wondered, *What person has demonstrated the skills that are needed for this area of church leadership?* Two persons were nominated: Barsabbas and Matthias. Peter refers to the decision between the two as if it has already been made and requests in prayer that God show them whom God has already chosen. For God is the *kardiognostes*, the knower of the hearts. H. Richard Niebuhr, in his book *The Purpose of the Church and Its Ministry*, refers to three components of representative ministry: inner conviction, corresponding gifts, and institutional invitation. While asking that God discern the level of inner conviction, Peter has facilitated a process that links qualified candidates (nomination) and institutional invitation (casting lots). (John Fiedler)

# A LIVING TESTIMONY

## 1 JOHN 5:9-13

A youth leader posed a question to a group of high school students—most of whom had grown up in the church—concerning their assurance of going to heaven. To the leader's surprise the overwhelming majority of the youth expressed uncertainty about their eternal life. Some of the reasons cited for their doubt included mistakes they had made in the past, current attitudes and actions they knew to be questionable, and a knowledge that they could not live a perfect life. This list is now decades old and comes from my own youth group experience. Ask the young people in your church, however, and I suspect that you will hear similar concerns voiced.

Like youth who constantly receive grades for their performance, we all get caught in trying to measure up, even with God. We've heard two pieces of the message: God loves us freely, and God expects us to live our lives in response to that love. Free love from God; right action from us. Fortunately, this is not a chicken-and-egg question. Free love from God most definitely comes first, for God's salvation is offered "while we were still weak" (Romans 5:6). The order is easy to forget, however, and we fall victim to the worry that we are not good enough for God's love.

The author speaking to us in 1 John 5:9-13 seems to understand the need of youth and Christians everywhere to hear a message of assurance. As verse 13 tells us, these things are written to us who believe so that we might know for sure that we have eternal life. Such assurance is offered to us who are already going to church, who already have confirmed our personal relationship with God. And the assurance is this: God has already given us eternal life by sending Jesus Christ.

Other people also witness to this truth. Think of the people whose love, example, direction, or inspiration fills your life.

Maybe you can think of a teacher, pastor, family member, or coworker. You might reminisce about an infant in your arms or marvel at the life of someone like Mother Teresa. Whomever you consider, they have influenced your relationship with God. They have taught you about devotion, generosity, graciousness, persistence, humility, and more. Their lives have provided you with testimony, evidence of God's presence in their lives and this world. But no testimony is greater than that which God gives directly to us through Jesus Christ. What an amazing God!

The author offers us this assurance but does not leave any room for us to abuse it. We cannot accept the unconditional promise of eternal life and then use it as an excuse to live however we want. As noted above, our lives, when lived in response to God's love, do assume the responsibility of right action. In verse 10 the author prods us not to make a liar out of God by claiming falsehoods concerning Jesus Christ. In the broader context of 1 John, the author seems to be referring to believers who denied that the divine as well as the human nature of Jesus Christ died on the cross. While that particular debate does not plague many present-day Christians, we must remain watchful in order not to make a liar out of God through other false claims. When we minister to others in the name of Jesus without seeking to balance care for spiritual and physical needs, we give false witness to the character of Christ. When we act out our religiosity with only academic thought or hearty emotion we give false witness to Christ.

Believers, rest assured that salvation is yours, freely and greatly shown to you by God through Jesus Christ. Believers, rest assured that you matter in the kingdom of God. Make your life a living testimony to the truth of God's love. (Karen Hudson)

## JOY BONDS WITH SANCTIFICATION

### JOHN 17:6-19

Jesus' prayer here offers us an open invitation to abstraction. Reading this passage could inspire deep thoughts on the nature of the unity of God and the Son and how the church models that unity. We could talk for hours about what it means to understand

God's Word as truth. We could develop a theory about the "world" and its operation. For some of us, this would be engaging. But I'm afraid that most people find discussions such as these tedious at best. Is there any "practicality" here that does justice to Jesus' poetry?

This prayer is undoubtedly abstract, but its abstract terms are put forth as part of an argument. Jesus is seeking to persuade God, not a difficult task given their explicit unity. But Jesus' other audience is the disciples, and so now includes us. So what does this text invite us to be or become?

First, Jesus prays that we may be one. This unity will come through God's protection. That is, unity will prevail if we are protected from the world's temptations to disunity. There is danger in this argument. If unity is of God, then disunity is a sign of capitulating to the world, of abandoning the community. Thus, the bringer of discord cannot be from God. The Hebrew prophets as well as Christian history contradict this view. Discord may have many meanings.

Beyond that danger, this vision of unity raises issues of power. While it would be nice to chastise some troublemakers (and you may well have a list!), such exercise of authority is more liable to fragment rather than solidify a congregation or denomination. The difficulty here is in putting a "practical" face on this unity without abandoning the church to authoritarian kinds of behavior or hopelessly romantic notions of universal consensus.

I think the key to understanding and describing the unity intended in this passage lies in looking at the other results for which Jesus asks God. Jesus pleads for us to be sanctified in truth. This sanctification obviously includes being made separate from the world. But it is also clear that this sanctification will take place *in* the world. Jesus notes that while he is to be no longer in the world, his followers would still be there. Furthermore, Jesus asks that his followers not be removed from the world, only that they be protected from the evil one. So, while the world is, for John, not our home, it is still the arena of our activity, where the drama of our sanctification will be worked out. In other words, sanctification will involve all sorts of practices that take place in the world, which will serve to make us holy, which will set us apart from the world.

But beyond the question of the ethical dimension lies an emotional response: "I am coming to you [God], and I speak these things in the world so that they may have my joy made complete in themselves." Sanctification cannot be separated from joy; the practices that will serve to set us apart from the world, which the world finds confusing or off-putting, will also give us great joy. For a church now encouraged to weaken its distinctiveness in the face of the supposed demands of the marketplace, this strikes me as exceedingly good news. We may never agree on which practices serve to make us holy or how to perform them, but above all the noise is God. If we look carefully, we may see marks of unity and hear shouts of joy. (Don Polaski)

# JUNE 8, 2003

*Day of Pentecost*

**Worship Theme:** For a world that sits in darkness, God sends the Holy Spirit to reassure God's people of Christ's living and resurrected presence in all creation and for all people.

**Readings:** Acts 2:1-21; Romans 8:22-27; John 15:26-27; 16:4*b*-15

## Call to Worship (Psalm 104:24-30, 34-35 RSV)

| | |
|---|---|
| *Leader:* | O LORD, how manifold are thy works! In wisdom hast thou made them all; the earth is full of thy creatures. |
| ***People:*** | **Yonder is the sea, great and wide, which teems with things innumerable, living things both small and great.** |
| *Leader:* | There go the ships, and Leviathan which thou didst form to sport in it. |
| ***People:*** | **These all look to thee, to give them their food in due season.** |
| *Leader:* | When thou givest to them, they gather it up; when thou openest thy hand, they are filled with good things. |
| ***People:*** | **When thou hidest thy face, they are dismayed; when thou takest away their breath, they die and return to their dust.** |
| *Leader:* | When thou sendest forth thy Spirit, they are created; and thou renewest the face of the ground. |
| ***People:*** | **May my meditation be pleasing to him, for I rejoice in the LORD.** |

202

*Leader:*    Let sinners be consumed from the earth, and let the wicked be no more!

**All:**    **Bless the LORD, O my soul! Praise the LORD!**

**Pastoral Prayer:**

O God of Wind and Fire, breathe on us once again that Holy Spirit of Pentecost that birthed your church. As we remember from whence we come, inspire us once again to be like those early believers who called upon your holy name and whom you saved from the time of trial. Remind us, day by day, that you save us in your love and mercy and that our task is to accept that gift in faith. As we exercise our living faith let us be your hands and feet in the world. Help us to reach out to others with the sweet love of Jesus burning in our hearts. May the fire of your Holy Spirit once again be loosed on our world. Let us sing the praises of the holy name of Jesus, in whose name we pray. Amen. (David Mosser)

# SERMON BRIEFS

## THE SPIRIT'S FIREWORKS DISPLAY

### ACTS 2:1-21

The apostles are all in one place: Jerusalem. The fact that they did not flee from the large city to their homes and fishing jobs in Galilee attests to their encounters with the risen Christ in the forty days after Passover. The disciples are no longer driven by fear. Instead the Holy Spirit enters into them and gives them the ability to speak many different languages. In the moment of Pentecost many nations are represented in one place through the power of language. In the narrative of the Tower of Babel (Genesis 11), God confuses the language of the people and scatters them all about the globe. Pentecost is the anti-Babel moment. The peoples from all over the world are brought together in the amalgamation of "language fireworks."

Accused of drinking in the morning [*methuo*, to be drunk],

203

Peter is quick to defend the integrity of the process as the fulfillment of Joel's prophecy. Yet, the mistaken notion carries some interesting points. Intoxication involves the experience of a new, different, and often energizing reality. Alcohol-induced states, of course, lead to addiction, impaired judgment, and the possibility of self-destruction. However, the uplifting of the Spirit can be quite beneficial in throwing off the drudgery and depression of the routine. Life lived in the spirit is always about transforming the ordinary into the extraordinary.

The disciples are speaking actual languages that are readily understood by the cosmopolitan mixture of Jewish pilgrims gathered in the city. The Holy Spirit imparted to them the ability to communicate the gospel around the ancient world; the church is born, and it is to "go global." Given this ability, the apostles are now able to find people outside of their home area. Christianity cares enough about people to "locate" them and speak to them in a language that is meaningful to them. This is more than a matter of language. It means using images, story, music, and art that best conveys the gospel to a given community. The Holy Spirit emboldens us to transcend cultural barriers and find our unity in Christ. In the gospel, the language of love becomes the universal message.

In the present age, faith communities struggle over the use of media in the effort to convey the gospel. Traditions of sacred music and preaching have been challenged by the use of modern music and projected images chosen to supplement the preached Word. Although the capability of the Holy Spirit to use media as a conduit should not be questioned, another valid issue is incarnation. Ours is a faith in which God cared enough to come "in person," and we would never file into a room, view a one-hour video, and call that worship. Disembodied voices and video images of persons captured in the past must not supplement the living presence of preachers and vocalists who are a present locus for the Spirit. The Spirit is poured out upon flesh. Beyond that, the communication's imperative remains to reach persons in their native language and native medium. By celebrating Christ in many ways and many languages, the global Christian community is brought together in one place.

Finally, the apocalyptic note of Joel's prophecy is unavoidable in its reference to the last days. God's spirit continues to pour out upon us resulting in prophecy, visions, and dreams. These all speak of the coming of the kingdom of God and must be accompanied by present action. We are reminded that even our best efforts, even our most successful church events, do not synthesize the kingdom of God. The Kingdom is always unleashed by God and the periodic inbreakings that we are allowed are the fruits of the Spirit. This invokes the age-old tension between works and grace. While we do not earn salvation and we do not manufacture the Kingdom, we are expected to supplement grace with acts of caring that do approximate the kingdom of God. Pentecost celebrates the explosion of spirit and vision that propelled the church into all reaches of the world. The Christian church started with a great fireworks display and that possibility continues. (John Fiedler)

# PRAYING ACCORDING TO GOD'S WILL

## ROMANS 8:22-27

Today we celebrate the Day of Pentecost. Paul, having just spoken of life in the Spirit in the preceding verses, admits that the Spirit's presence is not a panacea for all of life's ailments (v. 23, cf. v. 17). So, we might ask, what difference does the Spirit really make in our lives right now? Is God's Spirit simply a divine presence to keep us company while we live in perpetual anticipation of a future salvation? Surely Paul, a Hebrew among Hebrews, has not abandoned a foundational Hebraic thought that this life in the here and now matters to God.

Although Romans 8:22-27 is replete with language of waiting for a future rescue, this passage is fundamentally about the difference the presence of God's Spirit makes in our lives at this moment. Just as God asks us to keep our priorities straight by offering up a portion (or tithe) of the produce from our labors, God emphasizes God's commitment to us by giving the "first fruits of the Spirit" (v. 23). We are meant to savor that gift now, even if the full experience is yet to come. Whether you have opened a gift on Christmas Eve, had a bite of dessert before supper, or snatched any peek, you know about this "first fruit" experience. It comes with all the joy and fun that the full experience promises to bring later. And it makes a difference in that moment.

Right now, the presence of God's Spirit works to unite us to all creation (vv. 22-23). This entire world—sky, land, seas, plants, creatures of the sea, birds in the air, animals along the ground, humanity everywhere—strains toward God. The Spirit gives us a sense of belonging greater than we could ever imagine on our own. Although much of our yearning to belong focuses on other people, our experience of the Spirit offers deeper connections not only to humanity, but to all created order. Such ties, especially to the land, are disappearing fast. Native American culture teaches us extensively about connectivity to creation and its spiritual impact. We can also listen to farmers, homesteaders, geologists, and ecologists to revive an intimacy with the world in which we live.

God's unifying Spirit also gives us hope. Although hope is inextricably linked to the future, it makes a difference in our daily lives. Paul seems to prod us to look at our current situation, examining it for impact from the Spirit. Is there a new freedom from old habits, a sense of peace, a deepening relationship with God? Hoping that our future with God will look like what we now encounter in the Spirit is not true hope. The future is much greater than that! Nevertheless, such grand hope can only spring forth from an awareness of how the Spirit is already working in your life.

"Likewise the Spirit helps us in our weakness" by maintaining a clear connection with God (v. 26). Even when we have no idea what or how to pray, God's Spirit in us acts on our behalf. Society, in moving away from the childhood ditty "sticks and stones," is reclaiming the power of words. Words can build up and tear down any number of relationships from friendship to family to corporate alliances. The Bible is full of stories that acknowledge the power of words: the act of creation, the giving of blessings by the patriarchs, the parables told by Jesus, the disciples' desire to know how to pray, and so on. Yet in the midst of knowing that correct, righteous speech is important to God, we are assured that we cannot alienate God simply by blundering through a prayer. God's Spirit, praying according to God's will, has power that goes beyond any of our words. (Karen Hudson)

# THE SPIRIT AND TRUTH

## JOHN 15:26-27; 16:4b-15

"You can't handle the truth!" These words reverberate through the courtroom in a powerful scene from the film *A Few Good Men*. The prosecutor has just demanded the truth from a hostile witness who gives him that reply. While the scene in our Scripture is very different, Jesus is telling his disciples the same thing. Jesus is speaking with his disciples just before he goes to the garden where he will be arrested. He has shared much with them that they are unable to understand, and he senses their confusion. "I still have many things to say to you, but you cannot bear them now" (v. 16:12).

The disciples simply could not handle the truth. They had not yet seen Jesus' predictions of his own death and resurrection come true. All the things of which Jesus spoke seemed impossible. How could they understand his words about an Advocate when they could not grasp that he would soon be leaving them? So, Jesus decided to stop giving them information they could not process. Instead, he said, "When the Spirit of truth comes, he will guide you into all the truth" (v. 16:13a).

Though Jesus was speaking to his disciples about the days immediately following his death, the promise of an Advocate is for disciples in all times. This Spirit, whose coming we celebrate, brought truth not only to the Twelve but to all of us. That truth comes in many ways.

The most important truth the Spirit brings is the witness of Christ. Jesus told his disciples that the Advocate, who would come from God, would testify on Jesus' behalf. The Spirit does this in our own time as well. Many missionaries will attest that the Spirit is at work long before they arrive at their place of service. Those with whom they share the gospel have some sense of Christ's love long before they hear the words of Scripture. The Spirit works to guide all people into the truth, glorifying Christ by declaring him to everyone.

The Spirit also shows us the truth of the state of our own souls. Jesus told his disciples that "when [the Advocate] comes, he will prove the world wrong about sin and righteousness and judgment" (John 16:8). One of the jobs of the Spirit is to convict us of the untruths in our lives—the false ideas we hold, the sins we ignore. The Spirit acts in this sense as a prosecutor rather than a witness, pointing out the areas where we have failed. The courtroom imagery does not take us far enough, however, because this prosecutor is not concerned with our punishment but with repentance and healing.

Jesus also promised that the Spirit will share with us the truth concerning our future. "He will declare to you the things that are to come" (John 16:13). This does not mean that we can, with the help of the Spirit, foresee every turn of the path before us. If that were true, we would be much like the first disciples, unable to comprehend what we are being shown. We can't handle the truth, at least not in such a large dose. At times, God helps us take in a much larger view of the future; other times, we can only handle seeing things one step at a time. The Spirit reveals to us only what we are able to understand.

The coming of the Spirit marked a new stage in the journey of the disciples. They were given insight which emphasized the truth of all they had experienced when Jesus was with them. May we, too, receive new wisdom and comfort from that same Spirit who is still with us. (Melissa Scott)

# JUNE 15, 2003

## *Trinity Sunday*

**Worship Theme:** The doctrine of the Trinity attempts to reveal in human language who God is for God's people. At the last, however, we worship the mystery of a God who loves us.

**Readings:** Isaiah 6:1-8; Romans 8:12-17; John 3:1-17

### Call to Worship (Psalm 29:1-4, 9-11)

*Leader:* Ascribe to the LORD, O heavenly beings, ascribe to the LORD glory and strength.

***People:*** **Ascribe to the LORD the glory of his name; worship the LORD in holy splendor.**

*Leader:* The voice of the LORD is over the waters; the God of glory thunders, the LORD, over mighty waters.

***People:*** **The voice of the LORD is powerful; the voice of the LORD is full of majesty.**

*Leader:* The voice of the LORD causes the oaks to whirl, and strips the forest bare;

***People:*** **In the LORD's temple all say, "Glory!"**

*Leader:* The LORD sits enthroned over the flood; the LORD sits enthroned as king forever.

***All:*** **May the LORD give strength to his people! May the LORD bless his people with peace!**

**Pastoral Prayer:**

From the beginning of time, O Lord, your people have sought to define and describe you. We search our mind, and our tongues cannot begin to reflect your grandeur in our all-too-human speech. Yet we dare to describe you; for you are our God, and we strive to be your people. In days of old, your prophet saw you "high and lifted up" (Isaiah 6:1 RSV). Help us respond to you as Isaiah did when he said, "My eyes have seen the King, the LORD of hosts!" (Isaiah 6:5). Give us another vision of your exalted majesty and make us again confident that you have forgiven us from our sins. In addition to saving us from sin, save us for something better than our own self-seeking interests. Make us a people for others. Make us people after the fashion of Jesus, who gave his life for others. Help us pray daily in Jesus' holy name. Amen. (David Mosser)

# SERMON BRIEFS

## RUN, RISE, AND REST WITH GOD

### ISAIAH 6:1-8

"This is Trinity Sunday, and I'm going to explain the Trinity to you," said the young pastor at the beginning of the children's sermon. That got our attention. None of us, including the theology students, had ever heard the Trinity "explained" before. And, of course, it wasn't explained that day either. The preacher relied on a faulty illustration. Water that can change from one state to another—solid, liquid, and gas—has nothing in common with the living, moving triune community of God, who embraces us with a love that is beyond explanation.

The Trinity isn't explained in Scripture either, although there are suggestions throughout of God's moving and communal presence with us. God, according to Proverbs 8:27-31, had a helper and companion at creation. In Genesis 18 Abraham welcomes three strangers and knows that he has been with God. In the Gospels the disciples are commissioned to go to "all nations, baptizing them in the name of the Father and of the Son and of the Holy

Spirit" (Matthew 28:19), and in Paul's epistles he blesses us with "the grace of the Lord Jesus Christ, the love of God, and the communion of the Holy Spirit" (2 Corinthians 13:13). God comes to us as a loving, active, and encompassing community.

We are not expected to explain the inexplicable. The Trinity is the title of a story, the story of God's community and our relationship to God. Stories surprise us with the truth; they invite us in as participants, but stories are better left unexplained.

This is a day for dancing. Can you see three dancers moving in an intricate choreography of circling and spiraling around each other, dancers who will invite everyone here to move with them in a joyous dance of fellowship? This is a day for feasting, for sitting together around the table and praising the graciousness of the provider, the host, and the companion. Can you see us all walking through the door, going to the highways and hedges and bringing the wounded and the outcasts to sit in communion with us at the table?

We are asked to move and work with the Trinity everyday, to enter the embrace, to know the blessing. We are invited to live with God's community and extend it into all the world so that the love we share is there for everyone.

Reading the account of Isaiah's encounter with God reminds us that we are all called by God. Through our calling, our sense of living with God is clearly focused. For Isaiah at the beginning of his prophetic ministry, the reality of God's presence was awesome. The building shook on its foundations and was filled with smoke. This experience was not unlike the rushing wind and tongues of fire at Pentecost. Others have a less dramatic encounter. Elijah, for example, heard God not in the earthquake, wind, or fire but in a whisper; Jesus' disciples heard only his simple command, "Follow me" (Matthew 4:19 and parallels).

But what we share in our calling is that God is with us, asking, *Whom shall I send? Who will go for us?* Like Isaiah, we may feel unworthy of God's presence surrounding us. We may be weak with terror when the angels' voices echo the great triple Sanctus: "Holy, holy, holy is the Lord of hosts; the whole earth is full of his glory" (v. 3). Isaiah was cleansed with a burning coal so that he no longer need feel unworthy in God's holy presence. We are loved by the God who cleansed us through Jesus' sacrifice and brought us into communion through the Holy Spirit.

211

God is with us, and God is for us. God is our parent who loves us beyond measure, our brother who gives his life for us, and our giver of gifts who stays with us and sustains us. Can there be any response other than to enter into community with this God and live to bring others with us into that love? (Blair Meeks)

# GOD'S HOLY FAMILY—THE CHURCH

## ROMANS 8:12-17

Alcatraz, the scene for a variety of tales, witnessed a few remarkable escape attempts. In one case, an inmate spent months staking out his opportunities, preparing his passage out of the prison walls, and positioning himself to escape. Initially he was successful. After spending the night in the cold waters of the San Francisco Bay, however, the prisoner chose to turn himself in rather than suffer further in the bay.

Initially, Gentile converts to Christianity might have empathized with this prisoner. They heard Paul speak a message of salvation, peace, and freedom. Then came the daily "dos and don'ts" of how to live as a Christian. Of course, we remember that Paul is writing during the time that Christianity is trying to define itself within Judaism. It is not hard to imagine that more than one convert questioned whether the newly found freedom in Christ was really worth being bound by all the equally new regulations. We too can identify with feelings of burden rather than of release when we focus solely on righteous thought and deed.

Paul must have known that, at times, Christianity could seem akin to religious bondage. In Romans 8:12-17 Paul offers encouragement that in Christ we find the blessing of family rather than the curse of slavery. In God's Spirit lies the key to this blessing because it unites us with God and joins us with the life of Christ.

Ask any newlywed, college freshman, new employee, or recent church member and they will attest to the fact that becoming part of a "family" involves learning different customs. Whether you are new to Christianity or your family has been Christian for generations, living out a life in Christ requires us to have different habits from the world. Among other matters, we approach financial planning differently, have an alternate basis for justice, and consider morality in the unique light of Jesus. God's Spirit gives us the strength to live out these differences.

If ever we question whether life in the family of God is worth it or whether we are even included in this family, the Spirit testifies to and for us: We are children of God. Although the church uses slave language when speaking of Jesus paying the price for our sins, the Spirit gives us the invitation to think of ourselves as adopted children, not owned slaves of God. We need not be frightened of God as some terrifying master, but rather can approach God as a tender parent.

Being this close to God is an awe-filled possibility. This God is different from the other cool, mercurial deities of the first and twenty-first centuries. This God is steadfast whereas careers can be insecure. This God is forgiving when people can shrug you off for one fault. This God offers hope and promise while money is an illusive goal. This God provides tender security and a strong Spirit with whom we can return to the world with justice and mercy (cf. Micah 6:8). This God knows suffering and considers us glorified, not condemned, because of it.

Christians, we are children of God, part of the mysterious one-in-three family. Do not run away from the fear of failure in this family. The Spirit sustains us in daily household matters. God welcomes us with tender love. Christ proves to us that life, fully and eternally, is ours. (Karen Hudson)

## NICK AT NIGHT

### JOHN 3:1-17

To Nicodemus, Jesus' meaning was as dark as the night around them. Born from above? What could he possibly mean? "How can anyone be born after having grown old" (v. 4)? Those born of the Spirit are like the wind, according to Jesus. Nicodemus probably agreed wholeheartedly, since he could grasp neither the breeze nor the significance of Jesus' words.

Jesus must have shook his head in wonder at Nicodemus and

213

the others who failed to understand. We, with our knowledge that Jesus was the Christ, the Son of God, might be tempted to marvel at their lack of perception, as well. Before we give way to that temptation, perhaps we should examine our own lives more closely. Are there times when we have missed the word spoken clearly to us? Is our world, like that of Nicodemus, limited to the immediate and the physical?

The surest sign that we have failed to understand is the feeling that we know God completely. On Trinity Sunday there is no more appropriate time for us to admit our own failure to penetrate the mystery of God. Through the ages, Christians have debated exactly what the idea of God as Trinity means. The word is never mentioned in Scripture, yet the idea is present in both the Hebrew Bible and the New Testament. Creator, Redeemer, Comforter; Father, Son, Spirit; these and many other images have been used to make the Trinity something we can fathom. We are like Nicodemus, struggling with an idea that seems impossible. How can God be one God but also three? Perhaps the greatest lesson comes to us in the sheer immensity of the concept of Trinity. It is beyond our understanding. If the coming and goings of the wind are beyond our calculations, how much more so is God!

As we mature, we both understand more about God and realize that there is much more to God than we will ever understand. In C. S. Lewis's *The Chronicles of Narnia*, Aslan, a lion, is the Christ figure. When the little girl Lucy is reunited with him after a long separation, she notices that he is much bigger and questions him about it. " 'That is because you are older, little one,' answered he. 'Not because you are?' 'I am not. But every year you grow, you will find me bigger' " (C. S. Lewis, *Prince Caspian: The Return to Narnia*, book 2 in *The Chronicles of Narnia* [New York: Macmillan Publishing Co., 1970], p. 136). As we grow in our faith, becoming more spiritually mature, we gain a greater capacity for comprehending the awesomeness of God. We also understand that, like the wind, God will always be larger than our minds can understand.

Ultimately, Nicodemus seems to have understood that Jesus was the Messiah. He was with Joseph of Arimathea as they claimed Jesus' body and laid it in the tomb (John 19:38-42). He may never have understood fully what it means to be born again, to be born from above, but it seems he did hear and accept other words Jesus spoke that night: "For God so loved the world that he gave his only Son, so that everyone who believes in him may not perish but may have eternal life. Indeed, God did not send the Son into the world to condemn the world, but in order that the world might be saved through him."

What will we do today? Will we continue to confine God to the limits of our understanding, or will we follow Nicodemus's example? Even a journey begun in the darkness of night can lead us to the light of Christ. (Melissa Scott)

# JUNE 22, 2003

## *Second Sunday After Pentecost*

**Worship Theme:** Even when life seems overwhelming and nothing appears in our favor, faith in God will see us through our troubled waters.

**Readings:** 1 Samuel 17:(1*a*, 4-11, 19-23), 32-49; 2 Corinthians 6:1-13; Mark 4:35-41

### Call to Worship (Psalm 9:9-11, 12*b*-14)

*Leader:* The LORD is a stronghold for the oppressed, a stronghold in times of trouble.

*People:* **And those who know your name put their trust in you, for you, O LORD, have not forsaken those who seek you.**

*Leader:* Sing praises to the LORD, who dwells in Zion.

*People:* **Declare his deeds among the peoples.**

*Leader:* He does not forget the cry of the afflicted.

*People:* **Be gracious to me, O LORD. See what I suffer from those who hate me; you are the one who lifts me up from the gates of death.**

*Leader:* So that I may recount all your praises,

*People:* **And, in the gates of daughter Zion, rejoice in your deliverance.**

**Pastoral Prayer:**

O God of Infinite Horizon, in you "we live and move and have our being" (Acts 17:28). Grant us this day a vision of how we might, like David, contend against the foes of our time with courage and confidence. Remind us again that love is stronger than hate and that "perfect love casts out fear" (1 John 4:18). Give us a mind to understand your perfect love for us. Give us a heart to spread that love in which we stand to others who need an encouraging word in their time of need. Give us a will to face the untruth rampant in our society and meet it headlong with a word of hope, grace, and truth. Create a space in our lives where we can fellowship with those whose story of life is different from our own. Make the companionship of our congregation such that those who come to us for comfort find the words of life. This is our prayer, O God, in the name of Jesus. Amen. (David Mosser)

# SERMON BRIEFS

## ONE STRAIGHT SHOOTER

### 1 SAMUEL 17:(1a, 4-11, 19-23), 32-49

He was brash, loud, and downright annoying. Nobody argued with him. Why would they? He was bigger, meaner, and nastier than anybody in the World Wrestling Federation! His appearance made everyone shiver with fright. He was over nine feet tall, wore a bronze helmet and sported a coat of scale armor of bronze that weighed 125 pounds. On his timberlike legs were coverings of armor as well. He carried a bronze javelin slung over his back and its shaft was like a weaver's rod with the iron point weighing fifteen pounds! Is it any wonder they called him "a champion"? His name, *Goliath*, brought goose bumps to the Israelite army. Everyday for weeks he taunted the Israelite army of King Saul. Each morning the Israelites would line up in military ranks until they heard the voice of Goliath. Then they fled to their tents.

One day a mere boy in his mid- to late-teen years from the Judean countryside visited his older soldier brothers at Socoh in Judah, where this debacle was taking place. The text gives us the order of events that made Jesse's son David a national hero, a biblical heavyweight, and a spiritual giant, propelling him from obscurity into history's limelight forever!

## I. David's Confidence Was in God (vv. 32-37a)

The Israelite army including David's brothers and King Saul misplaced their confidence and were ill equipped to find it. They all looked for their confidence builder to be in their numbers, equipment, fortification, and other warlike material. Each of them had lost sight of the real basis for confidence—God. It took a teenager to remind them that confidence comes from within first. The motto Christians need to live by is, "I can do all things through Christ who strengthens me" (Philippians 4:13 NKJV).

Someone asked the pioneer missionary to China, J. G. Morrison, "Do you expect to make an impression on the vast Chinese Empire?" His classic reply was, "No, but I expect that God will."

The more we get into God's Spirit, power, and presence the more confidence we will have to overcome the obstacles we face in life.

## II. David's Comfortability with God's Plan (vv. 37b–40)

Goliath's battle plan was intimidation—his brute strength against an Israelite's brute strength. David didn't fight that way. He didn't meet Goliath on the giant's terms but forced the giant to meet him on his terms: five smooth stones. David understood that to meet this challenge he would do his best and leave the rest to God.

Cassius Clay was an outstanding boxer. I listened to his fights on the radio when I was in high school. He later changed his name to Muhammad Ali and was practically unbeatable during his prime. The sports announcer always commented that Ali made his opponent "fight his fight." Ali set the pace and the other boxer either kept up or ended up on the mat.

David refused to be intimidated by Goliath's appearance. Young David was outmatched by size, age, experience, and weapons, but in a moment of sheer abandonment, he approached Goliath in the power of God! With an attitude like his and a faith in the living God, David's plan succeeded.

What is it you fear? What obstacles do you face? Whose plan are you working on—your plan or God's plan? Discover God's personal plan for a successful life.

## III. David Conquers the Enemy with God (vv. 41-49)

One of the benefits of the Christian faith is that our God is not just somewhere in the sky unconcerned about us. No! God's presence strides alongside us as we meet our giants in life. We take aim with our rocks of faith and God delivers them to the right spot.

We either conquer with God, like David, or fail like the army of Israel against the Philistines. Remember, God is looking for some straight shooters! (Derl Keefer)

# WORKING TOGETHER

## 2 CORINTHIANS 6:1-13

There is a tendency to idealize the New Testament church. We are apt to say to ourselves, *If only we could be like them.* Yet the reality of the infant church struggling to maturity is quite different. In Paul's trouble and fractious relationship with the Corinthian church, we catch a glimpse of those inner struggles.

Following a plea to be ambassadors for Christ and reconciled to God, the passion of Paul pours out in his plea that God's grace not be in vain. The opening paragraph lays out a dominant theme of working together with God. The emphatic emphasis of verse 2 puts an exclamation mark on this. "Now is the acceptable time" because God is at work with and through us (v. 2b). Thus, in swift strokes, the apostle lays to rest any false notions that the work of Christ ought to wait for a better, safer, more advantageous time. Ignited by God's gift of Christ, the time of salvation is now!

In verse 3 the theme of working together with God shifts to a direct address to the troubled Corinthians. Verse 3 is both the opening defense of Paul's own ministry among them and a call to share in that ministry working together with God.

In the ancient world, personal identity was closely aligned with moral character and social usefulness. Paul again returns to his theme of working together with God: "as servants of God we have commended ourselves in every way" (v. 4a). In commending his own conduct, Paul is not boasting. To be sure, he is anxious to demonstrate that his own behavior is beyond reproach. However, there is a deeper sense of truth in this passage. Paul points to his own integrity and faithfulness as both witness and example. He has both talked the talk and walked the walk. By implication the Corinthians are to judge his personal consistency for themselves.

What follows, in a threefold structure, is an explanation of living as a servant of God. Here are the credentials by which Paul presents both himself and his ministry. Echoing softly in the background is the implication that these are to be the credentials of all Christians.

The brief phrase "through great endurance" brackets the whole list. Endurance is not passive. It is a way through the struggles to triumph. The first set of these—"afflictions, hardships, calamities"—are internal. They represent the deep struggles in the hearts of all Christians. The second set of three—"beatings, imprisonments, riots"—represent external hardships (v. 4b). In a day of Christian ease, these afflictions stand as a sharp reminder of the persecution suffered in building the church. Sacrifice is part of the redemptive work of God. The third set of credentials points to enduring courageous conduct, unceasing toil, and unwavering determination. They are attributes surely needed by present-day Christians.

In verse 6 we encounter the second triad that marks Christian character. The word often translated as *purity* does not imply our unwillingness to get our hands dirty in the hard work of Christ. Rather, it means personal integrity and blameless conduct. Knowledge is insight that is open to the will of God. It is important to note that none of these characteristic Christian credentials are offered in judgmental self-righteousness but rather by genuine love through the Holy Spirit in truth. They are attributes of the power of God at work within us.

Paul closes the paragraph with an appeal to righteousness in all situations (at the left and right hand). To be held in honor is to be recognized for personal merit. The sacrifice of working together with God leads to genuine living. Even in sorrow, the Christian rejoices.

This is an extraordinary passage of self-witness that calls the Christian back to high purposes of God in Christ. Our current age of rampant hedonism, self-indulgence, and the subjective dissipation of truth reflect much of the corresponding Corinthian struggle. Paul's challenge to work together with God is every bit as applicable now as it was then. An old hymn states the case:

The voice of God is calling its summons in our day;
. . . . . . . . . . . . . . . . . . . . . . . . . . . . . . . . . . . . . . . . . . . . . . . . . . .
From ease and plenty save us; from pride of place absolve
purge us of low desire; lift us to high resolve.
(*The United Methodist Hymnal* [Nashville: The United
Methodist Publishing House, 1999], p. 436)

(Mike Lowry)


# GOD'S CALM

## MARK 4:35-41

From the beginning, the primordial waters and sea were given great respect. The water was often viewed as a place where evil lurked. There was much uncertainty about the waters and about the storms that raged on them. Fisherfolk and sea traders alike understood the power and might that the raging sea could possess. Currents and storms left boats at the sea's mercy, and even the best of captains could be crushed under wind and waves.

In our passage, even the professional fisherfolk were surprised at the severity of the storm. They panicked, and so like most of us do, they expected Jesus and everyone else around them to react in the same way. Since Jesus wasn't panicked, their fear led to anger, for they felt that Jesus didn't care. They cry out, "Teacher, do you not care that we are perishing?" (v. 38*b*). What is so amazing is that after calming the storm, Jesus answers their question with another question: "Why are you so afraid? Do you still have no faith?" (v. 40 NIV). Jesus turns their question of his concern for them around. He reveals their own insecurities and lack of faith. Jesus has been calm amidst the storm, and it is the disciples who have shown their immature faith.

221

As Christians, even longtime Christians, we often unexpectedly find ourselves getting caught up in the storms of our lives: a loved one dies, we lose a job, our family is falling apart, we are depressed, or we get stressed out from all that life has dealt us. We are tossed and thrown for a loop, and we don't know how we will respond until we face such fierce situations. There are places in our lives that are filled with uncertainty and with great fear. This passage speaks to people of faith who are being swept away by the currents of life and beaten down by the waves of the storms. Jesus speaks up to those of us who, for whatever reason, lack faith. Why do you lack faith that God cares for you? The question is turned around on us, for we are the ones who still need to grow in our faith, to open our minds, and to soften our hearts.

As growing disciples, we are left in the boat to answer Jesus' question. Can we trust Jesus? Do we know that God is concerned, even when we do not perceive God's presence? Is our faith strong enough to count on God for our every need? When will the storms end? Can we find the "peace that passes our understanding" when life seems too much for us? When we walk through the valleys, does our faith profess, "Thou art with me?" Why do we so often seek everyone's help but only God's when life is overtaking us? Why are we so faithless when we are tossed about by the storms of life? Can we experience God's peace even amidst certain death? When will we realize that Jesus is Lord of all? When will we remember our faith? Jesus is in the boat with us! When will we let Jesus give us God's calm amidst our storms? (Ryan Wilson)

# JUNE 29, 2003

## *Third Sunday After Pentecost*

---

**Worship Theme:** Life is what happens to us when we make other plans. Even in the eventful life of Jesus, our Messiah still had the time to devote himself to others in need.

---

**Readings:** 2 Samuel 1:1, 17-27; 2 Corinthians 8:7-15; Mark 5:21-43

### Call to Worship (Psalm 130)

*Leader:*   Out of the depths I cry to you, O LORD.

**People:**   **Lord, hear my voice!**

*Leader:*   Let your ears be attentive to the voice of my supplications!

**People:**   **If you, O LORD, should mark iniquities, Lord, who could stand?**

*Leader:*   But there is forgiveness with you, so that you may be revered.

**People:**   **I wait for the LORD, my soul waits, and in his word I hope;**

*Leader:*   My soul waits for the Lord more than those who watch for the morning, more than those who watch for the morning.

**People:**   **O Israel, hope in the LORD! For with the LORD there is steadfast love, and with him is great power to redeem.**

**All:**    **It is he who will redeem Israel from all its iniquities.**

**Pastoral Prayer:**
To us who worship you in spirit and truth this day, O God of All Majesty, draw near in faith. In your gift of Jesus Christ, O God, you have given us a clue to the salvation of humankind. May we take solace in your love for us that while sin yet separated us from you, you took it upon yourself to seek us as your people. As in the days of Israel's kings, you provide for us in our time of testing. May we not be found wanting as you again speak to us the wonderful words of eternal life. May we take these sacred promises and communicate them to a hurting world so that all people may hear of your marvels. Grant us, in this worship hour, a glimpse of the Heavenly Host who watches over us and encourages us in our journey of faith. Grant us the peace of Jesus Christ who for our sake became sin to release us from sin's burden. Let us live as forgiven and redeemed people in Christ's name. Amen. (David Mosser)

# SERMON BRIEFS

## FIRST THE END—THEN A BEGINNING

### 2 SAMUEL 1:1, 17-27

Before every new beginning, there has to be an ending. Moses led the people of Israel out of Egypt and through the wilderness to the edge of the promised land. As they prepared to enter into the promised land it was a time for a new beginning. So the first verse of the sixth book of the Bible opens with, "Now after the death of Moses" (Joshua 1:1 KJV).

Joshua would lead the people into the promised land fighting the inhabitants. When the people of Israel began to settle in the land, it was a new beginning in their history. So we open the book of Judges with the verse, "Now after the death of Joshua" (Judges 1:1 KJV).

In 2 Samuel it is time for a new beginning. It was time for

David to become king. So the book opens with the words, "Now ... after the death of Saul" (2 Samuel 1:1 KJV). Before every new beginning there must be an end.

David was just a boy living in Bethlehem when the prophet Samuel came looking for Jesse's family. When he saw David, Samuel was moved by the Spirit of God and anointed David to be Israel's next king. David served in Israel's army and, in the beginning, was on good terms with Saul; then things changed. Now David was hiding in Ziklag while Saul and Jonathan battled against the Philistines on Mount Gilboa. David anxiously awaited news about the battle. Finally, a runner announced that Saul and Jonathan were dead. He had seen Saul die. He brought Saul's crown and arm amulet to David. These ornaments symbolized that David, just as the prophet Samuel predicted, was now to be king. David always believed his day would come and now it had. But before he seized power, before the time of a new beginning, it was time to grieve.

As people of faith we believe in new beginnings. We see the gift of new beginnings at Easter. We see the gift of new beginnings at Pentecost with the coming of God's Holy Spirit and the birthday of the church. Before we go on to new beginnings, it is important to take time to grieve what we have lost. I remember when my wife and I brought our first child home from the hospital. It was exciting to have a new baby in the family, but I noticed that my wife was quiet and seemed depressed. I asked her what was the matter, and she said, "I've come to realize that I'm not a little girl anymore. I'm now a mother who will always have responsibility for this child's life. I guess I've just come to realize a certain phase in my life is over." We all have many "endings" in our life. When people marry, when a baby is born, when the children leave home, when you lose your job, when your health fails, or when a loved one dies, something ends. Before we rush on to the new beginning that we believe God will give, it is important to grieve our losses.

As David remembered Saul and Jonathan, all he spoke about was the good. David's relationship with Saul had not been all positive. There had been much strife and struggle. David had grieved over that, but in this moment and for the public, David wanted to talk about what was good in Saul and Jonathan. When-

225

ever a member of my church dies, I sit down with the family in order to prepare for the service. I ask, "What are the stories you want me to share about your loved one?" I listen for the next hour as family and friends tell me good things about their loved one. It's not that the person was perfect; of course they had their faults, shortcomings, weaknesses, and struggles. It is important for them to deal with those, but at this moment of loss, they look into the person's life and see what was good. That's what David was doing with Saul and Jonathan.

Endings are not always easy. As people of faith we believe that after we grieve, it is God alone who gives us the gift of a new beginning. (Robert Long)

# GRACIOUS GIVING

## 2 CORINTHIANS 8:7-15

Although our text begins in verse 7, the larger context demands careful attention to the first part of the chapter as well. Paul opens by sharing news of the grace of the Macedonian churches. While struggling themselves, "their abundant joy and their extreme poverty have overflowed in a wealth of generosity on their part" (2 Corinthians 8:2). Paul continues that they gave voluntarily. He also lays out two principles for spiritual stewardship and generosity. First, "they gave themselves first to the Lord" (2 Corinthians 8:5). Second, they gave of themselves to others. This forms the crucial backdrop for the passage which begins in verse 7 with the plea that the Corinthians themselves should excel in "this generous undertaking."

Although verse 8 opens with the caution that the offering for others is not a command, Paul nonetheless states it in the strongest language. It is a "testing." Verse 9 heightens this sense of expectancy when Paul moves to exhortation using the grace of the Lord as a model for the Corinthian church. In almost blunt terms, the self-offering of Christ is to become a model for our financial offering toward others. Verse 10 returns to the theme of verse 8 in stating that this is only his opinion. However, Paul reinforces that it is a strong opinion that this work, so nobly begun, must now be completed.

Verse 11 introduces a new theme. Here, Paul explicitly states that one should give in accordance with his or her means. With verse 12, he returns us again to the theme that joyful, willful giving reflects one's commitment to Christ and a commitment to God's people. In a larger sense, this section of the passage invites us to have our deeds match our words. In the more colloquial phrase, we might say, "Put your money where your mouth is." Paul does so in the context of understanding that gracious giving is evaluated not on the basis of the amount given, but rather on the connection between the spirit of giving and the resources one has to offer. Verse 15 drives this point home. " 'The one who had much did not have too much, and the one who had little did not have too little' " (v. 15). Because the Corinthians have an abundance to share, they are expected as a faithful people to help their brothers and sisters in Jerusalem. It should be noted further that verse 15 is a quotation from Exodus 16:18.

Taken as a whole, Paul makes a strong, though not commanding, plea for the voluntary, joyful support of the needs of the poor beyond the local community of faith. The Christian's duty is not merely to one's own circle of friends or church community. Christian duty reaches to the wider world. The Gentile Christians of Corinthians are called to help the Jewish Corinthians of Jerusalem because of the abundance of God's gifts and, in so doing, are to use Christ as the model, giving according to their means in faithfulness to the work of the Lord.

Choices for freedom in ordinary lives are frequently, perhaps constantly, connected to money. The instruction to the Lord to those of us who live in the abundance of Western civilization is gripping. Our abundance is to be used to meet the needs of others. The gifts God has given us are not to control us, but to graciously be used as the Lord graciously gave of himself in the love and care of the poor and the needy. (Mike Lowry)

## GETTING IN TOUCH

### MARK 5:21-43

A woman gave a shabbily dressed stranger a $20 bill and said, "Don't despair." The next day the man handed her a wad of money. "What's that for?" she asked. He replied, "That's the money you won. In the second race Don't Despair paid 7 to 1."

Mark's Gospel is a gospel about and for those who despair. *Gospel* means "Good News," which is what despairing people need most.

The Scripture presents a woman who is in despair. She has three strikes against her. First, she's a woman in a culture where many doors are shut to women. Second, she's been ritually unclean for twelve long years. Those whom she touches also become unclean, so she's socially isolated. Her self-image must be very low. For her, as for us, self-image is destiny.

Jonathan Butler studied inner city students using art as a tool. When he asked a little boy named Wayne to draw a picture of himself and his family, Wayne drew a row of faceless triangles. Butler asked, "Can you draw me?" Wayne drew a man with a carefully detailed body and face. This kind of artwork is typical of children who live in the inner city. They see themselves as face-less beings without bodies but have exalted concepts of people they consider prosperous suburbanites. How would this woman with a flow of blood have drawn herself?

The woman has a third strike against her. She's broke. She has spent all of her money on medical treatment. Many of us can sympathize with her. How can she get the healing she needs? She can get it, she believes, by touching someone who has the power to heal. Maybe she needs only to touch the fringe of Jesus' cloth-ing. For her, a nobody, to touch Jesus would be like a woman of the working class touching the Queen of England. It's just not done!

Touch must be very important to her. Touching has a healing power, and is most powerful for those who feel untouchable. We humans *require* touch.

Alongside this need is another: our need as broken, unre-deemed mortals to be touched by God. Michelangelo's God reaches out to touch Adam across the ceiling of the Sistine Chapel. It's the moment of creation. Creation and healing are much alike: One brings life, the other *new* life. Each depends on the touch of God.

Mark says that the woman tells Jesus "the whole truth." Like Zacchaeus and many others, she spills out her story to Jesus. All of us have a story. It's the story of our trials, disappointments, and aspirations. Jesus has the courtesy to listen to our stories. Listening is a form of touching. It's one of the ways that Jesus engages us.

Jesus says, "Daughter, your faith has made you well" (v. 34). For Mark, *faith* is the way people are drawn into the new age. We don't need a lot, but we must have some. Faith is our openness to let God into our lives. It's the contribution that *we* must make.

When people open up and are touched by God, changes appear. First, there's a new, more positive self-image. Second, there's the discovery of community—an intimate community where people call us names like "daughter." Third, the healed are empowered, even compelled to reach out and touch others. Our tradition has a name for this process: *salvation*. It's what happens when the divine and the human touch.

What part of you is broken or unredeemed? Where do you hurt? Are you ready to be healed? For some of us it's time to reach out and touch Christ's garment as he passes by. Christ will know it if we do, and Christ will bless us as he did our dear sister! (Sandy Wylie)

# REFLECTIONS

# JULY

**Reflection Verse:** *"There was a Levite, a native of Cyprus, Joseph, to whom the apostles gave the name Barnabas (which means 'son of encouragement')."* (Acts 4:36)

Something of a miracle has occurred around the church where I am pastor. Over the last several years, five persons from this congregation have surrendered to the call to ministry. We had not had a person enter the ordained ministry in about a decade. Yet, five have surrendered in a matter of thirty months.

Each of the individuals' calls has been distinctive. The first fought the call for years, but finally said yes to God's invitation to attend God as a pulpit servant. Our church judicatory assigned him to a small church thirty miles or so west of here. He preached for a full year before cancer struck him down as he was "ratcheting it up" for the Lord. A second individual replaced the first at the small church on an interim basis. He functioned so well that he was assigned to a new church that included more responsibilities. The third person has now taken the pulpit in the same small church. Another candidate is a young woman, nurtured in the life of this congregation since her birth. A fifth person spoke to me recently about his call—stifled for nearly forty years. Thus the path of each person varied, but God led each to respond to God's call. Each person will make or has made a significant contribution to the Body of Christ that we call the church.

Whenever someone tells me that they are answering the call to the ordained ministry I tremble slightly. The reason, of course, is that I know what they are in for. In the middle years of ministry, we look back effortlessly to recollect our mistakes. It is easier still to second guess ourselves and suggest in silence, "If I had only made a better decision here or made a healthier choice there."

Nonetheless, I do believe that the Spirit of God does work in us and on us. As a pastor to persons answering the call, I feel a great burden for these people. Believe it or not, the aspiring candidates for ministry all seem to think that those already engaged in the full-time ministry somehow understand how God calls us—and why. Consequently, they ask deep and often thoughtful questions.

In reflecting on my own ministry, I asked the same kinds of questions of people whom I respected and whom I believed could help shed light on the mysterious call of God. Then I listened with care. Several older pastors said that ministry is a much more difficult call now than it was twenty or thirty years ago. The church expects the local preacher to be an expert in homiletics and biblical studies—that is a given. But now, congregations expect pastors to be proficient in pastoral counseling, long-range planning, finance, new member recruitment, building maintenance, personnel issues, worship, and music. They also want someone who can help them discipline their children and themselves. Several years ago, a congregational leader asked me, "Preacher, I drink too much. What should I do?" I was tempted to simply say, "Stop!" Add to these duties and expectations the proclivity for modern Americans to sue for incompetence or sexual harassment (and pastors have a dependable recipe for failure before anyone "opens the chute"). Older ministers say they are pleased that the high expectations people placed on them were at least reasonable. Thus, what do we tell those people entering the ministry?

After thinking long and hard about this issue, I have hit upon something that helps me beyond measure. When a word of encouragement comes my way, rare as it may be, I use it as fuel for months. When we think of an encouraging word, we think of God's grace mediated through another person. There is no more welcome gift to receive. Moreover, if encouragement is a welcome gift to receive, then surely encouragement is not a difficult gift to bestow.

In the story of Scripture, Barnabas is an encouraging biblical character. Barnabas's first act, as recorded in Acts, was to share the bounty of his sold property with the Jerusalem church. As we all know generous and cheerful givers are among the most encouraging people we ever encounter in church. Of all the complainers I have encountered, few are generous givers. There seems to be a direct correlation between how much someone gives to God's realm through the ministries of the church and the amount of complaining they do. Barnabas put his money where his mouth was. Luke contrasts Barnabas's encouraging behavior with that of Ananias and Sapphira who show us how misused money can be deadly.

Barnabas always seemed to be in the shadow of Paul. Paul was a natural born leader, but without Barnabas's steady and encouraging behavior it is possible that Paul would have never even encountered the Jerusalem apostles. By his steady and unyielding demeanor, Barnabas convinced the disciples in Jerusalem—those afraid of Paul—that Paul was okay. Luke tells us, "Barnabas took him, brought him to the apostles, and described for them how on the road he had seen the Lord, who had spoken to him, and how in Damascus he had spoken boldly in the name of Jesus" (Acts 9:27). So Barnabas became an advocate for Paul. Barnabas's action was pure encouragement.

In sensing how we can best help our brothers and sisters, the most faithful and useful thing we can do is offer encouragement for the ministry. Ministry is hard and often lonely. Ministry calls forth a multitude of diverse talents. Unfortunately, it is easy to get discouraged. Perhaps this is true because so many are in need of God's help, and God often mediates through the office of pastor. Yet, do many pastors have a pastor? This pastoral function is one we can offer. An encouraging pastor is a too-rare thing to find. However, when we find this encouraging pastor it is like the treasure of which Jesus spoke when he said, " 'The kingdom of heaven is like treasure hidden in a field, which someone found and hid; then in his joy he goes and sells all that he has and buys that field' " (Matthew 13:44). A simple word of encouragement to our colleagues in the ordained ministry is like finding a wonderful treasure quite without price. (David Mosser)

# JULY 6, 2003

## *Fourth Sunday After Pentecost*

---

**Worship Theme:** On our life's journey of faith, God's grace arms us with a spirit of wisdom. A wise heart and the truth are sufficient weapons against evil for those who follow Jesus.

---

**Readings:** 2 Samuel 5:1-5, 9-10; 2 Corinthians 12:2-10; Mark 6:1-13

**Call to Worship (Psalm 48:1-8)**

*Leader:*    Great is the LORD and greatly to be praised in the city of our God.

*People:*    **His holy mountain, beautiful in elevation, is the joy of all the earth, Mount Zion, in the far north, the city of the great King.**

*Leader:*    Within its citadels God has shown himself a sure defense.

*People:*    **Then the kings assembled, they came on together.**

*Leader:*    As soon as they saw it, they were astounded; they were in panic, they took to flight; trembling took hold of them there, pains as of a woman in labor,

*People:*    **As when an east wind shatters the ships of Tarshish.**

*Leader:*    As we have heard, so have we seen in the city of the LORD of hosts, in the city of our God,

*All:*    **Which God establishes forever.**

**Pastoral Prayer:**

Gracious Lord God, as we worship you this day send your spirit of truth and mercy into our midst so that we too can become more faithful and loving in your holy service. Let us experience some of the revelation of your love of which the apostle Paul speaks when he writes that the Lord said, "My grace is sufficient for you, for power is made perfect in weakness" (2 Corinthians 12:9). Help us, Lord, find assurance in this kind of grace. Send it not only upon us individuals gathered here in the name of Jesus but also, we pray, that you send your spirit on our whole assembly. May your salvation not only be for some of us, O Lord, but may your salvation be for *all* of us. Let the spirit of truth and love convict each of us to a new way of living, loving, and learning as disciples of the one in whose name we always pray, Jesus Christ. Amen. (David Mosser)

# SERMON BRIEFS

## WITH GOD EXPECT THE UNEXPECTED

### 2 SAMUEL 5:1-5, 9-10

Led by the spirit, Samuel came to Bethlehem in search of the person God had chosen to be the new king of Israel (1 Samuel 16). God told Samuel that the next king would come from the family of Jesse. So Samuel invited Jesse to come, and Samuel offered a sacrifice with Jesse's family. When the eldest son passed before Samuel he was tall and good-looking, but God told Samuel, "That's not the right one." Seven sons came before Samuel, yet he never felt God's Spirit move within him. Finally Samuel said, "Are all your sons here?" And Jesse said that his youngest son was out taking care of the sheep. And Samuel said, "We will not sit down until he comes here" (1 Samuel 16:11). When David came into their presence, Samuel knew that this was the one and he anointed him to be Israel's next king.

In the second chapter of 2 Samuel David had been anointed king by the leaders of Judah. But now in the fifth chapter, we read how David is going to be anointed by the leaders of the northern tribes of Israel so that David becomes the king of a united Israel. In the tenth verse we read, "And David became greater and greater." This really is the culmination of the story of how David moved from being the eighth child, the youngest in the family, to becoming the greatest of kings. There are two things we need to see.

First, it had not been a straight path to glory for the Lord's anointed. David may have been called by God but his life would still have plenty of ups and downs. As a young boy he would go and volunteer in Saul's army to fight the giant Goliath. With just a sling and five smooth stones, David would defeat the giant and bring a great victory to Israel. Yet before too long, Saul would turn on David and David would have to flee for his life. David would be considered an outlaw and a fugitive from Israel and have to go and live with the Philistines. We are reminded that simply because God leads our lives, it does not mean all will go smoothly. It is easy to see times when we seek to follow Christ in faith and things go wonderfully; yet other times difficult situations arise that can cause us great pain. But it is as people of faith, that during those difficult times, we do not give into despair. We continue to hope because we believe we are seeking God's will for our lives.

Second, the author of 2 Samuel wants to be clear that "David became greater and greater" because "the LORD, the God of hosts, was with him" (v. 10). We believe today that the Lord of Hosts is always with us! But the question is, *Are we open to listening and experiencing God's grace?* Up to this point David seems very genuine in seeking to follow God's will for his life, but there will come a time in David's reign when he will choose to follow his own way rather than listening to God. God had asked David to be "the shepherd of Israel," but the time would come when David would begin to live for himself.

The promise is that God will lead all of us and use us in a meaningful way. We will be the people of hope because we know that in good times and in hard times "The Lord, the God of Hosts" will be with us! (Robert Long)

# SUFFICIENT GRACE

## 2 CORINTHIANS 12:2-10

As a number of scholars suggest, this strange, perhaps autobiographical passage toward the close of 2 Corinthians ought to be treated with reverence. "I know a person in Christ," Paul writes. Is he speaking of himself? Or is this strange third-person recitation perhaps, as some have suggested, merely a way of laying aside any importance attached to special claims of revelation? It is hard to know. However, the reference to fourteen years ago in the opening phrase of this chapter ("It is necessary to boast") seems to indicate that this is Paul's autobiographical claim to his own mystical experience of the presence of Christ. In doing so, he undoubtedly puts himself on common footing with those he critiques so sternly in this epistle.

Whatever one's experience of revelation, the true point is driven home at the close of verse 5, that he "will not boast, except of my weaknesses." Paul will not allow individual claims of visions or revelations to substitute for the gospel of God's grace.

In verse 7, Paul emphasizes this by sharing his own experience of a thorn in his flesh to "keep me from being too elated." Much has been made of what this thorn in the flesh is. All such speculation misses the real focus of the passage. Paul does not write about it explicitly because his point is that his boasting is not in his own strength (even in overcoming the thorn in the flesh) but in God. Thus, verse 8 is given to drive home the central thrust of the text. "My grace is sufficient for you, for power is made perfect in weakness." The number *three* is of special significance because the ancient world asserted that no one could pray in vain to God three times in succession. Thus, Paul's threefold request reflects God's answer. God's grace is sufficient! This points to the truth that Paul's prayer is answered, not in the removal of the thorn but in the grace of God. God's radically free, forgiving, and redemptive love—and nothing else—is Paul's strength.

It is significant here that power and grace are synonymous in this passage. Power comes from Christ, not from our own goodness or greatness, our own eloquence or wisdom, our own courage or moral integrity. Thus, the great claim of verse 9 is established when Paul writes, "I will boast all the more gladly of my weaknesses, so that the power of Christ may dwell in me." Verse 10*b* in effect seals this conviction of boasting in weakness to lift up the sufficiency of God's grace: "For whenever I am weak, then I am strong."

In a day of televangelists and great claims of human glory, the truth of this passage forces us to reflect on our own false attempts to boast of our accomplishments rather than rest on the sufficiency of God's grace. We live in an age in which grace itself is distorted into cheap grace—pointless, meaningless, worthless. We live with the curse of distorted grace leading us to boast in our own accomplishments and to think that God exists to provide for our own needs, even at the expense of others. Paul would attack all such false claims and escort us back into the hands of a loving God. When we are weak, then we turn to God. When we are vulnerable, then we are open to love. When we are in need, then we are open to serve. When we are humble, then we most profoundly experience the presence of God's graceful love. God's power is made perfect in our weakness. (Mike Lowry)

# ARE WE ABLE?

## MARK 6:1-13

In our text Jesus calls his disciples and sends them on a mission. We read Mark's story with care because it typifies the mission of the church in all ages. Jesus instructs his followers to cast out evil spirits. Our doing battle with evil sounds like a tough job, and it is! How do we feel about our mission? Are we up to it?

Our answer probably depends on our assessment of the powers of good and evil in the world. During the twentieth century the pendulum swung to both extremes. The 1890s launched a two-decade time of wild optimism. There was widespread confidence that good had gained the upper hand. Christians were busily building the kingdom of God and welcoming what would surely be "the Christian Century." Ralph Waldo Trine launched the "positive thinking" movement. Katharine Lee Bates wrote a popular hymn containing the words "America! America! God mend thine every flaw." America's few remaining flaws could be fixed! Such was the spirit of the age.

Then there was a sudden, chilling change. It was caused most conspicuously by World War I. Optimism crumbled. The powers of evil seemed to be in control. Writers like William Butler Yeats rendered an entirely different assessment of the relative power of good and evil. In his poem "The Second Coming," Yeats portrayed a world in which evil had the upper hand. He died in 1939 as the worst atrocities of the century were barely getting underway!

Neither extreme of the last century serves us well at present. What serves us best is the Bible, which gives a balanced, truthful assessment of good and evil. It doesn't leave us in a fool's paradise or in a gloomy valley.

Mark is realistic about the power of evil. For him, Jesus is primarily a battler with evil. The first chapter includes several confrontations with evil spirits. Mark summarizes Jesus' ministry in 1:39: "He went throughout Galilee, proclaiming the message in their synagogues and casting out demons."

Mark is clear that evil is entrenched in our world. It's around us and in us! We should have no illusions. However, for Mark evil doesn't have ultimate power. There's something stronger. The New Testament calls it "the power of God," and it's unleashed in the ministry of Jesus.

*Tass* reported the strange case of Olga Frankevich. Olga fled the Soviet police in 1947 during a Stalinist purge. She eventually emerged from a house in the western Ukraine, where she had hidden under a bed for 45 years. Can you imagine hiding under a bed for 45 years? Olga reminds us of people in our churches who live timid lives, never aware that the power God offers them far exceeds the powers that harass them!

A man fulfilled the dream of a lifetime. He bought a Rolls Royce. As he was driving home, it hit him: He'd failed to learn the car's horsepower. He went back and asked the salesman, who said, "I've never been asked. I'll investigate." Failing to find the answer, the salesman wrote to London. Back came a letter. On the page was but one word: ADEQUATE.

I can see it now. A great church at (your address) in (your town) writes a letter to God: "Dear God, we want to attempt great things for you this year. But first we need to know how much power you're going to give us, so we know what to count on." We send the letter. Here comes a letter carrier with a letter. It's from God. We gather around and open it. The message says, "My power is adequate." (Sandy Wylie)

# JULY 13, 2003

## *Fifth Sunday After Pentecost*

---

**Worship Theme:** In the life of each disciple, moments occur when we must stand for the truth of Christ against the adversaries of God and God's people. God will vindicate those who stand for the truth.

---

**Readings:** 2 Samuel 6:1-5, 12*b*-19; Ephesians 1:3-14; Mark 6:14-29

### Call to Worship (Psalm 24:1-6)

*Leader:*   The earth is the LORD's and all that is in it, the world, and those who live in it;

***People:***   **For he has founded it on the seas, and established it on the rivers.**

*Leader:*   Who shall ascend the hill of the LORD? And who shall stand in his holy place?

***People:***   **Those who have clean hands and pure hearts, who do not lift up their souls to what is false, and do not swear deceitfully.**

*Leader:*   They will receive blessing from the LORD, and vindication from the God of their salvation.

***People:***   **Such is the company of those who seek him, who seek the face of the God of Jacob.**

### Pastoral Prayer:

O God, the Great Provider for God's people, we worship you today in a joyful spirit. We thank you for your everlasting grace that we find most fully in our Lord Jesus Christ. Help us reflect our deep thanksgiving for your mercy toward us in tangible ways. Let us give drink to the thirsty and food to the hungry. Make us attentive to the needs of those alienated, lonely, and bereft of human compassion. Make us the living proof that your Word has broken into our world. Make us the people who live out the words of Jesus in our world. Jesus spoke kind words to the aging and to children. May we also speak words of value and acceptance to those whom Christ valued and accepted. O Lord, help us learn a giving spirit from Jesus who taught that it is more blessed to give than to receive. Make us one with each other and unify our fellowship. In Jesus' name we pray. Amen. (David Mosser)

# SERMON BRIEFS

## LORD OF THE DANCE

### 2 SAMUEL 6:1-5, 12b-19

It is here in the sixth chapter that we read about one of the most significant events in the history of Israel. After conquering the city, David moved the Ark of the Covenant to Jerusalem. You remember how it was the ark that went before the people of Israel in the wilderness leading them towards the promised land and a new day. The ark was a symbol of God's presence. The people of Israel believed that their God, Yahweh, was the one and only true God. God could not be seen, and one of the commandments was that you should never make a graven image of God.

Yet the people of Israel needed to feel that God was near, so the Ark of the Covenant became the symbol of God's dwelling place. With the Ark of the Covenant they knew that God's presence was near. And that's why the ark was used to lead the people through the wilderness because it was said that God was leading the people to the promised land. When David moved the Ark of the Covenant into his new capital city of Jerusalem, he was making the statement that God now dwells in Jerusalem. Since God now dwelt in Jerusalem, the City of David, David was able to solidify the claim to be God's chosen one.

Like David, we have discovered that we need God's presence in our lives. If we are going to fulfill God's mission for us, then we have to experience communion with God. We experience God's presence through worship, study, and fellowship. Each of these things would ultimately take place in the temple that Solomon would build to house the Ark of the Covenant. Although we certainly understand that God's presence does not simply dwell in Jerusalem, the question remains, *Are we disciplined and intentional in our desire to open ourselves to God's presence now?*

Because David believed that God's presence dwelt in Jerusalem and would guide his kingship, David was singing and dancing for joy in front of the Ark of the Covenant. Sometimes we forget that the appropriate response to God's presence in our lives is one of singing and joy. During the Middle Ages with the growth of the monastic movement, Rome put out an edict that the way to act holy was to always dress in brown or black, to walk with one's hands folded, to always look at your feet, never to speak unless you were spoken to and only then in quiet and controlled tones. Without realizing it, we have come to believe that that's what it means to be religious. Many times, in our own mind, that's how we imagine Jesus acting. We forget that Jesus attended a wedding feast, changing the water into wine to keep the party going (John 2:1-11). We forget how David went before the Ark of the Covenant singing and dancing for joy. To all those who followed the Ark into Jerusalem, David gave a piece of bread and meat and raisins. They had a party.

We, too, have been invited to the party. When we open our hearts to experience the presence of Christ, then we, too, shall feel like singing and dancing. (Robert Long)

# DEVELOPING A POSITIVE SELF-IMAGE

## EPHESIANS 1:3-14

Why is it that so many Christians suffer from low self-esteem? Can you imagine Jesus having a poor self-image? Of course not. Neither does God want you to loathe yourself.

People have low self-esteem because they have not been able

to believe and receive the good news that the Bible says about them. People always act consistently with the way they view themselves.

First, Paul writes that you are a "saint." Saints are not perfect people. There are no perfect people (Romans 3:23). We all need to agree with God about the ways in which we have "missed the mark" and receive the cleansing power of God's forgiveness (1 John 1:8-9). But we also need to think of ourselves as saints. Remember: We act consistently with the way we view ourselves. So then, recognize your righteousness. "Consider yourselves dead to sin and alive to God in Christ Jesus" (Romans 6:11).

Second, Paul says you are spiritually blessed. Nothing that love can give you has been withheld from you (2 Peter 1:3). Nothing you need has been overlooked (Philippians 4:13). Paul does not say that one day God is going to bless you. He does not promise that you are going to receive part of what you need. He says God "has blessed us in Christ with every spiritual blessing" (v. 3). And when did God bless you? Paul says God "chose us in Christ before the foundation of the world" (v. 4). Before God created the universe, God had blessing you in mind! Can you believe that? Whatever you need in order to live the Christian life is within you because Christ lives in you. Rely on the spiritual resources that God says are within you.

Third, you are accepted in the beloved. Our relationship is not based simply on our acceptance of Jesus Christ. It is based on Christ's acceptance of us. We have experienced "adoption as his children" (v. 5). Think of yourself as an imperfect child in an orphanage. Jesus comes in, looks at you, loves you, and adopts you as his child.

*Accepted* is one of the most beautiful words in the English language. We all long to be accepted. But if you look for your acceptance from the people around you, your life is going to a roller-coaster ride. You are going to suffer from "the yo-yo syndrome." You will bounce back and forth between pride and depression because each person you meet is going to have a different view of you. Paul Tillich was right when he said that the task of the Christian is to "accept our acceptance." You've made it. You're in.

Fourth, you are forgiven. When you ask God to forgive you, then there is a sense in which God does forgive you. That is right.

You were forgiven two thousand years ago (Colossians 2:13-14). When you ask for forgiveness, you are only accessing what has been there since Jesus died on the cross. God's grace has been "lavished on us" in Christ Jesus our Lord.

Finally, you are sealed by the Holy Spirit. In the ancient world official documents were sealed. The seal is like branding; it is a mark of ownership. This seal is our assurance that God will not change God's mind about us (John 10:29; 17:9-15; Romans 8:35-39). Paul also described the Holy Spirit, who lives in us, as a "pledge" that the eternal promises made to us are true. (Jim Jackson)

# RISKY BUSINESS

## MARK 6:14-29

This story of John the Baptizer's execution prefigures the story of Jesus' execution. Both stories exemplify how the world receives God's messengers. "Exhibit A" in this discussion is composed of the prophets of Israel. Nobody liked the prophets! The *kings* didn't like them. Ahab's reaction to Elijah in 1 Kings 18:17 is typical. The kings were always doing wicked things. Consequently, prophets automatically brought them bad news. The *people* didn't like prophets either. Read Jeremiah 37–38, if you need evidence.

It's clear: To be God's messenger is to meet opposition. We need to know that living a life for Jesus Christ is risky business. The road is sometimes no smoother for us than it was for Jesus.

Reading this story of John's execution is like reading the morning newspaper. The characters are just like people we know. They represent the cold, hard world. There are three conspirators. First is King Herod Antipas, ruler of Galilee. As a typical king, he's arrogant and immoral. Whatever he wants, he takes—including Herodias, his brother Philip's wife.

Let's not work up any sympathy for Herodias. She *willingly* leaves Philip for Herod. As the story unfolds, her wickedness only multiplies. When John denounces her sin in marrying Herod, she resolves to kill him, making her the second conspirator. She's happy to use her daughter and husband as well as *murder* to get whatever she wants.

The third character is the royal daughter. Biblical manuscripts are unclear as to her name. Josephus, the historian, says it's Salome. We're not told what kind of dance Salome dances, but speculation has abounded. Some have characterized it as a dance of seven veils. Art, music, literature, and cinema have portrayed Salome as the child from hell.

So there you have it: three characters who are going to determine the fate of God's messenger. How would you like to have *your* fate in *their* hands? They represent the world—the ways of power and sin—and anyone who gets in their way is expendable.

Herod is the one who actually has the power to execute. Here's where we really see the parallel between John's death and Jesus' death. Both John and Jesus are condemned by a person of authority—Herod in John's case and Pilate in Jesus' case. Neither authority wants to kill God's messenger. In fact, both have respect and even fear for the messenger. But both rulers are weaklings; they get pushed into it. Both fear others more than they fear God. Rulers are usually willing to sacrifice people in order to maintain power.

Mark makes an important statement by the context in which he places this story. He sandwiches it between Jesus' sending out of the disciples to preach (Mark 6:6b-13) and their subsequent return (Mark 6:30). He's showing how the world receives God's messengers. Since you and I as Christians are messengers *by definition*, we'd better pay attention!

Nothing can spare us messengers from evil rulers. In fact, evil will track us down, even in the most sacred places. Archbishop Thomas à Becket (Dec. 29, 1170) in England and Archbishop Oscar Romero (March 24, 1980) in El Salvador were murdered in their own sanctuaries for opposing rulers. Similar stories abound.

We must never suppose that the world will automatically congratulate us for telling the truth or doing the right thing. God's messengers are always up against the indifference and evil of self-centered people.

Good news! Even in the face of grim realities like these, there's always reason to rejoice. The world can nail down God's messengers, but in the end the nails won't hold. *God* always has the last word. When the world is busy being the world, God is busy being God. And for that we say, Praise be to God! (Sandy Wylie)

# JULY 20, 2003

*Sixth Sunday After Pentecost*

---

**Worship Theme:** Even in the midst of momentary rest, we know that we, like Jesus, face a world of sickness and alienation. For us the world's needs are overwhelming evidence of the gospel's value to God's creation.

---

**Readings:** 2 Samuel 7:1-14*a*; Ephesians 2:11-22; Mark 6:30-34, 53-56

### Call to Worship (Psalm 89:20-26)

| | |
|---|---|
| *Leader:* | I have found my servant David; with my holy oil I have anointed him; |
| *People:* | **My hand shall always remain with him; my arm also shall strengthen him.** |
| *Leader:* | The enemy shall not outwit him, the wicked shall not humble him. |
| *People:* | **I will crush his foes before him and strike down those who hate him.** |
| *Leader:* | My faithfulness and steadfast love shall be with him; and in my name his horn shall be exalted. |
| *People:* | **I will set his hand on the sea and his right hand on the rivers.** |
| *All:* | **He shall cry to me, "You are my Father, my God, and the Rock of my salvation!"** |

**Pastoral Prayer:**

Glorious God, who builds divine dominions from the lives of your consecrated people, consecrate us for service to your realm this day. In our hymns, prayers, and preached word, speak again to us those wonderful words of life. Give us the ears to hear your word and the will to follow your paths. We know that the way is sometimes not easy, and often we are afraid. Yet in you, O God, is a power so deep and so wide that it ferries us along the rough currents as if they were smooth waters. Make us as our forebears. They knew of your great powers to cure the sick and feed the hungry. Feed that great spiritual hunger of our souls and bring to us a ready acceptance of the yoke of discipleship that you place upon us. Give us courage to bear up for the sake of the gospel. We pray this in the holy name of Jesus, our Messiah and Lord. Amen. (David Mosser)

# SERMON BRIEFS

## WHO IS IN CONTROL?

### 2 SAMUEL 7:1-14*a*

David has come a long way from being a shepherd boy in Bethlehem and the youngest of eight sons of Jesse to being the king of Israel who reunited the northern and southern kingdoms, established the capital of Jerusalem, and moved the Ark of the Covenant into the city. He has built himself a great palace, and without a doubt, he is the greatest king in the history of Israel. In this seventh chapter the writer tells us that the Lord gave David rest from all his enemies. So one day he looked out of his palace onto the tent that housed the Ark of the Covenant, and he thought, "I need to build a temple for the Lord." He called in his prophet Nathan and asked him what he thought about the temple idea, and Nathan immediately said, "I think it's great!" That night, when Nathan went home to sleep, God spoke to Nathan: "Today you acted more like a politician than a prophet. You didn't take the time to ask me what I thought." Thus, God gave Nathan a different answer to give to David. The next morning Nathan told David what God really thought.

God said, "I've never lived in a house but rather I've been able to go wherever I wanted, whenever I wanted." It's important to remember that a tent was a symbol for a nomadic life. Nomads are always on the move, no one controls them, and they go where they want, when they want. The question is, *why did David want to build a temple?* Was it out of a love and dedication to God or was it that David now understood that if one builds a temple and puts the Ark of the Covenant in the temple, then one claims that God is always in Jerusalem?

Often this is our great temptation. We want to control God. We want to claim that we have all the truth, and we can always predict and explain what God does and why. For centuries Christians have fought among themselves claiming that they have the whole truth. These people believe that others who think differently are wrong. However, John Wesley said that no one has all the truth. God is bigger than us all. How do finite creatures wrap our minds around the infinite? We can't! With God there must always be mystery. God said, "I have taken you from being a shepherd boy to being a king. You will not build me a house but rather I will build you a house" (or dynasty).

God said, "I will establish the throne of . . . [your] kingdom forever. . . . I will not take my steadfast love from [you]" (vv. 13, 15). Many scholars say that this may be the most significant story in all of the Hebrew Scriptures, for it is here that God declares his unconditional love. God is not saying I love you *if*, but rather I *will* love you. Period. The Protestant reformers pointed to this passage and deduced the doctrine of "justification by faith." They understood that no matter what we do, God will not stop loving us. These reformers suggested that within each of us there is something of value, and that if we turn again to God, then God will be there to help us. God shows his steadfast love by sending his son through the line of David. Jesus, born in Bethlehem of the lineage of David, comes to show again how God never abandons us. (Robert Long)

# THE PATH TO PERFECT PEACE

## EPHESIANS 2:11-22

How would you like to have peace—real peace, perfect peace? Paul tells us how *shalom* can be ours.

Paul writes we can have peace with God. Paul writes that we were once "aliens" and "strangers" to God. These are lonely words, aren't they? Do you remember feeling distant, almost at war with God? Do you remember the hopelessness ("without hope") this alienation produced? The good news is that the war ended when Jesus went to the cross. That means God has not been angry with you for two thousand years. The war is over. We were once "far off" but we "have been brought near by the blood of Christ" (v. 13). How do we receive this purchased peace? By having faith that what Jesus did on the cross was for us. Jesus' death was not just for the world; it was for us too (John 3:16; Romans 5:1).

We all remember the story about the development of the Transcontinental Railroad. This story tells us how the Atlantic and Pacific Oceans were connected by a railroad. Can you imagine the effort and coordination this took on both coasts between engineers, financiers, lawyers, real estate buyers, and workers? Finally they said, "It is finished." The Holy One's sovereignty took action to bring reconciliation between God and humanity. When the work of peacemaking was done, Jesus said, "It is finished" (John 19:30). Have you put your whole trust not in the hope of perfect performance but in the reconciliation Jesus accomplished on the cross?

Next Paul writes we can have peace with other people. Paul writes an amazing thing. He writes that when Jesus died on the cross, every dividing wall that separates us from other people was broken down. Think of the dividing walls that exist in our world: race, class, gender, education, language, economic, political, religious, and so forth. We count on these categories to give us a sense of identity, to distinguish us from other people. But think of all the hostility that exists in our world because of these categories. Think of the peace that our world would have if someone removed these walls of hostility.

Jesus did just that on the cross. We are now "one new humanity" through Christ. We are not to think of people in terms of labels any more (Galatians 3:28). Of course, there are differences between us, but there is more that unites us than divides us.

Finally, Paul asserts that we can have peace with ourselves. Our peace comes from belonging to Christ and being part of his great kingdom enterprise. Peace is not merely detachment as some religious groups teach. It is connectedness to the life of God and to the household of faith.

Paul uses an architectural metaphor to describe how important we are to God. He talks about the "holy temple." He says the apostles and prophets are the foundation, Jesus is the corner-stone (the stone that binds all the other stones together), and we are living stones (1 Peter 2:5). We are little temples (1 Corinthians 3:16; 6:19), joined together to completely make up the holy temple of God. We have an important role in the kingdom of God. There is a sense in which God's holy temple would be incomplete without us. Does it not give you peace to know how important you are in God's thinking? (Jim Jackson)

# WHO IN HELL NEEDS A SHEPHERD?

## MARK 6:30-34, 53-56

The Bible compares people to sheep. It's an apt comparison. Sheep may be the most helpless creatures alive. They're vulnerable to parasites and disease. They follow each other almost blindly and are easily panicked by predators. They overeat, lie down, and can't get up. They won't come in out of the rain. Sheep might be extinct except for one thing: They follow their shepherd.

Notice the details of our text. Jesus and the disciples are worn out, so he suggests that they go away to rest. But the crowd is one step ahead. They beat Jesus and the disciples to the retreat site! Jesus can't be pleased; but, as Mark states, "he had compassion for them, because they were like sheep without a shepherd" (v. 34).

Jesus doesn't have compassion because they're poor or sick, but because they're *lost*! Have you ever been lost, I mean good and lost? [Tell your favorite "being lost" story.]

There's also a lostness that has nothing to do with geography. In *Camelot*, King Arthur stares into space and says, "I can think no longer what to do but to ride the tide of events." This is the sort of lostness that says, "I've lost control of my family, my job, my emotions, my life—and I don't know if I can ever find my way." When you feel that way, you start grasping—like this crowd.

While sitting in a New York nightclub, W. H. Auden was overwhelmed with the desperation around him. He jotted these words:

> Faces along the bar
> Cling to their average day:
> The lights must never go out,
> The music must always play,
>
> . . . . . . . . . . . . . . . . . . . . . . . . . . . . . .
>
> Lest we should see where we are,
> Lost in a haunted wood,
> Children afraid of the night
> Who have never been happy or good.

("September 1, 1939," st. 5, from *The Collected Poetry of W. H. Auden* [New York: Random House, 1945], p. 58)

People get lost in haunted woods of their own incompleteness. Like sheep, they're easily misled. Consider nationalism, for example. Demagogues have always known how to exploit people's natural feelings of patriotism. Think about substance abuse and how millions of us have strayed into drug and alcohol addiction. Even religion is abused. Jonestown and Heaven's Gate demonstrate the incredible power of false shepherds.

We humans stray into all kinds of places. We have a name for such places: hell. In *The Great Divorce*, C. S. Lewis suggests that hell is not a place to which people are sent. It's a place where people land through bad choices. Hell is finding ourselves lost in some haunted wood.

I'm gripped by the image of little Virginia Dare, the first English child born in America. When her colony encountered hostile conditions in 1587, they felt that their only hope was for the governor to return to England to get help. It took him three years to get back. He found none of the original settlers. Theirs was the ultimate form of despair: to be lost in a haunted wood and realize that no one is coming.

A classified ad read: "Lost: One dog. Brown hair with mange.

Leg broken. Blind in right eye. Left ear bitten off. Answers to the name Lucky."

Lucky? Of course! That was a lucky dog. He was lucky because, even with all of those things wrong with him, somebody still wanted him and was doing everything to get him back.

Aren't you and I lucky! Jesus told a story about a shepherd who got home with 99 of 100 sheep. We would be satisfied with that, but the shepherd wasn't. God's mathematics is different from ours, and that's incredibly good news. Somebody still wants us. Somebody is trying to get us back. Somebody's coming. Why, I believe, Lucky is our middle name! (Sandy Wylie)

# JULY 27, 2003

*Seventh Sunday After Pentecost*

---

**Worship Theme:** Sometimes our faith is strong; often it is not. Whether strong or weak, Jesus comes to us across our troubled waters.

---

**Readings:** 2 Samuel 11:1-15; Ephesians 3:14-21; John 6:1-21

**Call to Worship (Psalm 14)**

| | |
|---|---|
| *Leader:* | Fools say in their hearts, "There is no God." |
| ***People:*** | **They are corrupt, they do abominable deeds; there is no one who does good.** |
| *Leader:* | The LORD looks down from heaven on humankind to see if there are any who are wise, who seek after God. |
| ***People:*** | **They have all gone astray, they are all alike perverse; there is no one who does good, no, not one.** |
| *Leader:* | Have they no knowledge, all the evildoers who eat up my people as they eat bread, and do not call upon the LORD? |
| ***People:*** | **There they shall be in great terror, for God is with the company of the righteous.** |
| *Leader:* | You would confound the plans of the poor, but the LORD is their refuge. |
| ***People:*** | **O that deliverance for Israel would come from Zion! When the LORD restores the** |

**fortunes of his people, Jacob will rejoice; Israel will be glad.**

**Pastoral Prayer:**

O God of Storm and Rainbow, give us this day your assurance and your love. Remind us that you have loved us with a love that will not let us go. In Jesus Christ, O God, you have proved for all people through all time that you care, nurture, and save your creation. As we move through life, let us be the people you created us to be. Make us loving and caring people after the fashion of Jesus Christ. Jesus came to give us the gift of abundant life. Help us, O Lord, recognize this life, seek this life, and receive this life. Give us a burning passion to reach out to you and exclaim like the five thousand, "This is indeed the prophet who is to come into the world" (John 6:14*b*). Allow us, O God, to hear Jesus' voice as if for the very first time. Let Jesus speak to us the words that lead to life eternal. We pray this in Christ's holy name. Amen. (David Mosser)

# SERMON BRIEFS

## OF CHAOS AND CREATION

### 2 SAMUEL 11:1-15

Inquiring minds want to know: *How did things as they are come to be?* That particular question is the bread and butter of science, of course, and of most psychological inquiry. Biblical scholarship is concerned with such matters, too. There are countless other examples. But the fact is, even we who are nonspecialists ask roughly the same question about our world—its systems, leaders, and stars—and about our own situations and selves. It is uniquely human to ask after the origins of life and of our lives.

Many times, our inquiries are answered with varnished versions of the truth—clichés, propaganda, and spin—especially when it comes to politics and politicians. "Consultants" would convince us, at least until the polls close, that their candidates have never done or said anything that would cast shadows on their character or impugn their leadership. Concerns or accusations are met with lawyering and parsing. No wonder the electorate has become cynical.

How different the biblical testimony! It is often noted that the Bible, unlike much ancient literature and most current public relations, will not spare even its greatest heroes—or us—the painful truth. Note how many preeminent figures are presented in somewhat unflattering terms: Moses is impatient (as well as a murderer), Jonah is defiant, Gideon is cowardly, and David is, well, David. These biblical accounts will not let us imagine that the king is better than he is. There is no "spin" here. In other words, "be sure your sin will find you out" (Numbers 32:23).

The biblical texts tell the truth, and the whole truth, but, that said, these stories do not trade in lurid details. They do not offer scandal for scandal's sake. Nor do they offer simple, arithmetic explanations to complex human equations. In the end, inquiring minds and faithful hearts will be allowed to see that deep ironies and mysteries are involved in all matters of sin and salvation. By these processes God's will is accomplished on earth.

We have, in the text, the beginnings of the "Throne Succession Narrative"; that is, these stories answer questions about how the monarchy came to be. Many scholars date these materials to the time of Solomon, or just after, when such questions would have been common. It is only the latest in a series of texts from Samuel depicting both the changing sociopolitical dynamics in Israel, and how, so soon after the rise of the Davidic line, the seeds were sown for a rapid demise of both David and the united kingdom. These stories are sad and ambiguous. Why did David stay at home when the other kings went out to battle? Was he feeling old? Tired? Worn out? Used up? No longer a fighter but a lover?

What did David see in Bathsheba? Another chance to be young? Another opportunity for conquest? Someone he had to have at any cost and, as Frederick Buechner ruefully notes, the cost would be incredible?

In the movie *Moonstruck*, Olympia Dukakis's character wonders why men have affairs. Her conclusion? "Because they fear death." If that is part of it, David may be "Exhibit A."

There are profound mysteries and deep ironies in this story, not to mention great sin and sparse hope. There also seems little to admire in the human condition. Yet, it is precisely from these "raw" materials—adultery and deception, murder and intrigue—in and through such chaos that God continues working to create a "holy" people. God's task is still in the works. (Thomas Steagald)

# HOW TO PRAY FOR YOUR LOVED ONES

### EPHESIANS 3:14-21

Here is a profound thought: There is a God, and God answers prayer. I believe that when we get to heaven and see things "complete" rather than "in part" (1 Corinthians 13:9-10), we are going to be disappointed that we did not pray more and better. We are never more like God than when we are praying (Romans 8:26-27, 34; Hebrews 7:25).

Paul teaches us in this passage how to pray for our loved ones. Sometimes we say we do not know how to pray because we do not know what God's will is. Well, God's Word is God's will. Would you agree with that? So, why do you not pray Paul's words for your loved ones? You can pray this prayer with confidence and boldness.

Pray, first, that they will have internal power. Do not spend all of your prayer time asking God to provide for your loved ones outwardly—position, power, popularity, prestige, or prosperity. There is nothing wrong with these benefits, but there is something even more important: inner well-being. If you are not strong inwardly, the temptations and pressures of life will cause your life to collapse. Paul wrote that even when "our outer nature is wasting away, our inner nature is being renewed day by day" (2 Corinthians 4:16).

Second, pray that your loved ones will have the indwelling Christ. Remember, these were Christians for whom Paul was praying. The word *dwell* means "to be at home" or "to have undisputed ownership." Paul prayed that Jesus would be given preeminence in their lives, that Christ will be their Lord. This is what our loved ones need more than anything else. They need to have a constant awareness of Jesus as the enthroned King of their lives. They need Jesus' presence, power, and purity reproduced in their lives.

The third thing we need to pray for our loved ones is that they will know God's love. Notice the dimensions of God's love that we should comprehend: its breadth ("world," John 3:16), length ("eternity," Psalm 90:2), height ("If I go up to the heavens, you are there," Psalm 139:8*a* NIV), depth ("if I make my bed in the depths, you are there," Psalm 139:8*b* NIV). We have so many emotional problems in life because we are not rooted and grounded in Christ's love. We think we are loved based on our performance, and this produces anxiety and fear. God's love for you is unconditional.

The final thing Paul writes that we need to pray for our loved ones is that they will experience infinite usefulness. God is able and willing to do more through us than we have ever been bold enough to ask or think (John 14:12-14). Read the account of Moses and the children of Israel in Numbers 11:1-23. Thank God that the Lord's arm is not short. God is able to use you in ways greater than you have ever imagined. Pray this prayer for your loved ones. Pray it boldly. It is God's will for them. (Jim Jackson)

# FEED US, O LORD!

## JOHN 6:1-21

Among Jesus' miracles, this is among the greatest, if not *the* greatest. In personal terms we can believe the healing of individuals had a profound impact not only on the person who received the healing but also on their family members. Walking meant a new life for beggars who were forced into that demeaning task due to a physical disability. Taken altogether, the miracles were about new life. The greatest lesson shown in this miracle is the new life found in trusting God and sharing that which God has shared with us.

The writer of John's Gospel shares his insight into the timing of the miracle. It was close to the time of the festival of Passover. Financially, Passover's implications were much like the time close to Thanksgiving for citizens of the United States. We know a big celebration is coming, and we begin to budget our money in terms of food purchases that we have to make. Some make budgetary decisions based on travel to loved ones' homes. For the crowd following Jesus, their desire was to travel to Jerusalem for the feast and festival of Passover.

We note that Jesus' main concern was for the people's hunger. Jesus asks Philip, "Where are we to buy bread for these people to eat?" John writes that Jesus already knew what he was going to do, but the testing of Philip and the twelve was important. The question seems to be, *Do we care enough to sacrifice from what we have, to care for others?* Immediately Philip's answer is obvious of his concern, for he says, "six months' wages would not buy enough bread for each of them to get a little" (v. 7). The crowd was just too huge. Too many followers and not enough money. Philip has already answered, "no, we cannot possibly care for these people, for we do not have the resources." Andrew says that he knows a boy who showed up with "five barley loaves and two fish" (v. 9). Yet, Andrew knew that that would not be enough among so many people. This already sounds like a finance committee meeting in most churches after a program committee steps forward with a positive and possible new idea.

Nevertheless, Jesus moves ahead. The people are told to sit. The count was about five thousand. Most scholars believe this is a counting of men only so the crowd could have been larger with women and children. The presence of children is evident by the provider of the resource for the miracle, the young boy. There was plenty of grass in the area, so it was a comfortable locale, in which to sit. The Lord Jesus took the loaves and fishes, and gave thanks. With a spirit of thankfulness to God for this blessing small as it was, Jesus distributes food enough for all. How can it be proved that indeed the miracle occurred? That all the people received enough to satisfy their hunger and then filled twelve baskets of leftovers, staggers the imagination. It has all the drama of an Old Testament miracle story exactly like the manna in the desert. Yet, it is the same God. The same God who loves and cares for creation, especially God's creatures, performs a New Testament miracle. The people receive it as a prophetic wonder, "indeed the prophet who is to come into the world" (v. 14*b*). That word spread fast the Gospel tells us. Jesus leaves immediately out of fear that the people would forcibly crown him as king. He withdraws to be alone.

The miracle of the feeding was done to glorify God. It was shared to show that God does indeed care even in situations that seem desperate. In the face of scarcity and hunger, God provided food and plenty of it. Jesus wanted none of the recognition nor anything associated with the miracle. He wanted all the honor to go to God.

As evening comes, the disciples set sail to Capernaum. Jesus, still alone, had not joined them. It is when the boat is three miles out from shore that Jesus appears to them walking on the water and coming near to the boat. The disciples react much in the manner most would react: with fear. Yet even in their fearfulness, Jesus speaks to them a word of peace, "It is I; do not be afraid" (v. 20). With Jesus with them they "immediately" reached the land toward which they were going.

In this one text, two very difficult-to-explain events occur. The multitude is fed with a small offering, and the disciples see Jesus master water in a way that dumbfounds them. Yet, the message is the same. When we allow God to be involved, great things can happen. Yes, not all the time will they be explainable, but they will still be wonderful. They will be signs that indeed God is with us. (Eradio Valverde)

# REFLECTIONS

# AUGUST

**Reflection Verse:** *"God is our refuge and strength, a very present help in trouble. Therefore we will not fear, though the earth should change, though the mountains shake in the heart of the sea." (Psalm 46:1-2)*

"When I was a child, I spoke like a child, I thought like a child," and we started school after Labor Day. This school schedule provided the whole of August for summer vacation in the grand calendaring scheme of things. We would go on our family trips or to summer camp in August in the 1960s with no thought that it might impinge on school days. However, in my part of the country school now begins around the second week in August.

I would guess that several factors come into play when changing the nature of the school calendar. Fewer American school children work on the family farm. Therefore, the late summer harvest is no longer a basis for the school calendars. Another argument that influences the new and more modern school calendar is that most schools have included more breaks. Schools in my area, for example, have a long Christmas break in addition to a winter and spring break. Finally, compared to the time when I attended public schools, the educational "powers that be" in my state have, over the years, increased the number of days necessary to complete a child's educational requirements.

All this talk of change reminds us that occasionally we, by the nature of the culture in which we live, must adjust the ways that we have always done things. I often hear pastors bemoan the lack of desire to change in their congregations, but it is often they who do not like to rock the boat. In many cases, it is the pastor who likes to keep things on an even keel.

Several years ago I learned about the power of change, when I found that by not paying close attention to our culture, I could blunder my way into one mistake after another. I decide to take the Sundays in August off from my regular pulpit duties. In the congregation were about a dozen retired pastors who were all too eager to fill the pulpit in my absence. Five volunteered to preach so I could spend a month reading, writing, and taking a break from my normal preaching schedule.

Later, I discovered that we had more first-time visitors during August than any other one month period. Several years ago, this would have occurred in September, but now it happens in August. Families relocate during the summer months and with the advent of earlier school beginnings, people new to our community sought a church home in August. Although my absence may not have been a factor in their decisions, often people who visit want to hear the senior minister preach. After all, they want to know with whom they will worship on a typical Sunday.

Preachers have a dual task. First we must immerse ourselves thoroughly in the Holy Scriptures. We need to understand what the biblical witness of faith says and how the context of Bible stories, statutes, and ordinances color the implications of sacred texts. Our other task, however, may be just as important. We need to be aware of the world around our congregations. Karl Barth once commented that faithful preachers carry the Bible in one hand and the daily newspaper in the other. I suppose Barth meant that preachers need to not only know the scripture but also understand the world to which holy writ speaks.

While it may be true that "Jesus Christ is the same yesterday and today and forever" (Hebrews 13:8), it is equally true that the world to which the Scripture speaks changes constantly. The Greek pre-Socratic philosopher Heraclitus once said, "It is not possible to step twice into the same river" ("Fragment 91," Heraclitus, in John Bartlett, *Familiar Quotations* [Boston: Little, Brown and Company, 1968] p. 77b). By this he meant that whenever one approaches a river it is different by virtue of the fact that new droplets of water form what appears to be the same river. In other words, everything is in constant flux or change. This may be especially true when we speak of social groupings of people. No matter how similar we look to outsiders, no two groups of people are alike.

Pastors live a balancing act between venerable traditions and the serendipitous unconventional. It is good to remember that a standard Christian doctrine is the unchanging nature of God, hence the reference to Psalm 46:1-2 in the Reflection Verse. Despite Process Theology, which urges deep thought about if and how God changes, for most of us it is a comfort to know that our God resides in a stable status. We can take comfort in knowing that in preaching we help many people cope with the lightning pace of change that swirls around us all. Our task may be to remain humble about what we know or thought we knew long ago. In this humility we continue to learn and grow as Christian leaders. As Plato said: "My child, you are still young, and time as it advances will cause you to reverse many of the opinions you now hold: so wait till then before pronouncing judgment on matters of most grave importance" (G. P. Goold, ed., R. G. Bury, trans., *Plato: Laws, Books VII-XII*, vol. 11 of *The Loeb Classical Library* [Cambridge, Mass.: Harvard University Press, 1999], p. 309). Humility of opinion is a characteristic best worn by servants of Jesus Christ. (David Mosser)

# AUGUST 3, 2003

## *Eighth Sunday After Pentecost*

**Worship Theme:** The epistle summons us "to lead a life worthy of the calling to which [we] have been called" (Ephesians 4:1). Therefore, we examine whether we have responded faithfully to God's claim on us. Have we done the work we were called to do?

**Readings:** 2 Samuel 11:26–12:13*a*; Ephesians 4:1-16; John 6:24-35

### Call to Worship (Psalm 51:1-4, 9-12)

*Leader:*   Have mercy on me, O God, according to your steadfast love; according to your abundant mercy blot out my transgressions.

**People:**   **Wash me thoroughly from my iniquity, and cleanse me from my sin.**

*Leader:*   For I know my transgressions, and my sin is ever before me.

**People:**   **Against you, you alone, have I sinned, and done what is evil in your sight, so that you are justified in your sentence and blameless when you pass judgment.**

*Leader:*   Hide your face from my sins, and blot out all my iniquities.

**People:**   **Create in me a clean heart, O God, and put a new and right spirit within me.**

*Leader:*   Do not cast me away from your presence, and do not take your holy spirit from me.

*People:*    **Restore to me the joy of your salvation, and sustain in me a willing spirit.**

**Pastoral Prayer:**

O Holy God, you call us from our worldly mind-set and give us a task. This task is to be a people who see your glory. We experience this glory each time we turn to you in prayer. You have forgiven us in our weakness and in your mercy. All you ask of us, Lord, is that we live lives that reflect the gospel of Jesus. Help us in our weakness. You know all too well that we are tempted each day, yet by the power of your spirit, you lead us toward your realm. Let us take strength from Jesus as he revealed to us what a person filled with your spirit might become. Help us, we pray, to not only listen to your word as it comes to us in worship but also hear your words of life. As we depart worship, encourage us by the prayers of the saints. Help us, like them, be faithful in each day's trials. In Jesus' name we pray. Amen. (David Mosser)

# SERMON BRIEFS

## WHAT GOES AROUND . . .

### 2 SAMUEL 11:26–12:13*a*

The most astute analysis I ever heard regarding the Nixon Administration was this: "It was characterized by grand vision and petty grievance." This seems an elegy for many things, not least of all the Church.

This description also seems an appropriate interpretation of David's life, as well. At least it rings true to what we see in this story as David's sins are forced into the scorching light of divine judgment.

"The thing that David had done"—namely, his scandalous affair with Bathsheba and the subsequent murder of honorable Uriah—"displeased the Lord" (v. 27*b*). It is a terrifying understatement and the occasion for Nathan's house call on the king. By this time, Uriah is buried. Bathsheba's mourning is over, and David has taken her as his wife.

David's love for Bathsheba seems genuine enough. In fact, in an ironic and cruel tangling of motives, it may be that David acted against Uriah in order to protect Bathsheba from stigmatization and even execution. Now, with the birth of their baby, a boy, perhaps David is hoping that the scandal has blown over, that the battle is won, and that life can return to normal in the royal house. Things seem to be going well enough, until God sends Nathan, who cannot leave well enough alone.

I imagine Nathan as old and bony, with long fingers and a hawk nose. Perhaps, Nathan possesses sharp eyes and a cackling laugh. He may not have looked anything of the sort, but it seems clear that Nathan feared no one but God, especially not an aging and adulterous king to whom he would give no quarter if that were God's verdict. He goes nose to nose with the king, eyeball to eyeball. It is the king who blinks.

Remember the parable: the poor man with a little lamb, more a child or pet than livestock; and the rich man who is loathe to diminish his own flock, so he cruelly takes the poor man's one lamb; and David is furious to hear of such injustice. David proclaims that the man who had done such a thing deserved to die. The irony: David's wrath shows nothing less than his own "grand vision." He really does have a sense of propriety and justice. But when Nathan points his bony finger and says, "Thou art the man" (v. 7a KJV), David surely realized how small and petty he had become.

For if his sins, heinous as they were, were no greater than what many others have committed, his guilt is profounder because of his identity and role. His funeral song for Saul and Jonathan was suddenly a song for himself: How the mighty had fallen. A great man, God's own, diminished almost beyond our ability to look.

The consequences of his sin will be fourfold, grievous, and almost Newtonian: Because he had Uriah killed in war, his own wars will never end; because he destroyed a family, his own family will be continually sundered; as he took another's wife, another will take his wives; and as Uriah was struck down, so shall it happen to Bathsheba's baby. The sins of the father, visited upon the head of the son.

Trapped by Nathan's parable, fallen David does a remarkable thing: He confesses. He does not blame or excuse, but confesses outright. In that confession God exalts him again somewhat. The confession does not change anything—except perhaps for David himself—but his willingness to do so may explain why God chose David over Saul, and why this murderous and adulterous king was yet a man after God's own heart. (Thomas Steagald)

# A FORMULA FOR FELLOWSHIP

## EPHESIANS 4:1-16

Christian unity is a God-given gift. We cannot produce it, but we can lose it. We are responsible for protecting and preserving the unity that God has given us. We are to make "every effort to maintain the unity of the Spirit in the bond of peace" (v. 3). There is nothing sweeter than being among believers where this unity exists (Psalm 133:1). Conversely, there is nothing worse than being around believers where suspicion, accusation, and factionalism prevail.

Unity is not about uniformity, agreeing about everything, or being alike. God does not have a cookie cutter. God's goal is not about stamping us out alike. Our differences are gifts to the Body of Christ. Have you ever been to a symphony? When the members of a symphony are warming up, discordant sounds fill the air. But when the conductor's stick is raised, the musical confusion goes away. We must learn to believe that those believers who disagree with us, who are part of another group, are also part of God's symphony (Mark 9:38-40).

How can we "maintain the unity of the Spirit in the bond of peace"? First, we can learn to love one another. Love is not about how we feel toward people. It is about a decision of the will regarding how we will treat one another. The Scripture is clear that we are to treat each other in a loving way (John 13:35; 1 John 4:20).

The alienation and anger between the various sects of Christianity should be an embarrassment to every Christian. Jesus prayed for the unity of his church (John 17). For the most part, our theological disagreements are but a smoke screen. The real problems between us are about ego, power, and control—the failure to love.

Notice the words used in Ephesians 4:2: "humility and gentleness, with patience, bearing with one another in love." Could these words be used to describe your attitude toward believers of a different faction?

Second, we maintain Christian unity by agreeing in the central truths of the faith and choosing not to be dogmatic about peripheral beliefs. What are the central things about which we are to agree? Paul suggests there is one body (for instance, the Catholic Church), one Spirit, one hope, one Lord (Jesus), one faith, one baptism, one God.

Virtually every denominational group believes in the central truths of the faith as taught in the Apostles' Creed. Most of our disagreements are about style, methods, polity, and peripheral doctrines.

Third, we can maintain the unity of the Spirit by setting one another free to use our gifts in ministry. Each Christian is a minister. The basis of our ministry is not ordination but baptism.

You have gifts for ministry that are unique and God-given. They are not mere talents or abilities; they are supernatural spiritual gifts of grace. We are to use these gifts to "build up the body of Christ" (v. 12).

We do not need more people to serve on committees. We need people who are called to serve and build up the people sitting in the sanctuary at present. The job of pastor-teacher is to help people discover, develop, and deploy their spiritual gifts. (Jim Jackson)

## TIME TO EAT?

### JOHN 6:24-35

Imagine a satisfying meal. It fills your heart and stomach. In Spanish we have a saying, "Panza llena, corazón contento," literally, "full stomach, contented heart." We know that after a full meal we tend to get sleepy. This may have been what happened to the crowd after the miraculous feeding. Jesus and his disciples slipped out across the sea to Capernaum without them noticing. Once they discover this, they make their way to the same place.

They wanted to know how this had been possible. It may have even been a reprimand of the sort, "Teacher, how could you leave us alone?" To their astonishment the honesty of Jesus hits them hard. "You're not looking for me for the right reasons," Jesus says. "You ate your fill of the loaves, and for that reason you have followed me." He knew they had seen a sign that touched them and that they wanted more. They had been nourished physically but missed the spiritual portion altogether. To this Jesus says, "Do not work for the food that perishes, but for the food that endures for eternal life, which the Son of Man will give you" (v. 27).

It took work to follow Jesus. It was work that took this multitude to the mountain to be fed. And it was work getting across the sea to Capernaum. This fit the legal definition of the Hebraic understanding of work. Jesus tells them that the work they should be doing is that which will result in food that endures for eternal life, which the Son of Man (Jesus) can give them. Now they have something to ask for, and they ask, "What must we do to perform the works of God?" (v. 28).

There are two ways to understand this question. One is to ask *how can we do the same things you are doing?* The second is to ask *what is "God work" that gives us this "bread" to which you refer?* Jesus answers both questions. "This is the work of God, that you believe in him whom he has sent." Belief as work. That was Jesus' answer. To have a spiritual certainty in your mind and heart about God and God's son is all the work you have to do. It continues to plague all Christians—from those who think they're not doing enough to those who think they're doing too much. Jesus is telling the well-fed though weary crowd, just believe in what God has done for you through me. Was that enough for the crowd? Is it enough for you? No. There's always at least one more question. This question though also had a demand attached. "What sign are you going to give us then, so that we may see it and believe you? What work are you performing?" (v. 30).

They continue with a comparison from their Bible about how their ancestors had eaten manna in the desert. It was their way of saying, "our ancestors received a sign, what sign will you give us? We must be shown something tangible and believable. If you give us that, we will believe you." Again, the issue of faith and belief. Does eyesight have to be involved in faith in order for the mind and heart to believe? This is an interesting thought, especially since their reference to their ancestors' experience in the desert was a faith reference. No one present during Jesus' time had been present then. They had not seen. They had simply heard and believed. It was taught to them as "written, 'He gave them bread from heaven to eat' " (v. 31). It is then that Jesus shares the teaching of the bread of life. From God comes the bread that gives life. To make the point clearer, Jesus declares, "I am the bread of life. Whoever comes to me will never be hungry, and whoever believes in me will never be thirsty" (v. 35).

God had provided for their physical hunger in a setting where it seems no relief was available. In situations of spiritual drought, God shares fullness of life through Jesus. Spiritually, as well as physically, God takes care of those who believe. (Eradio Valverde)

# AUGUST 10, 2003

## *Ninth Sunday After Pentecost*

---

**Worship Theme:** Just as David loved his son Absalom, so too does the Lord love all God's people. God provided the "Bread of Heaven" in Jesus so we could feast with one another as we feast with the Lord.

---

**Readings:** 2 Samuel 18:5-9, 15, 31-33; Ephesians 4:25–5:2; John 6:35, 41-51

### Call to Worship (Psalm 130)

| | |
|---|---|
| *Leader:* | Out of the depths I cry to you, O LORD. Lord, hear my voice! |
| *People:* | **Let your ears be attentive to the voice of my supplications!** |
| *Leader:* | If you, O LORD, should mark iniquities, Lord, who could stand? |
| *People:* | **But there is forgiveness with you, so that you may be revered.** |
| *Leader:* | I wait for the LORD, my soul waits, and in his word I hope; |
| *People:* | **My soul waits for the Lord more than those who watch for the morning, more than those who watch for the morning.** |
| *Leader:* | O Israel, hope in the LORD! For with the LORD there is steadfast love, and with him is great power to redeem. |

*People:*     **It is he who will redeem Israel from all its iniquities.**

**Pastoral Prayer:**

Merciful God of David, Paul, and Jesus, you spread a gift of bounty before each of us and call this wonderful gift *our life*. Help us graciously receive your gift of life and use it as good stewards. Help us live each day to its fullest. Help us spread your love to others. May the love David had for his son Absalom inspire us within our own family of faith. Inspire us to be driven by your love. Stir us to spread this love to our homes, communities, and beyond. Give us a sense of mission for the whole world. Help us use the truth as a bridge to our neighbors. Generate in our common lives as church members such examples that people want to know about the gospel that animates us. Most of all let us not simply speak of love; make us loving people. We pray this, as we pray always, in the name of Jesus the Christ. Amen. (David Mosser)

# SERMON BRIEFS

## THE SINS OF THE FATHER, THE HEAD OF THE SON

### 2 SAMUEL 18:5-9, 15, 31-33

Perhaps you saw the movie *Gladiator*. Near the beginning of that powerful and violent epic is the terrible scene in which the aging Caesar Marcus Aurelius philosophically confesses to his worthless son Commodus something to this effect: Your faults as a son are my failures as a father. Caesar realizes that if he had been more of a father to the boy, the boy might have been more of a son to his father, and he admits as such—just before Commodus kills him.

Patricide notwithstanding, Caesar's fear is a deep dread most fathers know.

Theologically, of course, "the sins of the father" are not "visited

271

upon the head of the son." That ancient notion, operative in Israel's early history, was dispelled by the prophet Jeremiah. Ezekiel would reiterate, as would the New Testament, affirming instead that all souls are, to use the forensic word, *competent* before God. That is, "people die for their own sin," and any sour-grape eater has only himself to blame when his teeth are set on edge.

Still, it must be said that, psychologically and practically, there can be a terrible truth to the ancient axiom. *Gladiator's* Caesar saw it. So did the Deuteronomic historian. For this theological interpreter, David was a strong man in many ways and a great leader, especially in battle. But he was also possessed of sinful weaknesses, as evidenced both in the "flesh" and in his fitful relationships with his children.

Later, as an epilogue to the text, Joab chides David for showing "love of those who hate you and for hatred of those who love you" (2 Samuel 19:6a). It is precisely that kind of weakness and confusion that left not only David's life and family but also the kingdom itself in disarray.

"The sword shall never depart from your house" (2 Samuel 12:10), Nathan told David, and indeed it had not. "I will raise up trouble against you from within your own house," God said through the prophet, and indeed God had (2 Samuel 12:11).

Since Nathan's visit, there had been almost continual turmoil and strife, and almost all of it family related. There was the one skirmish against the Ammonites, but the real trouble came when David's firstborn son, Amnon, raped his half sister Tamar. When David failed to take action against Amnon, Tamar's brother Absalom conspired to kill Amnon. With his brother's blood on his hands, Absalom fled Jerusalem. But over time, Absalom was allowed to return to the royal city, where he conspired to overthrow his father, David, and assume the throne. Because of the attempted coup, David and his loyal servants fled the city, while Absalom occupied the palace. Absalom thus fulfilled the remaining portions of Nathan's prophecy.

After the fashion of his father, Absalom's vanity proves both his rising and his falling. The charisma of the young man won him popular support before the coup—and may even have all the more thoroughly endeared him to David—but his delay gave the victory to his father. Joab, whose field Absalom had burned, killed the pretender without a moment's hesitation, and the coup was deuteronomic history.

Informed of Absalom's death, David's wrenching lament comprises more than grief for a son. It is that, surely. But many fathers may hear grief for more: all that has been and all that hasn't. They may also hear David weeping over all the vanities, sins, and failures that have left him to rule a ruined family and kingdom. David now serves a regretful memory. "Would I had died instead of you," he wails (v. 33*b*). We get the sense he really meant it.

However, David did not die. He returned to Jerusalem again to continue his rule. And it is God who, though invisible in the text, takes despair and turns it into hope for David and Israel's future. (Thomas Steagald)

# GOD'S ACTION

## EPHESIANS 4:25–5:2

Our college-aged daughter was asked if she was saved. "That's none of my business," she replied. Paul would love her. She wasn't unkind to the questioner, saying it was none of *his* business. She was just saying that salvation is *God's* business. It is God's gift, through grace.

The questioner didn't quite get it, so he asked her *when* she was saved. "On Good Friday," she replied. Salvation is *God's* act, in Christ.

### I. Our Problem

Why is it that even though we are Christians, we continue to be bitter and slanderous, giving opportunity to the devil and grieving the Holy Spirit?

Sometimes it seems we are worse with our fellow Christians than with the rest of the world, saying and doing malicious things in church meetings that we would not dare say or do in the secular world.

It would be much easier if God had us programmed with a "Replace" button, like a computer. As soon as we are converted to Christ, we could pull down on the menu to *Falsehood* or *Wrath* and just give the command "Replace All" with *Love*. Living a Christian life isn't that simple.

## II. Preaching Sideroads

There are some blue highways for preaching in this passage.

One of the most scenic side roads is the difference between anger and sin. The writer says it's okay to be angry, but not sinful, as long as you let go of the anger before the day is done. We could preach a long time on how far one can go in anger, and in what direction, before it becomes sin.

Our author is just being realistic. People do get angry. The problem is expressing that anger in hurtful ways. That's where malice and slander and falsehood and unkindness enter in.

It's probably best to stay on the main highway for preaching on this text, which is "grieving the Holy Spirit of God." It's clear that our Pauline writer thinks such grief is caused by falsehood, theft, evil talk, bitterness, wrath, anger, clamor, slander, and malice (RSV).

## III. Solution

Our author doesn't even ask why we do this evil talk, this sinful talk, this false talk that grieves the Holy Spirit. He just says, "Stop it." It is not the way of Christ, and those of us who claim to follow Christ simply cannot act that way. The way of Christ is the way of love—being kind to one another, forgiving, being tenderhearted. The way of the devil is falsehood and anger and malice.

Often the preacher's task is just to remind us of what we already know: in this case, that the way of Christ is the way of kindness. Kindness doesn't always come naturally (Remember original sin!). Kindness takes work, but it's good work. It's the work of following Christ.

Another fork into the woods immediately beckons to us. Don't we have to practice honesty and "tough love"? Are they compatible with kindness?

Author David Belgum tells of a young man who was having a birthday party. He was a Christian and felt guilty about not inviting certain people because he didn't like them. By way of explanation he started telling all that was wrong with them. "Wait," said Belgum. "You *don't* have to invite them to your birthday party. You *do* have to be kind."

I recently gave my wife, Helen, a gift, a bracelet. I made it myself. It says, WWAGD? That means, What Would Aunt Gertrude Do?

Helen says: "It's sometimes hard to know what Jesus would do. Aunt Gertrude is so unfailingly kind that if I do whatever she would do, it will be what Jesus would do."

Malice? Just stop it! Kindness? Just do it! (John Robert McFarland)

## BREAD OF LIFE—FOR THE SOUL

### JOHN 6:35, 41-51

In every church there will always be at least two types of people after a sermon. One type "got it" and were blessed by the sermon. The other type consists of those who, no matter what the preacher might say, "didn't get it" and leave either disappointed or frustrated. Sadly, there is a third group in some churches, and that's the group that has already decided that the preacher cannot ever say anything to feed them spiritually for some reason or another. The text from last Sunday gives us a portrait of that in Jesus' audience. Of course, we cannot know how everyone felt about Jesus' declaration about his being the "bread of life." It may be that some believed, understood, and were blessed by it and left it at that. Others may have wanted to know more about what Jesus is truly saying. And sadly that third group mentioned is present here and named by John simply as "the Jews."

"The Jews" said that this was an outrageous statement given the fact all knew well who Jesus was because they knew his mother and father. Given the probable fact that all in the audience were "Jews," we tend to believe that "the religious leaders" of the Jews are "the Jews" whom John mentions. They begin to

275

attack Jesus' comments, especially the one about him coming "down from heaven." The practical view of life is, of course, that one is born of a mother and a father. Any additional explanation to the process is left to science. For one to claim that he has come from heaven is an outrageous claim, yet Jesus uses this discussion to address his relationship to God. For most who were familiar with his birth stories, this claim was not so outrageous. For others it was a declaration made only by one who is completely mad.

What Jesus wants to share is that he came from God, and all those who would believe in him would have a new relationship with God. Jesus begins to let them know of his messianic purpose, to give his body as the ultimate paschal sacrifice for the human race. The manna eaten in the wilderness strengthened the people, but ultimately they died. The satisfaction of that meal did not last. Jesus speaks of a meal that would satisfy forever. Those who would believe on him and accept him, as the Lamb of God, would not die. This image remains, although now it has the special significance of Jesus' pending death as payment for our sin. Jesus uses the image of bread as something that all in his audience would understand. Bread was central to everyday life in Israel, but it was also central in their religious life. The celebration of Pentecost featured bread, as did the celebration of the Passover, which featured unleavened bread. All God-centered, all God-given. As Jesus explains, this is the ultimate feeding, the giving of God's son for the good of all the world. A feeding that will not need repeating. A satisfaction as only God alone can provide. All this comes after the miraculous feeding to further emphasize the theme of this chapter of John, that God will provide for our every need be it material or spiritual.

In God we find our strength and nourishment. In God we also find life. To those who believed, they received the feeding and the nourishment that is life in abundance while here and life eternal after this life. That people can walk away from that meal without eating and being satisfied is a deep sadness. Our task is to invite others to join us in this celebration of life. (Eradio Valverde)

# AUGUST 17, 2003

*Tenth Sunday After Pentecost*

---

**Worship Theme:** Abiding in Christ is the honor of everyone who calls on the name of the Lord. We worship God for the gift of Jesus. By God's gift of Christ, our lives have meaning and purpose.

---

**Readings:** 1 Kings 2:10-12; 3:3-14; Ephesians 5:15-20; John 6:51-58

**Call to Worship (Psalm 111:1-4, 7-10)**

*Leader:*    Praise the LORD!

*People:*    **I will give thanks to the LORD with my whole heart, in the company of the upright, in the congregation.**

*Leader:*    Great are the works of the LORD, studied by all who delight in them.

*People:*    **Full of honor and majesty is his work, and his righteousness endures forever.**

*Leader:*    He has gained renown by his wonderful deeds; the LORD is gracious and merciful.

*People:*    **The works of his hands are faithful and just; all his precepts are trustworthy. They are established forever and ever, to be performed with faithfulness and uprightness.**

*Leader:*    He sent redemption to his people; he has commanded his covenant forever. Holy and awesome is his name.

*People:*     **The fear of the LORD is the beginning of wisdom; all those who practice it have a good understanding.**

*All:*        **His praise endures forever.**

**Pastoral Prayer:**

Almighty God, we hallow your name. May we feel your holy presence in our midst as we respond to your grace through our prayers, our preaching, and our hymn singing. Grant us your presence so our lives may have both meaning and value. O Lord, you know our hurry in all we do. None here has enough time to fulfill our obligations. O God, it is tempting for us to forget to pay our homage even to you weekly. Yet, without divine focus our life loses its center. Remind us, in this hour, how much we depend on your guidance for daily life. Make us the people you created us to be. Assist us to become what our families and communities need to reveal abundant life. Help us use our days and hours as faithful stewards. You, O Holy One, have given us dominion over our time. Inspire us to redeem our time to the glory of Jesus Christ, in whose name we pray. Amen. (David Mosser)

# SERMON BRIEFS

## UNDESERVED BLESSINGS

### 1 KINGS 2:10-12; 3:3-14

Solomon, like many biblical characters, is an ambiguous figure. Depending on when and where we find him, he can be viewed as either an extraordinary leader who relied upon God and followed the law or as a fallible human leader who made poor choices. There are two sides to this king of Israel. One side seeks to walk closely with the God of his father David, and the other seeks to walk only in ways that will ensure his own personal gain. The amazing stories of Solomon building the temple are tempered by the fact that he built his own home first and spent twice as long doing so. The stories of Solomon following the Law are undercut

Slawed

AUGUST 17, 2003

by his taking foreign wives in blatant disregard of the holy statutes. Solomon, like his father David before him, is a sinful human being that God blesses and uses despite himself.

Our first clue that all is not right in Solomon's life comes in verse 3 of chapter 3. We are told that "Solomon loved the LORD, walking in the statutes of his father David; only, he sacrificed and offered incense at the high places." The word *only* looms large in that sentence. Solomon seeks to worship God, but scholars note that "He went to Gibeon to worship, even though the ark was already in Jerusalem! Solomon cannot be easily exonerated for having gone to that great high place" (Choon-Leong Seow, *The New Interpreter's Bible*, vol. 3 [Nashville: Abingdon Press, 1999], p. 39). Solomon's leadership is already in serious jeopardy, if for no other reason than he is setting a poor example for the worshiping community. Yet, it is precisely this flawed leader, who does not worship at the ark in Jerusalem, whom God comes to visit.

"At Gibeon the LORD appeared to Solomon in a dream by night; and God said, 'Ask what I should give you' " (v. 5). Miraculously, God comes to Solomon and asks what he desires. This is the pivotal point in the narrative. Despite everything, God continues to seek to work in Solomon's life and to bless the people through him. It is always this way with God. It is not our worthiness that encourages God to visit us but our need of God that moves God's compassionate giving.

Perhaps God seeks us in our most vulnerable moments, when we have need of grace, because that is when we are most receptive. The writer of 1 Kings tells us that in that moment of divine visitation, Solomon understood and responded in humility. Solomon recognized the immenseness of his task and confessed the improbability of his kingship—"Although I am only a little child; I do not know how to go out or come in" (v. 7b). He deeply felt his need of guidance and asked for the thing that pleases God most, "Give your servant therefore an understanding mind to govern your people, able to discern between good and evil; for who can govern this your great people?" (v. 9). Solomon sought after the wisdom, that he might rule in ways that pleased God.

The rest of the story is the stuff of legend. God blesses Solomon with wisdom and with all the other gifts that he might desire. God promises that, "No one like you has been before you and no one

279

like you shall arise after you" (v. 3:12*b*). Solomon's fame continues even now. However, the most amazing part is that Solomon and the nation of Israel do not live happily ever after. Solomon continues in his very human ways. Like those before him and after him, he triumphs and he stumbles. But don't keep your eye on the king of Israel, keep your eye on the king of the Universe, for the blessings continue to flow despite us all. (Wendy Joyner)

# SING WITH ALL YOU HAVE

### EPHESIANS 5:15-20

Our author in this passage answers three questions: (1) *How can we live wisely?* (2) *How can we make the most of our time?* (3) *How can we be filled with the Spirit?*

Remarkably, the writer answers each question with the same, quite surprising, word: Sing!

How many of us were taught that singing is the hallmark of wise living? Wasn't that what the foolish grasshopper did, sang the summer away while the industrious ant kept quiet and worked?

Were we taught to make the most of our time by singing? No, we're supposed to be in bed early, and up early, and make lists, and consult palm pilots.

Filled with the Spirit? Well, maybe, but that's related more to tongue speaking or those lists in 1 Corinthians 12 and 13.

The people our author wrote to were used to getting drunk on wine. Their drunkenness wasn't wise, it wasn't efficient, and it wasn't spiritual. But they did it [and still do it] because a partial good time is better than no good time at all. As Jesus said, "They have their reward" (Matthew 6:2 KJV). They felt good, until the hangover kicked in and they found out later they had danced on the table with an oil lamp balanced on a foolish head.

Our author has a solution. He speaks here of replacement. He knows that people don't replace a partial good time with nothing at all. The resulting vacuum leaves too much room for the devil to operate.

So, he writes, replace wine, the false good time, the false

"high," with the Holy Spirit, the true good time, the natural "high." The way you do that is with music-psalms, hymns, and spiritual songs, making melody to the Lord with all your heart. That is the way we avoid foolishness and make the most of our time, avoiding the evil that is in our days.

This counsel runs counter to a lot of Christian history, doesn't it? Christians have usually been suspicious of music, not without reason. There is a lot of bad music around and always has been. But when John and Charles Wesley wanted to tell the love of Christ to people who knew only drinking songs, they put new words to those songs. It was no longer "Let's Do Something Cheap and Superficial," but "Let's Do Something Deep and Sacrificial."

One of my friends sang a solo in church recently, "Just a Closer Walk with Thee." He sang beautifully. You'd never know that when he was younger, a teacher told him he should never sing because he sounded so awful. Because of that comment, he didn't sing for thirty years. My friend, however, read Ephesians 5:15-20. Now he's a regular in the choir and a soloist.

Why would anyone tell a child, or anyone else, not to sing because they sing badly? The point of singing is not to sound good; it's to make melody to the Lord and give thanks to God.

I sing very poorly, especially after having a tube down my throat for two weeks following surgery. So I now sing loudly, and I lead singing. My theory is that those who are hesitant to sing will be encouraged if they hear someone who sings so badly singing without fear.

To sing, to make melody to the Lord in your heart, is to live wisely and make the most of one's time.

A music critic once said of Johnny Cash: "He *does* make an honest attempt to hit every note." That's all God asks of any of us. God asks us to make an honest attempt to hit each note of the Lord's melody. (John Robert McFarland)


## EATING TOGETHER WITH JESUS

### JOHN 6:51-58

The human body is something special for most of us. We seek a body that is healthy, and we fret when we are sick and weak.

We protect our bodies when we know they could be injured through an activity or accident. And we avoid cuts at all costs. If you're like most people, you suffer when your body receives a cut. Those of you who work with paper fear even the dreaded paper cut! We cannot imagine purposefully injuring ourselves for any reason. The sight of blood for many is a definite cause for looking away. One cannot begin to imagine what it would mean to give our flesh for someone to eat. This was the reaction from those who heard Jesus' words about his flesh. Jesus says in this passage that he is the "living bread that came down from heaven" (v. 51). Given freely and shared with the world, Jesus says, it serves to give eternal life to all who would eat of it. To the astonishment of everyone, this bread he mentions is his own flesh. Jesus refers to his blood as being the "true drink" (v. 55).

Yet, it bothered the Jews, for cannibalism then, as now, is a subject not easily discussed. We read in history books about incidents where severe hunger drove people to survive on the flesh of those who perished, all the while cringing while it was being read. We cannot imagine that sort of hunger. Our feelings about humanity keep us from even thinking that we could eat the flesh of another person. It is said that a young Central American painter in the 1920s forced himself to eat the flesh of the deceased in hopes of receiving added life to his own body. Thankfully, it was a secret experiment that did not prove him right. The Jews were advanced enough to know that the eating of flesh was forbidden. It made no social or civil sense to eat the flesh of another person for any reason. And to hear this man proclaim that his flesh was the "living bread," served only to anger them. Yet, it is precisely in this context that Jesus offers life in the thoughts of morbid death practices.

We know now that these references were to the elements of Holy Communion. In that sacrament of the Last Supper, as Jesus instituted later, we take the bread and drink from the cup with the knowledge that it was shared with us out of love, as the ultimate sacrifice for humankind from God. Even the disciples did not fully understand at that moment of the Last Supper, but later the words rang true with the words of life that Jesus had shared. We seek the words that remind us of the *why* behind this sacrament and how we as Christians hold as true and dear the words of our Lord. Jesus tells us that through faith and celebration of his life, death, and resurrection, we have eternal life. In this passage Jesus explains that through the eating of his flesh and the drinking of his blood, we will be raised up with him on the last day. It is Jesus' promise to live through us as we receive him. This is a life that will not end with our death but will continue beyond this life to eternity. It is an invitation to the fullness of life that only the Son of God can give. Can we pass up such a love as this? Can we honestly turn away from the one who gave himself for us? (Eradio Valverde)

# AUGUST 24, 2003

## *Eleventh Sunday After Pentecost*

**Worship Theme:** Christians are people who abide in Christ. As Solomon revered the ark of the Lord's covenant, so too do we revere the new covenant God makes with us in Jesus Christ.

**Readings:** 1 Kings 8:(1, 6, 10-11), 22-30, 41-43; Ephesians 6:10-20; John 6:56-69

### Call to Worship (Psalm 84:4-10, 12)

*Leader:* Happy are those who live in your house, ever singing your praise.

**People:** **Happy are those whose strength is in you, in whose heart are the highways to Zion.**

*Leader:* As they go through the valley of Baca they make it a place of springs; the early rain also covers it with pools.

**People:** **They go from strength to strength; the God of gods will be seen in Zion.**

*Leader:* O LORD God of hosts, hear my prayer; give ear, O God of Jacob!

**People:** **Behold our shield, O God; look on the face of your anointed.**

*Leader:* For a day in your courts is better than a thousand elsewhere.

**People:** **I would rather be a doorkeeper in the house of my God than live in the tents of wickedness.**

*All:*      **O LORD of hosts, happy is everyone who trusts in you.**

**Pastoral Prayer:**

O Lord God of the Universe, make us thankful that we dwell in your holy house. Remind us daily of the covenant that you make with us through the life, death, and resurrection of Jesus Christ. As you make covenant with your holy people of old, may we be inspired by their steadfastness and wary of their stumbling blocks. We know too well that temptation lurks for us, and sin waits at our doorstep. Yet you in your mercy have created our hearts for you, O God. Our choice is sometimes clear, but often obscure. Give us a holy vision to discern the divine truth and be guided by your spirit. Keep us in your fold, and may the Good Shepherd, who hears our prayers and intercedes for us, guide us on our way. May we abide with Jesus now and always. In Jesus' name we pray. Amen. (David Mosser)

# SERMON BRIEFS

## HOPES FOR GOD'S TEMPLE

### 1 KINGS 8:(1, 6, 10-11), 22-30, 41-43

The Old Testament lection finds us at what is arguably the very heart of the book of 1 Kings, Solomon's prayer of dedication over the completed temple. Years of yearning, of hoping, and of praying for a centralized place of worship have come to an end. Solomon stands before the entire assembly of Israel and invokes God's blessing upon this place. It is a time of excitement and new beginnings. It is a time for the nation of Israel to consider once again their covenant with Yahweh and to contemplate what this place might be in their lives together. In his prayer, Solomon mentions several things that instruct God's people. They are helpful not only as we consider the importance of our worship spaces but also as we consider our motivations and calling in any new work or ministry within the church.

First of all, Solomon reminds us that God is bigger than any one building or person or program. The theology of the temple in

1 Kings has quite a history of development, but here in Solomon's prayer we find the assertion that "Even heaven and the highest heaven cannot contain you, much less this house that I have built" (v. 27b)! God ultimately transcends any human attempts to contain or localize God's presence. God is elusive and all-powerful. The temple, as well as our modern-day churches, are places where we may go to feel close to God, but God's work and movement is not limited to our human structures. As Choon-Leong Seow writes,

> The Temple is neither God's residence nor the place where the petitioner personally encounters the deity. Rather, it is a place at which the needs of the petitioner coincide with the willingness of the deity to respond. . . . it is merely the place where God's presence may be known, where the authority of God is proclaimed (*The New Interpreter's Bible*, vol. 3, p. 75).

The temple is not to be equated with God's presence but is a means to discovering it.

This leads us to a second point in Solomon's prayer, the request that the temple be a place of prayer. How often do we take for granted that our houses of worship are to be places of prayer? It is easy to forget the power that lies in these sacred spaces, for it is here that human need meets with the desire of God to bless and care for us. Solomon thanks God for God's faithfulness in the past and asks that God might continue to be present to this beloved people. Solomon boldly seeks "that your eyes may be open night and day toward this house" (v. 29). How would our ministries change if we were to open our hearts to the transforming power of prayer?

Finally, Solomon begins a litany of situations in which God's sustaining presence might be needed in the lives of individuals and the community as a whole. What is edifying here, however, is that Solomon does not simply deal with those that are already a part of the chosen community. He acknowledges the universal reign of God, and seeks that the temple might be a place of blessing for all people. He asks of the Lord, "When a foreigner comes and prays toward this house, then hear in heaven your dwelling place, and do according to all that the foreigner calls to you, so that all the peoples of the earth may know your name and fear you" (vv. 42b-43a). The temple is not simply to be for those who already enjoy a relationship with God. God's gathered people are always outward looking, seeking to be a blessing to those who still have need of God's presence. (Wendy Joyner)

# FIGHTING SIN

### EPHESIANS 6:10-20

## I. The Context

Our writer has given instructions for how to live the Christian life, and now he sums up.

## II. The Problem

We are in a battle against evil. It's not enough just to follow the instructions given in this letter. Those are good for the struggle against flesh and blood enemies, but there is a bigger battle, a spiritual battle. One must put on spiritual armor, the whole armor of God.

This is not just defensive armor. This is armor for someone who is going out to do battle, not sitting home behind high walls, hoping the enemy doesn't find him or her.

## III. The Enemy

Sin, original sin, that's the enemy.

Sin is separation from God. It's a state of being, not simply individual bad acts. The acts are manifestations of our separation from God.

We call sin "original" because it comes with the human territory. If you don't believe that, just watch a two-year-old for a while. Saint Augustine said that, "The so-called innocence of children is more a matter of weakness of limb than purity of heart."

Augustine led us down an original sin side road, however. By linking it to sex, he tried to account for why we are in a state of separation right from the start. Because all people are conceived through the sex act (at least before test tubes) then, Augustine thought, that's how original sin gets transmitted.

Augustine tried to answer an unanswerable question. We don't know why we start off in a state of separation from God. We just know it's true. It's both corporate and individual. Sin is in the world and in our lives.

This is what John Calvin meant by "total depravity," not that there is no good in us or that we are incapable of good acts, but that because of original sin, our faculties—will, intellect, and so forth—cannot be trusted. They are infected by sin so that we cannot really even think or pray rightly. We need the Holy Spirit to help us.

So the battle is against real, objective sin. It's not simply within us, not just our bad choices. It's the cosmic powers of this present darkness.

## IV. The Armor

There is evidence that our author was using the astrological categories of his day to get this point across. Astrology is still with us, but a battle against astrology misses the point of this passage, which is that because there is real, objective sin "out there," we need real, objective salvation from "out there."

That's where the whole armor of God comes in. That armor is the necessary help from beyond our own lives and world truth, salvation, righteousness, peace, faith, Spirit/Word. These are the gifts of God for use in the battle.

## V. The Decision

Having put on the armor of God, we are not free from wounds. The battle is fierce. We shall tire. We shall be injured. There are times we shall turn tail and run.

Then, however, we look down and see the armor and remember whose side we are on. We ask forgiveness and return to the fray, for that's where the action is. As we face death at the side of God in the war on evil, we receive life.

A soldier in arctic training is dropped into the wilderness with a survival pack. In the midst of the 50-degree-below-zero weather, he has to strip naked to put on the pack. If he does, he will survive. The only way he can live is to expose himself to that terrible cold, that possibility of death. (John Robert McFarland)

# ALL OR NOTHING

## JOHN 6:56-69

It is no wonder that the early church was accused of cannibalism and bizarre pagan rituals. Jesus' words are hard to swallow, and the images they evoke turn the stomach. He knows it, of course, and the shock value is apparently intentional. Jesus turns to his complaining, grumbling, hesitant disciples and points to the reality of God. To paraphrase verse 62, *If you were to see me as I was before I became one of you, would that make this any easier to swallow?*

## I. Faith Is Always Involved in Following Jesus

What you believe matters. The eucharist or Lord's Supper is a means of grace that reminds us of the commitment, sacrifice, and love expressed in Christ's incarnation. The birth, death, resurrection, and ascension of the Christ are all symbolized in the observance of Holy Communion. The bread and cup become the symbols of incarnation. The broken bread and poured juice or wine are the broken body and spilled blood of Jesus. We consume the elements and take in God's love and then live out Christ's love through our discipleship. We rise to serve and live as faithful people in the name of the risen Christ.

I was visiting a woman who was a cancer patient. Her diagnosis was recent, but she appeared to be handling her situation with reason and composure. When I offered her the sacrament I shall never forget her response, "That is merely the trappings of religion. I have no need of that." Certainly, not everyone views the symbols and sacraments of faith with the same depth of meaning, but I felt pity for this woman who seemed oblivious to the grace conveyed through acts of faith and discipline.

We need spiritual disciplines to remind us of who we are and whose we are. We need them to give birth to deeper faith, greater insight, daily devotion, growing commitment. Faith is always involved in following Jesus. Prayer, scriptural study, devotional reading, worship, baptism, the Lord's Supper, footwashing, confession, and meditation can all be means of growing in our pursuit of the Christian way.

## II. Commitment to the Christ Is All or Nothing

There is no halfway discipleship. You cannot "sort of" follow Jesus anymore than you can be a "little bit pregnant." Faith is a reality, and belief is either/or: either you do believe or you do not.

The spectrum of understanding along which one's beliefs may reside can be extremely diverse. This is the reason we use terms like *conservative* or *liberal*. Still, Christian faith involves the basic understanding of acceptance of God's love as revealed through the Christ. One either accepts the gift of love or rejects it. There is no halfway grasping or "sort of holding on."

A class of sixth-grade students was exploring the Christian faith as they moved toward their time of profession of faith in Christ. Individually, each one was given the opportunity of talking with their pastor and deciding whether or not they would make their confession of faith before the congregation. One young man, with tears in his eyes, said that he was not ready. He said that he did not believe. I asked him what was holding him back. He said that he had doubts, that he did not understand the mystery of God and Christ. I realized that this young man had a deeper understanding than did any of the others in his class.

He took faith seriously and sacredly. His doubt revealed a deep and exploring faith that refused to be satisfied with pat answers or easy explanations. We visited again over the course of several weeks, and he was later confirmed in his faith as a disciple of Jesus Christ. He understood the importance of commitment, and he wanted to profess his faith when he felt that he could give it his all.

None of us ever achieve Christian perfection along the way, we simply move toward it. Being followers of Jesus Christ means that we are works in progress, doubters and believers together. We have good days and bad days. Our discipline can be spotty and our faith even erratic at times. Being Christian means that we have discovered the love of God through Christ and that we choose to grow more like the one who gave his all for us. (Gary Kindley)

# AUGUST 31, 2003

*Twelfth Sunday After Pentecost*

---

**Worship Theme:** The God of Jesus Christ wants his covenant people to worship in the spirit of love and mercy. Ritual words, as important as they may be, are no substitute for loving hearts.

---

**Readings:** Song of Solomon 2:8-13; James 1:17-27; Mark 7:1-8, 14-15, 21-23

### Call to Worship (Psalm 45:1, 6-9)

*Leader:*    My heart overflows with a goodly theme;

**People:**    **I address my verses to the king; my tongue is like the pen of a ready scribe.**

*Leader:*    Your throne, O God, endures forever and ever.

**People:**    **Your royal scepter is a scepter of equity; you love righteousness and hate wickedness.**

*Leader:*    Therefore God, your God, has anointed you with the oil of gladness beyond your companions; your robes are all fragrant with myrrh and aloes and cassia.

**People:**    **From ivory palaces stringed instruments make you glad; daughters of kings are among your ladies of honor;**

*All:*    **At your right hand stands the queen in gold of Ophir.**

### Pastoral Prayer:

O Loving Lord of All Creation, remind us that it is your love that binds our heart to your divine presence. What sets a

THE ABINGDON PREACHING ANNUAL 2003

believer apart is the recognition that you alone love us with a love that will never leave us. Nothing in all creation can separate us from your love shown in Jesus Christ, our master and our sovereign. Grant us a vision of the realm of God and make us citizens of it. Remind us that citizens of your realm are those who hear and obey Jesus' words of eternal life. Make eternal life that which drives us to be better and more faithful in our discipleship. Help us confess that our discipleship is your gift to us, for we can do nothing apart from your spirit. We count on your spirit to intercede for us. Thank you for the gift of the Holy Spirit. May our lives reflect the mercy of your guiding hand. (David Mosser)

# SERMON BRIEFS

## THE POETRY OF GOD'S LOVE FOR US

### SONG OF SOLOMON 2:8-13

A group of adults in our church recently met to discuss theological themes in Southern fiction. We have been able to glean many insights from contemporary writers, and one of our recent conversations concerned the effectiveness of different artistic media. One man remarked that "music and poetry take us to an entirely different level of meaning than prose." In that moment, he articulated something we had all experienced in spiritual journeys, the ability of more abstract media and images to speak to our souls. Our rational, linear world sometimes expects us to relate to matters of faith in a cognitive way. However, passages like this one in the Song of Solomon remind us of the gift of the Spirit, moving in and through the beauty of poetry to inspire and evoke deep feeling.

The dialogue in Song of Solomon is between two lovers, seeking to find ways to woo each other and to be in relationship with one another. It is the language of deep emotion, and it reminds us of the sacredness of human love. On yet another level, we can, like the early church mystics, draw parallels with humanity's relationship to God. We are wooed by God, and the mystery of the divine love is captured beautifully in this language of desire and affection. Through the use of poetry, relationship with God is described in ways that open us up to a more "heart centered understanding" of the divine convenant. We must simply wade into the language and try to feel what it evokes.

"Arise, my love, my fair one, and come away; for now the winter is past, the rain is over and gone. The flowers appear on the earth; the time of singing has come, and the voice of the turtledove is heard in our land" (vv. 10*b*-12). Hear the words of the speaker as she revels in the promise and hope of springtime and new life. It is a time of celebration, and all creation breaks forth into song. Perhaps there have been times of barrenness and struggle; but now her heart is full, for the winter is past!

What a marvelous image to capture the mystery of our redemption and the love of God for all creation. Springtime, with all its gifts, reminds us that God is present in all places, during all the seasons of life. We engage all our senses as we experience the wonder of God's love for us. Listen closely, and you can hear the birds in the trees. Inhale deeply, and the perfume of flowers will fill your lungs. Taste the ripe fruit off the trees, and look at the explosion of color on the hills. Feel the warmth of the sun on your skin, and listen for the voice of your beloved calling your name. God's love surrounds you in a multitude of ways. Experience the reality of God's promise in all of creation, for "I am about to do a new thing; now it springs forth, do you not perceive it?" (Isaiah 43:19*a*).

Perhaps the best way to approach this passage is for us simply to acknowledge that we must sometimes listen with our bodies and our hearts. We must pay attention to receive what the divine lover has for us. In her commentary on Song of Songs, Renita J. Weems challenges us to do just this as she writes, "to behold beauty and to hear the sacred in our routines, we must take care to lean closer and see God's face and to hear God's voice in our lives" (*The New Interpreter's Bible*, vol. 5 [Nashville: Abingdon Press, 1997], p. 395). (Wendy Joyner)

# STAY PURE, ACT WITH LOVE

## JAMES 1:17-27

## I. A Giving God

It is important as we look at this text to keep the preceding verses in mind. James declares that God does not tempt us, but in our own deprived state, we succumb to temptation. God is the giver of good things, and James goes so far as to say all good things. God calls Christians to be givers. As we grow in our relationship with Christ and grow closer to God, we learn that it is truly better to give than to receive. The joy of giving is an emotion that is difficult to forget. When people are discouraged, they can recall a kind act that they may have done for someone else and receive an additional blessing from that act. Usually, when we receive a gift, the possibility exists for that gift to disappear into the clutter of our lives. The gift received is easily forgotten while the gift given is seldom forgotten. One Christmas, my father gave one such gift. He had a book of my mother's favorite poems put together and printed for the whole family. I still have the gift (the book of poems), but the memory of his act is more vivid in my mind than even the gift that is tangible. James also speaks of God's steadfastness. In describing the "Father of lights," James portrays God as one who does not change. God is present in our lives at all times. When we live as God calls us to live, we avoid the pitfalls of sin and temptation. We reflect the light of God to others we encounter.

## II. A Lesson in Discernment

How often do we speak before the other person is finished talking? Some people just love to hear the sound of their voice. In verse 19, James begins his version of the Sermon on the Mount. Pay attention. Listen. Absorb what you have heard. Speak only after some thought. Do not get angry. As Jesus said, "Love your enemy"; James proclaims that we rid ourselves of our hate, our discontent, or anything that might cause us to miss the mark of God's righteousness. Some people have the uncanny ability to let the words of another "go into one ear and out the other." I suppose that sometimes this may be a positive, especially when the words of the other person are monotonous, hurtful, or without reason. But the Word of God is another story altogether. We are to live out our faith in our actions. If we proclaim Christ with our mouths and live a life of hypocrisy, we do more harm than any verbal witness could ever do.

### III. A Cry for Social Action

In two verses, James summarizes the words of the prophets of Israel. Isaiah, Micah, Amos, Jeremiah, and others cried out for the people of Israel to love God with their very being instead of through their routine actions. The psalmist declares,

> For there is no truth in their mouths;
> their hearts are destruction;
> their throats are open graves;
> they flatter with their tongues.
> (Psalm 5:9)

James is challenging the Early Church, and us as well, to be faithful to the words of Jesus. He calls for us to care for the "orphans and widows in their distress." We are called to care for those in our world who have become disenfranchised by society. Furthermore, James calls for us to stay pure in the world in which we live. It is a challenge for Christians to live their life for God while fighting the secular distractions that are encountered each day. (John Mathis)

## OVERCOMING OURSELVES

### MARK 7:1-8, 14-15, 21-23

Calvin, the youngster in Bill Watterson's delightful cartoon series "Calvin and Hobbes," marches up to his mother wearing a helmet and cape. He tells her that whatever happens today he's ready for it.

We can't always know what life will send our way. Something could happen today, something that would shake us, something for which we would want to be ready.

Calvin would seem to believe that the greatest threat to his well-being will come from forces outside him. Thus, his need for the "suit." There are at least two dangers in such thinking. One is that it sets us up to play the victim. Stephen R. Covey contends that we are effective when we claim our behaviors as evidence of choices we've made (*The 7 Habits of Highly Effective People* [Simon and Schuster, 1989]).

The second danger in perceiving the larger threat from outside is that it makes self-confession more unlikely. "Dennis the Menace" is often pictured facing a corner and wondering why he is always the one to get in trouble. Until we become responsible for our behavior, nothing changes.

Jesus would appear to believe that the biggest threat to our wholeness comes from within. Jesus said, "There is nothing outside a person that by going in can defile, but the things that come out are what defile" (v. 15). The Pharisees were offended because they observed that the disciples didn't wash their hands before eating. Pharisees believed eating without first washing made one ritually unclean in the sight of God and, thus, liable to suffering, even destruction. Jesus disagrees and tells them to look inward first, that nothing external to them (like failing to wash one's hands before eating) can defile them in God's eyes. Uncleanness has nothing to do with what we take into our bodies and everything to do with what comes out of our hearts.

I've often prayed, "God, show me where to take my stand. What are my fiercest enemies? Militarism? Drugs? Racism? Stress?" Invariably I'm directed to look inwardly: impatience, an overinflated ego. "These are your worst enemies," says God. Don't misunderstand! Militarism, drugs, racism, and stress are important issues calling for my faithfulness. But first, I must take the inward journey if I'm to make an authentic difference in the world around me.

Nothing external to me can "defile" me, says Jesus. Still, there are forces out there that will seek to "undo" me. So I'll need to take care with the choices and responses I make to what happens to me. If nothing more, I always have choices as to the meaning or sense I make of what comes my way. It's a truth I've seen lived out innumerable times over the years: some bitter and broken in response to a tragic circumstance, others full of light and love.

God give me the grace to claim those choices that will bless, especially given Jesus' warning that the biggest obstacle to my wholeness will likely be me. (Kelly Bender)

# REFLECTIONS

# SEPTEMBER

**Reflection Verse:** *"For I resolved to know nothing while I was with you except Jesus Christ and him crucified. I came to you in weakness and fear, and with much trembling. My message and my preaching were not with wise and persuasive words, but with a demonstration of the Spirit's power, so that your faith might not rest on men's wisdom, but on God's power." (1 Corinthians 2:2-5 NIV)*

September is the month that many clergy return from vacations rested, revived, and hopeful about the work of God and the ministry of the church. Many clergy during the month of August travel with their families, take care of things around the house, or just lay around the house and sleep. Some of the more active play golf, fish, or engage in other leisure activities. Many preachers use the summer months to read and study God's Word. Most of this activity tends to re-create us, and we find ourselves at least somewhat rejuvenated and anticipating new possibilities in the coming months in our churches and in our preaching. During this downtime, we often get a fresh word from God and are ready to pursue a heightened sense of God's purpose and direction.

The text in 1 Corinthians 2 reminds me of how I feel when I come back to church life in September. Paul says, "For I resolved to know nothing while I was with you except Jesus Christ and him crucified." In September I often feel fresh and my members remark about how dynamic my preaching is. The rest and the relaxation afford me the opportunity to remember why I entered ministry in the first place. I thank them for the generous compliment and say, "I resolve to know nothing among you except Christ and him crucified." Rest allows us to get back to the source of it all.

Let's look at the context of our passage. Paul's relationship with the Corinthian Church was a very rocky one at best. Unlike the

298

church in Galatia, for example, Paul's relationship with Corinth had many challenges, questions, and painful encounters. Paul started the church of Corinth (Acts 18). As was his custom, Paul nurtured and developed leadership in a new church, and then went on to his next missionary stop. Paul got word in Macedonia that there were big problems in Corinth, that there was a party spirit—some followed Paul, some Apollos, and some Peter. Paul also heard that there was sexual immorality among them and that a speaking-in-tongues crowd had raised itself up in spiritual superiority. Paul sent a letter to them correcting some of this behavior, and they had the audacity to reject his letter. In response to Paul's letter, the Corinthians criticized him and challenged his integrity. They responded that Paul was not as good a speaker as the Greek rhetoricians. They accused Paul of being slow of speech. They then presented Paul with several questions that they wanted addressed. Paul addressed these questions and penned the letter that we know as First Corinthians.

Often in congregational life we deal with various kinds of critics, saboteurs, and painful challenges to our integrity. In every church, there is a "Corinthian" element that is high maintenance and requires much prayer on our part. On vacation, we spend time with God and renew our souls. When we encounter God, we come again in touch with our call. We hear the voice of God speak, and we often gain confidence and strength. Like Paul, we come back and say to our critics and our opposition, "We know nothing but Christ and him crucified." We rise above the politics, resentments, hurt feelings, and grudges. We preach and proclaim Christ and Christ alone. Because we have been with God, we are able to admit that at least some of the criticisms are right and true. We get a sense of our fragility, unresolved issues, and lack of skill in certain areas. Paul says, "I came to you in weakness and fear, and with much trembling." In essence Paul was admitting that he was not perfect, that he had flaws and defects that were a part of his nature. But Paul knew that the message was not dependent on the perfection of his human form. Paul says, "My message and my preaching were not with wise and persuasive words, but with a demonstration of the Spirit's power, so that your faith might not rest on men's wisdom, but on God's power."

This is how I feel when I return from vacation. My preaching is not resting on wise and persuasive words but on a demonstration of the Spirit's power. Paul means his preaching is based on a mystical display of the Spirit's power deep in the life of the believer. His preaching has the force of something supernatural that breaks through to the human spirit. It is something more than what we say in words alone; it is the power of the Holy Spirit grasping, seizing, convicting, and redeeming the human heart. It is the power of the revelation of God through which God reaches the human soul.

When I come back from vacation, I feel as though my preaching is a demonstration of the Spirit's power. It is not based on wise and persuasive words of human wisdom but rather what I have seen and heard from the very mouth of God. I cannot wait to get back to the pulpit to see what God is getting ready to do.

Dear Lord, I know that there are many clergy who do not take significant vacations and times of rest. Show us the connection between rest, renewal, time with you, and a demonstration of the Spirit's power in preaching. Help us to know that if we do not get rest, then we will rely on wise and persuasive words. God, as we read this meditation, grant us true rest that we may stand before the people of God and say, "For I resolved to know nothing—except Jesus Christ and him crucified." (Frank Thomas)

# SEPTEMBER 7, 2003

## *Thirteenth Sunday After Pentecost*

---

**Worship Theme:** As our lesson from Proverbs reminds believers concerning the rich and the poor that, "the Lord is the maker of them all." Therefore, people who have a heart for God also have a heart for the less fortunate.

---

**Readings:** Proverbs 22:1-2, 8-9, 22-23; James 2:1-10 (11-13), 14-17; Mark 7:24-37

### Call to Worship (Psalm 125 RSV)

*Leader:*    Those who trust in the LORD are like Mount Zion, which cannot be moved, but abides for ever.

**People:**    **As the mountains are round about Jerusalem, so the LORD is round about his people, from this time forth and for evermore.**

*Leader:*    For the scepter of wickedness shall not rest upon the land allotted to the righteous, lest the righteous put forth their hands to do wrong.

**People:**    **Do good, O LORD, to those who are good, and to those who are upright in their hearts!**

*Leader:*    But those who turn aside upon their crooked ways the LORD will lead away with evildoers!

*All:*    **Peace be in Israel!**

### Pastoral Prayer:
Sometimes, Gracious God, we are overly concerned with our good name. We try to protect our reputation by doing all sorts

of things to enhance it. However, when we are honest with ourselves, and when we discern the divine in our lives, we confess that it is you alone who give a good name to your people. We know that Jesus does everything well. In his spirit, help us, O God, follow Jesus' teachings and life. Give us a will that yearns to do right by those with whom we come into contact. Remind us that Jesus loved the little children as well as those who stood apart from whom we see as "socially acceptable." Grant us the wisdom to embrace all people, for they too are those for whom Christ died. As we journey through life, give us the courage to reach out to others as you have first reached out to us. We pray this in the strength of Jesus' holy name. Amen. (David Mosser)

## SERMON BRIEFS

## WHAT'S IN A NAME?

### PROVERBS 22:1-2, 8-9, 22-23

I suppose that at some point in our lives, most of us try to determine the origin of our names. We might ask our parents about how they chose our name. We might do genealogical research to determine where our name can be found in previous generations of our families. We might even try to determine the meaning of our name. Our names can tell us a lot about where we come from and what our parents hoped for us. The most important thing about our name, however, is that it continues to be significant for us throughout our lives because it is how we are known. It is a means of establishing who we are in relation to others.

Biblical writers understood the importance of a name. Yet, our Scripture reading talks at length about not only our names but also our treatment of the poorest among us. At first glance, these two themes might not seem related, but a seldom explored dimension of naming is that we also have something to do with our own naming. How we are known to others is determined by our own actions, attitudes, and disposition. In examining this passage in Proverbs, Raymond C. Van Leeuwen writes that, our " 'name' includes reputation. . . . Israel was an honor-and-shame culture, and one's name meant personal identity as it was recognized and respected (or not) in the community" (*The New Interpreter's Bible,* vol. 5 [Nashville: Abingdon Press, 1997], p. 197).

Personal identity is still central to us in terms of our relationship to others. In our society, we sometimes make promises based on "our good name." We speak of our character and reputation as things to be protected. We worry about our "name" in our community because ultimately this is all we have that is truly ours. This understanding reminds us that if our name is a part of our personal identity, then our moral and ethical choices make a difference in how we are known to ourselves and in the world around us.

The writer of Proverbs here encourages us to take a look at our choices related to economic justice and social dimensions of mercy. Our actions, attitudes, and disposition toward others reveal a lot about our true identity. The wisdom of these sayings is that we are to be ever vigilant in terms of our relationships toward those who are not prosperous in the eyes of the world. We are encouraged to realize our common humanity with all people, regardless of community standing for "the Lord is the maker of [us] all" (v. 2*b*). We are reminded that we will reap what we sow and that God will bless those who are generous, "for they share their bread with the poor" (v. 9*b*). We are warned about the judgment of God, "for the Lord pleads their cause and despoils of life those who despoil them" (v. 23). The God we worship calls us to serve those who are in need and to live in such a way as to bless them rather than curse them. These ethical concerns are central, for our personal identity reveals the love we have for those in need.

"A good name is to be chosen rather than great riches, and favor is better than silver or gold" (v. 1). We can and do choose our names. We are "called" by the way we live. Our name is chosen, in part, by how we relate to those who are nameless in our society. (Wendy Joyner)

# FAITH WANTED: DEAD? OR ALIVE?

## JAMES 2:1-10 (11-13), 14-17

### I. Living the Dream

We are to love our brothers and sisters in the world unconditionally. In the eyes of God, all of us are the same. Martin Luther
King, Jr. cried out for equality for all people. His dream was a day
when all people would live together and pay no attention to race
or color. The dream in the book of James is that we in the church
will live together in harmony without "acts of favoritism." James
challenges us to disregard wealth or standing and to treat everyone who comes into the church the same. We have struggled
with this through the years. One of the blessings of the Free
Church is when a congregation lives according to these texts.
God blesses us when no regard is paid to wealth or social status.
Sometimes those who cannot provide monetarily to the church
have some other gift of service they can provide. Moreover, in
today's world, are we going to concern ourselves with what people wear to church, or are we going to concern ourselves with
getting our sisters and brothers to come to faith? Are we going to
step out on faith and be willing to live outside our comfort zones
and open the church to everyone in the community? The challenge is just as real now as in first-century Palestine.

### II. Living According to All of the Law

In continuing his discussion on partiality, James comments on
the nature of sin. No part of the law is greater than any other part
of the law. It is difficult for Christians to believe that each sin is
the same to God. If we sin in the simplest way, perhaps telling a
white lie, we sin as someone who has committed the most horrible sin. Jesus told us "You shall not commit adultery." Furthermore, Jesus said, "You shall not murder." James reiterates these
words to remind the members of the church in Jerusalem that
the rules have not changed. Because the Lord is no longer with
them, the church must strive to live in honor of the gospel that
Jesus proclaimed. Verse 12 is James's version of John 8:7*b*, "Let

anyone among you who is without sin be the first to throw a stone at her." We are to forgive others who transgress against God as God forgives us when we sin. We are to show mercy to others. So often, we are quick to point out the faults of others, forgetting that we too are not perfect. James proclaims that mercy triumphs over judgment.

## III. Living Faith

In verses 14-17, James speaks of a living faith. The Jewish heritage of James might suggest these passages are speaking of works righteousness, but he is not proclaiming that a dead faith is without salvation. A further look at these texts shows that James is differentiating between a faith that is dead (pew sitters) and a faith that is living (spiritually mature Christians). A dead faith may lead to salvation, but it also leads to a Christian life that is mundane and unexciting. As disciples, we seek to experience the living Christ in our daily lives. Our actions come from our love of God, not from our guilt or selfish pride. We may experience a better relationship with God as we serve the Lord. As with any relationship, if we take an active role, it becomes more meaningful. An experience with the living Christ through the indwelling of the Holy Spirit seldom is a passive action. A certain amount of active listening is required even when we are still and feel the presence of God. Faith alone is dead. A living faith is exciting and a joy to share. (John Mathis)

## DOGGED LOVE

### MARK 7:24-37

When I was a boy I desperately wanted a new bicycle for my tenth birthday. I had a bike, but it was a hand-me-down, from my older brother; and it wasn't even a 3-speed bicycle. I'm afraid I pestered my folks, pleading my case until my mother, frustrated with me, said, "Would you stop pestering me for the bicycle! Mercy!"

Have you ever pestered God? Have you ever wanted something so desperately from God and feared you wouldn't get it that you felt you had no recourse but to be tenacious in your petitions to God?

In our Gospel lesson, a woman comes to Jesus for her daughter's sake. She will have to pester Jesus to have her request granted. Hers will be a dogged love, stubbornly determined.

The mother is Gentile (a non-Jew); the daughter suffers from an "unclean spirit" (other translations call it an evil spirit). Our tendency is to give scientific, medical explanations for behaviors that the ancient world attributed to demonic spirits. Clearly, the daughter is ill, and her mother has heard about Jesus and believes he can heal her. So, she falls to her knees at Jesus' feet and begs him to help. And Jesus, always compassionate, especially to the hurts of children, says, "Of course, I will help. Take me to her!" Right? No! Jesus says, "Let the children be fed first" (Matthew's account adds "the lost sheep of Israel" [15:24]), "for it is not fair to take the children's food [his attention intended for God's people, the Jews] and throw it to the dogs" (v. 27).

The Jews are God's people, and Gentiles (like this woman and her daughter) are "dogs"? These words attributed to Jesus? Could Jesus really have said them? Yes, if we can allow him to be fully human—even as he was fully God. Jesus, fully human, and thus subject to the pride and prejudice of his culture and religion, as we all are, Jew and Gentile alike.

But the woman will not take no for an answer. It is her daughter who needs help, so she is prepared to persist. "Sir," she says, "even the dogs under the table eat the children's crumbs." In other words: *Surely, Jesus, your God, the One you call "Abba" (Father) has enough compassion to share a little with those of us who are not Jewish!*

Jesus, God in human flesh, must have been surprised, even stunned by the woman's request. In his mind's eye, Jesus might have rehearsed his faith tradition's more inclusive themes, its concern for justice for the marginalized of society: the widow, the orphan, the poor, the stranger.

Perhaps Jesus was reminded of his own decisions to sup with those typically excluded from table fellowship, for instance tax collectors and prostitutes.

The woman's dogged love pays off. Jesus replies, *You are very brave. Your stubborn persistence has served your daughter well. Go home and find her whole.*

Who or what, do you value so much that you would be willing to pester God about it with your own dogged love? Persons you love, no doubt. And what about the unlovely, the unlovable? Jesus illustrated that even they deserve the crumbs that fall from our fellowship tables. God desires for them to be whole.

The need for our dogged love, even to the point of pestering God, has to do with our need to persist, to so value someone or something that we must persist. We don't have to awaken God's sense of what's right or just. God doesn't promise to give us everything for which we persist. I don't want my faith to be finally determined by what I ask for and get, do you?

My grandmother offered persistent prayers that a niece would come to know and love the Lord. For years grandmother prayed, "storming the heavens," on behalf of her niece, whom she loved dearly but didn't respect. Love is a gift, respect is earned. I knew her niece. It appeared to me that my grandmother's prayers weren't working. But still she persisted. One day, I said to my grandmother, "Why do you continue to pray? It isn't doing any good!" My grandmother said, "Maybe not for her—but look at the good my prayers for her are doing for me."

By the way, I didn't get the 3-speed bicycle, either. (Kelly Bender)

# SEPTEMBER 14, 2003

*Fourteenth Sunday After Pentecost*

---

**Worship Theme:** The knowledge of who Christ is—for us—is the beginning of wisdom.

---

**Readings:** Proverbs 1:20-33; James 3:1-12; Mark 8:27-38

### Call to Worship (Psalm 19:1, 7-10, 14)

*Leader:*    The heavens are telling the glory of God; and the firmament proclaims his handiwork.

*People:*    **The law of the LORD is perfect, reviving the soul;**

*Leader:*    The decrees of the LORD are sure, making wise the simple;

*People:*    **The precepts of the LORD are right, rejoicing the heart;**

*Leader:*    The commandment of the LORD is clear, enlightening the eyes;

*People:*    **The fear of the LORD is pure, enduring forever;**

*Leader:*    The ordinances of the LORD are true and righteous altogether.

*People:*    **More to be desired are they than gold, even much fine gold; sweeter also than honey, and drippings of the honeycomb.**

*All:*    **Let the words of my mouth and the meditations of my heart be acceptable to you, O LORD, my rock and my redeemer.**

308

**Pastoral Prayer:**

Precious Lord, remind us that our lives are restless until we find who Jesus is for us. In our journey of faith we may see many parts of who Jesus is. For some of us, Jesus is like the prophets of old. For some, Jesus is the great miracle worker and healer of human infirmities. For some, Jesus is a great teacher and dispenser of divine wisdom. However, Lord, remind us that Jesus is the Messiah. As our Messiah, Jesus gives us the pathway to eternal life. We confess that Jesus, as our Messiah, is our way to salvation. Keep us on the path that leads to you, O God, and may we follow Jesus as both the invitation and the way to fullness of life. Make us mindful of the poor, and may we lift up the afflicted in our daily prayers. Grant us the privilege of partaking of your divine wisdom, we pray, O Lord, in Jesus' holy name. Amen. (David Mosser)

# SERMON BRIEFS

## LISTENING FOR WISDOM'S VOICE

### PROVERBS 1:20-33

Years ago, while living in Kenya, I would make a weekly shopping trip to the outdoor market. The market is a large square in the middle of town. Inside its walls, there are hundreds of sellers, surrounded by stacks of fruits and vegetables. What I remember most vividly are the sounds of the market, particularly the sound of human voices calling out to me. First were the young men, taking me for a tourist on safari: "Buy this carved elephant? Good price!" I would keep going, their voices still calling after me. I would make my way between the sellers and, before I had time to catch my breath, other voices would call out, "You there. Taste this mango. Very sweet. Buy my bananas!" I would then attempt to decide which voice to heed, which seller would get my business, how much to buy, and what price to offer. As I walked away from one voice, I was confronted by more voices, urging me to consider their produce and their price. In the end, I would leave exhausted from the barrage of voices and with too much in my bag to comfortably carry home.

That market of competing voices is something like the world in which we live. Think about how many different voices cry out to us for our attention and consideration. Some voices promise success, money, or power. Others call out for compassion and justice. Some urge self-preservation, some self-destruction. It is difficult to sort out the voices and decide which one is right. It can be overwhelming and confusing. How in the world do we choose which voice to listen to, which "goods to buy" and take home with us?

Thank goodness there is a voice that can be heard above the others. The book of Proverbs calls her Wisdom. There she goes—right out into the middle of life, crying loudly to get our attention: *LISTEN TO ME! How long will you refuse to heed my voice? I am the way to understanding and right choices and good living. I am God's Wisdom Voice, sent to turn you to the right path. Pay attention to what I say.*

God cares enough about our choices in the market that God sends the Voice of Wisdom. Wisdom persuades us to choose "the fear of the LORD" (v. 29). When we pay attention to Wisdom, we become better able to distinguish which voices are right and wrong, and decide which way is God's way. It takes a conscious decision and an effort of will to be attentive to Wisdom's voice. But when we listen to Wisdom, we find peace and security.

One day when I was still new in the Karatina market, confused by all the voices, I suddenly heard a familiar voice. "May I help you with your shopping?" I turned. There was Lucy, a young woman my age, smiling at me. The relief I felt was immense. Lucy guided me through the aisles, waving off some who called, taking me to her favorite sellers, showing me the best fruit, and telling me what to pay. I left with just the right amount in my bag. Thank goodness I heard Lucy's voice above the others and that I listened to her wisdom.

God so loves the world that God sends out Wisdom, so that her voice might find us amid the barrage of voices. How gracious that God would come calling us, in the markets of our lives, reach out a hand and lead us to the best fruit. May we hear and respond. (Laura Jernigan)

# ONE OR TWO FACES?

## JAMES 3:1-12

### I. Fear and Trembling

It is amazing that anyone who reads these words of James would volunteer to teach or preach the Word of God. James says that those who teach "will be judged with greater strictness" (v. 1*b*). The question is, *what judgment will be stricter?* The apostle Paul challenges us in Philippians 2:12 to "work out your own salvation with fear and trembling." In a similar way, James challenges those who feel the call of the Lord to teach and preach the gospel. We are to be careful to proclaim the true gospel of Jesus Christ and not to proclaim an individual idealism or agenda. James uses many examples to express his opinion that our little mouths control our larger bodies. A small bit controls a horse when it is placed in its mouth. A tiny rudder controls a boat or ship. Although our mouths are tiny, they can tell many a tall tale. How many of us have exaggerated the simplest stories to bring glory upon ourselves? Teaching the gospel is a job to be done with "fear and trembling." We should remain in prayer and seek the guidance of the Lord to lead us.

### II. Careful Words

In the drier regions of the western United States, forest fires are a great concern. One day while driving in a park reserve outside of Fremont, California, I became very concerned that a tiny spark from my automobile might ignite the dry grass on the hills of the park. I know that I was probably being an alarmist, but a great fire can start from the smallest spark. James knew this and compared the tongue to that spark. There must have been many within the early church that could not hold their tongues in check. This should not surprise us; how many people do we know who could do a better job of watching their words? Words have the ability to cut like a knife. We can encourage one another with our lips, but instead we criticize and gossip. Perhaps James's words should be of some comfort to us. In his opinion, no one is exempt from this "restless evil, full of deadly poison" (v. 8*b*).

311

Since we all possess this capability to harm with our words, we need to choose our words carefully. Let us be on watch, so that we do not gossip, do not boast, or do not hurt.

## III. The Two-Faced Person

James continues his discourse on the evils of our mouths. Again, it is obvious that some problem existed in the first-century church in regard to what people were saying. James suggests that people were praising God one minute then cursing a fellow human being the next. It is important to look at what James is saying here. He is not saying that we curse simply fellow believers or only those who do not believe. Instead we curse all of humanity "who are made in the likeness of God" (v. 9). James's words are reminiscent of the Sermon on the Mount. His teachings, like the teachings of Jesus, are not easy. In verse 10, James's words are like a scolding mother to her child who has behaved badly. To support his claim that the mouth cannot bless and curse at the same time, James lists several contradictions in the world. Fresh and brackish water do not come from the same spring; a fig tree does not produce both olives and figs; and finally, fresh water does not come from salt water. How many more contradictions could we find to support James? Unfortunately, or fortunately, God made human creatures as walking, talking contradictions. We possess an innate ability to praise God in one breath and curse others in the next. (John Mathis)

# CROSS CRY

### MARK 8:27-38

We have all heard the story of a woman who went to a major department store to buy a piece of jewelry. "I'd like a gold cross," she said to the sales clerk behind the counter. The clerk looked beneath the glass casing at the rich assortment of offerings and asked, "Would you like a plain one or one with a little man on it?"

George G. Hunter III has warned us that nearly half of our neighbors have either no Christian memory or a distant Christian memory (*How to Reach Secular People* [Nashville, Abingdon

Press, 1992]). The significance of the cross and Christ crucified on it have been largely lost to our culture. Not that the cross as a popular symbol is lost! We see it everywhere, worn or displayed. Some athletes cross themselves before a game, while candy confectioners make chocolate crosses to be eaten during Holy Week.

For Peter and the disciples, devout Jews, the cross was a symbol of suffering and shame, of utter weakness. Knowing that view of the cross is crucial to our understanding the Gospel.

Jesus and his disciples are at Caesarea Philippi, in the northern reaches of present-day Israel, near the borders of Lebanon and Syria. Jesus asks his disciples, "Who do people say that I am?" (v. 27b). They answered him, "John the Baptist; and others, Elijah; and still others, one of the prophets" (v. 28). In other words, forerunners to the Messiah, the long-awaited anointed one of God sent to redeem Israel. Jesus is seen as among those sent to prepare the way for the Messiah. There is comfort, if not convenience in that. Think of houseguests for a moment. Until they arrive, life continues pretty much as it always was—there is some clean up and preparation but no disruption, not yet. Once they arrive, your life's routine is changed. By thinking of Jesus as one still preparing the way, commitments can be put off or delayed. But Peter sensed that things had changed forever, though he didn't realize how much. So when Jesus asked his disciples, "Who do you say that I am?" Peter replied, "You are the Messiah" (v. 29), only to promptly blow it by insisting that the Messiah could not suffer, could not lose, could not die on a cross.

It wasn't so much that Peter loved Jesus and didn't want to see him suffer. Peter didn't see how Jesus' prediction that he would be rejected by the religious leaders and crucified could accomplish anything. Besides, Messiahs don't die for the people; people die for their Messiahs. Peter must have thought, "I've left everything: my successful fishing company, my family. I've sacrificed too much to have this enterprise dead-end." So Peter took Jesus aside to try to talk some sense into him, and there Peter caught Jesus' wrath. "Get behind me, Satan!" Jesus said (v. 33b).

Apparently, Jesus saw evidence in Peter's rebuke that evil was seeking the allegiance of his top disciple as a way of undermining Jesus' mission. Evil will seek a foothold even, especially, in a circle of people seeking to follow Jesus. So, Peter and the disciples had to decide about the cross, as do we.

Philip Yancey asks, "Do we look at Jesus' powerlessness [on the cross] as an example of God's impotence or as proof of God's love?" Is it a symbol of suffering and shame and nothing more? Or is it the very presence of God's redeeming love? Yancey writes, "The Romans, bred on power deities like Jupiter, could recognize little godlikeness in a crumpled corpse hanging on a tree." The Romans lined the roads of the Empire with rotting corpses on crosses as a reminder of their might. For "devout Jews, bred on stories of a power Jehovah," death by crucifixion could evidence martyrdom at the hands of the Empire but never Messiahship. In fact, Justin Martyr, an early church theologian, argued that "Jesus' death on a cross made a decisive case against his Messiahship for the Jews"; Jesus' crucifixion was a mark of weakness! (*The Jesus I Never Knew* [Grand Rapids: Zondervan Publishing House, 1995], p. 204).

Before you decide on this issue, consider this: Claiming the cross as God's redeeming work in Jesus will call for you to take up your cross in the future. Do you want Jesus in your life? Jesus tells us in this lesson that three behaviors will be required. First, we will have to deny ourselves. That's a behavior more obviously needed for some of us than for others. Second, we will have to take up our cross. It will be our choice, and it will mean choosing to suffer unjustly for the sake of another. Third, we are to follow Jesus. Peter forgot that; he tried to take charge, become Jesus' manager, and advise him on his next career move. This faithful behavior will mean seeking to discern Jesus' will for our days and our lives. Jesus warns us that following him won't come naturally, and it will run counter to popular culture.

When I was a boy, I learned to cross my fingers behind my back as to relieve my responsibility for saying something I didn't really mean. Later, I learned to cross fingers in front in hopes that it would bring good luck. Imagine my surprise when I first learned the early church, facing persecution from the Roman Empire, used crossed fingers as a sign (known to them, unknown to the Romans) of their trust in the God revealed to them in Jesus Christ! Come to me Jesus, so that I can follow you. Let me not gain everything the world values only to lose my very soul. (Kelly Bender)

# SEPTEMBER 21, 2003

## *Fifteenth Sunday After Pentecost*

---

**Worship Theme:** Jesus welcomes all people into the realm that is God's. If we follow Jesus, then we serve not only the poor but also the children, the widows, and the resident aliens among us.

---

**Readings:** Proverbs 31:10-31; James 3:13–4:3, 7-8*a*; Mark 9:30-37

**Call to Worship (Psalm 1)**

*Leader:*    Happy are those who do not follow the advice of the wicked,

**People:**    **Or take the path that sinners tread, or sit in the seat of scoffers;**

*Leader:*    But their delight is in the law of the LORD, and on his law they meditate day and night.

**People:**    **They are like trees planted by streams of water, which yield their fruit in its season, and their leaves do not wither.**

*Leader:*    In all that they do, they prosper.

**People:**    **The wicked are not so, but are like chaff that the wind drives away.**

*Leader:*    Therefore the wicked will not stand in the judgment, nor sinners in the congregation of the righteous;

**People:**    **For the LORD watches over the way of the righteous, but the way of the wicked will perish.**

**Pastoral Prayer:**

God of Judgment and Mercy, we are a peculiar people. We often clamor for justice for others but beg for mercy and forgiveness for ourselves. In our honest moments, not one of us would cry out for our own justice; we know too well we each need mercy. Grant us a wider vision of what it means to be united with all your people, O Lord. Remind us that the people created in your image are our brothers and sisters whom you unite in your divine love and mercy. Help us confess our sins so that we may be forgiven. In your forgiveness, O God, are the seeds of newness of life. Give us the wisdom and discernment to grasp the new life you offer us in Christ Jesus. Make us people who know what to do with our second chance at the blessed salvation you offer us freely. We pray in Jesus' name. Amen. (David Mosser)

# SERMON BRIEFS

## LIVING WISDOM

### PROVERBS 31:10-31

We meet a remarkable woman in the text. Some call her "the good wife" or "the capable wife," but others call her "a woman of strength, worth, or substance" (Christine Roy Yoder, "Wisdom as a Woman of Substance: A Socioeconomic Reading of Proverbs 1–9 and 31:10-31" [Ph.D. Diss., Princeton Theological Seminary, March 2000]). She is the star of a poem that concludes the book of Proverbs. Each verse of the poem begins with a different letter of the Hebrew alphabet, signifying her complete worth. She is far more precious than jewels. She is active and productive. She trades, buys, sells, and makes a profit. She clothes her family in crimson cloth, worn only by the wealthy. She manages a staff of servants. She speaks with kindness and gives to the poor. Because of her wise management, her husband does well and finds a position of honor in the city gates. Her children call her blessed and her husband praises her.

Near the end of the poem, we learn this Super Woman's secret: "Charm is deceitful, and beauty is vain, but a woman who fears the LORD is to be praised" (v. 30).

Can you imagine those lines appearing on the cover of a top-selling women's magazine or in a rock video aimed at teenage girls? The message of the media and pop culture is this: My worth as a woman is based on the beauty factor: what my body looks like or what clothes I wear. But this woman knows something different. Her worth is based on her relationship with God. She is praiseworthy because she fears the Lord.

In Proverbs, "the fear of the Lord" is a catchword for the godly life. To fear God is to be in a relationship to God that issues forth in right living. When you fear the Lord, your life reflects the goodness and righteousness of God. To know how to live rightly, to know what is pleasing to God, you must attain wisdom. Wisdom then guides you in your daily interactions, decisions, and dealings in the world.

Getting wisdom is the whole point of the book of Proverbs. And interestingly, Wisdom is portrayed in the book as a female character; a sought-after bride, a woman of worth with a price worth more than precious jewels. Woman Wisdom will bring her husband long life and prosperity. The man who acquires her and prizes her highly will benefit, for Wisdom gives wealth to those who love her and fills their storehouse treasuries. Attain Wisdom, and you will receive God's blessings on earth.

The woman that is praised at the end of the book of Proverbs is a real woman who looks a lot like Woman Wisdom in her activities and benefits. There is a correspondence between the two! She is a living embodiment of Wisdom. She fears the Lord, and so lives rightly and enjoys the good life.

We who fear the Lord and live rightly will embody wisdom as well. If we base our worth on our relationship with God and walk in God's ways, we will know overflowing abundance for others and ourselves. The culture may not buy it. But for those who do, her way is worth more than precious jewels.

So, go after Wisdom. Take her hand. Prize her highly. And she will look well to your ways all your days. (Laura Jernigan)

# DOWNWARD MOBILITY

## JAMES 3:13–4:3, 7-8*a*

## I. Wisdom from Above

Why do we do anything? What is our motivation? Are our actions done out of love or out of selfish ambition? James posed these questions to the early church. It is important to James that believers understand their motivation. We are to realize that it is through God that we are capable of serving others with our good works. Many great works have been done in the church out of selfish ambition. The wisdom of God is that the Lord allows these acts to be accomplished even while those accomplishing them do so for the wrong reasons. James makes a distinction between wisdom from above and earthly wisdom. Earthly wisdom is that which comes from humanity—selfishness, envy, boastfulness, and falsehood. James proclaims that this wisdom is not spiritual wisdom. It is "devilish" and of this world. In verse 3:17, James proclaims that, "wisdom from above is first pure, then peaceable, gentle, willing to yield, full of mercy and good fruits, without a trace of partiality or hypocrisy." This wisdom is pure in that it is holy and from God. This wisdom is peaceable in that it seeks justice and not selfish gain. This wisdom is gentle in that it cares for others in the world. This wisdom is willing to yield in that it is concerned first with others and places itself as a secondary interest. This wisdom is full of mercy in that it is willing to forgive. And finally, this wisdom is full of good fruits in that it shows love, joy, peace, patience, kindness, generosity, faithfulness, gentleness, and self-control. We need to ask ourselves, "Who is wise and understanding among [us]?" (v. 3:13). For us to have the ability to serve God as the Lord calls us to serve, we must rely on wisdom from above and not on earthly wisdom.

## II. Peacemaking

I believe that many books could be written about verse 18. How many persons throughout history have sown a harvest of righteousness by their peacemaking. Jesus was the ultimate purveyor

318

of peace. Dietrich Bonhoeffer struggled in Nazi Germany to speak out against the atrocities of Hitler and the German church that supported Hitler. Mother Teresa worked diligently for years with the poor and sick of Calcutta. Many in the United States fought to end slavery during the early growth of our nation. God uses many faithful people to be peacemakers, but more important the Lord uses everyday people, ordinary saints, to bring peace into the world. When we strive to live in God's will, we can be peaceful. James proclaims that when we covet the things of this world, we become "engage[d] in disputes and conflicts" (v. 4:2).

### III. A Closer Relationship with God

If you are seeking a closer relationship with God, what should you do? If you fall in love with someone, do you ignore that person? The lesson in James 4:8a is a simple plan for anyone seeking a deeper and more meaningful relationship with the Lord. "Draw near to God, and he will draw near to you." We must seek God's will for our lives and resist the things of this world and the prince of this world. James writes that we do not have what we want not because we do not ask but because we ask for the wrong reasons. We are seeking things that bring us pleasure, but we truly do not know what will make us happy. When we ask for God's will for our lives, it is amazing how much joy enters into our lives. Many people find that corporate ladder climbing has left them unfulfilled. They believed that the more money they made and the more possessions they owned, the happier they would be. They found out they were wrong. There is a new trend toward downward mobility. People are seeking lives and jobs that are more fulfilling. James knew in his day, as we are finding out in our time, that we need to simplify. "Draw near to God, and he will draw near to you." (John Mathis)

## JOY FULLY SERVING

### MARK 9:30-37

In the comic strip "Calvin and Hobbes," by Bill Watterson, Calvin tells Hobbes that people would be less self-centered if they focused more on others than on themselves. Then Calvin suggests that everyone simply focus their attention on him as an alternative.

Calvin just doesn't get it! Neither did the disciples, according to our Gospel lesson. Jesus is anticipating heading south, toward Jerusalem. He has again talked about how he will suffer. It's important that Jesus and his inner circle be on the same page. The text tells us that, still, the disciples don't understand and are afraid to ask. I remember times when I didn't understand but was afraid to ask—math classes, mostly, in junior and senior high school. I didn't want to come off as more stupid than I already felt!

Maybe the disciples knew so much they were afraid to know any more. It's not unlike the typical response when receiving an alarming diagnosis from a doctor. The gist may be so negative that we are afraid to ask any questions; afraid to understand all the details; afraid to know any more. I say that because the text tells us the disciples had been arguing among themselves as to who was the greatest. Could it be that they had understood enough of Jesus' pronouncement to sense his eventual demise so that conversation and conflict had ensued as to who would be best qualified to lead?

We don't know. What Mark does tell us is that when Jesus confronted them they were all too ashamed to reply. They had no defense. So long as they thought Jesus wouldn't know, what did it matter? When in Jesus' presence, the inappropriateness of their behavior was painfully obvious. There is a lesson here, isn't there? When knowing Jesus' presence, our behaviors are likely to be more appropriate, even faithful?

Jesus took their inappropriate behavior seriously because the text says, "He sat down to teach." William Barclay, a biblical theologian, writes that when rabbis assumed the role of master teacher, they would sit down. When Jesus sat down, it clearly communicated to his disciples to listen; that what is to follow will be of utmost importance.

And what did he say? If you want to be great in the kingdom it won't come by being first in line, first to be served. Rather you will need to place yourself "last of all and servant of all" (v. 35).

Jesus wasn't against ambition, he refocused it. Instead of ambition to rule he substituted ambition to serve. Instead of ambition to have things done for us, he substituted ambition to do things for others.

Caregivers who are forever and always doing things for others, even to the point of neglecting self, take note. There is a difference between serving out of a genuine desire to help and helping because of a need to be loved by those you help. Jesus names it later in Mark 12:31 as finding that balance between love of self and love of others.

And, just in case the disciples still hadn't gotten the message, Jesus, knowing that some of them were visual learners, took a child in his lap and said, "Whoever welcomes one such child in my name welcomes me" (v. 37a). Jesus didn't give a children's message. The child was the message. The message wasn't that children are the greatest in the Kingdom. Rather, all who receive a child will be especially close to Jesus.

A congregation I once served sponsored a breakfast club every weekday morning for "at risk" children, often for as many as two hundred. Studies had shown that a healthy breakfast could raise a child's school performance by as much as 20 percent. Lots of volunteers were required to provide the program, so I took my turn, always reluctantly, out of a sense of duty. I didn't like the wake-up call (we had to be at the church's fellowship hall by 6:30 A.M.), and I didn't like a number of the kids. Too many of them, from my perspective, were rude and ill-mannered.

But one of the volunteers, a retired schoolteacher and member of the church, was there every day. One morning, I watched as she responded to a child who had just dumped a bowl of oatmeal on a little girl's head. When confronted, the culprit threw a fit. He was out of control: kicking, screaming, and cursing. I watched as this woman hugged the child from behind, sat on the floor with the child between her legs, in what social workers call a "therapeutic hug." She rocked him and sang to him while he continued to throw his fit. Finally, when his rage was spent, he was taken to the time-out room. I said to her, "I don't know how you do it." She replied, "My arms weren't the only arms around that child. Jesus was holding him too. When I added my arms to the circle I felt especially close to Jesus, and it filled me with joy." She modeled for me that when I serve, however reluctantly, in the name of Jesus, Jesus will be discovered close by. There will then be more than enough joy to serve around. (Kelly Bender)

# SEPTEMBER 28, 2003

*Sixteenth Sunday After Pentecost*

---

**Worship Theme:** Jesus tells gospel believers that they are the salt of the earth. But Jesus also asks, "If salt has lost its saltiness, how can you season it" (Mark 9:50)? Are we still the salt of the earth?

---

**Readings:** Esther 7:1-6, 9-10; 9:20-22; James 5:13-20; Mark 9:38-50

### Call to Worship (Psalm 124:1-8)

| | |
|---|---|
| *Leader:* | If it had not been the LORD who was on our side—let Israel now say—if it had not been the LORD who was on our side, when our enemies attacked us, |
| ***People:*** | **Then they would have swallowed us up alive, when their anger was kindled against us;** |
| *Leader:* | Then the flood would have swept us away, the torrent would have gone over us; |
| ***People:*** | **Then over us would have gone the raging waters.** |
| *Leader:* | Blessed be the LORD, who has not given us as prey to their teeth. |
| ***People:*** | **We have escaped like a bird from the snare of the fowlers; the snare is broken, and we have escaped.** |
| ***All:*** | **Our help is in the name of the LORD, who made heaven and earth.** |

**Pastoral Prayer:**

O God, our hope for years to come, impart to us a willingness to think through what it means to be Jesus' disciples. Too often we come to our places of worship and ask what God can do for us. Help us turn our lives and questions toward a larger task. What is it we can do for God and God's people in our lives? Day by day, circumstances confront us with opportunities to proclaim Jesus' name in small ways that make a big difference in the lives of hurting people. Give us the determination to again be your people. Restore in us that divine fire that will set the world afire for the sake of Jesus' realm. Give us occasions in which we can make the world a different place for the sake of the gospel. You, O God, have reconciled the world to yourself. We pray that we can be agents of your divine reconciliation. We pray this in the holy and righteous name of Jesus. Amen. (David Mosser)

# SERMON BRIEFS

## UNFLAUNTED FAITHFULNESS

### ESTHER 7:1-6, 9-10; 9:20-22

The story of Esther is important for each of us. If you are Jewish it is the origin of the observance of Purim, a day of feasting, celebration, and service to the poor. If you are a student of ancient history, it is a revealing look into ancient culture. If you are a student of human personality, it is a testimony of how little humanity has changed through the centuries. There are schemers, dreamers, and people who never quit—no matter what the odds. If you are a person of faith, it is a heroine's story, an example of faith that perseveres and overcomes.

### I. Faith Takes Courage

Esther is Queen to the Persian King Ahasuerus. An evil and subtle plot arises in this kingdom that would bring an end to the Hebrew race there. Only by Esther's courage and character is the anti-Semitic plot foiled and her people saved. Esther risked her life and her lifestyle. She served and lived at the pleasure and whim of the king. What are we willing to risk for faith?

A well-paid government contractor gives up his six-figure salary to answer a call to Christian service and becomes a church business manager. A *summa cum laude* graduate of a prestigious liberal arts university humbly rebuffs lucrative offers from Fortune 500 companies, which were wooing her upon graduation. Instead, she gives two years of her life and career to quietly serve as a missionary to the poorest of the poor along the border between the United States and Mexico. Two well-paid yuppies in a Texas metropolis have their hearts touched by their church's stewardship campaign. They sell their $400,000 home and $45,000 cars to live a more modest lifestyle so that they can generously support their church's ministry. What are we willing to give up for faith?

## II. Faith Takes Commitment

Faithfulness unflaunted is the unobtrusive, unspectacular, everyday, ordinary daily discipleship that keeps the earth moving and life worth living. Fidelity and love are demonstrated by those who faithfully make a craft, bake a pie, repair a pew, clean a classroom, make a phone call, invite a friend, visit a nursing home, pick up trash, mail a card, or pray for others. Faithfulness unflaunted seeks no reward, serves God and others rather than self, and solicits no recognition or spotlight.

A dear friend and her husband, gave up three years of their life to care for the woman's aging mother who had developed Alzheimer's disease. Her mother required round-the-clock attention for her own safety and to prevent her from wandering off onto a highway or into the woods. When her mother died, her daughter remarked how much she missed her. "Aren't you relieved from your labor?" I asked. To which she simply replied, "Yes, but I still miss my mother." Daily commitment seeks no relief or reward beyond the satisfaction of fulfillment, purpose, and accomplishment of the goal at hand.

## III. Faith Reveals Character

In what or whom do you place your faith? Do you most trust money and possessions, prayer and holy intervention, or relationships and human resourcefulness? Do you feel more comfort in holding on to something you can own or in being blessed by the warmth of human touch, a radiant smile, and a caring word? Esther believed in herself, her heritage, her God, her people. She was not willing to deny who she was in order to "play it safe." Haman placed his faith in his own scheming, plotting, and preparations. His thirst for royal power and praise fueled his actions and led to his own undoing.

In the Greek version of this story, the king's heart is turned in Esther's favor by the providence of God. Esther was faithful to God and to her people. God was faithful in return. Faith reveals character, the character of the one who believes and the nature of the God in whom we place our trust and belief. (Gary Kindley)

# SPECIAL PEOPLE

## JAMES 5:13-20

Rugged individualism is often the role model favored as a way of life in American society. Cultural heroes like Daniel Boone and Davy Crockett were the role models for many young children growing up in the 1950s. Movie stars like John Wayne, Clint Eastwood, and Harrison Ford have often played the part of the complete person who needs nothing and needs no one to be successful.

Men and women in much of American society are taught to keep their emotions in check, to be strong, and not to let others know we need anything.

Into such a world comes the church with a totally different point of view. Instead of individualism, the church offers community. Instead of competition, which individualism always encourages, the church teaches cooperation. The church is the alternative community inviting persons to a life that involves them with one another in ways that make life better for all.

The epistle of James offers instruction for the practice of religious beliefs. James reminds us that "faith without works is dead." Part of the work of faith is the practice of faith. And the practice of faith means helping one another live whole lives. We share the suffering of one another, and the joy. We care for the sick with attentive presence. We help one another with sin burdens by hearing confessions and lovingly calling sisters and brothers back to "the truth." The instruction of James, like much of the rest of the teaching of the New Testament, is that we need one another. We have a common ministry to be lived out in the community of faith that affects the lives of all members.

Far from being an invasion of privacy, the instruction of James offers a way of living that enables us to draw from the strength of one another. The church is a body knitted together by love and concern for all the members. Of course for love to be love, it must be practiced by involving ourselves in each other's lives. In my ministry I have often heard wonderful compliments at the door of the church for the sermon just preached. But the ministry that people remember, really remember, after years have passed is not the words of a particular sermon. Rather, they speak of the times when Christian presence was brought to some life situation.

There are two stories that capture the spirit of James in the text before us. One is about a little girl who was late for the evening meal with her family. Her father scolded her for her tardiness and demanded to know why she was late. She explained that her friend had dropped a cherished doll on the sidewalk, and the doll had been broken beyond repair. "So you stopped to help her pick it up?" asked her father. "No," said the little one. "I stopped to help her cry."

This is what the church does when it is the church in the most Christlike sense. We bear the burdens of one another, rejoicing and crying with one another in an expression of redemptive community.

The other story is from a Special Olympics event. Boys and girls are about to run a race. On the sidelines are parents and friends shouting encouragement to the runners. The race begins but before the children run very far, a little boy trips and falls on the running track. And all the children in the race stop. The parents and others are shouting, "Don't stop! This is your chance to win! Run!"

But the special children seem deaf to these words of instruction. Instead, one little girl kneels before her fallen companion and begins to ask over and over, "Are you all right?" The other children, seeing her care, also kneel and ask, "Are you all right?" They gently touch the fallen little one, brushing off the sand of the track, all the while repeating the question of love and concern, "Are you all right?"

Finally the fallen racer begins to respond to this special ministry and says through his tears and sobs, "I'm all right."

All the while the race watchers are shouting, "Run! You can win now. This is your chance." But the children seem not to hear.

The runners help the little boy to his feet. And then an amazing thing happens. These special children join hands across the track and run the race as one, crossing the finish line together.

Is there any better image of the church at its best than this? Perhaps it takes special people to do what James is teaching. By God's grace may we be that special people who care for one another in easy and difficult times. It is really the only way to live that matters. It is the only way to get to the finish line that counts. (Chris Andrews)

# A SMALLER WORLD NEEDS BIGGER PEOPLE

## MARK 9:38-50

This is a passage that most of us dislike because it suggests that Jesus, at least in Mark, draws boundaries considerably more gracious and expansive than we would draw. Part of human nature is to have insiders and outsiders. Theologically speaking, the insiders agree with us and the outsiders do not. The problem is that God has a completely different set of boundaries than we do. In this text, the followers of Jesus encounter a man who is not a disciple and apparently has somewhat different beliefs, yet he is healing people in Jesus' name.

The problem is that God is helping a number of people, despite the fact that we disagree with their theology. A woman who worked for us had the most simple, even primitive, theology imaginable. However, she had raised six children, sent them to college, worked every day without the benefit of much education, and supported her family even after her husband had been killed in an auto accident. Her faith brought her an incredible strength and a full life, however had she written my sermons or taught my Bible study, I would have been scorned.

The text suggests that if we were to make a list of the people we ignore, these are the people Jesus is interested in. The text suggests that if we were to ignore the lines that society has drawn between people, we would be in line with God. This lesson suggests that if we were to ignore established religious convention in order to help someone, God would be pleased. The text suggests that it is dangerous for you to just hang around with people like yourself.

This God about whom Mark writes is a God not of one state, or of one country, or of one continent. This God is a God of the whole world. Our theology and our viewpoint is often too narrow. God wants disciples who are willing to take chances and step out in adventure in order to expand God's kingdom. The expansion of that Kingdom involves a love that is larger than any of us. Our job is to constantly challenge ourselves and those around us to consider the remarkable, far-reaching, inclusive love of Mark's ninth chapter.

A favorite chaplain talked of the time when thirteen religious groups met in the basement of the university chapel. There were all kinds of competing viewpoints—Baptists, Methodists, Lutherans, Jews, Presbyterians, Catholics, Campus Crusade, Intervarsity, and so forth. Naturally, there was a wide range of viewpoints on every topic and a great deal of heated discussion. The chaplain overheard one person wonder if this was what heaven is like. If the standard is the ninth chapter of Mark, the answer is surely Yes!

One popular religious consultant has warned that if we concern ourselves only with our needs rather than in reaching out to those who need us and God, we shall become extinct. How many churches have died because they had an inward-looking, rigid theology? How many churches have died because the energy was directed inward and not outward?

Jesus' message in the ninth chapter of Mark is extremely appropriate for a world that is becoming smaller. As the world becomes smaller, it needs more and more people who are becoming bigger. (Wayne Day)

# REFLECTIONS

❦

## OCTOBER

**Reflection Verse:** " *'Come to me, all you who are weary and burdened, and I will give you rest. Take my yoke upon you and learn from me, for I am gentle and humble in heart, and you will find rest for your souls. For my yoke is easy and my burden is light.'* " *(Matthew 11:28-30 NIV)*

When I return from vacation in the month of September, I declare and proclaim with great zeal and fervor, "I know only Jesus Christ and him crucified." I have spent time with the Lord and have been renewed in God and can therefore also say, "My message and my preaching were not with wise and persuasive words, but with a demonstration of the Spirit's power." But by the end of September, I am caught again in the hustle, bustle, and complexity of congregational life. By the end of September, the pace has so quickened that I find preparation time for the sermon difficult to come by. I am fighting to hold on to the statements from 1 Corinthians 2. I am face-to-face with the fact that I am overcommitted and overextended. There is a drain on my spiritual passion.

How quickly we can fall into the trap of an overloaded and overcommitted life. It has only been a month since vacation, but we notice that we are weary. Most of us suffer from soul fatigue, or what has been termed *compassion fatigue*. I am usually fighting with guilt because I have promised myself and my family that I would not resume a life of frantic activity. In the midst of my failure, I hear Jesus say, "Come unto me all ye that labor and are heavy laden, and I will give you rest" (Matthew 11:28 KJV).

The term *labor* has the connotation of hard struggle and toil. *Burden* is to be overloaded and weighted down with many things like the beasts of toil. Ministry can often feel like labor. Ministry can be an experience of hard struggle and toil. Being a pastor and preacher can sometimes feel as though we are burdened and weighted down with many things. I notice that when I live in frantic activity and overcommitment, I skim relationships and am less engaged with people; I short my time and intimacy with God; and I am tired and weary and can easily fall into sin. But Jesus says, "Take my yoke upon you and learn from me . . . for my yoke is easy and my burden is light." What does Jesus mean when he says this? What does Jesus' meaning have to do with the funerals, hospital visits, administrative meetings, counseling, conflict resolution, sermon preparation, sermon delivery, and so on that is part of the responsibility of the everyday pastor? I am a pastor; what does Jesus mean by *rest*?

We must first recognize that Jesus says, "Come to me." It does not say come to a stress management class, although that might help. It does not say go back on vacation, although that would not be a bad idea. Jesus does not even say come to church. Jesus says, "Come to me. I will give you rest." Jesus says, "I will partner with you, and I will preserve you." The image of a yoke recalls a harness with two stations: one animal pulls from one harness and the other animal pulls from the other. Jesus says, "Take my yoke upon yourself because if you take one side, I will take the other. I will be a partner with you in this gospel. You will not have to pull all the weight." Jesus tells us about his ministry and says, "I never lived in a hurry. I never lived running from one deadline to the next." Jesus makes a distinction between his yoke and the heavy yoke of legalism that the Pharisees laid on people. Jesus says, "My yoke is easy and my burden is light."

Rest is indispensable in preaching. I know that we all do it without rest sometimes. I have long days and late nights, and sermon preparation somehow falls to the bottom of the agenda. By the time I get to preparing the sermon, I am weary, and sometimes it is only by the grace of God that I get through it. God has been far more gracious than I have ever deserved. But here is Jesus saying, "Come unto me all ye that labor and are heavy laden, and I will give you rest. . . . for my yoke is easy, and my burden is light" (vv. 28, 30 KJV).

In order to preach effectively, I am a proponent of fewer counseling sessions and fewer administrative meetings. I am a proponent of one day off per week and one sermon preparation day as well, which means that the preacher is not in the office for two days a week. I am a proponent of more time with the family and more time for exercise. I am a proponent of sabbatical time and renewal retreats and conferences. I am a proponent of clergy getting more rest and taking absolutely every day of their vacation. I am a proponent of us doing less crazy things for the church. I once taught a Sunday school class in the middle of preaching two sermons on Sunday morning—that was crazy! I once did administrative meetings Sunday after service or sometimes early on Sunday mornings—that was crazy. I did all kinds of crazy things that hampered my preaching by eroding my rest.

We are not in this preaching task alone. We are not by ourselves in the unfolding preaching drama. But for us to pull our part, we must have rest. God does not require frantic activity and overcommitted lives, "for [his] yoke is easy and [his] burden is light."

Dear God, I admit that I do not know how to rest. Come into my life and speak to me and show me what your rest looks like. I admit that I am weary and burdened. I admit my preaching has suffered because of the pace of my life. Help me to let some things go. Help me to keep my promises to my family. (Frank Thomas)

# OCTOBER 5, 2003

## *Seventeenth Sunday After Pentecost*

---

**Worship Theme:** Suffering comes to all people sooner or later. The issue about suffering is not whether we suffer but whether our suffering has a redemptive purpose.

---

**Readings:** Job 1:1; 2:1-10; Hebrews 1:1-4; 2:5-12; Mark 10:2-16

**Call to Worship (Psalm 26:1-7, 11-12 RSV)**

*Leader:* Vindicate me, O LORD, for I have walked in my integrity, and I have trusted in the LORD without wavering.

*People:* **Prove me, O LORD, and try me; test my heart and my mind.**

*Leader:* For thy steadfast love is before my eyes, and I walk in faithfulness to thee.

*People:* **I do not sit with false men, nor do I consort with dissemblers;**

*Leader:* I hate the company of evildoers, and will not sit with the wicked.

*People:* **I wash my hands in innocence, and go about thy altar, O LORD, singing aloud a song of thanksgiving, and telling all thy wondrous deeds.**

*Leader:* But as for me, I walk in my integrity; redeem me, and be gracious to me.

333

*All:*        **My foot stands on level ground; in the great
              congregation I will bless the** LORD.

**Pastoral Prayer:**

Dear Lord of Life and Beyond, we praise your holy name. You
have called us out as your people and given us our names at baptism. At Holy Communion you feed us with the Bread of
Heaven, Jesus Christ. Daily, as we study your holy Word, we are
fed by the Word that dwells at the heart of the church. Day by
day, however, Lord, we see the suffering of innocents. Our
friends and family suffer affliction and alienation in ways that go
far beyond our mortal reason. Help us understand that suffering
may have redemptive purpose, although it is difficult for us to
imagine what it may be. Redemptive suffering does not lessen
the pain. Yet, in it you remind us of Jesus' suffering in which you
vindicated the Messiah. So too in our suffering may you provide
us a place and opportunity to make our witness. Ease us toward
you and the eternal realm that awaits all who are faithful. We
pray this in Christ's holy name. Amen. (David Mosser)

# SERMON BRIEFS

## THE JOB WITHIN

### JOB 1:1; 2:1-10

The questions are older than Job: Why do human beings suffer? From whence come the slings and arrows of life? What
causes human pain? Who can rescue us from life's random
errors? "Life's random errors?" Dr. J. Truett Gannon, Senior Professor of Ministry at the McAfee School of Theology in Atlanta,
observes that in life, random, seemingly mindless errors inject
themselves into the human condition. Viruses, bacteria, paralysis,
accidents, misfortune, cancer, Alzheimer's disease, and dozens of
other maladies, both named and unnamed, afflict us on the
human journey. To whom can we turn?

The unanswerable conundrums of our common humanity are
older than Job and as current as the morning paper. The book of Job

has been described in many ways: a play (Archibald MacLeish's *J.B.*), an epic poem, a treatise on suffering, and a historical account of an ancient wise man. What is this text, this tale we will hear as holy Scripture these next few weeks? What if the book of Job is a story about every human being? What if this is your story and my story?

The ancients had a curious way of interpreting life. Prosperity was a sign of God's blessing; suffering and misfortune, a sign of God's judgment. Those who fared well in life marched across the stage of time basking in God's smile. The poor, the outcast, the less fortunate trudged through life beneath God's frown. Lest we be too harsh on our ancient friends, we prefer the K.I.S.S. theory (Keep it Simple Silly) to the prosperity-misfortune dilemma ourselves. "You got a promotion? A new house? An inheritance? God has surely smiled on you." Or when the tide turns in life—cancer, AIDS, divorce—we can't avoid wondering, "What did they do to deserve that?" It's simple all right. But is it healthy?

The writer introduces us to Job, a man "blameless and upright, one who feared God and turned away from evil" (v. 1:1). Our kind of person, for sure. Job was a person who would be welcomed into any civic club, congregation, or community. Chambers of Commerce go far with people having Job's profile. Who wouldn't want Job for a neighbor? That is, until all hell breaks loose around him.

Something threatening is going on without Job's knowledge. Satan, or "the Accuser," comes before God and bargains for Job's soul. Satan accuses Job of loving and obeying God for purely selfish reasons. Job, Satan argues, is not a true believer. Rather, Job is a man whose faith is mortgaged to his fortune. Take everything away from him, the Accuser suggests to God, and Job will "curse you to your face" (v. 5).

What if this episode staged in heaven never took place? What if the storyteller sets up this meeting between God and Satan because we who hear the story believe that's the way it is. But what if that's not the way it is at all? Playwrights do this all the time. They bring us in on a mutually agreeable conspiracy in order to demolish our untested notions. Urban legends—God won't put more on you than you can take; What goes around comes around; God helps those who help themselves—are just that: legends.

Unspeakable tragedy descends on Job as it often does on us. At some deep level, Job lives within us all. The tale is told to give us a text through which we can face the suffering that comes our way with simple courage and uncommon faith. Why do good people suffer? This is a profoundly troubling question. In my judgment, a more transformative question is, *What is God calling me to become through suffering?* That is the question Job will be asking us these autumnal October Sundays. (Timothy Owings)

# NO ONE OR NOTHING GREATER

### HEBREWS 1:1-4; 2:5-12

These verses very much set forth the theme of this whole letter: the superiority of Christ. It's true that in the past God chose many different ways to be revealed, even through human beings like the prophets. But now God has chosen something far superior to all those ways; God has come in God's own son. The Son is Jesus, the fullest revelation of God that we have been given. In flesh and blood, we see and hear God and what God desires for us and from us. Indeed, all else in the past is measured by this new revelation.

Why is this new revelation so far above all others?

First, Jesus is God's son. Who better to reveal God and God's will than a child who has lived in the constant presence of the Parent? Jesus said in John 10:30, "I and the Father are one" (NIV) and in John 14:9, "He that hath seen me hath seen the Father" (KJV). In Jesus, we see God as never before.

Second, Jesus is far superior because he is now "heir of all things" (v. 1:2). All the physical and spiritual blessings of God are his inheritance and, by implication, also passed down to those who follow him, who are gathered into God's family.

Third, Christ is the one from before time through whom God created all things. This is perhaps a reference to the teaching we find in John 1:1-14 of how Jesus is the Word, or agent, God used to create the world (see also Colossians 1:16).

Fourth, Christ is the reflection of God's own glory, which calls to mind Moses coming down from the mountain having been transformed by his communion with God.

Fifth, more than just a reflection of God's glory, Jesus is the expressed image of God. The idea behind this is the impression that a seal creates in wax. It leaves its exact likeness there. So, in Christ, we see the image of God, what God is like. Christ is God's self-portrait.

Sixth, Christ's word sustains all things. Just as Jesus was the Word that created all things, Jesus is also that power that holds everything together, that supports and sustains the universe (see Colossians 1:17).

Seventh, referring to the priestly work of Christ: Jesus is the one who has "purged our sins."

Eighth, the writer then reminds the reader just where Christ sits now, after his ascension—at the right hand of God. Christ is Priest and King! As such Christ deserves the highest honor, praise, and devotion.

Verses 1:4 and 2:5-12 are interesting passages contrasting Christ with the angels. It may be that some of the readers of this letter thought Jesus was simply another such being—an angel, a messenger no different than any other. But the writer says that no angel was ever called God's "own son," therefore no angel deserves the honor and position rightly afforded to Christ. God brought about salvation for the world through one who accepted a place lower than the angels, becoming a human being. He did so in order to carry out God's plan to bring saving grace to human life. God created people for a loving relationship with God. Sin has shattered that. Nothing we do can restore it. So God did all that was needed in Christ. No wonder we call him "Lord." (Bass Mitchell)

## MATTERS OF THE HEART

### MARK 10:2-16

We are taught as children that marriage is a matter of the heart. Someday, each child will grow up, and perchance fall in love, get married, and have children; the process is cyclical. It all sounds so simple. Perhaps it would be simple if our hearts always functioned perfectly, but unfortunately, they do not.

THE ABINGDON PREACHING ANNUAL 2003

What could be a simple cyclical process has become progressively complicated with broken hearts and many marriages ending in divorce.

To remind us that divorce is not just a modern issue, the Gospel of Mark gives us a glimpse of the divorce rate in Jesus' time. Jesus is approached by the Pharisees with a question about the law surrounding marriage and divorce. Jesus' answer takes us back to the time of creation—the beginning of all life and relationships. It is as if Jesus is saying, as a good teacher might, "Let's go back to the basics." Jesus teaches that marriage is not, and never has been, a matter of the heart. God created males and females to be together; God puts two people together so that they may complement and support each other. Jesus even goes so far as to issue a charge, as he says, "what God has joined together, let no one separate" (v. 9). This is quite a strong statement regarding divorce. If the Pharisees came to Jesus to seek out specific ways to dissolve a marriage, they would leave disappointed.

Sometimes God's laws are just too simple for humans to follow. In this text, Jesus shows us that somewhere along the line, marriages became matters of the heart. Moses wrote a certificate permitting divorce—the destruction of a God-ordained covenant, because of "your hardness of heart" (v. 5). We, as humans, became restless and could not maintain relationships as they have been since the beginning.

The disciples, wanting to make sure they understand this basic concept, ask Jesus again about marriage and divorce. Again, Jesus explains to them in the plainest of terms, if a man divorces his wife and marries another, he commits adultery. And for emphasis, Jesus gives equal attention to wives as he says, "If she divorces her husband and marries another, she commits adultery" (v. 12). This statement stands in contrast to the Pharisees' original question: "Is it lawful for a man to divorce his wife" (v. 2b). Jesus both empowers and condemns husbands and wives within divorced marriages.

Jesus cannot seem to make his stance on marriage more clear or simple. Marriage is a matter of God, not a matter of the heart. Divorce, it seems, is not for humans to grant.

At the close of this story, the disciples are turning away parents and their children who want to see Jesus. He rebukes his disciples and invites the children to surround him. With this action, Jesus explains that the kingdom of God belongs to those who believe like children. Ironically, it is children who understand the most simplistic and basic of concepts. They do not grasp abstract laws and principles like theologians, scholars, or even Pharisees.

Jesus lays his hands on the children and blesses them. He shows them love, probably because they unconditionally love him in return. They do not complicate matters with rules or laws. They believe Jesus' words as he speaks them. It is as if Jesus looks at the children and sighs, "Finally, someone who understands." (Victoria Atkinson White)

# OCTOBER 12, 2003

## *Eighteenth Sunday After Pentecost*

---

**Worship Theme:** In God's Word all possibilities for human creatures exist. As disciples dwell in the truth of God's Word they dwell in both humility and security.

---

**Readings:** Job 23:1-9, 16-17; Hebrews 4:12-16; Mark 10:17-31

**Call to Worship (Psalm 22:2, 3-5, 11; Hebrews 4:16)**

| | |
|---|---|
| *Leader:* | O my God, I cry by day, but you do not answer; and by night, but find no rest. |
| ***People:*** | **Yet you are holy, enthroned on the praises of Israel.** |
| *Leader:* | In you our ancestors trusted; they trusted, and you delivered them. |
| ***People:*** | **To you they cried, and were saved; in you they trusted, and were not put to shame.** |
| *Leader:* | Do not be far from me, for trouble is near and there is no one to help. |
| ***All:*** | **Let us therefore approach the throne of grace with boldness, so that we may receive mercy and find grace to help in time of need.** |

**Pastoral Prayer:**

Great God of Heaven and Earth, hear our prayer this day. We often suffer because we do not feel the assurance that we want to feel in our relationship to you. In Jesus you have come to give us

340

a glimpse of the heavenly places and offer to us a foretaste of life eternal. Yet, in our idol of security, we want more. We want a sign, or we want words of assurance, or, even worse, we lust after some kind of divine guarantee from you. However, in our anxiety your word comes again to us. Give us ears that hear the great promise of the ages. Your have promised us that in Christ Jesus nothing can separate us from your love. Help us hear and receive again this wonderful promise of life. Let us take this promise and live it and share it with others day by day. We pray for this and everything in the name of Jesus. Amen. (David Mosser)

## SERMON BRIEFS

### GOD'S PRESENCE: A GIFT

#### JOB 23:1-9, 16-17

God hiding. That's Job's dilemma, even ours. Sitting in the ashes of our life's calamities, friends come to offer their sympathy, counsel, scorn. We listen. We listen carefully. But the volume of counsel, compassion, or criticism together cannot equal one word, one syllable from God. We long to be heard and to hear; to be understood and to understand. Thirsty, desperate, exhausted we demand a hearing.

The lovely tenor aria, "If With All Your Hearts," in Felix Mendelssohn's *Elijah*, is based on Jeremiah 29:13, "And ye shall seek me, and find me, when ye shall search for me with all your heart" (KJV). And Job 23:3, "Oh that I knew where I might find Him! that I might come even to his seat" (KJV). It is a lovely aria; however, Job petitions with all his heart, but God is not so easily found. How neat and tidy it would be if we could reach God at our convenience.

Job has another problem. Not only is God hidden—" 'If I go forward, he is not there; or backward, I cannot perceive him' " (v. 8)—God is silent. Paul S. Fiddes, principal of Regent's Park College, Oxford University, in his book, *The Creative Suffering of God*, reminds us that God's silence does not mean God's absence. Some of life's most profound moments of intimacy—between husband and wife, between parent and child, between God and the soul—are often blatantly silent. In Phillips Brooks's beloved Christmas carol, "O Little Town of Bethlehem," we sing, "How silently, how silently, the wondrous gift is given; so God imparts to human hearts the blessings of his heaven" (*The United Methodist Hymnal* [Nashville: The United Methodist Publishing House, 1999], 230).

Job is not so sure. In fact, Job is angry: bitter anger, demanding anger, verbose anger. Job wants answers to suffering's questions, not sympathy; resolution, not advice; healing, not criticism. If only Job could have one word from God, one fill-in-the-blank answer, Job would be satisfied. Or, would he? So sunken in despair is the old man, he accuses God of terrorizing him. "If only I could vanish in darkness" (v. 17). "If only," indeed.

Our text throws an all-too-familiar reality into the order of worship this Sunday. Although we have donned our Sunday clothes, made our way to the house of worship, and done our best to focus on God, the nauseating bitterness served to us by life is not so easily dismissed from our souls. A child has died, a cancer has returned, a friend is going through the worst kind of emotional trauma. Three hymns, a couple of prayers, and a sermon do not bring healing. We are hurt, lost, angry, disappointed, hungry. To make matters worse, we can't even get a syllable from God.

There are times that all we can do in church is get through the service. It's not that the hymns are unfamiliar or the anthems tedious. No, we're not talking about liturgical dissatisfaction. Rather, Job walks into our service today and tells us that it's okay to complain to God, to unravel all the twisted, sordid details of our suffering. It's perfectly acceptable and appropriate to unload on the Almighty, so long as we give God the privilege of coming alongside us in silence.

When our service is over and you make your way to your car, be careful not to critique the liturgy too harshly or criticize the preacher too quickly. What actually may be going on is that life has crushed all that was lovely, beautiful, and precious. Right now, in what may seem like terrifying silence, the God of Abraham and Sarah, Jesus and Paul, and the other victims of a thousand injustices quietly wants to walk with you through the darkness that is all around you. Listen carefully and lean into that presence. (Timothy Owings)

# WITH A WORD AND A PRAYER

## HEBREWS 4:12-16

What do you say to a church trying to hold on in the face of discouragement and weariness? How do you encourage them to keep their faith strong in the midst of persecution and struggle? This was the challenge the writer of Hebrews faced. To answer it, the writer discussed the nature and meaning of Jesus Christ. Christ was their answer. In these verses, the writer provides two challenges to help them hold on.

## I. With the Word

The believers were to pay attention to the Word of God. Like a two-edged sword, it pierced the inner depths of a person, judging them rightly and thoroughly. No one could escape the judgment of God. Like a wrestler who renders his opponent helpless, all stand helpless and accountable before this God.

We can't fool God. God knows what we are like, what we think, what we do. The Word of God looks us in the eye and says, "Face up to who you are." No games, no deceit. Only honesty! If we have sinned, we confess our sins. If we need love, we reach out for it. If we are struggling with the faith, we seek help. The Word of God—the Bible—challenges us to open ourselves up to the ways of God.

Someone once said that they liked the Bible because it was "an honest reading of the facts." It doesn't beat around the bush. If we have lived on the other side of God, it calls us sinners. If we have trusted God, it calls us children of the faith. The Bible pushes us to give our best to God.

## II. With Prayer

The writer provided the church with good news. Jesus was their high priest who would take their prayers to God. As a priest was to represent the people before God, so Jesus would function. What a high priest they had! Jesus had "passed through the heavens" and ascended to sit at the right hand of God. He was a high priest who knew from experience what they were facing, as he "in every respect has been tested as we are" (v. 15*b*). Jesus also knew how to help the people overcome because he had come through the tests "without sin." This was the believer confession, the belief that Jesus had done all of that for their sakes.

Since that was so, they could pray boldly, with the confidence that God would hear their prayers. Jesus presented their petitions to God. Then Jesus would also turn and give them "mercy and . . . grace . . . in time of need" (v. 16*b*). What a hope! Their prayers would be heard—and answered.

This is good news for us. Christ, who knows us and sympathizes with us as no other, will take our prayers to God. We will be heard. God will answer us and give us what we need (not want) to live our Christian lives.

When my younger son was a boy, he had childlike faith and felt he could talk to God about everything. If he had a question, he prayed to God about it. When someone talked about a need, he would pray about it right then. When he had a problem, he would stop and pray about it immediately. Then he would say, "There, that's taken care of."

What childlike faith! Why do we lose it when we grow up? For it is the way of faith. Trust the Word of God—and pray! (Hugh Litchfield)

# TO WHOM MUCH IS GIVEN

## MARK 10:17-31

The story of the rich man trying to inherit eternal life is traditionally used to admonish the wealthy. It is natural to paint an ugly picture of this man. One could imagine him in brightly colored robes, perhaps with gilded accents; he is clean shaven with a good composure. He speaks eloquently and probably commands respect when he is in a crowd. He has most likely had an easy life with an exotic and lavish upbringing. It is easy not to like him. It is easy to think of him as having horded his wealth, not giving to the poor or to his church. He may be getting to the end of his life and wants to ensure his eternity. Surely, we would like to think, that is why he approaches Jesus.

A closer look at this passage and Jesus' words and actions toward the rich man shows a different story. As the man approaches Jesus, he calls him "Good Teacher." He knows who Jesus is and what his ministry is about. When Jesus addresses him he says, "You know the commandments," identifying that he is a knowledgeable man. After the man claims to have kept all the commandments, the text reveals, "Jesus . . . loved him and said, 'You lack one thing.'" Jesus does not condemn him or belittle him for the way he has handled his wealth. Rather, Jesus loves the man and affirms him for following the commandments but does mention that the man lacks one thing. Instead of focusing on what he has not done, Jesus loves him for the commandments he has honored.

When hearing that he must sell his possessions and give the money to the poor before he follows Jesus, the rich man is shocked and leaves Jesus in a grievous state. This prompts a harsh statement from Jesus as he exclaims that it will be difficult for the rich to enter the kingdom of God. This proclamation perplexes the disciples, perhaps because it does not apply to them. Thus Jesus makes his exclamation more personal. "Children, how hard it is to enter the kingdom of God!" (v. 24b). This statement applies to everyone; this exclamation means everyone, including the disciples, will have a difficult time entering the kingdom of God. Jesus' focus is no longer on the rich man trying to enter the kingdom of God; rather Jesus explains that everyone needs God's help when trying to accomplish, as Jesus calls it, the impossible.

This passage concludes with a distorted version of what has come to be a key phrase of the Christian faith. We typically quote, "So the last will be first, and the first will be last," as it is written in the Gospel of Matthew (20:16). But Mark 10:31 reads: "But many who are first will be last, and the last will be first." There is great importance in Jesus using the word *many* in this verse. Since Jesus does not say that *all* who are first will be last— only "many" of them—perhaps there is hope for the rich man of this story.

Too often we would like to think that those who are ranked first in this life—those who are wealthy and seem to have easy lives—will have their time of hardship in the future. They will be last in line for the kingdom of God, behind people like some of us who have dedicated our time and energy to the perpetuation of Jesus' ministry. Jesus' final statement in this story helps us to not be so judgmental. Because Jesus loved and affirmed the rich man, he gives him hope in the kingdom of God. Perhaps we should also follow Jesus' example. Jesus loves and affirms those who do their best to obey the commandments and who may come up short. We follow Jesus' example, lest we also find ourselves last. (Victoria Atkinson White)

# OCTOBER 19, 2003

## *Nineteenth Sunday After Pentecost*

---

**Worship Theme:** The power of God is most ingeniously displayed by disciples' service toward other people. Those who would be first in God's realm are those who serve God's people.

---

**Readings:** Job 38:1-7 (34-41); Hebrews 5:1-10; Mark 10:35-45

**Call to Worship (Psalm 104:1-9, 24 RSV)**

*Leader:*    Bless the LORD, O my soul! O LORD my God, thou art very great!

*People:*    **Thou art clothed with honor and majesty, who coverest thyself with light as with a garment,**

*Leader:*    Who hast stretched out the heavens like a tent, who hast laid the beams of thy chambers on the waters, who makest the clouds thy chariot, who ridest on the wings of the wind, who makest the winds thy messengers, fire and flame thy ministers.

*People:*    **Thou didst set the earth on its foundations, so that it should never be shaken.**

*Leader:*    Thou didst cover it with the deep as with a garment; the waters stood above the mountains.

*People:*    **At thy rebuke they fled; at the sound of thy thunder they took to flight.**

*Leader:*    The mountains rose, the valleys sank down to the place which thou didst appoint for them.

*People:*    **Thou didst set a bound which they should not pass, so that they might not again cover the earth.**

*All:*    **O LORD, how manifold are thy works! In wisdom hast thou made them all; the earth is full of thy creatures.**

**Pastoral Prayer:**

O God, you have turned our understanding of the world upside down by the proclamation of the gospel. We often think that real power resides in wealth or influence or strength of command. Yet, in your holy Word, you remind us that those who wield real power are those who serve others. Give us a will to be servants of others for the sake of Jesus Christ. Let us swallow our pride that has become a stumbling block to many of us. Let us have the mind of Christ who emptied himself for the sake of others. Give us the strength to humble ourselves and follow the example of Jesus, who always put other's needs ahead of his own. Unite us as a people who understand that true discipleship is in loving one another as Christ has first loved us. Give us the courage to be your people in Jesus' holy name. Amen. (David Mosser)

# SERMON BRIEFS

## GOD'S HOPE FOR A STORM-TOSSED LIFE

### JOB 38:1-7 (34-41)

The writer of the beloved Psalm 121 asks the question on many of our lips. "I will lift up mine eyes unto the hills, from whence cometh my help" (Psalm 121:1 KJV). The answer comes quickly. "My help cometh from the LORD, which made heaven and earth" (Psalm 121:2 KJV).

Job has endured much. The arrows of misfortune have stung all the more as his so-called friends have offered little consolation or comfort. In anger, Job has raised his fists to God, wondering if his wife's first counsel was not his better option. "Curse God, and die!" was her suggestion (Job 2:9). Job has pummeled heaven with words, confusion, pain, abandonment. Now what?

Now, God speaks. Like the painful, sobering moments of disillusionment we face, God speaks "out of the whirlwind." This is not "the still, small voice," the "gentle whisper" that addressed Elijah (1 Kings 19:12 NIV). Rather, God speaks out of the whirlwind of Job's storm-wrecked life. In tatters, with boils festering, and with his head covered in ashes, Job hears the One with whom he must deal, the Lord God of Israel. Now, God fires questions to Job: " 'Where were you when I laid the foundation of the earth?' . . . 'Have you commanded the morning since your days began?' . . . 'Where is the way to the dwelling of light?' " (vv. 4a, 12a, 19a). Job, once so full of words he could only spit them out like bitter bile, is now silent. He has nothing to say.

What is God saying to us in this text, so ancient and full of mystery? What if God's questions to Job are God's questions to us? We too have only stuttered in silence. As we sit in the dust of our tragedies, life's broken glass all around us, what do we do? As God summons Job to brace himself, to be mortal before God's almighty majesty, so God summons us. The Holy One of Israel, God Almighty speaks to us not when life is still, calm, together, but rather from the storm, in the midst of tragedy, sitting down with us in the dust of our humanity. God comes to us not *as* the whirlwind but *out of* the whirlwind.

Here is a message for storm-tossed lives. Times come when we accuse God, as did Job, of bringing life's calamities upon us. I have heard faithful believers ask "God's will" questions when an accident ends the life of a promising teenager or when cancer cuts short a young life. Our questions of God may lead us nowhere. On the other hand, God's questions of Job each lead to a place called trust. From the whirlwind, God invites Job to trust that God's ultimate purposes for life will come to fruition in God's time. The soul's storm wreaks its havoc. God comes from the storm, not as a relief effort but with God's self, uncommon grace, and assuring presence.

Beloved mentor and friend, now of blessed memory, Dr. Chevis Horne, was pastor of First Baptist Church, Martinsville, Virginia, for more than three decades. He told the story of a Vacation Bible School picnic that the church sponsored in a city park one bright, breezy summer day. Without prompting, a preschooler walked up to her pastor, looked up into his warm, inviting face, and said, "God wonders me." Job's disaster-ridden tale tells us that even when the storm comes, when all that is lovely and beautiful is ripped from our hearts, we can look into the face of God, believing God has more wonder to give us than any storm can destroy.

God calls for the Job inside all of us to wonder again at God's power, to trust God's ultimate purposes, to live through the circumstances life brings us with hope. (Timothy Owings)

# PRIESTLY DUTIES

## HEBREWS 5:1-10

I overheard two women talking in a restaurant about a problem one of them was having. Her friend asked, "Have you talked to your priest about it?" "Oh, no! He wouldn't understand." Enthusiastically, the other woman replied, "Have I got a priest for you!" She proceeded to tell her friend about her new priest, one she knew could help her friend.

That is what this passage is about. The writer reminded the church that they had a great high priest in Jesus. Jesus' priestly duties were compared with the earthly priesthood.

## I. Appointed by God

Priests didn't become priests by making a job search and deciding that it would be a good career to undertake. They became priests because they were called by God. God chose the persons to lead the people. Likewise, Jesus was designated by God to be a high priest after the order of Melchizedek, a mysterious priest in the Old Testament who was appointed in a special way by God (Genesis 14:18, Psalm 110). Jesus was God's choice to be the ultimate high priest.

It is our faith that God calls ministers to serve. God calls everyone to serve in some way—as teachers, mechanics, bus drivers, and so forth. But God also calls some into full-time vocational service as ministers. They are called to represent God before the people and to represent the people before God. A minister does not choose the profession, the profession chooses the minister.

This understanding of God's call is important. Ministry is hard, and without that sense of call, it would be tempting sometimes to quit. A minister friend went through some terrible times—difficult work in the inner city, a church split, and character assassinations by many—but through it all, he served faithfully. He said, "I cannot quit. God called me here, and here I will serve." Such is the way of the priest.

## II. Understanding Life

The human priest knew what the people were going through because he was one of them. He experienced the same temptations, the same problems, the same guilt, the same need. As a result, he dealt gently with the congregation.

Jesus also knows what it is to be human. He faced all of life's experiences: loneliness, rejection, despair, physical pain, and death. Although he did not give in to sin, Christ knew what everyone faced and understood their lives like no one else.

We are understood! No matter what we are going through, Jesus understands. He has faced it and sympathizes with us. He was fully human. He has walked through where we walk.

For years, I ministered to people who had lost loved ones. I cared and tried to help. Then suddenly, my father died. I suddenly understood the pain of that experience. From that moment on, I was a more effective minister in times of sorrow. I had been there.

Jesus has been there. Jesus knows what we need.

## III. Sacrifice for Others

A priest would offer sacrifices in the temple for his own sins and for the sins of the people. Through the sacrifices, forgiveness was given. Jesus did not need to make any sacrifices for his sin. He did not sin. Therefore, he became the eternal, perfect sacrifice for sin. Jesus paid the price of sin for all. After Christ's sacrifice, no other sacrifices were needed. Jesus brought forgiveness to all.

Here is the sum of it: Who can wash away our sin? Only one—our high priest. Jesus! What a special priest he is! (Hugh Litchfield)


# RECOGNITION OF SERVICE

## MARK 10:35-45

Do you remember when you were fourteen years old, and you just knew that life would be better when you turned sixteen because then you could drive? Perhaps when you were seventeen, your eighteenth birthday seemed ages away; you thought you would never become a legal adult. One of the characteristics of youth is wishing for the important milestones that seem so far in the future. We end up wishing away some of the most wonderful times of our lives—the times when life is simple, and we have few responsibilities or pressures on us. The immaturity that comes with youth means that we miss the significance of contentment; we are constantly looking for better things in our future.

Although they are adults, we find James and John acting immaturely as they approach Jesus with a childish request. Perhaps as a child you can remember saying to an adult, "I am going to ask you something, and no matter what it is, I want you to say yes." This adult would then know that some outrageous question was on the way, to which the answer would undoubtedly be no. Nevertheless, James and John ask Jesus for places of honor at his right and left sides. They are seeking recognition for their dedication and service to Jesus and his ministry. They even go so far as to say they want to be in your Jesus' glory.

Jesus knows that their request is outrageous. He says to them, "You do not know what you are asking" (v. 38). He asks them if they can handle such a great responsibility by drinking from the same cup and experiencing the same baptism. They of course, think they are up to the challenge and claim they are able to do as Jesus does. Like children with imaginative requests, James and John truly believe they are ready for all that comes with the right and left places of glory next to Jesus. They think they have been good and faithful followers of the Messiah, thus, they have earned this honor.

The irony of this passage is that James and John have no idea of how the places of honor at Jesus' left and right are decided. Jesus says it is not even his decision to make; they are places that have already been prepared. He then tells them the kind of person who will have these places of glory. "Whoever wishes to become great among you must be your servant" (v. 43*b*). This is not the attitude James and John have had. They believe that because they have been faithful followers of Jesus, they deserve a place of honor. Actually, their behavior is the exact opposite of those whom Jesus considers to be great.

The behavior of these disciples is not indicative of a mature faith. They claim to be able to do the things Jesus does, but they miss the point at the center of his ministry. Servanthood is one of the key messages Jesus has tried to instill in his disciples. James and John have completely missed it. Before they are even in the running for a place of glory and honor next to Jesus, they must realize that service, rather than recognition, should be their goal.

In searching for a place of honor in times to come, James and John miss the beauty of Jesus' presence with them in the present moment. Their immature faith blinds them to the significance of the time at hand, instead they are wishing away their time with Jesus. Let us not fall into the same trap these disciples did by looking too intently on the things in our future, lest we miss the wonderful things that lie before us today. (Victoria Atkinson White)

# OCTOBER 26, 2003

*Twentieth Sunday After Pentecost*

---

**Worship Theme:** God calls all people to become part of God's realm in Jesus Christ. We respond when we confess our weakness and turn toward God's strength.

---

**Readings:** Job 42:1-6, 10-17; Hebrews 7:23-28; Mark 10:46-52

**Call to Worship (Psalm 34:1-8)**

*Leader:* I will bless the LORD at all times; his praise shall continually be in my mouth.

**People:** **My soul makes its boast in the LORD; let the humble hear and be glad. O magnify the LORD with me, and let us exalt his name together.**

*Leader:* I sought the LORD, and he answered me, and delivered me from all my fears.

**People:** **Look to him, and be radiant; so your faces shall never be ashamed.**

*Leader:* This poor soul cried, and was heard by the LORD, and was saved from every trouble.

**People:** **The angel of the LORD encamps around those who fear him, and delivers them.**

*All:* **O taste and see that the LORD is good; happy are those who take refuge in him.**

**Pastoral Prayer:**

You, O Lord, have knitted together a quilt of humanity from millions of pieces of bone, and marrow, and DNA. You have

354

miraculously joined people of every nation, tongue, tribe, and perspective. We are part of your great handiwork, O God. Remind us as we worship this day, that each of us—your created individuals—are part of the grand scheme of creation. You have created us for you, and we will not rest until we find ourselves in your keeping. Bring to our remembrance your story of old. Bring to our awareness that through countless generations you have led your people and sustained them in their times of need. Let us join their unending song of praise for you and your mighty works done on behalf of your creation, O God. Create in us a new awareness of our connection and make us again a people who seek you in all our decisions and actions. We pray this in Jesus' name. Amen. (David Mosser)

# SERMON BRIEFS

## JOB'S END, A NEW BEGINNING

### JOB 42:1-6, 10-17

The story of Job comes to a surprising end. Job has lost it all, questioned everything, faced everybody only to come to the place where he confesses his faith in the sovereign mercy of God. Unlike most stories of riches to rags, Job's fortune is restored twofold. "The Lord gave and the Lord has taken away. Blessed be the name of the Lord" (Job 1:21b NASB). Does God relate to us this way? I'm not sure. In fact, I'm so troubled by much of what I read here that I struggle to hear a Word from God that makes sense in light of whom I know God to be in Jesus Christ.

The kernel of wisdom woven into our text may best be found in verse 5. " 'I had heard of you by the hearing of the ear, but now my eye sees you.' " Like so many of us, Job—enjoying life with healthy children, a rising economic fortune, a good reputation—thinks little of life's meaning until his way of life is destroyed. Satan speaks what we all think at times: *Do we serve God because we believe God has blessed us?*

In fact, we all have "God ideas" that our ears pick up from others. Early on, we hear "God is great, God is good, let us thank

355

him for our food. By His hand we all are fed, thank you God for daily bread." The comfort those words give us at a table set by our mothers and fathers also gives us information about God. Who is God? God is good; God is great.

Then tragedy strikes. In our teen years, a good friend dies in an automobile accident. As young adults, we become cynical about church. In our formative years, we learned that the Bible is a trustworthy book, only to discover as adults that the Bible has its challenges. We hear with our ears of a God who is good, only to discover with our eyes the brutality of daily life.

We hear of God's love; but not until we see God's love feeding the poor, caring for the man with AIDS, or tutoring the fatherless child do we see God's love. We hear that God cares for us all. But not until we see God's care in the middle of the night in an emergency room, or at the casket of a friend's dead father, or in the consoling words of a friend do we believe that God cares.

The Church through the ages has done well at speaking what we believe people need to hear. Like Job's less-than-comforting friends, we who are numbered among the faithful are adept at telling people what they should do, ought to do, or need to do. Feeding the hungry, tutoring the at-risk child, embracing the homeless, reaching across racial lines of division, and dozens of other "oughts" populate the Christian community's "most wanted" list of societal virtues.

What God may be calling us to be—from someone as unlikely as Job—is to give visual expression to our want list. Although this culture is increasingly disinterested in organized religion, it is deeply curious about spirituality in all its expressions. A living spirituality, a dynamic intentionality about ministry may well be the way we bear our witness to God's love in this secular, self-centered culture.

I don't know. Maybe fortunes lost can be restored. Surely some are. Maybe when someone loses it all, they get it all back. All my life, I've heard much about God that is still needing visual verification. I hear a voice from across the dusty millennia saying that's exactly what it took for him to believe again. "I had heard of you by the hearing of the ear, but now my eye sees you." So get busy living what your ears hear, and who knows, you may yet see. (Timothy Owings)

# THE FOREVER PRIEST

## HEBREWS 7:23-28

In these verses, the writer returns to a favorite subject: the supremacy of Christ over everything. Christ's superiority as a high priest is emphasized. Earthly priests die, but not Jesus. He continues in office forever. They could count on Jesus to be their high priest eternally. This was good news to a struggling church. It is good news for us. What will this forever priest do?

## I. He Will Save Forever

Jesus faced life in all of its fullness. He underwent its temptations and challenges and pains. He triumphed over them. When sin tried to bring him down, Jesus resisted it. When heartbreak and suffering assaulted him, Jesus overcame it. When death appeared, Jesus conquered it. This high priest knew how to help people live abundantly and triumphantly. Therefore, Jesus was able to save those who trusted him.

Jesus knows what to do for us. For example, a man's wife died suddenly. Many feared he would not be able to survive that loss. However, he had a friend who had gone through the same experience. He believed this friend would help him through his grief because he had gone through it himself. In a sense, his friend saved him from giving up.

Do we need saving from sin? Do we need saving from suffering? Do we need saving from death? Jesus has come through all of those experiences triumphantly. If we trust Jesus, he will help us through these crises of life.

## II. He Forever Intercedes for Us

Jesus lives to forever make intercession for us. Picture Jesus as able to approach God at any time to plead our case. Jesus has that kind of access to God. Jesus is on our side, pleading for us.

I imagine myself sitting on the witness stand in the court of God's judgment. The charges are read against me. I have no ground to stand on. The verdict is given—guilty! I have no hope.

357

But then Jesus intercedes for me. Jesus pleads for me, telling how he died for my sins. Even though I blew it many times, my feeble faith in Jesus was enough. Jesus is able to change the verdict from guilty to saved. Without Jesus' help, that would not happen.

Jesus wants to do that for each of us forever. We have a priest who will plead our cases before God. Jesus is on our side.

### III. He Forever Forgives

Jesus offered himself as a sacrifice for our sins. This perfect priest paid the price for our sin. Jesus waits, ready to forgive us. Whatever we have done, whatever we have been, if we seek his mercy, Jesus gives it. That is true forever! We will need his mercy for that long.

Stephen Arrington, a former navy frogman, took several wrong turns in life and became involved in smuggling cocaine into this country. He landed in prison and experienced its horror. One night, he lay on his bunk wondering how he could ever atone for what he had done, how he could ever face honest people again. He wondered if God could still care. So he asked, "Are you still there for someone like me?" "ALWAYS!" was the reply that flooded his body and soul (*Journey into Darkness: Nowhere to Land* [Lafayette, La.: Huntington House Publishers, 1975], p. 174).

*Always!* That was the word for the early church—and for us. Jesus is ready to always save, intercede, and forgive. We have a forever priest! (Hugh Litchfield)

## A LEAP OF BLIND FAITH

### MARK 10:46-52

We see them everyday—on the street corner, under bridges, and outside the convenience store. We consider them the lowest of our society; they are unemployed, homeless, dirty, and alone. They are left to beg for money and food to keep themselves alive. Sometimes one will be brave enough to ask us for help, and in our busyness of life, we consider them an inconvenience. It is easy to think they have always been in need. Probably, they have never been our coworkers, our friends, or even in our family. We are not connected with them; they are not like us.

We find a similar situation in this text. Bartimaeus, a blind beggar, hears that Jesus is leaving Jericho, and he calls out for help. But instead of simply asking for a handout from Jesus, something peculiar happens. As the text shows us, Bartimaeus immediately knows three things about Jesus. He knows his name, thus probably knows his reputation as a healer. He knows he is from Nazareth, meaning he knows Jesus' upbringing. And he calls him the Son of David, showing that he knows Jesus' lineage. How startled would we be if a beggar called out to us with this much knowledge of who we are? As if knowing these things about Jesus is not enough to shock those around him, Bartimaeus asks Jesus for mercy. The beggar knows what Jesus is capable of doing; he knows that Jesus is a granter of mercy.

At this request, the crowd surrounding Jesus and Bartimaeus reacts as many of us would when a person of importance is approached by a beggar. They sternly tell him to be quiet and not to bother Jesus. In turn, Jesus responds to Bartimaeus with respect and inquiry. Jesus does not presume to know why he wants or needs mercy from him. Instead, he calls Bartimaeus to him to ask what he wants. Bartimaeus's request of Jesus gives us great insight into who this beggar really is. He says, "My teacher, let me see again" (v. 51b). Bartimaeus calls Jesus, "My Teacher," a title revealing endearment and indicating a personal relationship between the two men. He also says, "Let me see again." We suspect that Bartimaeus has not always been blind—perhaps he has seen Jesus before or previously been a witness to Jesus' power. What wonderful insight we are given within this story through knowing more about Bartimaeus. He is no longer a faceless beggar on the street, asking for handouts from Jesus. In knowing some of his story, he becomes less of an inconvenient beggar and more like us and those in the crowd surrounding him.

Upon receiving his sight, Jesus says to Bartimaeus, "Your faith has made you well" (v. 52). Jesus does not begin to take credit for this healing, rather he credits the faith of the one who has been healed. What a witness Jesus' actions are at this point in the story. Those in the crowd and the ones who have been following Jesus probably presume that they have great faith in their leader. They are, after all, the ones who have left their families and their homes to follow their Teacher. Yet, it is the faith of a beggar, one of the lowest of the society, that is great enough to bring about healing.

How does one acquire such a strong faith, one that can heal the blind on request? Perhaps this story is appropriately placed after the story of the rich man trying to inherit eternal life. The rich man had many possessions, which he did not want to leave behind to follow Jesus. Bartimaeus, on the other hand, was a beggar, he had nothing to leave behind and nothing to lose before following Jesus. In a literal sense, Bartimaeus's faith was blind, meaning it was without reservation or hesitation. He knew from the beginning who Jesus was and what Jesus could do for him. With a leap of faith, Bartimaeus had nothing to lose and everything to gain. (Victoria Atkinson White)

# REFLECTIONS

# NOVEMBER

**Reflection Verses:** *"Be patient, therefore, beloved, until the coming of the Lord." (James 5:7a) " 'Are you the one who is to come, or are we to wait for another?' " (Luke 7:19)*

Waiting is something we human beings ought to be pretty good at. We get plenty of practice, especially at this time of year! We wait in traffic and check out-lines. We wait for people to arrive for the Thanksgiving feast or for our names to be called for a restaurant table. Dieters wait until the holidays are over. Children wait for Christmas. We ought to have waiting down to a fine art. If you look around, however, at how we behave while waiting in line or in traffic, you would see that waiting is *not* one of our finer points. When we are waiting for something—anything—we are not on our best behavior.

Our text from the letter of James urges us to be patient in our waiting. All human beings have to wait for something important. James nods toward the farmer who is waiting for "precious" crops to grow. He reminds us that the prophets of old told us for whom and what we are waiting. We wait for a word from God. It is a word that God will speak in God's own time. It might not be a word we expect to hear. When God does not act as we think God should or come to us in a manner that we expect, we lose patience even with God. James knows that when that happens, we tend to "grumble."

We are better at the grumbling than we are at the waiting. We grumble because waiting takes up valuable time, and time is a precious commodity these days. Why wait when we could be doing something more productive? When waiting seems foolish and futile or when we do not know whom or what we are waiting for, unwanted weeds sprout on the landscape of the human heart: anger, despair, disillusionment, doubt, and distrust, even of God.

Every now and then a playwright or poet will reveal how human beings behave when they wait. In a play called *The Chairs* by Eugene Ionesco, lights come up on a sparsely furnished apartment. Two characters simply called "Old Man" and "Old Woman" enter. They know somehow that the end of their lives are coming, so they are spending their final hours preparing for the arrival of a great orator. They believe that only such a person can come to speak of the significance of human life as they have lived it. It seems that everyone from the janitor to the Pope has been invited to come hear the Orator speak on their behalf.

In an eerie bit of theatrics, we see the old couple engaging in elaborate pantomimes. We watch them greet imaginary guests and fill the stage with chairs that only phantoms sit in. Finally the highly acclaimed Orator arrives! He is the only other "real" character to make an appearance on the stage! The couple trust their message to the Orator so completely that they leap out of the window to their deaths.

The Orator steps forward. He stands on a platform in front of a stage full of empty chairs. We then discover that he is not capable of uttering words, only gibberish! Finally he gives up, writes some nonsense on the wall, and exits. When the curtain closes on that play, we are left with some troubling questions: Is human life simply a farce? Do our words, gestures, and actions seem as silly as do those of the characters in the play? Is life full of foolish posturing on an empty stage where God never shows up?

I wonder if John the Baptist was thinking like this as he languished in Herod's prison? John had been waiting for a long time to see the face of God's Messiah. He believed that once God's Messiah came, God would start acting clearly and decisively in the world as John knew it. John imagined what that decisive action would look like. God's Messiah would arrive with an ax in one hand and a winnowing fork in the other, chopping, clearing, and burning chaff with fire (Luke 3:7-9, 15-17). When he had baptized Jesus and announced that Jesus was the Promised One, John must have expected Jesus to start acting like the Messiah he had envisioned.

Now John heard reports from his own disciples that Jesus was not carrying out that sort of program. Jesus was moving around in the margins, not making a general assault on the centers of power. Jesus was healing not destroying, restoring life not taking it away, opening eyes and ears, preaching to the poor and offering them hope. This was not the sort of Messiah that John had been patiently waiting for! Now, in the darkness of that prison, John doubts that his life had meaning. He wonders if Jesus is the one God promised. "Are you the one who is to come, or are we to wait for another?" John grumbles.

This is the time of year when we wait for God to come. Yet, we want God to come on our own terms. We want God to act in ways that conform to our own political opinions and priorities. When that does not happen, then we grumble and complain to God and to each other. We withhold our worship and our witness until God acts like we think God should or we wonder if God will show up at all!

James urges us to wait patiently for the coming of the Lord. Luke promises us that God will come but may do so in ways that we might not expect. God's coming in the person of Jesus Christ might be unsettling and may cause us to reexamine how we are living our lives and what we are expecting God to do. When God does come, it is not to say that our lives are empty and full of nonsense. God comes to speak a word of love and grace in the drama of human existence by sending Jesus.

It is Jesus who gives the final word on the meaning of John's life and in fact on our own. "Among those born of women there is no one greater than John; yet the one who is least in the kingdom of God is greater than he" (Luke 7:28 NIV). (Richard Ward)

# NOVEMBER 2, 2003

*Twenty-first Sunday After Pentecost*

---

**Worship Theme:** As disciples, Jesus asks us to love our neighbors as ourselves. To fulfill this request is the fulfillment of the law.

---

**Readings:** Ruth 1:1-18; Hebrews 9:11-14; Mark 12:28-34

## Call to Worship (Psalm 146:1-10 RSV)

*Leader:*   Praise the LORD! Praise the LORD, O my soul!

***People:***   **I will praise the LORD as long as I live; I will sing praises to my God while I have being.**

*Leader:*   Put not your trust in princes, in a son of man, in whom there is no help.

***People:***   **When his breath departs he returns to his earth; on that very day his plans perish.**

*Leader:*   Happy is he whose help is the God of Jacob, whose hope is in the LORD his God, who made heaven and earth, the sea, and all that is in them;

***People:***   **Who keeps faith for ever; who executes justice for the oppressed; who gives food to the hungry.**

*Leader:*   The LORD sets the prisoners free; the LORD opens the eyes of the blind. The LORD lifts up those who are bowed down; the LORD loves the righteous.

*People:*  **The LORD watches over the sojourners, he upholds the widow and the fatherless; but the way of the wicked he brings to ruin.**

*All:*  **The LORD will reign for ever, thy God, O Zion, to all generations. Praise the LORD!**

**Pastoral Prayer:**

Almighty God and Creator of the Universe, give us this day a task in your realm. Make us your disciples who follow the way of truth and liberty. Remind us that your love and being is revealed most fully in Jesus Christ, but also remind us that your perfect will for us can also be read in the pages of nature and the sacred law. The law does not provide salvation for us, but it is a reliable guide to living in community. Remind us that you desire that we follow the spirit of the law and not simply the letter of the law. Place us near the kingdom of God and inspire us to act out our faith in our daily lives. Make us good stewards over both the mysteries of the gospel and those resources that you have given us to build up your kingdom. We pray this in Jesus' precious name and for his sake. Amen. (David Mosser)

## SERMON BRIEFS

### FROM EMPTY TO FULL: NAOMI'S STORY

#### RUTH 1:1-18 (19-22)

The book of Ruth really begins with the story of Naomi, which begins in want, loss, and emptiness.

We have hints of Naomi's past, a life that was full: a husband, sons, plenty to eat in Bethlehem, "The House of Bread." Naomi means "Sweetness," but we quickly see her personality change into "Bitterness." The precipitating loss and famine lands Naomi and her family in the strange land of Moab, forced to leave the House of Bread. The next losses come so quickly that it is hard to absorb them: the death of Naomi's husband then the deaths of both of her sons. The unnamed, but ever-present loss, is the lack of fertility, for no babies are born to either of her sons and daughters-in-law. Naomi is alone in a foreign land. Naomi is a widow, without a husband or sons to provide for her or protect her, without grandchildren to continue her family, with no one to call her own, with no hope for the future.

Naomi decides to return to Bethlehem with her daughters-in-law, Ruth and Orpah, for she has heard that the Lord has "considered his people and given them food" (v. 6*b*). This is her only hope for survival, to go and depend on the charity of her people. But worse, Naomi has a triple burden: Ruth and Orpah are childless widows also. Three widows seeking assistance from the kindness of others pushes the limit. In the middle of the journey, Naomi tells Ruth and Orpah to turn back to Moab and seek a better future in their own land. What can she provide them? What can she promise them? Nothing. Naomi voices her despair and states her complaint against God: "It has been far more bitter for me than for you, because the hand of the Lord has turned against me" (v. 13*b*). In Bethlehem, she says to her people, " 'Don't call me Naomi ["Sweetness"], . . . Call me Mara ["Bitterness"]. I went away full, but the Lord has brought me back empty' " (vv. 20-21*a* NLT).

Many of our stories begin in despair and hopelessness. We can understand Naomi's complaint: being struck down, tasting bitterness, feeling alone. Naomi's story begins with emptiness. But it does not remain there. There are hints of hope even in this bitter beginning. In the midst of her despair, Naomi hears of the God that is caring and providing for God's people back in Bethlehem. Could it be that God will provide for Naomi? Another hint of hope is in the surprising decision of Ruth to remain with Naomi. Naomi cannot yet see how Ruth's decision will affect her life for good. How could Ruth, an outsider and dependent herself, be able to help the helpless? Yet Naomi allows Ruth to set out with her for Bethlehem, and the possibilities are left open.

What hints of hope have we glimpsed in our own stories? Perhaps there is the conviction of an unseen but caring hand in our lives, one that we can only name "God." Perhaps there have been surprising people who have surrounded us and walked with us, giving us the strength to go on.

We must listen to learn the rest of Naomi's story. Will God take care of her? Will the two widows find bread in Bethlehem? Will

Ruth, an outsider, be accepted? Is there any way that Naomi's family will continue?

Will Naomi be made full again? Can our stories take a turn for good? We have yet another hint. Naomi and Ruth arrive in Bethlehem at the start of the barley harvest. *Harvest*: fullness in the fields. Perhaps there is hope for Naomi and for ourselves. (Laura Jernigan)

# CLEANSING!

### HEBREWS 9:11-14

"You need to clean up your life," a counselor told the drug addict. The young addict said, "But how do I do that?"

What an important statement that is! How does one clean up a life caught in the addiction of drugs? Or stop hating others, or ruining their marriage, or being dishonest? How can they change?

These verses from Hebrews help provide an answer to that question. In emphasizing the supremacy of Christ, the writer touches on the idea of cleansing. Two kinds of cleansing are contrasted.

## I. Outer Cleansing

In their religious tradition, there were certain rites of purification one needed to undergo to receive forgiveness of sin. They would offer the blood of goats and bulls and sprinkle in the ashes of a heifer. Through the presentation of these sacrifices, priests declared forgiveness. However, the cure was only temporary. The next day, they would need to offer the sacrifices again. Outwardly, they had done what they were supposed to do, but that forgiveness did not last. They went out and committed the same sins again. The rituals did not have the power to keep them from failing once more.

In our day, there are some rituals we go through to make us feel better about our sinfulness. We go to church regularly, we pray every day, we tithe, we try to do good works for others—

hoping that such actions will make us feel better inside. For a while, they might. However, it doesn't last. We continue to sin, which causes us to feel guilty and ashamed. All those outer actions did not cleanse the heart inside. We need something else.

An alcoholic once said to me, "I want to stop. I try to stop. But I just can't!" Telling him to put the drink away was not enough. He needed more cleansing than that.

## II. Inner Cleansing

Jesus entered into a perfect sanctuary—not a temporary tent—to make a once and for all sacrifice for our sins. His action was not a quick fix. It was an eternal remedy. Christ gave his blood to "purify our conscience from dead works to worship the living God" (v. 14b). Jesus did not require us to perform some outer ritual to find forgiveness. He performed the ritual himself. Jesus took our sin so that we could be purified inside. Now we have the power to resist and overcome sin. We are cleansed from the inside out.

This is what makes Jesus superior to all. Jesus enables us to overcome. If we trust Jesus, amazing things can happen. An alcoholic can put down that next drink. Hatred in the heart can be replaced by love. Marriages can be reconciled. Forgiveness can happen. Whatever we need cleansing from, Jesus is able to give it. It is the only way we will ever be clean.

A friend shared this story: He saw a soap commercial where the advertisers found a homeless man in a gutter, unshaven, dirty, smelly. They took him and cleaned him up—gave him a bath with that special soap, shaved him, and gave him some new clothes. He looked good. They pointed to him as an example of how using their soap could transform a person. Someone followed up on that commercial and found the same man a week later—lying in the gutter, unshaven, dirty, smelly. He had been cleansed on the outside but not on the inside.

Once again, the hymn is right. "What can wash away my sin? Nothing but the blood of Jesus." (Hugh Litchfield)

# MOVING TOWARD THE KINGDOM

## MARK 12:28-34

For days, the scribes, Pharisees, and Sadducees have been peppering Jesus with questions and looking for ways to trap him. Now, here is a scribe with an honest question and an open heart to the answer. The scribe asks Jesus which commandment is the first of all. Jesus responds with the familiar words of the Shema, "Hear, O Israel: The LORD our God, the LORD is one" (Deuteronomy 6:4 NIV). Then Jesus proclaims love as the greatest command—love of God and love of neighbor. Unlike the others who had been questioning Jesus, this unnamed scribe agrees with the Lord's teachings. The scribe correctly surmises that love of God and neighbor are more important than burnt offerings and sacrifices. For this affirmation and insight, Jesus declares the scribe "not far from the kingdom of God" (v. 34).

The text does not tell us whether this man became a follower and disciple of Christ or not. Many sermons have faulted the scribe for being "so close but yet so far." However, rather than condemning the man, Jesus affirms his movement toward the kingdom. As with so many of Jesus' stories, the emphasis shifts from the main character to us. Are we moving toward obeying and living the greatest commands or do we merely agree in theory? Are we asking questions from a genuinely seeking heart or are our motives more like those of the Sadducees and Pharisees?

Lamar Williamson, Jr., writing on the book of Mark, provides excellent insight into the relevance of this text for our context. Williamson asserts that the significance of this text is its disturbing challenge to the basic presuppositions of Western culture and the fundamental self-centeredness of each one of us. Although many of us agree with Jesus' assessment of the greatest commands, none of us come close to living these standards as Jesus did. God affirms us for our agreement with the principle, but God also calls us past our rituals and "sacrifices" to a radical life of love for God and others (Lamar Williamson, Jr., *Mark*, vol. 2 of *Interpretation Bible Commentary—New Testament* [Louisville: Westminster John Knox Press, 1983]).

The following story illustrates this love. It was told to a United

States Colonel while he was in Vietnam. Although he had no proof, he accepted it as fact.

During the Vietnam War, several children in an orphanage were injured in a mortar attack. One girl needed a blood transfusion to survive. The American doctor and nurse, speaking only limited Vietnamese, explained to the children the need for a blood donor. Finally, after a visible struggle, an eight-year-old boy named Heng volunteered. The nurse laid him on a pallet, swabbed his arm, and began to draw his blood. After a moment, the boy began to sob. The Americans asked Heng if it hurt, and he replied, "No." He continued to sob, but language barriers prevented the Americans from determining what was so wrong. At this point, a Vietnamese nurse arrived and began talking to Heng. A few moments later the boy stopped crying, and a look of relief spread across his young face. The nurse explained to the Americans that Heng thought he was dying. He thought that he had been asked to give all of his blood so that the little girl could live. The Americans were amazed. "Why would he be willing to do that?" asked the American nurse. The Vietnamese nurse repeated the question to Heng. He answered simply, "Because she is my friend."

We have no greater love than this, that we are willing to lay down our lives for our friends. May we be moving toward the kingdom and obedience to Jesus' radical command to love. (Tracy Hartman)

# NOVEMBER 9, 2003

*Twenty-second Sunday After Pentecost*

**Worship Theme:** The Lord has created people to live with a humble spirit and to love other people for Jesus' sake.

**Readings:** Ruth 3:1-5; 4:13-17; Hebrews 9:24-28; Mark 12:38-44

**Call to Worship (Psalm 127)**

| | |
|---|---|
| *Leader:* | Unless the LORD builds the house, those who build it labor in vain. |
| *People:* | **Unless the LORD guards the city, the guard keeps watch in vain.** |
| *Leader:* | It is in vain that you rise up early and go late to rest, eating the bread of anxious toil; |
| *People:* | **For he gives sleep to his beloved.** |
| *Leader:* | Sons are indeed a heritage from the LORD, the fruit of the womb a reward. |
| *People:* | **Like arrows in the hand of a warrior are the sons of one's youth.** |
| *Leader:* | Happy is the man who has his quiver full of them. |
| *People:* | **He shall not be put to shame when he speaks with his enemies in the gate.** |

**Pastoral Prayer:**

As we enter into your sanctuary, O Gracious God, give us the spirit of true worship. Let us worship you in spirit and truth. Give us in this hour the voice to sing praises to your holy name. Give us in this hour the heart that humbles itself before you, O God, and a heart that prays from the depths of our being. In this hour of worship, O Lord, give the preacher the words that will open holy Scripture to us and make its claim upon our lives. Give us in this hour the will to follow the instruction of Jesus, who told his disciples, "It is more blessed to give than to receive" (Acts 20:35*b*). In this hour of worship, O Lord, remold and shape our lives so that we will conform to your will for us. Make us again your people and put us on the path that leads to eternal life. We pray this and every prayer in the name of Jesus, our Lord and our Messiah. Amen. (David Mosser)

# SERMON BRIEFS

## FROM EMPTY TO FULL: RUTH'S STORY

### RUTH 3:1-5; 4:13-17

Ruth is one of two women in the Bible with a book bearing her own name. She is the ancestress of David and of Jesus. That Ruth became such is surprising, for she was not a daughter of Israel. She was a Moabite, a people that were outsiders to God's promises. Yet, by her faith and own initiative, Ruth was given a full measure of God's grace. She stands as a model of faith for both insiders and outsiders.

We first meet Ruth in Moab, the daughter-in-law of Naomi. Both women have lost husbands, and both are childless. The two widows are powerless, on the edge of poverty, and without men to provide protection for them. They are facing the end of their family line. When Naomi decides to return to her native place of Bethlehem, she urges Ruth to go back to her own people. It is the sensible thing to do, for Ruth has better prospects for marriage and children in Moab. Ruth, as an outsider, has no security or future in Naomi's land. But despite all this, Ruth makes a surprising choice. In words of poetic devotion, Ruth binds herself to a helpless and hopeless woman with no identifiable future, risking her own future out of compassion for the other (Ruth 1:16-17). Naomi tries to persuade her otherwise, but Ruth clings to Naomi and pledges her solidarity. So they set out, empty-handed.

The two widows arrive in Bethlehem, their future bleak. But it is the beginning of the barley harvest. Full fields are in view. Ruth takes action and gains permission to glean. As a widow, she is allowed to follow the harvesters and gather the sheaves that are left behind. It happens that the field where she gleans belongs to Boaz, a wealthy man who also happens to be a relative of her late husband. And it just so happens that Boaz shows kindness to the widow from Moab, not only letting her glean but also arranging for her to gather more than usual. Boaz even prays for Ruth to find a full reward from the God of Israel under whose wings Ruth has sought refuge.

Ruth returns with her hands full of barley. When Naomi learns that the man who showed kindness is a relative, she gives thanks to God, for Boaz is by law a kinsman and redeemer for her husband's family. Although Boaz has no obligation to marry Naomi, since she is not his brother's wife, Naomi sees possibilities in the favor Boaz has shown to Ruth. Naomi devises a plan for Ruth to present herself as wife to Boaz, asking him to honor the role of family redeemer. Ruth accepts the plan and follows through with it. She approaches Boaz under the cover of darkness and asks him to spread his cloak over her, signifying a proposal of marriage.

Imagine the risk Ruth took! Boaz could have thrown her out. But with gutsy faith, Ruth asks for a future. Boaz accepts his role as redeemer and fulfills his own prayer for Ruth by marrying her. Ruth gives birth to a son, Obed. Naomi, once bitter and hopeless, takes the child to her own breast.

Ruth, the outsider, acted as redeemer and became the redeemed. She took action by faith in a God she claimed as her own, showing compassion for the helpless and then claiming her place and a future with the people of God. May we model our own faith after Ruth, acting boldly to help the helpless, putting our trust in God, and claiming a future of full reward. (Laura Jernigan)

# HEALING AND WHOLENESS THROUGH CHRIST

## HEBREWS 9:24-28

The issue of forgiveness is important to us. Forgiveness is important when people act or speak in ways that hurt us. Generally, we are much more clear about what must happen for others to be forgiven than we are clear about what we must do to restore ourselves to someone's good graces. We would do well as preachers to help the congregation consider how we find the healing of forgiveness and how it affects our capacity to forgive.

When we are wronged, we often want the other person to hurt as we have been hurt. We seek some vindication that will indicate to the world that we do not deserve such treatment. At the very least, we want an apology, the more public the better. It is not inconceivable for us to begin to think of ways we can put this person in their place or seek some restitution. Even if the offender has remorse, it is difficult for us to keep from reciting the litany of our pain so that their transgression is not forgotten.

What are we like when we are the offender? The hardest words ever to be collected in a sentence are "I am sorry." Besides, we may say, offense was not what we intended. We did not mean to hurt anyone. Why should we worry about being forgiven if we did not intend it? We wonder why the person we offended cannot let it go, and ironically we can become angry when they cannot help us to feel better about ourselves.

Hebrews tells us that it was the task of the High Priest to offer sacrifices that would restore the people to God's favor. It was an endless task. Sacrifices had to be offered regularly because of the waywardness of the people. The seeking of forgiveness had to cost the sinner something important. The sacrifice had to be done in the sanctuary so that God could see the symbol of remorse. The High Priest would intercede for the people. He would plead their case.

All that has changed and been replaced with the coming of Christ. As the intercessor for all, Christ's once-and-for-all death is the last word in God's saving work. For the author of Hebrews, our death is the passage to another phase, which is judgment. For

Christ, death is the passage to the next phase of his work in God's planned salvation. From the sacrifice of Christ we receive the gift of forgiveness.

It becomes important for us to reflect on what this means for us. It announces the path to the healing that we are seeking. Healing comes to us because we confess our sinfulness. We are freed from the burden of making excuses. We do not have to hide from God any longer. We see in Christ that it is not God's intention that any perish. We are restored.

The sacrifice of Christ also restores us to one another. Healing comes to our relationships out of our gratitude, which create in us the capacity to forgive. We are freed from the false notion that causing others pain through retribution will make us whole again. Our wholeness comes through the holiness of Christ, who has given himself for our sake. (Bob Holloway)

## SELF-DENIAL

### MARK 12:38-44

There is a story of a lady who had kept a turkey in her freezer for over two years. Finally, she called the 1-800 number on the wrapper and asked the company if the turkey was still OK to eat. The customer service representative replied that while it would be safe, it probably would not taste very good. "Oh," replied the lady, "then I think I'll give it to the church."

In a humorous way, this story gets to the heart of the text: our hypocrisy. Jesus contrasts the hypocrisy of the scribes and Pharisees with the genuine and total gift of the widow in the temple. Unlike the rich man who would not give up his wealth to become a disciple, the widow belongs to the kingdom. During stewardship season, this text can be used to reinforce the principle that all we have belongs to God and that we are merely stewards of it. In this passage, giving as an optional activity or giving out of our excess is not an option. Although the gifts of the wealthy were large, Jesus condemned them because they were likely calculated based on the law of the tithe and a long tradition of how to determine it. The widow made no such calculations; she gave her all.

This passage also dispels the often-quoted notion that giving will increase our own blessing. While Jesus commends the widow who gave her all, he gives no indication that her circumstances will change. The message is that we need to give our best and our all with no expectation of return.

Those not addressing stewardship issues can review this passage from a larger context. In Mark, Jesus' last act of public ministry is commendation of the widow in the temple. Her gift foreshadows the one Jesus is about to make: the gift of his own life. "In Mark, this poor widow becomes a type of him who, 'though he was rich, yet for (our) sake he became poor, so that by his poverty (we) might become rich' " (2 Corinthians 8:9) (Lamar Williamson, Jr., *Mark*, vol. 2 of *Interpretation Bible Commentary—New Testament* [Louisville: Westminster John Knox Press, 1983], p. 234). By comparing himself to the widow, Jesus also reinforces the idea that he will not be the military-political ruler that the Zealots and many others were expecting. Rather, Jesus is the humble servant who lives a simple life in total obedience to God.

A third option for preaching this passage centers around the injustices that existed in the social and religious realm of the day. Jesus condemns the church leaders who set themselves apart through special clothing and greetings and who clamored for places of honor at banquets and in the church. Jesus especially condemns these acts when they are a part of a larger system that supported such hypocrisy through the oppression and abuse of the poor. Unfortunately, modern parallels are abundant. Instead of this hypocrisy, Jesus commands true disciples to deny themselves, take up their crosses, and become servants of all. (Tracy Hartman)

# NOVEMBER 16, 2003

*Twenty-third Sunday After Pentecost*

---

**Worship Theme:** People desire to know the eternal timetable for the world and themselves. In the divine plan, God's time is the right time.

---

**Readings:** 1 Samuel 1:4-20; Hebrews 10:11-14, (15-18), 19-25; Mark 13:1-8

### Call to Worship (Psalm 16 RSV)

*Leader:*    Preserve me, O God, for in thee I take refuge.

***People:***    **I say to the LORD, "Thou art my Lord; I have no good apart from thee."**

*Leader:*    As for the saints in the land, they are the noble, in whom is all my delight.

***People:***    **Those who choose another god multiply their sorrows; their libations of blood I will not pour out or take their names upon my lips.**

*Leader:*    The LORD is my chosen portion and my cup; thou holdest my lot.

***People:***    **The lines have fallen for me in pleasant places; yea, I have a goodly heritage.**

*Leader:*    I bless the LORD who gives me counsel; in the night also my heart instructs me.

***People:***    **I keep the LORD always before me; because he is at my right hand, I shall not be moved.**

*Leader:*      Therefore my heart is glad, and my soul rejoices; my body also dwells secure.

*People:*      **For thou dost not give me up to Sheol, or let thy godly one see the Pit.**

*All:*      **Thou dost show me the path of life; in thy presence there is fullness of joy, in thy right hand are pleasures for evermore.**

**Pastoral Prayer:**

God of All Creation, we worship you this holy day. We offer our worship in thanksgiving and praise. We pray this day that you will abide with us and in us during our time of worship. Remind each of us assembled here this day that "the sacrifice acceptable to God is a broken spirit; a broken and contrite heart, O God, you will not despise" (Psalm 51:17). Give us the resolve to be your people in a world that has such shortsightedness that it misses your wonders and your handiwork. Let us be those persons who live such righteous and sober lives that others who see us catch a glimpse of the work of Jesus in us. Let us remember the poor and needy. May we sacrifice our bounty and ourselves so that the hungry and those without shelter may find relief in our expression of love for you. Grant us peace and make us worthy to be called Christ's followers. In Jesus' name we pray. Amen. (David Mosser)

# SERMON BRIEFS

## PREVAILING PRAYER

### 1 SAMUEL 1:4-20

Stephen Leacock once said, "There is only one beautiful child in the world, and every mother has it." Children play such a precious role in a family. They should bring sunshine and happiness in the life of a parent. Unfortunately, in present society children are too often seen as an inconvenience, something to be used for profit, or in the extreme cases, experimental guinea pigs for scientific research. Many are abandoned, beaten, or simply ignored. Blessed are children who are wanted, cared for, and loved! Fortunately God has still given most people a sense of need for children.

The birth story of Samuel begins with an instinct for motherhood from a woman named Hannah, whose name means "fixed" or "settled." Interestingly, her life for years was unsettled because she had no child to love. She was married to a man named Elkanah who practiced polygamy. His other wife's name was Peninnah, meaning "jewel" or "pearl," and she had several sons and daughters. However, Hannah was Elkanah's precious pearl, for he had a special love for Hannah. As much as Elkanah loved Hannah, his other wife Peninnah hated her with a special hatred. The rivalry was obvious. Peninnah flaunted the fact that she had children in Hannah's face, but the specific day mentioned in the text was probably the worst. Hannah cried and felt bitterness in her soul and a longing in her heart. That troubled spirit led her to prayer. That's not unusual.

Christians respond in prayer when trouble strikes and circumstances go beyond personal control.

## I. A Prayer of an Anguished Heart

Hannah felt trapped in a situation that seemed hopeless. The Bible comments, "So it was, year by year" (v. 7a NKJV). Many people feel snared in their situation. They feel caught in circumstances with no apparent relief in sight: habits that bind them in a circular rotation, jobs going nowhere, finances that refuse improvement, relationships that hinder rather than help, and health that deteriorates. Many people can relate to Hannah's circumstances.

## II. A Prayer of Faith

Like so many before her and so many after her Hannah appears to want to play the game of "Let's Make a Deal" with God. She would play the part of Monte Hall and God would be the contestant. If he would just give her a child—and specifically a male child—she would trade that child in as a "professional minister" for temple work. But what Hannah was saying was, "God, I believe you can handle any and all situations of my life.

379

Here is my heart, frustration, and anger. I give it all to you." Hannah's faith focused on God.

"Faith alone is the trigger that releases divine power. . . . Our trying, struggling, or promising won't work—faith is what God is after. Faith is the key to our relationship with him" (Jim Cymbala with Dean Merrill, *Fresh Faith: What Happens When Real Faith Ignites God's People* [Grand Rapids: Zondervan Publishing House, 1999], p. 41).

Hannah possessed that faith!

### III. A Prayer Answered

Eli's words, "Go in peace, and the God of Israel grant your petition which you have asked of Him" (v. 17 NKJV), bring a sense of hope and change her attitude! Elkanah becomes the vehicle of fulfillment to the promise of God's messenger. How often I have talked with childless couples—and cried with some—only later to learn of an unexpected miracle that resulted in a baby for the couple either through the natural process or an adoption.

God acted on Hannah's request and she bore a son naming him, appropriately, Samuel, meanings, "asked of God." Adam Clarke wrote, "This name would put both the mother and the son in continual remembrance of the Divine interposition at his birth" (Adam Clarke, *Joshua to Esther*, vol. 2 of *Clarke's Commentary* (New York and Nashville [Abingdon-Cokesbury Press, n.d.], p. 208).

When God answers our prayers—and God will—we need to thank and praise God for answered prayer!

Hannah received her answer to prayer but the greatest excitement about prayer is not so much that we receive the answer, but in being the type of individual God can trust and use with that answer. (Derl Keefer)

## THE GREAT MEDIATOR

### HEBREWS 10:11-14 (15-18), 19-25

Stephen was a friend in elementary school. He was a mediator. Whenever there was a conflict or fight between classmates, he had a way of breaking it up and even, sometimes, bringing them back together. He had a gift. So it did not surprise me to learn that he became a counselor. He's still bringing people together.

In the Scripture reading the writer continues his argument that, in every way, Christ, our great High Priest, is superior to any other high priest and anything that high priest may do. As high priest, Christ is the great mediator. Christ is the one who brings us back into the relationship with God for which we were created.

## I. The Perfect and Only Sacrifice

Every priest, even the high priest, had to repeatedly prepare and offer sacrifices in the temple. This could never cease to be the case. But it was all useless. None of the sacrifices, even if offered every minute of every day, could achieve what they were meant to: forgiveness of sins.

But then, along comes Christ. In the most Holy of Holies in heaven, Christ came and offered a sacrifice, his own life, so that no other sacrifice need ever be made again. Rather than having to then come back and do it all over again like other priests, Christ now sits at the right hand of God and continues to intercede for us. The other priests could never sit, for their work was never done. Now, what priest can compete with that? What high priest has ever been able to say or do anything like that?

## II. Mediator of a New Covenant

The priest is the one who seeks to mediate between God and the people, to be ever renewing that covenant or relationship. But in Christ, God has made a new and better covenant, which is a fulfillment of the promise the Hebrew writer quotes from Jeremiah 31. This covenant is written on the hearts and minds of believers. This High Priest, through the power of the Spirit, brings a new and intimate relationship with God. This new relationship is not based on law but rather on God's grace and love. This new covenant or relationship with God is such that Christ brings us into God's own presence where we are cleansed. Perhaps the writer has baptism in mind here. Certainly the image of the high priest entering the Holy of Holies is in mind. The high priest is the only one who can enter. But not so for Christ. Christ brings us into the Holy of Holies. Christ opens the way for all. So we can draw near with boldness to God's presence, God's very throne, knowing that in Christ we have been brought there and made clean. God is accessible now because of Christ. The veil or curtain that separated us from the Holy of Holies has been opened for all time.

## III. So Hold Fast

Verse 23 is the heart of what the writer wishes to see happen. In light of all this theology, he writes, "Hold fast." They cannot give up or give in now. They have made a good start in their faith in Christ. Now is no time to quit. Now is the time, in fact, to support one another, not to stop gathering as some had done but to keep gathering, to keep worshiping , and to keep serving together as God's people. They could not make it alone. They needed the strength that comes from Christian fellowship. (Bass Mitchell)

# KEEP AT IT!

### MARK 13:1-8

Perhaps you have seen the bumper sticker that says, "Jesus is coming—look busy!" Although humorous, this one-liner points to our text and the complicated web of issues it raises for preachers. Texts such as this one have long been popular with those fascinated with the end of the world. Similarly, it has been largely ignored by modern, more practical minds. The preacher's challenge is to help congregations find a relevant word in the text as it comes to us.

The first eight verses must be seen in the context of the entire chapter. In the first verse, the disciples are admiring the temple. In verse 2, Jesus tells them that the temple will be destroyed—it will no longer be the center or focal point of faith for those who choose to follow Christ. In verse 3, the scene shifts from the temple to the Mount of Olives—further signifying a shift away from the temple. Four disciples ask Jesus when the temple will be destroyed and when all of the things Jesus said would be accomplished. In their minds, the destruction of the temple is clearly linked to the end of all things. In his response, Jesus makes it clear that the two events are distinctive from each other.

Jesus' discourse begins in verse 5 and is divided into two sections. The first section (5-23) begins and ends with warnings to beware, for the end has not yet come. In the second section (24-37), Jesus says to watch, for although the time is unknown, the end is indeed coming. This chapter is Jesus' farewell discourse in Mark. In Matthew and Luke, Jesus' final words command us to be engaged in spreading the gospel. In John, the disciples were commanded to tend the flock. In Mark, the final message is to watch for the coming of the Son of man. From now on, the coming of the Son of man in glory replaces the Temple as the locus of hope for the full realization of the kingdom of God (Lamar Williamson, Jr., *Mark*, vol. 2 of *Interpretation Bible Commentary—New Testament* [Louisville: Westminster John Knox Press, 1983]).

It is in this larger context that we find our verses. Although Jesus disconnects the destruction of the temple from the end of the world, he does not answer the disciples' question about when such events will occur. Instead, Jesus instructs them on how to behave when difficulties arise. Jesus reminds them in no uncertain terms that trouble will come. False teachers will seek to lead them astray—beware! Wars will occur—do not be alarmed! There will be natural disasters—this is not the end of the world! Even now, a major world crisis prompts discussions, writings, and predictions that the end time has arrived. Many Christians succumb to the temptation to use apocalyptic material to try to make sense of traumatic events. Jesus' response to this reaction would be the same to us as it was to the disciples: The end time is not signaled by such events. We are to watch, yes, but our primary concern is to give witness to the gospel.

However, in our witness we are warned not to become complacent. Lamar Williamson states, "Perhaps facing the unexpectedness of the ultimate divine invasion can lift believers above institutionalized expectations to a more vital watchfulness. Mark 13 speaks to those who expect too much and to those who expect too little. It is especially pertinent for those who have forgotten to expect anything at all" (Williamson, *Mark*, p. 243). (Tracy Hartman)

# NOVEMBER 23, 2003

## *Christ the King Sunday*

---

**Worship Theme:** God has crowned Jesus as the Sovereign of Glory. Those who are under the reign of Christ are those who are true disciples.

---

**Readings:** 2 Samuel 23:1-7; Revelation 1:4*b*-8; John 18:33-37

**Call to Worship (Psalm 132:1-5, 13-18)**

> *Leader:* O LORD, remember in David's favor all the hardships he endured; how he swore to the LORD and vowed to the Mighty One of Jacob,
>
> *People:* **"I will not enter my house or get into my bed; I will not give sleep to my eyes or slumber to my eyelids,**
>
> *Leader:* Until I find a place for the LORD, a dwelling place for the Mighty One of Jacob."
>
> *People:* **For the LORD has chosen Zion; he has desired it for his habitation:**
>
> *Leader:* "This is my resting place forever; here I will reside, for I have desired it.
>
> *People:* **I will abundantly bless its provisions; I will satisfy its poor with bread.**
>
> *Leader:* Its priests I will clothe with salvation, and its faithful will shout for joy.

*People:*   **There I will cause a horn to sprout up for David; I have prepared a lamp for my anointed one.**

*All:*   **His enemies I will clothe with disgrace, but on him, his crown will gleam."**

**Pastoral Prayer:**

Everlasting God, we worship the king. In the prophecy about the Messiah we read that you have named the Christ "Wonderful Counselor, Mighty God, Everlasting Father, Prince of Peace" (Isaiah 9:6*b*). Help us Lord, see this Jesus about whom the prophets spoke. May this Christ be a living presence in our lives and in the life of our congregation. Draw us together and unite us in this vision of God, who took human form. Let us take the yoke of Christ upon ourselves, and teach us what it means to be a servant of others. Forgive us our foolish pride when we chafe under the weight of humility. Rather teach us that righteousness begins with a heart for the poor, the orphan, and the widow among us. Let us have that spirit in our heart that Jesus imparted to those who took up their cross to follow the Christ in living form. Make us one with you, O Lord, and one with each other. We pray this in the powerful and sovereign name of Jesus. Amen. (David Mosser)

# SERMON BRIEFS

## AND THE TWO SHALL BECOME ONE

### 2 SAMUEL 23:1-7

On the American side of the Atlantic, the term *separation of church and state* (though not actually appearing in the Constitution), has a constitutive and axiomatic authority. Between the Body Politic and the Body of Christ we raise a stout wall, such that even devout church members begin to get nervous when the preacher's sermons seem to mix "religion and politics."

One of the consequences of this "Enlightenment principle" is that many Christians live with a kind of "two kingdoms" mentality, according to which a bifurcation exists between civics and spirituality. In this reasoning, we conceive faith primarily as a private matter and not germane to discourse in the public square.

How odd a notion, at least from the biblical perspective. For the Bible, theology is political, and politics are theological. Granted, there is a huge difference between a theocratic monarchy and a modern (or postmodern) democracy, so that there are no easy fusings of biblical and current horizons with regard to social issues.

Still, we must affirm that God's proclamation of peace—which we will hear so very clearly in Advent and Christmastide—is for peace on earth. What we celebrate, in fact, is both pronouncement and anticipation of God's redeeming and reordering the earth in accordance with the original purposes of Creation.

When last we encountered David, it was soon after his battle with his insurrectionist son, Absalom. That particular lesson concluded several weeks of lessons that chronicled the rise and, by some methods of accounting, demise of the great king. At the time of his death, the kingdom will still be substantial and strong; but David's reign and his relationships are, in a very real sense, reduced to rubble by sin and savagery, by palace intrigue and personal *hubris*.

At the end, the promises and prophecies of 2 Samuel 7—anchored as they are in the steadfast love of God and anticipating a peaceful, just, and abiding reign for David, his progeny, and his people—might seem a distant and hollow pronouncement. And yet, in these "last words of David" we have more such pronouncements. We do not have a revisionist reading of David himself, not a spin doctor's epigraph on a failed administration, but a fuller anticipation of a better reign to come. These "bookend" hymns of praise, providing the parameters of David's monarchy, prove not empty at all, but full of hope and praise for the God who makes them. And if, in between, we are disappointed and disgusted with the failures of David, we are nonetheless moved by his confidence that God will yet bring the promises to pass.

Here is the thing: These promises, these prophecies of peace and goodwill and justice, are God's promises. For better or worse, David has been God's servant, sometimes faithful and sometimes not. But God is the steadfastly faithful one. It is God, ultimately and finally, who will forever reign as the holy and eternal King of

Israel and the world. And if God executes that reign through another—as we believe and celebrate in the season ahead of us—it will be through the Eternal Son, who will not faint or grow weary until he has established justice in all the earth.

It is that our Old Testament lesson anticipates a new beginning, a new reign, a new covenant established through a righteous king: a son of David, to be sure, but even more the Son of God, who will rule over a redeemed creation. All hail, Christ the King! (Thomas Steagald)

# LOOK UP AND LIVE!

## REVELATION 1:4b-8

In a recent article from *Atlantic Monthly* (March 2001), the author maintains that landscape art betrays the painter's worldview as much as it captures nature's reality. In the centuries that artists have painted the Pacific Northwest, they have moved from seeing a pastoral peace worthy of the English countryside, to the wild romance of the early 1800s, to the lines and angles of railroads and steamships inevitably dividing and humanizing the land. Landscape art not only describes topography but also reveals the artist's inner world: his or her commitments, faith, and personality.

The "landscape art" of the Apocalypse acquaints us with an author who has been seized with a peculiar vision of the world. John of Patmos did not learn it at a parent's knee, nor was it gleaned from the corners and classrooms of conventional culture. It is "the revelation of Jesus Christ" (1:1, 2). In that vision, John's world was ablaze with the wildfire of God's presence. John followed the command to write down what he saw and continued the presence of the eternal witness, Jesus Christ. For those with "eyes to see" and "an ear to hear," God's presence bubbles to the surface in the midst of our common life, and people are changed. We can thank God for revealing this in John's vision of the risen Christ.

## I. The faithful seer lives in the midst of the revelation of Christ's presence, where others see the commonplace.

The couplet reminds us: "Two men looked out through prison bars. One saw mud, the other saw stars." John was the starry-eyed visionary behind those prison bars. He was stuck on the island of Patmos, surrounded by the vaunted power of the Roman Empire. When the world's empire has you locked up, does it make any sense to speak of Jesus as the king, "who is, and who was, and who is to come"? (v. 8 NIV). But, someone must have the courage to tell of the vision, risking ridicule, exile, or worse. Yes, those prison bars are real, and unyielding. In this iron world there are times when we feel as though the evil kingdom of Babylon has taken out a long-term lease on our institutions. However, John wants us to know that God is powerfully present, just below the surface, and God is, was, and will be. That settles things for believers.

## II. Jesus Christ is the "faithful witness" who sees it all: past, present, and future, death and life.

John's vision was temporary. What he saw was the lamb upon the throne. But Christ's penetrating sight is present in all of life. Jesus will continue to be the martyr-witness. A witness does nothing more than tell what he or she sees. The witness borne by Jesus will continue to be conveyed to the people of the church.

## III. In God's good time, and in our joining in faithful witness to the vision, "every eye will see him" (v. 7).

We carry and continue the witness of Christ Jesus. We continue to see the unseen. Others see a dreary, dissected world of the principalities and powers. The believer sees through the eyes of the spirit that:

> The world is charged with the grandeur of God.
> It will flame out, like shining from shook foil.

(Gerard Manley Hopkins, "God's Grandeur" from *A Dictionary of Environmental Quotations*, comp. Barbara K. Rodes and Rice Odell [New York: Simon & Schuster, 1992], p. 193)

Does this revelation make sense in the midst of our sturdy, iron-bar world? Of course, it does not make sense until we look back and realize that the "eternal" Roman Empire, which had imprisoned John, would disappear like vapor within three hundred years of the writing of his vision. The vision of the fall of Babylon (Rome) came true when a confused and angry Visigoth general named Alaric walked into Rome and took it without a fight. Rome fell, and Christ lives on! It is Christ's revelation that continues to bring life to God's world. (Don Holladay)

## PILATE'S PEACE

### JOHN 18:33-37

Who is a king and what constitutes a kingship? In this passage, the conversation between Jesus and Pilate revolves around this very issue. The narrative begins in verse 33 with Pilate summoning Jesus and asking him, "Are you the king of the Jews?" Pilate had experienced an uneasy relationship with the Jews. On more than one occasion, they had complained to the emperor about him. In questioning Christ, Pilate reveals his own fear about a Jewish uprising.

In typical fashion, Jesus answers Pilate's question with a question. In effect, he becomes the examiner. Pilate becomes the one being interrogated. "Do you ask this on your own, or did others tell you about me?" (v. 34). In his answer, "I am not a Jew, am I?" (v. 35), Pilate distances himself from the Jews he governs. He reminds Jesus that it is his own people who have handed him over. Instead of answering Jesus' question, he asks another, "What have you done?"

Throughout his ministry, Jesus has been seeking to dispel the popular notion that he will be the political ruler who will free the Jews from Roman oppression. In Jesus' answer to Pilate, he shows again that his kingdom is not to be a political or social one, but a spiritual and eternal one. In describing his kingship or reign, Jesus states that it is from God, not a ruler located in Jerusalem. Jesus reminds Pilate that if his kingdom were a political one, Jesus would have servants and legal counsel working to free him. No such persons appear on Christ's behalf.

In verse 37, Pilate again asks, " 'So you are a king?' " Again, Jesus does not directly answer the question. Instead, Jesus tells Pilate that his purpose was to testify to the truth—the true knowledge of God. Jesus then adds that everyone who belongs to the truth, or to God, listens to his voice. The implication is that Pilate, who is not listening to what Jesus is trying to say, does not belong.

Again, Pilate misses the point. Changing the subject, Pilate asks Jesus, "What is truth?" Throughout the rest of his encounter with Jesus, Pilate continues to question Jesus without every getting to the heart of who Jesus is or about the true nature of Jesus' kingship. Although Pilate finds no reason to condemn Jesus to death, he ultimately caves in to the jeering crowds and sacrifices Jesus in order to keep peace and protect himself.

The question is, *where do we find ourselves in this story?* Too often, we are Pilate. Although we are curious and perhaps even annoyed and inconvenienced by this man Jesus, we don't really want to know the answer to the question, "Are you a king?" Perhaps, we are afraid of what it will mean to follow such a king. Perhaps, we know what it will mean, and we consciously choose not to follow the command to have the mind of Christ and willingly lay down our own lives. Perhaps, like Pilate, we cave in to the pressure to keep the peace and protect ourselves rather than doing what we know to be right. Jesus, the good shepherd, calls us to the still waters and the overflowing banquet table. However, we, like Christ, may have to walk through the darkest valley to get there. (Tracy Hartman)

# NOVEMBER 30, 2003

*First Sunday of Advent*

**Worship Theme:** During the season of Advent, God calls the church and its people to watch and wait. *Being alert* is the watchword of this season, which anticipates the announcement of the coming of Messiah.

**Readings:** Jeremiah 33:14-16; 1 Thessalonians 3:9-13; Luke 21:25-36

**Call to Worship (Psalm 25:6-10 RSV)**

*Leader:* Be mindful of thy mercy, O LORD, and of thy steadfast love, for they have been from of old.

*People:* **Remember not the sins of my youth, or my transgressions;**

*Leader:* According to thy steadfast love remember me, for thy goodness' sake, O LORD!

*People:* **Good and upright is the LORD; therefore he instructs sinners in the way.**

*Leader:* He leads the humble in what is right, and teaches the humble his way.

*People:* **All the paths of the LORD are steadfast love and faithfulness, for those who keep his covenant and his testimonies.**

**Pastoral Prayer:**
On this day of high anticipation, O God, we gather to hear the good news. Help us watch with alert eyes and with open hearts

for your word that breaks in on our mundane lives. Day by day, and too often, we go through life's motions with little reflection on the great and wondrous things you provide for us at every turn. Small things weigh down our spirits and souls; we forget you and all your benefits to your people. You have made a solemn covenant with us to be your people just as surely as you will be our God. Allow us to approach your throne of grace as forgiven and redeemed people. Let us acquire the joy that is ours for the gathering. May we share the joy of Jesus with a world in deep need of the happiness that your divine hope provides. Most of all, make us again a people who listen for and receive your promise of the coming of the Lord. We pray this in the name of Jesus, our Messiah. Amen. (David Mosser)

# SERMON BRIEFS

## PRE-CHRISTMAS SALE HOPE

### JEREMIAH 33:14-16

The season of Advent is a season of hope. Something is dawning on the horizon of our lives—can we see it? The very meaning of the season is about something or someone coming. The word *advent* is derived from the Latin word *adventus*, which literally means *coming*.

In this Advent season, the church lifts its collective head and squints toward the horizon. We take a long view, turning our gaze toward that which is approaching. On this first Sunday of Advent, our view may be a little cloudy. The horizon is far away, and although we can see that something is happening, we cannot quite make out what it is.

To discern what is approaching, we listen to the words of the prophet Jeremiah. His words excite us because he promises salvation: "In those days and at that time I will cause a righteous Branch to spring up for David; and he shall execute justice and righteousness in the land" (v. 15). The name of this approaching one is "righteousness."

Thus, in Advent, the church proclaims the approaching righteousness of God. It is a crucial proclamation because it is a real source of hope. The world, our lives, our days cannot live without hope. Anticipating what God is going to do energizes us for faithful and fruitful living.

Ironically, we anticipate the future by remembering the past. We remember the glory days of Israel under King David's leadership. We strain forward in order to see "a righteous Branch" spring forth. But this is a particular kind of remembering. In this season we do not remember that which has happened in the past in a historic sense. We remember in a way that changes us. It is the memory of a lover's kiss, the memory of a child returning home after too long an absence, the memory of the words of forgiveness for some wrong committed. The power of this kind of memory can make us cry or laugh or even feel contentment. It is memory that never grows old. We tell the stories of it again and again because each time we tell the story we experience the power of the memory in our lives.

Each year the season of Advent calls the community of faith to prepare for the visit of God's salvation. Our work is to anticipate that which God will do to bring fulfillment to all people. We are preparing for the event in the stable at Bethlehem which brings together "the hopes and fears of all the years," as Phillips Brooks's "O Little Town of Bethlehem" so beautifully puts it.

Hope is never cheap. It demands the great energy of faith. This is true because we need hope when we face desperate circumstances. Jeremiah draws on the deep energy of his own faith as he proclaims that, "the days are coming" (v. 14a NKJV). It must have been a difficult ministry because he was speaking to people who had lost hope. Exiles in a strange land do not find hope easily. Into this condition of lostness, the prophet dares to speak his word of hopeful newness that will come to pass because of God's salvation. Like Jeremiah, the Church must draw on its energy of faith as it offers to the world a vision of the newness that God brings in the birth of Christ. The proclamation must be bold so that our anticipation can be without hesitation. "The days are coming," and we must make ready. So, lift your heads and let your hearts be strengthened. God is doing a new thing, and to us has come the joyous and holy task of helping the world get ready for the most blessed event of history! (Chris Andrews)

393

# ENCOURAGING ONE ANOTHER

## 1 THESSALONIANS 3:9-13

As children growing up we all remember the old saying: "Sticks and stones may break my bones, but words will never hurt me." Although this defensive response may sound good, the reality is that words do have the power to hurt—or to heal. Timothy has returned to Paul in Corinth with a report from the church in Thessalonica. It is a good report. Despite some theological disputes regarding the *parousia*, the church is thriving in the face of persecution from the Jews. Paul is pleased with their progress and the pericope for this first Sunday of Advent is a word of great encouragement for the spiritual growth of those who are faithful.

In the context of the Advent season's theme of waiting and watching, what better word for us than the need for us to encourage one another in our spiritual growth? In a setting of persecution, Paul seeks to gently nurture this new congregation as it seeks to grow in reaching out to others. Paul shares his joy at their growth and work. Paul also pledges to come soon to see them and to celebrate and continue to nourish them in their faith. These are good words for us even now. We live in a culture that is quick to judge and one in which the tabloids are ready and waiting to divulge and exploit the latest gossip. On television we can now watch a game show host ridicule people for pure entertainment value. We know how easy it is to feel isolated and unworthy in such a culture. Advent is about seeking to proclaim that all is not lost. We do have a hope that is eternal and true. However, such hoping is not done watching the clock. Rather, such a hoping demands a response of actively living out in life what we know to be true in our heart.

Paul's perspective is one of praise and nurture for those who need to know that they are a part of God's work in the world. Paul believed that God was at work in history. Paul's letters are full of his sense of that work and the need for people to join in that work. As Paul hears the good news from Thessalonica, his response is one of praise and one of promise that they will continue. Paul is excited about the new converts to the faith and their faithful response in the wake of persecution and hatred. The waiting of Advent is not about sitting on a fence post daydreaming of what may happen next. The waiting of Advent is about growing in the love of God, sharing that love with others, and partnering with God in proclaiming the meaning that love brings. Etty Hillesum, Dutch Jew, voluntarily went to and died in a Nazi concentration camp because she felt, "a camp needs a poet, one who experiences life there, even there, as a bard and is able to sing about it" (Arno Pomerans, trans., *An Interrupted Life: The Diaries of Etty Hillesum 1941–1943* [New York: Pantheon Books, 1983], p. 190). The following is a diary entry as she watches the Nazi net tighten around the Jews.

> Monday morning, 10 o'clock. . . . The latest news is that all Jews will be transported out of Holland through Drenthe Province and then on to Poland. . . . And yet I don't think life is meaningless. And God is not accountable to us for the senseless harm we cause one another. We are accountable to Him! . . . And yet I find life beautiful and meaningful. From minute to minute.
>
> . . . Sun on the balcony and a light breeze through the jasmine. . . . I shall linger another ten minutes with the jasmine, and then to see the friend . . . who can still suddenly present me with an aspect so new that I catch my breath with surprise. How exotic the jasmine looks, so delicate and dazzling against the mud-brown walls.
>
> I can't take in how beautiful this jasmine is. But there is no need to. It is enough simply to believe in miracles in the twentieth century. And I do, even though the lice will be eating me up in Poland before long. (Pomerans, *An Interrupted Life*, pp. 127-28)

Paul celebrates and seeks to nurture such a perspective as he hears the good news from Timothy about the power of God being lived out through a church in Thessalonica. Regardless of how things may appear, the word of God proclaims a word of hope, encouragement, praise, and joy. Our world is waiting desperately to hear such words. (Travis Franklin)

## GOD'S HIDDEN WORK

### LUKE 21:25-36

The first Sunday of Advent is all about beginnings and endings, which begin all over again. The preceding week ended the liturgical year with Christ the King Sunday celebrating the final victory of God in Christ over all who oppose God's reign. One worship cycle ends and, with the coming of Advent, another begins.

Yet this beginning looks frighteningly like the ending/beginning of Christ the King Sunday. Advent begins with Luke quoting Jesus on the last days. With the exception of the opening story of the "widow's mite," Luke 21 is devoted to Jesus' warnings about the end time. The picture Jesus paints must have looked very familiar to Luke's readers in the years after the Roman wars and the destruction of Jerusalem. Readers and worshipers in our time find Jesus' words to be strange and disturbing. Some continue to look for timetables and clues to date the end of the age. Others skim quickly through these apocalyptic passages to hurry on to the more familiar stories. Neither approach will do.

Preaching this text can find its focus in the call to remember the great biblical loop that extends from creation to new creation. The church begins Advent, focused not on the baby to come, but on God's great design to finish creation in a blast of glory. As the worship year begins, the worshiper is called to remember that the cycle has a destination, and that destination is the reign of God. The sermon sets the stage not just for the holiday season or for "hanging the green," but for the entire salvation story. The text invites the church to begin with an eye toward the end.

The preacher might explore what living in Advent might mean with an eye to the end. Interestingly, the text has Jesus warning his listeners, "Don't spend all of your time thinking about eating or drinking or worrying about life" (v. 34 CEV). What an apt caution at the beginning of the holiday season! If the church were to live in Advent with an eye to the incarnation and the world's consummation, what a different Advent it might be. God will not only join us as word made flesh but will also promise that the purposes of creation are being worked out in the incarnation on the journey to God's final victory. The preacher might explore local or global events or customs to illustrate how the church might live in a different reality, full of the confident faith that God's reign is coming.

Examples abound. Advent in the United States is a frenzied celebration of the temporary. Decorations dry out and become fire hazards. Piped-in holiday music quickly becomes tiresome.

Gifts given and received are forgotten before the twelve days of Christmas are past. For most, the season is full of activity and empty of promise. In this text from Luke, Jesus calls the church to center on the long view and the assurance of "the final triumph of righteousness." As the culture begins its annual holiday madness, Christ invites his people to something much better. Human life and destiny cannot be reduced to good cheer and hangovers. God is at work. The creation is being fulfilled. Christ is coming both as child in the manger and as Lord of Lords. Begin appropriately with an eye to the true prize, and the weeks of Advent will bless rather than exhaust. (Carl Schenck)

# REFLECTIONS

# DECEMBER

**Reflection Verse:** *"'Do not be afraid, Zechariah; your prayer has been heard. Your wife Elizabeth will bear you a son, and you are to give him the name John.'" (Luke 1:13 NIV)*

Singing Christmas carols opens the old photograph album of my memory. In one image, I see myself as a child mourning the death of my grandfather at Christmastime. In another, I am at home from college wondering if the Vietnam War will ever end. I turn another memory page, and there I am with my spouse holding our sick and fitful child through his first Christmas. In every memory there are Christmas carolers outside, gripping candles in the cold darkness, standing like a priestly order, and singing songs of God's promise of peace. William Faulkner once wrote, "The past is never dead. It's not even past" (William Faulkner, *Requiem for a Nun* [New York: Random House, 1951], p. 92). That truth comes home to us whenever we sing Christmas carols.

In this story from Luke's Gospel, the Evangelist draws back the curtain of time to show us an old priest at work a long, long time ago. It is in the twilight of the day; Zechariah is in the twilight of his life. He is getting ready to approach the altar. He wants to remember every detail so that he can give a full account to those who will ask what it was like to be in the holy place. Who knows? This may be the last time his turn comes to be there.

The altar is about three feet high and square. Its wood comes from the durable acacia tree, the kind of tree that God promised would grow in the wilderness. The altar shimmers with gold. The light reflecting off the gold comes from a lamp stand with seven branches. On the table are twelve loaves of unleavened bread arranged in two rows of six, and with each row, pure frankincense gives off the fragrance of eternity.

Behind him there is a curtain, beyond which he will never

enter. The privilege of entering the Holy of Holies is reserved for the High Priest, who may enter it only once during the year—on the Day of Atonement. As for Zechariah and the members of his more modest priestly order, they are in charge of "ordinary" prayers offered twice daily, once in the morning and once in the evening. Twice a year Zechariah and his wife, Elizabeth, travel from their home in the hills to Jerusalem and there join the other members of Abijah's order (Luke 1:5) to accept the responsibilities of their priesthood.

Here was an ordinary priest doing his duty by leading ordinary prayers. But, something extraordinary is about to happen! On this day, in one moment of his priestly routine, God chooses to disclose God's self to Zechariah in a remarkable way. You have to wonder what might have been going through Zechariah's mind in the moments before God's messenger appeared. He must have felt that his life was a living contradiction. On the one hand, he and his wife had been faithful in all things. Yet, on the other hand, they had no children! They were blameless but barren! This did not add up in the belief system of that day. His very name, Zechariah, literally meant, "God remembers." Here, near the close of his life of faithful service, God will remember Zechariah.

Zechariah prepares by discarding the burnt residue left in the bowl from the morning prayers. Then he replaces it with the fresh incense that will bear the evening prayers of the people into the presence of God. The old priest presses the bowl of incense down onto the hot coals. As the fragrance rises in the dim flickering light and as the crowd waits outside, he prays the assigned words in a voice cracking with age and long years of expectation: "May the God of mercy come into the sanctuary and accept with pleasure the sacrifice of His people!"

"May the God of mercy come!" prays Zechariah and the words of this ancient priest become our own words of invocation during this season. "May the God of mercy come!" We pray in the silence of our hearts perhaps, asking God to meet us in our time and place in the sanctuary of our own lives.

Perhaps we dare to pray such things only once a year when the days are shortened by darkness, and we hear the surprising sound of our own voices singing ancient carols. Or perhaps we have found ways to enter a holy place more often—whether it is the light-filled sanctuary of weekly worship or the stolen stillness of daily devotion—but the worship is routine, and we have come to expect very little to happen. Maybe we have even forgotten how to find any place for the holy in our lives. We no longer travel the ritual pathways the ancients have laid out for us. Our trips down those pathways took us too far into doubt and left us feeling lost and abandoned. Worship in personal darkness becomes barren after a while. Still we ached for One to come and give light to all of us who were sitting in darkness and in the shadow of death.

Whoever we are, and wherever we have been, Luke invites us to follow this old priest into a holy, secluded place within this story. There he leads us in prayer: "May the God of mercy come!" And God does come. God comes to show mercy to a priest who thought he was forgotten and to his wife, ashamed of her barrenness. God comes to show mercy to this generation as God has come in all others. God comes to show mercy to parents who have forgotten how to love their own children and to children who have forgotten that they are loved. God comes to show mercy to all who have forgotten how to show compassion and who no longer know what (or who) they are to get ready for. The God of mercy does come but never in a way that we fully expect or for which we fully prepare. God always comes in a way that may even confound or inhibit our capacity to speak about it. Look at Zechariah trying to explain what happened in Luke 1:22. This attempt at human speech provides a clearer picture of how we try to talk about our meeting with the Holy One! Isn't this what worship is anyway? A few words that do not fully explain and some gestures that can only point to the mystery of God? We get some clues from Elizabeth of how to speak of God. God looks with favor on us even when we feel shamed, abandoned, or forgotten.

This is a God who is worthy of praise. Here is a God who promises to enter the story of our lives, to meet us in the secluded and hidden sanctuaries of our hearts, and to set our lives in motion with the same spirit that blows through the cold dark country of Advent. In that spirit we pray again with the old priest: May the God of mercy come "to guide our feet into the path of peace" (v. 79). (Richard Ward)

# DECEMBER 7, 2003

*Second Sunday of Advent*

**Worship Theme:** As the church prepares to receive the Messiah, God commands the church to "prepare the way of the Lord" (Isaiah 40:3). In the Lord's coming, all injustice will be right, all despair turned to hope.

**Readings:** Malachi 3:1-4; Philippians 1:3-11; Luke 3:1-6

**Call to Worship (Luke 1:68-79 RSV)**

*Leader:*   "Blessed be the Lord God of Israel, for he has visited and redeemed his people,

**People:**   **And has raised up a horn of salvation for us in the house of his servant David,**

*Leader:*   As he spoke by the mouth of his holy prophets from of old, that we should be saved from our enemies, and from the hand of all who hate us;

**People:**   **To perform the mercy promised to our fathers, and to remember his holy covenant, the oath which he swore to our father Abraham,**

*Leader:*   To grant us that we, being delivered from the hand of our enemies, might serve him without fear, in holiness and righteousness before him all the days of our life.

**People:**   **And you, child, will be called the prophet of the Most High; for you will go before the Lord to prepare his ways, to give knowledge of salvation to his people in the forgiveness of their sins,**

*Leader:*     Through the tender mercy of our God, when the
              day shall dawn upon us from on high.

**People:**   **To give light to those who sit in darkness
              and in the shadow of death, to guide our
              feet into the way of peace."**

**Pastoral Prayer:**

O God of Glory, we rejoice in this most lovely time of the year.
We prepare for family and friends with whom we will make
merry. Yet, in this time of merriment, remind us why our celebra-
tions are appropriate. Keep our hearts focused on the good news
that you deliver in the promised Messiah. Remind us that as we
gather with coworkers and those in our household, other people
have no one with whom to celebrate. Remind us to be watchful
for those grieving souls who spend this holiday without that significant other who has made their life so full of bliss. As we sing
the hymns of Advent, remind us of the wonder of the Christ
Child whom you promised through the prophets. Keep our
minds clear to the implications of the fulfillment of your
covenant pledge in the Christ. Make us the people you created us
to be. We pray this in Jesus' name. Amen. (David Mosser)

# SERMON BRIEFS

## A MIXED BAG

### MALACHI 3:1-4

Life is a mixed bag. It is full of ups and downs, but most of us
don't like the downs. Someone once said to me, "I wish Christmas
would not come." At first we may think, "How awful. This is supposed to be a season of joy." Just think about it for a minute. Do you
not get a little tired of everything? We have been getting ready for
Christmas for weeks, even months. We have been searching diligently to find that "perfect" gift for that certain someone. No matter
how much time or money we have to spend, we just cannot find it.
The stores have had Christmas decorations up since late October.

On Christmas morning children and adults will sit in the middle of all the litter of unwrapped gifts and think, "Is that all?" We will even rummage through the wrapping paper to make sure we have not missed something. Just a few minutes later, we will not be able to find the gifts we have opened. One Christmas, as a boy, I just had to have a certain red fire truck. Well, sure enough, it was under the Christmas tree. The very next week I left that fire truck in the driveway where a car ran over it. Life is a mixed bag. Christmas is a mixed bag. Regardless of how joyful a season this may be, counselors know that the time after Christmas is a time of tremendous depression for many people.

There should be a greater anxiety in our hearts, however, than simply having ups and downs in this season. That anxiety is the coming of our Lord. Why should we be anxious about Jesus' coming? Because when God comes, things change. Scripture tells us that God does not put new wine into old wineskins. Malachi is very clear about the refiner's fire. We are going to get next to the fire, and it will singe us. How can these words become words of hope and joy?

Not only does our human experience tell us that life is a mixed bag of ups and downs. It also tells us that many of the best things in life come at a price. Many who have been through heart problems know that when you get on "the other side" there is rehabilitation. Rehabilitation is a lot of exercise and a lot of pain. However, it brings health and hope into a threatened life. Also, athletes know that if you are going to be ready to do well in your sport, you have to put in many hours of practice with sore muscles the next day.

There are things in our lives that need refining before we can really experience the joy of God with us. Some of these things are hatred, prejudice, dry eyes in the face of human need, poverty, war, racism, and economic injustice. What are some of the things in your life that need refining before you can experience the joy of God's coming?

Some families have a custom of preparing special breads or cookies or other handmade gifts for family members and friends during this season instead of giving gifts bought at the store. The perfect gift is not necessarily the one that costs the most, but the gift given out of love.

God gives us the gift of refinement because God loves us. God wants us to experience the joy of this season. That is why God calls us to experience the refiner's fire. (Tim Russell)

# GOD IS UP TO SOMETHING!—ARE YOU?

## PHILIPPIANS 1:3-11

Paul addresses this most personal of his letters to the church at Philippi for their support and love during his imprisonment. He also seeks to identify the foundation of the good work they are doing and will continue to do. That foundation, for Paul, is God. The source of every good work among them springs from the love of God as it seeks expression in and through them. Paul knows that the reason for the offering they sent to him and for the support that they give him has at its source God. Paul expresses his sense of that in verse 6, "God began doing a good work in you, and I am sure he will continue it until it is finished when Jesus Christ comes again" (NCV). This is not only the theme of this passage but also a theme consistently found throughout Paul's work.

What better word to hear at Advent than a word to remind the church of who the source of our good work together is. In this time of expectant waiting, we need to be reminded that such waiting involves us in responding now to what God is doing among us. It is easy in these days preceding the Christmas experience to forget who is most important. With everyone worrying about what to buy the kids or where the money is coming from this year or who will be at whose house for Christmas, the church needs to remind us of who is most important in this time of year and in any time of year. Paul reminds the church at Philippi that it is not about them or about what they are doing. Life is about God and about what God is doing. Advent helps us in our watching and waiting with God to approach that climactic event of God's ultimate work expressed in the birth of a baby in Bethlehem.

An evangelist tells the story of how, as a young boy, he came home for supper after school, and there, seated at the table, was a stranger. It seems his mother, in her shopping spree that afternoon had found this man, had seen that he needed help, and had invited him to their home for a warm meal. The evangelist talks about how the stranger looked up and said, "Ma'am, I can't begin to tell you how much I appreciate you inviting me here. And how I wish there were more people in the world like you." To which the young boy's mother responded, "Oh, there are more people like me; you just

404

have to look for them." The young man looked across the table at the mother and said, "I didn't have to look for you. You found me."

The heart of Paul's joy and thanksgiving for this church, which he loves and which continues to reach out to him in support, prayer, and love, is that God's love has found him through them. Paul rejoices with them at the undeniable reality that once again God is up to something and that something has found him and touched his life in the midst of the darkness and despair of a prison cell.

In our waiting may we realize that the real and most significant message we seek to experience and to proclaim must be focused on the truth of what God is doing in the world. Any focus other than that is misguided and shallow. But such an affirmation of what God is doing begs the question, *If God is up to something, then are we?* (Travis Franklin)

# A GOOD WORD

## LUKE 3:1-6

The Gospel lesson presents at least two excellent avenues to the sermon. Either speaks well to the worshiper captured by the misguided values of the culture's observance of the holiday season.

Throughout Luke's Gospel is the repeated theme of the great reversal of fortune. The Magnificat celebrates the hungry being filled and the rich being sent away empty. Luke's Beatitudes are concrete promises of reversal of circumstances. Luke 3 begins with a review of the rulers and power brokers of the time. Then Luke moves quickly on to the important character: the unknown desert hermit. The people one would expect to be at the hinge of history turn out to be rather unimportant. The obscure desert prophet stands at the very center of God's saving work in the world. Here, as in so many places in his Gospel, Luke turns the world and the social pecking order upside down.

A prophetic approach to the sermon could have the preacher proclaim God's concern for the weak, the poor, the forgotten in contrast with the culture's obsession with the rich and famous. A look at the daily newspaper reveals how society keeps its eye on the powerful and the rich. The conventional wisdom says that the rulers of this age are key to the future. The holy wisdom calls attention to those whose passion for God calls them to work among the poor and forgotten. Most worshipers feel the important parts of their lives are the efforts they make in the political or economic realm. Luke challenges the worshiper to consider that the important venues of life are where God is bringing good news to the poor, the forgotten, and the hurting. Those who would be great might just be the ones who work in obscurity among those the society has forgotten. This sermon approach challenges the worshiper to repent of misguided attention to the powerful and to embrace the weak. God is changing the world, to be sure, but often in ways the world would not expect.

A second sermon approach is more pastoral. It springs from John's quotation of Isaiah 40. Isaiah's vision of the return to Zion addresses the broken condition of the exiles. The return itself is envisioned as a great procession across the brutal Arabian Desert made possible by God's action to lift every valley and level every mountain creating a virtual highway across the wasteland. Sometimes it is the worshiper who feels exile and needs to hear of God's promise of restoration. In every pew are exiles from family, faith, or hope in the holiday season. Separations are more keenly felt during the holidays than at any other time of the year. Many need to be brought home to Zion. Many feel lost and far from home at some level of their lives. We find deep wounds even among the affluent and the successful. All need to hear that God cares about the ways they are lost and in exile. Everyone needs to hear that God seeks to lift them up in the valleys of life and to sustain them in the desert wastes. If the pews are occupied by those in economic or political exile, then the promise is obvious. If those in the pews are the outwardly comfortable, they are often persons estranged from God and their best selves. A pastoral word to the lost and broken is a good word anytime, especially as the church awaits the coming of the Christ Child. (Carl Schenck)

# DECEMBER 14, 2003

## *Third Sunday of Advent*

**Worship Theme:** In the Messiah, God will execute God's judgment on all humankind. For those found faithful, this is good news indeed. However, for those who have lived with dishonor, the news may not be so good.

**Readings:** Zephaniah 3:14-20; Philippians 4:4-7; Luke 3:7-18

**Call to Worship (Isaiah 12:2-6)**

*Leader:*    Surely God is my salvation;

*People:*    **I will trust, and will not be afraid, for the LORD GOD is my strength and my might; he has become my salvation.**

*Leader:*    With joy you will draw water from the wells of salvation.

*People:*    **And you will say in that day: Give thanks to the LORD, call on his name; make known his deeds among the nations; proclaim that his name is exalted.**

*Leader:*    Sing praises to the LORD, for he has done gloriously; let this be known in all the earth.

*All:*    **Shout aloud and sing for joy, O royal Zion, for great in your midst is the Holy One of Israel.**

**Pastoral Prayer:**
This is a day of rejoicing. O Lord, teach us to pray with your great apostle Paul who wrote, "Rejoice in the Lord always; again I will

say, Rejoice" (Philippians 4:4). Out of this great joy of salvation, given to us as a free gift in Christ Jesus, let us remember the poor and the needy. Everything we have and hope to be comes from your gracious hand, O God. And because you have made us stewards, help us fulfill this role in your realm. We want to be better people, but sometimes life makes our path difficult. Give us the courage to look at people like Mary and Joseph and be inspired by what they willingly sacrificed for their dream of a just and peace-filled world. Fill us with your spirit during this season as we prepare our hearts, minds, and lives for the coming of the Messiah. Let us prepare the Christ a place in our lives so that he may reign in us and for us. We pray this in Jesus' holy name. Amen. (David Mosser)

# SERMON BRIEFS

## I'LL BE HOME FOR CHRISTMAS

### ZEPHANIAH 3:14-20

My son Neil keeps few calendars, but he does keep his Advent calendar with care. From Thanksgiving Day onward, Neil crosses off each calendar day with the utmost precision. He is counting down the days until Christmas. For the faithful, this is a countdown of delight. Most people look forward to the pleasure of Christmas in ways that few of us often reflect on deeply. However, our subconscious is at work. We crave these days like few others. Have you ever noticed how the singing improves in our church in direct proportion to our good humor? During this time—prior to Christmas—even television seems better than it has any right to be. In addition, otherwise dour folks seem almost jovial. It all has to do with the expectancy of Christmas. In fact, we are not there yet. But the anticipation is sometimes as wonderful as the arrival at this holy of days.

Zephaniah captures part of the deepest longings of our human pilgrimage. He uses phrases like, "Rejoice and exult with all your heart" and "Sing aloud" to express what we are incompetent of uttering with our human prose and poetry. Perhaps this is the reason all of us want to sing the carols of Christmas on the day after Thanksgiving. We desire the euphoria of Christmas. To the consternation of well-trained choir directors, the bleak and sober tones of beautiful Advent hymns simply do not exhilarate us like those songs of Christmas do.

Our prophet Zephaniah presents the great promises of God in capsule form: "The LORD has taken away the judgments against you" (v. 15a); "you shall fear disaster no more" (v. 15b); "[the Lord] will renew you in his love" (v. 17b); "I restore your fortunes before your eyes" (v. 20b); and best of all, the Lord tells the people, "I will bring you home" (v. 20a). These words appear especially hope-filled to the people for whom Zephaniah writes because they are people who feel doomed. Presumably, Zephaniah prophesied in the time of Josiah (Zephaniah 1:1). This was a time when the sting of Israel's and Judah's devastation was clearly in the people's shared memory. Consequently, optimism appeared futile. Yet within Zephaniah's cold prophecy of judgment, with special emphasis on "the Day of the Lord," there is a warm reminder of hope. Hope is the text's content before us now—the Lord God will eventually rectify all the people's fortunes.

For people today, there is a sense of hopelessness that too often pervades our society's thinking. Perhaps, we hear just too much bad news too much of the time. However, the child in each of us remembers better days. We ache desperately for those days. This aching for better days may be part of the fuel that propels even the most hardened people toward churches on Christmas Eve. We want to know a different ending to our story that we often only anticipate in fear. Zephaniah speaks to us like he did to people so long ago. God has the final word. God speaks this final word at Easter, but here at Christmas, the shepherds, angels, and Mary sing the opening oratorio. God is with us. Hallelujah!

Anne Murray, country western and pop singer, sings what is my favorite Christmas hope. When I listen to "I'll Be Home for Christmas," it is difficult for me not to remember Zephaniah's words to a distant set of my own relatives reeling from exile: "At that time I will bring you home, at the time when I gather you; for I will make you renowned and praised among all the peoples of the earth, when I restore your fortunes before your eyes, says the LORD" (Zephaniah 3:20). (David Mosser)

# GOD REALITY

## PHILIPPIANS 4:4-7

The letter to the Philippians is the most personal of Paul's letters to the churches. While Paul was in prison he had received an offering from the church and their continued word of support and prayer. So now Paul concludes this letter of thanksgiving and joy with his admonition of the source of that joy—God. The joy Paul mentions is not just any joy; it is the fullness of joy in the Lord. The peace Paul lifts up is not just any peace; it is God's peace. The thanks Paul suggests is a thanks to God for all that God is doing. Once again Paul highlights for the church at Philippi what must be at the heart of the Christian's life: a deep and abiding sense of who God is and of what God is doing among us.

The reality of life for Paul, which he offers to the church he loves so dearly, is a *God reality*. Paul writes out of a sense of the kingdom of God present with him wherever he may be, in whatever he may be doing. Frederick Buechner in his book, *Wishful Thinking*, defines the kingdom of God by writing, "It is not a place, of course, but a condition." The reality of Paul's life is the truth of God present with him in life. That presence is a condition, a lifestyle. So, when Paul sums up his thanks to this church, he cannot prevent himself from testifying as to his joy, his thanks, his peace (even in the prison cell) of this Kingdom condition that defines all that he is, all that he believes, all that he knows. Dietrich Bonhoeffer, the great theologian, wrote, "when Christ calls a man he bids him to come and die." Paul's witness to the church at Philippi is the condition of God's kingdom that lives within him and that claims all of him. Nothing, for Paul, is understood or expressed outside of that reality. It is what drives his perspective and his life.

The Advent experience of watching and waiting must be done in a *God reality*. It is the *God reality* that defines how we watch and how we wait. Paul writes in verse 5, "Let everyone see that you are gentle and kind. The Lord is coming soon" (NCV). The gentleness and kindness Paul advocates is done in response to the reality not only of who God is now but also in who God is going to be when the Lord returns. *God reality* claims not just all of us; it must claim the past, the present, and most certainly the future. Reality TV has become a phenomenon of our age. The reality television genre is permeating the networks. Paul defines reality by trusting in the truth of God and the claim that such a proclamation must make on not just a sliver of life but on all of life. This Advent, may the joy, the peace, and the thanks we proclaim be that of the God of love, who aims to have us all. Such proclamation finds its fullest expression in the birth of Jesus, who has come to fully reveal this *God reality* we dare to proclaim. (Travis Franklin)

## CONCRETE COMPASSION

### LUKE 3:7-18

John the Baptist is trouble during Advent. Most come to worship wanting to sing familiar Christmas carols, hear about the Christ Child, and feel good inside. John offers none of these comforts. Rather, John is the madman of the desert. Rather than comfort, he offers attack. Instead of praise for participation in the religious customs of the time, he suggests stones could be made more faithful. While it might be affirming to praise the worshiper for attendance, John instead questions their motives and calls them poisonous snakes. The preacher is tempted to turn to the Old Testament or epistle lesson for some more palatable material for the growing Christmas crowds. Is it possible that the choir might sing a cantata this week instead of having a sermon?

Yet, the lectionary and the gospel offer no escape from John's harsh words. Facing them might not be pleasant or popular preaching, but the faithful must face them. The preacher would do well to confess reluctance to deal with these texts. While John may have gotten away with attacking his listeners, the preacher is not John the Baptist. The best starting point with dealing with texts of this sort is to acknowledge the preacher's own discomfort with the text and the way it attacks the preacher as directly as the person in the pew.

After openly addressing the uncomfortable nature of the texts it may be possible then for the worshiper to listen to them anew, not as a victim of the preacher's wrath, but as a fellow disciple seeking God's work in a hard word. For when one listens beyond the harsh rhetoric of John's preaching, one can hear a message most of us need to hear. In this sermon, John is addressing a subject with which all faithful people struggle. How does one appropriate the lofty ideals and stirring phrases of the faith with the practical everyday realities of life in the world? This is John's theme, and it is a message needed during the holiday season.

John's admonition is simple. We are to put our idealism to work in everyday acts of compassion, justice, and simple living. The sermon could unpack the life situation of the various persons John addresses in verses 11-14. Certainly at holiday gift-giving season, there is a word from God calling God's people to simple lifestyles. Too much holiday gift giving is a poorly disguised trading of luxuries among the affluent. John would have us give to the poor and live more simply ourselves. Justice is the theme of John's word for the tax collectors. How might we do justice this season? A look at the news of the day would give many illustrations of the need for justice workers in Advent.

John's message is one each generation needs to hear. Instead of getting caught up in the trinkets and trivia of the holidays, God longs for those who can keep to the business of the faithful. God calls for repentance from the self-serving ways we practice as holiday festivities. God calls us to concrete acts of compassion that have more substance than a dollar or two in the collection plate for the needy at Christmas. Christian discipleship is much more than romantic visions of babes in the manger in the Advent season. Compassion, justice, and simplicity are harder now than in any other month of the year. They are also more holy. (Carl Schenck)

# DECEMBER 21, 2003

## *Fourth Sunday of Advent*

---

**Worship Theme:** The great promise held by believers is that God's justice and righteousness will overcome the sin and despair of the world. It is this promise that we celebrate most fully at Advent.

---

**Readings:** Micah 5:2-5*a*; Hebrews 10:5-10; Luke 1:39-45 (46-55)

### Call to Worship (Luke 1:47-55 RSV)

*Leader:*   "My spirit rejoices in God my Savior,

**People:**  **For he has regarded the low estate of his handmaiden.**

*Leader:*   For behold, henceforth all generations will call me blessed;

**People:**  **For he who is mighty has done great things for me, and holy is his name.**

*Leader:*   And his mercy is on those who fear him from generation to generation.

**People:**  **He has shown strength with his arm,**

*Leader:*   He has scattered the proud in the imagination of their hearts,

**People:**  **He has put down the mighty from their thrones, and exalted those of low degree;**

413

*Leader:* He has filled the hungry with good things, and the rich he has sent empty away.

**People:** **He has helped his servant Israel, in remembrance of his mercy,**

*Leader:* As he spoke to our fathers,

*All:* **To Abraham and to his posterity for ever."**

**Pastoral Prayer:**

Come Thou Long-Expected Jesus, we sing as a prayer, dear Lord. Now let it be so. We have awaited this day the whole long year. The joy of this season and its anticipation is deep within our bones. O Lord, you know we sing better, we feel better, and we pray better as we wait for your coming with expectation. We become almost like children as we anticipate the fulfillment of your ancient promises in the Christ whom you have named Jesus. Like Joshua of old, may he be for us the one who leads us toward and into the land of promise. Remind us to care for the lonely and alienated this Advent and Christmas season, O Lord. For it is in our sharing that we find our truest selves. We want to be your people, so incline our ears to the story of the good news found in our Scripture. May we, in these holy days, live lives that befit the gospel. May we spread the good news by the cheer we share with those who have little. Remind us that it is more blessed to give than to receive. We pray this in the holy name of Jesus, our Messiah. Amen. (David Mosser)


# SERMON BRIEFS

## WHO WOULD HAVE EVER THOUGHT?

### MICAH 5:2-5*a*

Micah was a prophet of the southern kingdom of Judah. He had a sense of God's impending judgment as a consequence to the hateful injustice of the people. It is a time of controversy and uneasiness especially in light of the work of Isaiah in the north and the fate of the Northern Kingdom. Micah's message announces God's certain judgment to be sure, but there is also an element in his message of signs of hope for the future. Our Advent passage is taken from that promise of a futuristic hope.

The message for our consideration is one of God's actions in the midst of doom and despair. Micah seeks to remind the people that although judgment is imminent, God will bring forth from that judgment a hope that will not only bring God's peace to Judah but also to the world. Micah makes it clear that this promise of a new ruler will find its beginning in the smallest of places, Bethlehem. The emphasis here is on what God can do with the smallest, the least likely. Such a brilliant prophecy seeks to use that which is unlikely to become the tool of God's blessing of hope. This device places the focus on the power of God and what God can do with very little. Certainly as we wait and watch we need to remember that God will be at work in the places and through the people we least expect. Such seems to be the way of God. This theme needs to be part of the message we seek to proclaim in this season of Advent.

In Viktor E. Frankl's book, *Man's Search for Meaning*, he tells a story that illustrates how God shows up in the strangest and most unexpected ways. Frankl was a prisoner in a Nazi concentration camp during World War II. He tells of how he and some other prisoners were moved on a work detail from Auschwitz to a Bavarian work camp.

> One evening when we were already resting on the floor of our hut, dead tired, soup bowls in hand, a fellow prisoner rushed in and asked us to run out to the assembly grounds and see the wonderful sunset. Standing outside we saw sinister clouds glowing in the west and the whole sky alive with clouds of ever-changing shapes and colors, from steel blue to blood red. The desolate gray mud huts provided a sharp contrast, while the puddles on the muddy ground reflected the glowing sky. Then, after minutes of moving silence, one prisoner said to another, "How beautiful the world *could* be!" (Viktor E. Frankl, *Man's Search for Meaning* [New York: Washington Square Press, 1964], pp. 62-63).

This is the message of Micah in the face of despair and impending doom. Micah reminds the people of God that somehow, someway,

God will once again redeem and reclaim that which is broken, lost, hurt, wounded, destroyed. Even in the midst of death and dying, through a sunset, God reminded a group of prisoners not to give up hope, for indeed the world could be beautiful!

This Advent people need to hear once again that hope is possible through the constant, loving, redeeming work of God. Our watching and waiting this season needs to be focused where we many times forget to look. It is such a paradox that during Christmas, when we should be celebrating all that is right with the world, it becomes so easy to lose ourselves and lose sight of what is important among self-imposed deadlines, meaningless traditions, and ridiculous expectations. Micah reminds the people to look to Bethlehem for their future hope. Who would have ever thought to look to Bethlehem? (Travis Franklin)

# THE GREATEST SACRIFICE

## HEBREWS 10:5-10

My father was a good man, a giving man. I recall one Christmas wanting more than anything an English Racer bike. It was very expensive, and I knew I would not get it because we did not have a lot of money. However, on Christmas morning it was there under the tree. My father had taken on extra jobs, working day and night, to get me that bike. Such love. Such sacrifice. Love—real love—is always that way, isn't it? It gives and gives and gives.

The text is about another love that led to the greatest sacrifice of all. The main point here is that Christ sacrificed himself—his own body—as the sinless Lamb of God, not some mere animal. Animal sacrifices were always wholly ineffective. They had to be done over and over again. Not so with the sacrifice Christ made. Christ makes the perfect and greatest sacrifice that the writer sees promised in Psalm 40:6-8, which he quotes. In fact, the writer places the words on the lips of Christ himself as if he spoke them. The message is simple enough: The whole levitical system of sacrifices, animals, grain, or whatever, was never really able to accomplish what was needed or desired from God—forgiveness. So Christ is sent to be, in his own body, the sacrifice that brings this forgiveness.

In every way, Christ was able to do what no other human could. Christ led a life of perfect obedience to God. The Law and all the sacrifices were intended to move persons toward such obedience but ultimately failed, for human beings are sinful. Paul writes much about the failure of the Law to do anything but make us aware of how far we miss the mark in obeying it. But Christ does the will of God, and in his sacrifice he shares that perfect obedience with us. Now our relationship with God is not based on sacrifices or even our perfect obedience to the law. That former way has been abolished now, the writer says, and in its place we now possess the way of Christ, the way of grace and forgiveness through his sacrificial death. The old has passed away and the new has come, Paul writes. We are now new creations because of Christ, and not because of any deeds on our part. In fact, all those deeds utterly fail. The writer here uses the word "sanctified." Because of what Christ has done for us—something we could never do for ourselves—we are now made holy, set apart, consecrated to God and for God's service. It is as if Christ took on our sins as filthy rags and gave us his perfect robe of obedience to God. So now when God looks at us, God sees the righteousness of Christ and not our sins. All because Christ loved and still loves us.

I think of this each time I partake of Holy Communion. I remember in seminary when a professor came out one evening and led us in Holy Communion. He sat a simple clay chalice on the table and a loaf of bread. "The body and blood of Christ," he said. "Broken and shed for us." No elaborate ritual or liturgy. Then he said, as he invited us forward, "Remember that Christ loved you so much that he died for you." I believe that was the first time I really heard, understood, and experienced Communion. I have not been able since to forget the sacrifice he made for me and for the whole world. Never forget just how much you are loved. (Bass Mitchell)

## A HOLY FAMILY REUNION

### LUKE 1:39-45 (46-55)

At last the lectionary gets to Mary and Jesus during this Advent season. Our usual hurry to get on to Christmas and avoid the pain of waiting has driven most of us to the refuge of Christmas carols weeks before. The lectionary requires patience on the part of the preacher and the worshipers. Now at last, the birth is in sight, and the characters are the familiar ones of the "Christmas story."

Mary's visit to Elizabeth is filled with riches. First, one might ask, "Why are these two women so happy?" Their words are ones full of joy, but their circumstances are anything but happy. Elizabeth is better off. She is finally pregnant after years of the social disgrace of infertility. But at her advanced age, pregnancy is dangerous. Her life is at stake and is threatened by her child. Mary at least is young, but perhaps too young. She is also pregnant, but she is unmarried and facing the harsh social stigma of village life in Galilee. Yet, these two women seem full of joy.

These two wise women are happy because they believe with all of their being that God is at work in their lives. They believe their pregnancies are a part of God's great design to save God's people. They even believe that the challenges they face are a part of God's larger plan.

This message is a great one for Advent. In every congregation there are those who find Advent difficult because of all kinds of personal problems. The temptation for the preacher is to ignore their pain and concentrate on the joys of the holiday. The temptation for those in pain is to believe that they are out of step with the season and that their troubles are not recognized or honored in a time of emphasis on joy. The gospel for them is to hear from the church that their pain is recognized and their struggles are somehow related to God. This is not to say that problems are sent from God. Rather, the message is that, even in trouble, God never abandons God's people.

Elizabeth and Mary's lives were full of trouble. Their faith allowed them to see that God had not abandoned them to trouble but was working in them to bring new life. The message is not that God brings trouble but that God is lovingly present seeking to redeem trouble and transform it into new possibilities. So it was for Elizabeth and Mary. So it is even now.

Further, these wise women could see beyond their own situation to the larger picture of God's redeeming work. Luke has Mary singing a psalmlike hymn of praise to God extolling God's mighty work bringing relief to the weak and needy. The coming

Christmas season brings hope and promise that God does not abandon God's people. In fact, God's presence, God's Immanuel, comes to the old pregnant woman whose husband is speechless, to the young pregnant peasant without a husband, and to the socially outcast shepherds who see the Christ Child. This season is all about God coming in unexpected ways. For those who wonder how God can be present in their trouble or pain, they need only to look at the characters of the Advent/Christmas drama and see God's presence everywhere. An Advent faith is not a confidence that all will be well; it is a faith that God is in all. (Carl Schenck)

# DECEMBER 28, 2003

## *First Sunday After Christmas*

**Worship Theme:** In the company of believers the church finds out who it truly is. Worship is the beating heart of congregational life. Let us praise God together.

**Readings:** 1 Samuel 2:18-20, 26; Colossians 3:12-17; Luke 2:41-52

### Call to Worship (Psalm 148 RSV)

*Leader:* Praise the LORD! Praise the LORD from the heavens, praise him in the heights!

**People: Praise him, all his angels, praise him, all his host!**

*Leader:* Praise him, sun and moon, praise him, all you shining stars!

**People: Praise him, you highest heavens, and you waters above the heavens!**

*Leader:* Let them praise the name of the LORD! For he commanded and they were created.

**People: And he established them for ever and ever; he fixed their bounds which cannot be passed.**

*Leader:* Praise the LORD from the earth, you sea monsters and all deeps, fire and hail, snow and frost, stormy wind fulfilling his command!

**People: Mountains and all hills, fruit trees and all cedars!**

*Leader:*   Beasts and all cattle, creeping things and flying birds!

**People:**   **Kings of the earth and all peoples, princes and all rulers of the earth!**

*Leader:*   Young men and maidens together, old men and children!

**People:**   **Let them praise the name of the LORD, for his name alone is exalted; his glory is above earth and heaven.**

*Leader:*   He has raised up a horn for his people, praise for all his saints,

**All:**   **For the people of Israel who are near to him. Praise the LORD!**

**Pastoral Prayer:**

O God of the Holy Family, you have baptized us into the faith of Christ and given us the task of being your people. Give us this day the power of Christ's spirit as we worship you, Creator, Sustainer, and Redeemer. In you we find our true center and in you, O Lord, we find our meaning and value for life. May we all participate in the life of our church and be baptized evangelists of the good news. May our words and actions invite others to be a part of the Christian life. Grant us a fresh spirit and give us a portion of your divine energy to live fully in the life that Christ offers us. As we worship this day, may our hearts and minds turn toward divine things. Create in us an enthused spirit to share good tiding that we ourselves have heard and received. Let the mind of Christ be ours. We pray this in Jesus' holy name. Amen. (David Mosser)

## SERMON BRIEFS

# DEDICATING A NEW YEAR!

### 1 SAMUEL 2:18-20, 26

The focus of the text is on the ministry of the boy Samuel and his increasingly spiritual wisdom. As a new year approaches, it's important to take stock of where we have been in our spiritual journey the past year. It also is valuable that we look toward the future. On this new year's walk with God, there are some insights we can learn from the beginning ministry profile of Samuel.

### I. This New Year Dedicate Yourself to Service

The author of this book forms quite a contrast between Eli's sons, Hophni and Phinehas, and Eli's adopted son, Samuel.

Eli's boys were priests in the temple of God, but according to verse 12, they "were wicked men; they had no regard for the LORD" (NIV). As we continue to read about these two scoundrels we understand they also had no regard for their fellow human beings. The author chronicles just one of the incidents of how these two treated "all the Israelites who came to Shiloh" (v. 14b). When the sacrifice to God was given, just as the priest plunged his fork into the meat, the fat was to be burned off as an offering to God. But these two unholy priests demanded it all with no regard for God's part of the sacrifice. If the person offering the sacrifice didn't give it to them, then they would tell him that they would take it by force!

The contrast between these two and the young boy Samuel was sharp. The text in verse 18 gives the picture clearly, "But Samuel was ministering before the LORD."

Servanthood gives, while selfishness hoards. Servanthood reaches outward into the hearts of people. A servant church should develop where people live, and it should be your personal goal to help that develop this year. A servant church is one person at a time within the group developing a servant heart.

A church that genuinely and authentically becomes a church of the Good Shepherd develops, much to its surprise, a legendary character on the community grapevine. It becomes a church that is more interested in helping than being helped. . . . more interested in loving than being loved. . . . more interested in giving than in getting. It becomes one of the distinctive churches in the community—a church that gives itself away in effective missional service. (Kennon L. Callahan, *Twelve Keys to an Effective Church* [San Francisco: Harper & Row, 1983], p. 9)

This year pray that your church will have a lot of Samuels attending.

## II. This New Year Dedicate Yourself to God's Presence

Samuel bathed himself in the presence of God. The *Westminster Shorter Catechism* states: "Man's chief end is to glorify God, and to enjoy him forever" (*The Confession of Faith of the Presbyterian Church of the United States*, "The Shorter Catechism" [Richmond, Va.: John Knox Press, 1944], p. 387). You cannot enjoy an absentee God! God's presence is a fresh touch upon any life. We are to seek God's presence continually!
Seek God's Presence by making yourself available to God.
Seek God's Presence by inviting God to live in your heart.
Seek God's Presence by submitting to God's authority.
Seek God's Presence by having a prayerful attitude.
Seek God's Presence by meditating on God's Holy Word.
Seek God's Presence by singing a song of praise.
Seek God's Presence by meeting with fellow believers.
Simply Seek God's Presence! God is near!

## III. This New Year Dedicate Yourself to Spiritual Growth

The writer relates, "And the boy Samuel continued to grow in stature and in favor with the LORD and with men" (v. 26). The child was becoming a person of God. Samuel dedicated himself to grow in God's grace.
Richard Lee wrote, "God's grace also comes in every hue and every color! Whatever the need, whatever the weakness, whatever the tint or hue of your sorrow or difficulty, there is corresponding grace to match it! Multicolored trials. Multicolored grace.
"He has grace for every trial, strength for every weakness, joy for every sorrow. And He never runs out! He always has more

than enough" (*Windows of Hope* [Sisters, Ore.: Multnomah, 1992], p. 46).

You have 365 days to grow in God's grace—start today! (Derl Keefer)

# THE KINGDOM'S NEW CLOTHES—OR, IN THE ALTOGETHER, NOW

## COLOSSIANS 3:12-17

It used to be popular to remark, "Clothes make the man (or woman)." But the attire of which Paul speaks isn't very *GQ* or chic. In fact, I doubt you'll see Paul's followers looking as though they stepped out of the pages of *Vogue*. You won't find them in the notions department at Macy's or in the aisle of Martha Stewart products at K-Mart. Not even Joan Rivers or her daughter could comment on how well these garments suit their wearers. This isn't *haute couture* from the salons and runways of Paris and New York; this is being in the altogether.

Sitting in the waiting room at the eye clinic, vision blurred from dilation drops, the occupants groaned over the latest controversy surrounding the material girl of pop music, Madonna. Her then latest music video was too blatant even by MTV standards, as the video depicted her taking her grandmother out on the town for a crime spree, complete with car crashes, shooting, looting, and pillaging. It's really "Material Girl cum Attila the Hun out for a spin." People who had seen the full-length version of this music video actually said they liked it. One young man said he could relate to it: The idea of someone out on the town with family members causing chaos was appealing. "Controversy sells," said another. A young woman who picked up on the same theme said Madonna's whole career has been controversy, and this music video was the pinnacle achievement of that career. I had little doubt most of the people watching this CNN report were wondering what the world was coming to.

Yet this is exactly what Paul is trying to broach on behalf of the Christians who resided in Colossae: Seek the things that are above rather than the things beneath the dignity and integrity of the Christ and the kingdom. What is below leads to dysfunction (if not perdition). What is above brings one to wholeness, to the practice of being in the altogether.

Think of the wisdom of Hans Christian Andersen's marvelous tale, "The Emperor's New Clothes," wherein an unwitting ruler is duped into wearing an "invisible" suit of clothes but is proclaimed naked as a jaybird by an innocent, honest young lad. Danny Kaye's rendition of it recently haunted my memory while pondering this text, particularly that singular phrase, "in the altogether." One thinks of Job's saying, "Naked came I from my mother's womb, and naked shall I return" (Job 1:21), but nakedness wasn't really what "altogether" implied in the Kaye song, Andersen's story, and assuredly not Paul's letter to the Colossians. In fact, *altogether* means just that: "all" plus "together," or whole. This is what Paul tried to convey to the good people in Colossae—and to us, too, if we're paying attention. Be clothed in all these essentials, especially love and the peace of Christ. Then, in the kingdom's new clothes, we shall be altogether whole. As George Zimmer says at the end of his Men's Wearhouse commercials, "I guarantee it." (Eric Killinger)

# THE SHORT VERSION

## LUKE 2:41-52

We just do not have very much information about Jesus between the birth narratives and when Jesus begins his public ministry. Only Luke includes this short version of what is surely a very long story.

All we know about Jesus growing up is this one story. It is a good story. It has drama and movement. It leaves us, however, wanting to hear more. It is a story about family. It is a story about trust. Perhaps it is a story about us.

We all know that any holiday when the family is together for a protracted period of time is a time of stress. That certainly is the case for Jesus' family. They are in Jerusalem for the feast of the Passover. In all of the hurry, Jesus' parents assume that he is with relatives. When they arrive home, Jesus is not there. Can you imagine the panic in their hearts? Have you had such an experience? Every parent can identify with the mixed emotions of anger and relief when Jesus' parents find him three days later in the Temple.

Young Jesus, however, seems impervious to their frustration, "Why were you looking for me? Didn't you know that I must be in my Father's house" (v. 49 NCV)? The Scripture says that Mary and Joseph do not understand what Jesus is saying, but Mary keeps "these things in her heart" (v. 51*b*).

There are many things in life we do not understand. Spending time together during holidays should help the family, but many times it does not. Perhaps the greatest puzzle is trying to understand the hearts of other people, even our own children.

Families begin, mature, and create new families. Individuals are born, mature, and take their own paths. Some therapists tell us that the patterns of family systems have ways of repeating themselves. We do not understand that fully. On the other hand, we can see it happening if we just look at our family trees. With patience, hope, and trust, however, we can find meaning in life if we have the assurance that we are in God's house. We are not in this life alone as individuals or as families. God is with us. This is God's world. This is God's house.

That brings us to the short version of the long story of Jesus' maturing. Jesus grows in wisdom and in stature and in favor with God and other humans. Wouldn't that be a wonderful epitaph for all of us? If we could just spend our lives growing, we could come to the end with a feeling that our lives have had some meaning. All too often, we reach points in our lives where we stop growing. We reach a point where we are overconfident or, conversely, we feel all our strivings are fruitless. There was a bridge in southern France that crossed the Rhone River. One end of the old bridge was inadequately secured, so that in a time of floodwater it was swept away. With only half the structure intact the bridge was useless for crossing the Rhone. To this day a popular saying survives: "On the bridge of Avignon they dance in circles."

They dance in circles because they have no place to go. With Christ, we have a place to go. We have some more growth to do. We can continue all our lives to increase in wisdom and in stature and in favor with God and other humans. That is the pattern Jesus has shown us. That is the challenge of this passage. That is the challenge of the life God has given us. That is what it is like to live in God's house, God's world. That is the short and the long of it. (Tim Russell)

# BENEDICTIONS

## Advent Season

Go now in peace knowing that the days are surely coming when the Lord fulfills the promises made of old. As we depart this house of worship may we each remember that "The Lord is our righteousness" (Jeremiah 23:6). As we go forth may the Spirit of God be with us to the end. Amen.

Live bountifully on the Lord's sustenance. As God provided manna for Israel in the wilderness and Jesus provides for us our daily bread as the Bread of life, so may we too go into our hungry world and share the Bread of life. Go forth in the gospel of Jesus Christ. Amen.

As we depart in peace, may the spirit of Jesus' grace surround your life so that others see the light of Christ in you. Serve the Lord with gladness as you spread the love of God to a world in need of good news. Amen.

"The grace of our Lord Jesus Christ be with you all" (2 Thessalonians 3:18).

## Christmas Season

"Let the peace of Christ rule in your hearts, to which indeed you were called in the one body. And be thankful. Let the word of Christ dwell in you richly; teach and admonish one another in all wisdom; and with gratitude in your hearts sing psalms, hymns, and spiritual songs to God. And whatever you do, in word or deed, do everything in the name of the Lord Jesus, giving thanks to God the Father through him" (Colossians 3:15-17).

On the cusp of a new year, O Lord, continue to guide us into the unknown future with the certainty that you have directed our footsteps in the past. Make us today a grateful people who honor you with our lives. May our lives reflect the blessing poured upon us each day. Amen.

## Season After Epiphany

Let us rejoice in bathing in the light of Jesus Christ who comes to us as God manifest. May our eyes be opened to the rich variety of wonder that life in Christ offers. May our hearts receive the light of the good news as the Lord uses us to illumine the world's darkness. In the name of the Creator, Sustainer, and Redeemer. Amen.

In Jesus, we have seen heaven unlocked and the angels of God ascending and descending upon the Son of Man. As we live in the promises of God may we share the good news with our brothers and sisters. May God, Son, and Holy Spirit, inspire us to become the people God created us to be. Amen.

May the "LORD watch between you and me, when we are absent one from the other" (Genesis 31:49). Amen.

## Lent Season

"The LORD bless you and keep you; the LORD make his face to shine upon you, and be gracious to you; the LORD lift up his countenance upon you, and give you peace" (Numbers 6:24-26). Amen.

O Lord, as we scatter from this sacred sanctuary, allow us to serve you in newness of life. Remind us to minister to our fellow creatures with the sweet love of Jesus burning in our hearts. Make us one with one another and one with you in the name of God, the Son, and the Holy Spirit. Amen.

"The grace of the Lord Jesus Christ, the love of God, and the communion of the Holy Spirit be with all of you" (2 Corinthians 13:13). Amen.

[or]

"The grace of the Lord Jesus Christ, and the love of God, and the communion of the Holy Ghost, be with you all. Amen." (2 Corinthians 13:14 KJV).

## Easter Season

May the joy in the Lord be all of ours to share with God's creation. Today God raised Jesus from the grave. So too may God raise us to new life in Christ. Amen.

"Now may the God of peace, who brought back from the dead our Lord Jesus, the great shepherd of the sheep, by the blood of the eternal covenant, make you complete in everything good so that you may do his will, working among us that which is pleasing in his sight, through Jesus Christ, to whom be the glory forever and ever. Amen" (Hebrews 13:20-21).

O Lord, allow us to skip with joy and hope as we hear and apprehend the good news that even the grave could not hold Jesus Christ, the firstborn of the dead. May we live in this promise that life in you conquers even death itself. Render in us the capacity to share this gospel of good news with a world lost in sin and death. In the name of God, the Son, and the Holy Ghost. Amen.

## Season After Pentecost

"May the God of peace himself sanctify you entirely; and may your spirit and soul and body be kept sound and blameless at the coming of our Lord Jesus Christ" (1 Thessalonians 5:23).

We now commend you all to God's love and mercy. Claim the promise of God and live in God's Spirit, for this is the pathway to life. Go now with full assurance that your sin is covered, and you have new life in Christ Jesus. Amen.

To the church the Lord reminds us to "grow in the grace and knowledge of our Lord and Savior Jesus Christ. To him be the glory both now and to the day of eternity. Amen" (2 Peter 3:18).

In Christ, God has paved the way to eternal life. Accept God's claim on you and live in fullness of life. For to such a time as this you were born; fulfill God's destiny and God's plan for your life. Believe in the gospel and proclaim it with all your being. Amen.

## Other Occasions

"Now to him who is able to keep you from falling, and to make you stand without blemish in the presence of his glory with rejoicing, to the only God our Savior, through Jesus Christ our Lord, be glory, majesty, power, and authority, before all time and now and forever. Amen" (Jude 1:24-25)

Remember, my beloved in the Lord, that it was Paul who reminds us who we are. We are the people of love. "And now faith, hope, and love abide, these three; and the greatest of these is love" (1 Corinthians 13:13).

## TEXT GUIDE*
## THE REVISED COMMON LECTIONARY (2003—YEAR B)

| Sunday | First Lesson | Second Lesson | Gospel Lesson | Psalm |
|---|---|---|---|---|
| 1/5/03 | Jer. 31:7-14 | Eph. 1:3-14 | John 1:(1-9), 10-18 | Ps. 147:12-20 |
| 1/12/03 | Gen. 1:1-5 | Acts 19:1-7 | Mark 1:4-11 | Ps. 29 |
| 1/19/03 | 1 Sam. 3:1-10 (11-20) | 1 Cor. 6:12-20 | John 1:43-51 | Ps. 139:1-6, 13-18 |
| 1/26/03 | Jonah 3:1-5, 10 | 1 Cor. 7:29-31 | Mark 1:14-20 | Ps. 62:5-12 |
| 2/2/03 | Deut. 18:15-20 | 1 Cor. 8:1-13 | Mark 1:21-28 | Ps. 111 |
| 2/9/03 | Isa. 40:21-31 | 1 Cor. 9:16-23 | Mark 1:29-39 | Ps. 147:1-11, 20c |
| 2/16/03 | 2 Kings 5:1-14 | 1 Cor. 9:24-27 | Mark 1:40-45 | Ps. 30 |
| 2/23/03 | Isa. 43:18-25 | 2 Cor. 1:18-22 | Mark 2:1-12 | Ps. 41 |
| 3/2/03 | 2 Kings 2:1-12 | 2 Cor. 4:3-6 | Mark 9:2-9 | Ps. 50:1-6 |
| 3/9/03 | Gen. 9:8-17 | 1 Pet. 3:18-22 | Mark 1:9-15 | Ps. 25:1-10 |
| 3/16/03 | Gen. 17:1-7, 15-16 | Rom. 4:13-25 | Mark 8:31-38 | Ps. 22:23-31 |
| 3/23/03 | Ex. 20:1-17 | 1 Cor. 1:18-25 | John 2:13-22 | Ps. 19 |
| 3/30/03 | Num. 21:4-9 | Eph. 2:1-10 | John 3:14-21 | Ps. 107:1-3, 17-22 |
| 4/6/03 | Jer. 31:31-34 | Heb. 5:5-10 | John 12:20-33 | Ps. 51:1-12 |
| 4/13/03 | Isa. 50:4-9a | Phil. 2:5-11 | Mark 14:1-15:47 | Ps. 31:9-16 |
| 4/18/03 | Isa. 52:13–53:12 | Heb. 10:16-25 | John 18:1–19:42 | Ps. 22 |
| 4/20/03 | Acts 10:34-43 | 1 Cor. 15:1-11 | John 20:1-18 | Ps. 118:1-2, 14-24 |
| 4/27/03 | Acts 4:32-35 | 1 John 1:1–2:2 | John 20:19-31 | Ps. 133 |
| 5/4/03 | Acts 3:12-19 | 1 John 3:1-7 | Luke 24:36b-48 | Ps. 4 |
| 5/11/03 | Acts 4:5-12 | 1 John 3:16-24 | John 10:11-18 | Ps. 23 |
| 5/18/03 | Acts 8:26-40 | 1 John 4:7-21 | John 15:1-8 | Ps. 22:25-31 |

*This guide represents one possible selection of lessons and psalms from the lectionary. For a complete listing see *The Revised Common Lectionary*.

| Sunday | First Lesson | Second Lesson | Gospel Lesson | Psalm |
|---|---|---|---|---|
| 5/25/03 | Acts 10:44-48 | 1 John 5:1-6 | John 15:9-17 | Ps. 98 |
| 6/1/03 | Acts 1:15-17, 21-26 | 1 John 5:9-13 | John 17:6-19 | Ps. 1 |
| 6/8/03 | Acts 2:1-21 | Rom. 8:22-27 | John 15:26-27; 16:4b-15 | Ps. 104:24-34, 35b |
| 6/15/03 | Isa. 6:1-8 | Rom. 8:12-17 | John 3:1-17 | Ps. 29 |
| 6/22/03 | 1 Sam. 17:(1a, 4-11, 19-23), 32-49 | 2 Cor. 6:1-13 | Mark 4:35-41 | Ps. 9:9-20 |
| 6/29/03 | 2 Sam. 1:1, 17-27 | 2 Cor. 8:7-15 | Mark 5:21-43 | Ps. 130 |
| 7/6/03 | 2 Sam. 5:1-5, 9-10 | 2 Cor. 12:2-10 | Mark 6:1-13 | Ps. 48 |
| 7/13/03 | 2 Sam. 6:1-5, 12b-19 | Eph. 1:3-14 | Mark 6:14-29 | Ps. 24 |
| 7/20/03 | 2 Sam. 7:1-14a | Eph. 2:11-22 | Mark 6:30-34, 53-56 | Ps. 89:20-37 |
| 7/27/03 | 2 Sam. 11:1-15 | Eph. 3:14-21 | John 6:1-21 | Ps. 14 |
| 8/3/03 | 2 Sam. 11:26–12:13a | Eph. 4:1-16 | John 6:24-35 | Ps. 51:1-12 |
| 8/10/03 | 2 Sam. 18:5-9, 15, 31-33 | Eph. 4:25–5:2 | John 6:35, 41-51 | Ps. 130 |
| 8/17/03 | 1 Kings 2:10-12; 3:3-14 | Eph. 5:15-20 | John 6:51-58 | Ps. 111 |
| 8/24/03 | 1 Kings 8:(1, 6, 10-11), 22-30, 41-43 | Eph. 6:10-20 | John 6:56-69 | Ps. 84 |
| 8/31/03 | Song of Sol. 2:8-13 | James 1:17-27 | Mark 7:1-8, 14-15, 21-23 | Ps. 45:1-2, 6-9 |
| 9/7/03 | Prov. 22:1-2, 8-9, 22-23 | James 2:1-10 (11-13), 14-17 | Mark 7:24-37 | Ps. 125 |
| 9/14/03 | Prov. 1:20-33 | James 3:1-12 | Mark 8:27-38 | Ps. 19 |

*This guide represents one possible selection of lessons and psalms from the lectionary. For a complete listing see *The Revised Common Lectionary*.

432

| Sunday | First Lesson | Second Lesson | Gospel Lesson | Psalm |
|---|---|---|---|---|
| 9/21/03 | Prov. 31:10-31 | James 3:13–4:3, 7-8a | Mark 9:30-37 | Ps. 1 |
| 9/28/03 | Esther 7:1-6, 9-10; 9:20-22 | James 5:13-20 | Mark 9:38-50 | Ps. 124 |
| 10/5/03 | Job 1:1; 2:1-10 | Heb. 1:1-4; 2:5-12 | Mark 10:2-16 | Ps. 26 |
| 10/12/03 | Job 23:1-9, 16-17 | Heb. 4:12-16 | Mark 10:17-31 | Ps. 22:1-15 |
| 10/19/03 | Job 38:1-7 (34-41) | Heb. 5:1-10 | Mark 10:35-45 | Ps. 104:1-9, 24, 35c |
| 10/26/03 | Job 42:1-6, 10-17 | Heb. 7:23-28 | Mark 10:46-52 | Ps. 34:1-8 (19-22) |
| 11/2/03 | Ruth 1:1-18 | Heb. 9:11-14 | Mark 12:28-34 | Ps. 146 |
| 11/9/03 | Ruth 3:1-5; 4:13-17 | Heb. 9:24-28 | Mark 12:38-44 | Ps. 127 |
| 11/16/03 | 1 Sam. 1:4-20 | Heb. 10:11-14 (15-18), 19-25 | Mark 13:1-8 | 1 Sam. 2:1-10 |
| 11/23/03 | 2 Sam. 23:1-7 | Rev. 1:4b-8 | John 18:33-37 | Ps. 132:1-12 (13-18) |
| 11/30/03 | Jer. 33:14-16 | 1 Thess. 3:9-13 | Luke 21:25-36 | Ps. 25:1-10 |
| 12/7/03 | Mal. 3:1-4 | Phil. 1:3-11 | Luke 3:1-6 | Luke 1:68-79 |
| 12/14/03 | Zeph. 3:14-20 | Phil. 4:4-7 | Luke 3:7-18 | Isa. 12:2-6 |
| 12/21/03 | Micah 5:2-5a | Heb. 10:5-10 | Luke 1:39-45 (46-55) | Luke 1:47-55 |
| 12/28/03 | 1 Sam. 2:18-20, 26 | Col. 3:12-17 | Luke 2:41-52 | Ps. 148 |

*This guide represents one possible selection of lessons and psalms from the lectionary. For a complete listing see *The Revised Common Lectionary.*

433

# CONTRIBUTORS

**Tracey Allred**
3810 Hermitage Road, Apt. E
Richmond, Virginia 23227

**Chris Andrews**
First United Methodist
    Church
930 North Boulevard
Baton Rouge, Louisiana
    70802-5728

**Kelly Bender**
Paradise Valley United
    Methodist Church
4455 East Lincoln Drive
Paradise Valley, Arizona 85253

**Bob Buchanan**
Parkway Baptist Church
5975 State Bridge Road
Duluth, Georgia 30097

**Thomas Lane Butts**
First United Methodist
    Church
405 Pineville Road
Monroeville, Alabama 36460

**Joseph Byrd**
Stewart Road Church of God
1199 Stewart Road
Monroe, Michigan 48162

**Gary Carver**
First Baptist Church of
    Chattanooga
401 Gateway Avenue
Chattanooga, Tennessee
    37402-1504

**Mike Childress**
St. Andrews UCC
2608 Browns Lane
Louisville, Kentucky 40220

**Joseph Daniels**
Emory United Methodist
    Church
6100 Georgia Avenue, NW
Washington, DC 20011

**Wayne Day**
First United Methodist
    Church
800 West Fifth
Fort Worth, Texas 76102

**John Fiedler**
First United Methodist
    Church
1928 Ross Avenue
Dallas, Texas 75201

**Travis Franklin**
The Methodist Children's
    Home
1111 Herring Avenue
Waco, Texas 76708

**Tracy Hartman**
Baptist Theological Seminary
3400 Brook Road
Richmond, Virginia 23227

**John Holbert**
Perkins School of Theology
P.O. Box 750133
Dallas, Texas 75275

**Don Holladay**
St. John's United Methodist
  Church
1200 Old Pacos Trail
Santa Fe, New Mexico 87501

**Bob Holloway**
First United Methodist
  Church
313 North Center
Arlington, Texas 76011

**Karen Hudson**
5709 Drayton Drive
Glen Allen, Virginia 23060-6381

**Jim Jackson**
Chapelwood United
  Methodist Church
11140 Greenbay Drive
Houston, Texas 77024

**Laura Jernigan**
1776 Stonecliff Court
Decatur, Georgia 30033

**Wendy Joyner**
Fellowship Baptist Church
466A Highway 280 East
Americus, Georgia 31709

**Derl Keefer**
6803 Lakeshore Drive
Raytown, Missouri 64133

**Eric Killinger**
129 Fairfax Street
Warrenton, Virginia 20186

**Gary Kindley**
First United Methodist
  Church
P.O. Box 205
Colleyville, Texas 76034

**Hugh Litchfield**
North American Baptist
  Seminary
1525 South Grange Avenue
Sioux Falls, South Dakota
  57105

**Robert Long**
St. Luke's United Methodist
  Church
222 Northwest 15th Street
Oklahoma City, Oklahoma
  73103-3598

**Mike Lowry**
University United Methodist
  Church
5084 DeZavala Road
San Antonio, Texas 78249

**John Robert McFarland**
425 20th Place Southwest
Mason City, Iowa 50401-6428

**Alyce McKenzie**
Perkins School of Theology
P.O. Box 750133
Dallas, Texas 75275

**John Mathis**
High Hills Baptist Church
211 South Halifax Road
Jarratt, Virginia 23867

**Blair Meeks**
501 Clear Springs Court
Brentwood, Tennessee 37027

**Bass Mitchell**
Rt. 2 Box 68
Hot Springs, Virginia 24445

**David Mosser**
First United Methodist
  Church
P.O. Box 88
Graham, Texas 76450

**Timothy Owings**
First Baptist Church
P.O. Box 14489
Augusta, Georgia 30919

**Don Polaski**
Union Theological Seminary
3401 Brook Road
Richmond, Virginia 23227

**Tim Russell**
  (Deceased)
The United Methodist Church
P.O. Box 67
Weatherford, Texas 76086-
  0067

**Carl Schenck**
Manchester United Methodist
  Church
129 Woods Mill Road
Manchester, Missouri 63011-
  4339

**Mary Scifres**
3810 67th Avenue Court
  Northwest
Gig Harbor, Washington
  98335

**Melissa Scott**
Colonial Avenue Baptist
  Church
4165 Colonial Avenue South-
  west
Roanoke, Virginia 24018

**Thomas Steagald**
P.O. Box 427
Marshville, North Carolina
  28103

**Frank Thomas**
Hope For Life, Inc.
1825 Riverdale Road
Germantown, Tennessee 38138

**Eradio Valverde**
Trinity United Methodist
  Church
6800 Wurzbach Road
San Antonio, Texas 78240

**Richard Ward**
Iliff School of Theology
2201 S. University Boulevard
Denver, Colorado 80210

**Mark White**
302 North Estes Drive
Chapel Hill, North Carolina
27514

**Victoria Atkinson White**
302 North Estes Drive
Chapel Hill, North Carolina
27514

**Ryan Wilson**
First Baptist Church
P.O. Box 828
Columbus, Georgia 31902-0828

**Sandy Wylie**
New Haven United Methodist
Church
5603 South New Haven
Tulsa, Oklahoma 74135-4100

# INDEX

## OLD TESTAMENT

# NEW TESTAMENT